Experimental Auctions

Economists, psychologists, and marketers are interested in determining the monetary value people place on non-market goods for a variety of reasons: to carry out cost-benefit analysis, to determine the welfare effects of technological innovation or public policy, to forecast new product success, and to understand individual and consumer behavior. Unfortunately, many currently available techniques for eliciting individuals' values suffer from a serious problem in that they involve asking individuals hypothetical questions about intended behavior. Experimental auctions circumvent this problem because they involve individuals exchanging real money for real goods in an active market. This represents a promising means for eliciting non-market values. Lusk and Shogren provide a comprehensive guide to the theory and practice of experimental auctions. It will be a valuable resource for graduate students, practitioners, and researchers concerned with the design and utilization of experimental auctions in applied economic and marketing research.

Jayson L. Lusk is Professor and Willard Sparks Endowed Chair in the Department of Agricultural Economics, Oklahoma State University.

Jason F. Shogren is Stroock Distinguished Professor of Natural Resource Conservation and Management, and Professor of Economics and Finance, University of Wyoming.

Quantitative Methods for Applied Economics and Business Research

Series Editor
PROFESSOR PHILIP HANS FRANSES
Erasmus University, Rotterdam

Researchers and practitioners in applied economics and business now have access to a much richer and more varied choice of data than earlier generations. *Quantitative Methods for Applied Economics and Business Research* is a new series aimed at meeting the needs of graduate students, researchers and practitioners who have a basic grounding in statistical analysis and who wish to take advantage of more sophisticated methodology in their work.

Forthcoming titles
Stewart Jones and David Hensher (eds.), *Credit Risk Modelling: A Primer*

Experimental Auctions

Methods and Applications in Economic and Marketing Research

Jayson L. Lusk and Jason F. Shogren

CAMBRIDGE
UNIVERSITY PRESS

CAMBRIDGE
UNIVERSITY PRESS

University Printing House, Cambridge CB2 8BS, United Kingdom

One Liberty Plaza, 20th Floor, New York, NY 10006, USA

477 Williamstown Road, Port Melbourne, VIC 3207, Australia

4843/24, 2nd Floor, Ansari Road, Daryaganj, Delhi - 110002, India

79 Anson Road, #06-04/06, Singapore 079906

Cambridge University Press is part of the University of Cambridge.

It furthers the University's mission by disseminating knowledge in the pursuit of education, learning and research at the highest international levels of excellence.

www.cambridge.org
Information on this title: www.cambridge.org/9780521671248

© Jayson L. Lusk and Jason F. Shogren 2007

First published 2007

A catalogue record for this publication is available from the British Library

Library of Congress Cataloging in Publication data
Lusk, Jayson.
Experimental auctions : methods and applications in economic and marketing
research / Jayson L. Lusk and Jason F. Shogren.
p. cm. – (Quantitative methods for applied economics and business research)
Includes bibliographical references and index.
ISBN–13: 978–0–521–85516–7 (hbk.)
ISBN–10: 0–521–85516–0 (hbk.)
ISBN–13: 978–0–521–67124–8 (pbk.)
ISBN–10: 0–521–67124–8 (pbk.)
1. Auctions.   2. Consumers' preferences–Mathematical models.   I. Shogren, Jason
F.   II. Title.   III. Series.
HF5476.L87   2007
330.072 4–dc22   2007002291

ISBN 978-0-521-85516-7 Hardback
ISBN 978-0-521-67124-8 Paperback

Acknowledgments

Participating in an auction is a collective process and so is conducting one. We have had the good fortune of learning about experimental auctions with a number of colleagues and students including: Todd Cherry, Keith Coble, Tom Crocker, Scott Daniel, Ty Feldkamp, Sean Fox, Sara Gunnersson, Dermot Hayes, Lisa House, Darren Hudson, Wally Huffman, Sara Jaeger, Jim Kliebenstein, Cannon Koo, Muhammad Koohmaraie, John List, Christy Lusk, Dana Marcellino, Michael Margolis, Darrell Mark, Chris McIntosh, Bryan Melton, Jim Mintert, Melissa Moore, Burt Morrow, Bailey Norwood, Greg Parkhurst, Matt Rousu, Ted Schroeder, S.Y. Shin, Lucine Tadevosyan, Abe Tegene, Bruce Traill, Carlotta Valli, Bob Wilhelm, and Christine Wilson. Sara Jaeger provided helpful comments on a number of the chapters. Seminar participants at the Journées d' Économie Expérimentale at Bureau d'Economie Théorique et Appliquée, Université Louis Pasteur, Strasbourg provided helpful comments on the material in chapters 9 and 10.

This book is dedicated to our families their support and patience during the writing of this book.

Contents

List of figures   *page* ix
List of tables   x

1   Introduction   1
   1.1   Introduction   1
   1.2   Why experimental auctions?   3
   1.3   What is an experimental auction?   5
   1.4   Purpose of this book and boundaries of coverage   17

2   Incentive compatible auctions: theory and evidence   19
   2.1   Introduction   19
   2.2   Theory of incentive compatible auctions   20
   2.3   Evidence from induced value auctions   27

3   Value theory   34
   3.1   Introduction   34
   3.2   Valuation under certainty   34
   3.3   Valuation under uncertainty   37
   3.4   Valuation in a dynamic environment with uncertainty, limited information,
       and irreversibility   43
   3.5   Summary   44

4   Conducting experimental auctions: some preliminaries   46
   4.1   Introduction   46
   4.2   Experimental design   47
   4.3   Sample size determination   55
   4.4   Experiment setting and context: field versus laboratory   57
   4.5   Conclusions   61

5   Conducting experimental auctions   62
   5.1   Introduction   62
   5.2   Training and practice   62
   5.3   Endowment versus full bidding   65
   5.4   Choosing an auction mechanism   69
   5.5   Multiple good valuation, demand reduction, and field substitutes   76
   5.6   Learning and affiliation in repeated bidding rounds   80
   5.7   Negative values   92
   5.8   Conclusions   94

6 Data analysis   95
    6.1 Introduction   95
    6.2 Censored regressions with auction bids   95
    6.3 Quantile regression with auction bids   100
    6.4 Panel data regression with auction bids   103
    6.5 Other types of data analysis with auction bids   106
    6.6 Conclusions   112

7 Valuation case studies   113
    7.1 Introduction   113
    7.2 Informing Policy I: beef tenderness grading system   113
    7.3 Informing Policy II: valuing safer food   121
    7.4 Informing Policy III: tolerance for genetically modified food   129
    7.5 Marketing I: forecasting market share of a new product   137
    7.6 Marketing II: preferences for fresh food with multiple quality attributes 141
    7.7 Marketing III: the value of farm financial records   149
    7.8 Controversial goods I: demand for genetically modified food in three
         countries   154
    7.9 Controversial goods II: irradiation   163
    7.10 Controversial goods III: food from animals treated with growth
         hormones   169
    7.11 Concluding comments   174
         Appendices   175

8 Auction design: case studies   196
    8.1 Introduction   196
    8.2 Preference learning   196
    8.3 Willingness to pay, willingness to accept, and the auction mechanism 199
    8.4 Second price auction tournaments   209
    8.5 Preferences: fixed or fungible?   217
    8.6 Gift exchange   225
    8.7 Calibration of real and hypothetical auction bids   229
    8.8 Hybrid auctions and consequential bidding   239
    8.9 Concluding remarks   245

9 Validity of experimental auctions   247
    9.1 Introduction   247
    9.2 Auction bids and economic theory   248
    9.3 Reliability   252
    9.4 Convergent validity   255
    9.5 Anomalies   261
    9.6 Summary   267

10 The future of experimental auctions   269
    10.1 Introduction   269
    10.2 Ten questions worthy of future research   270
    10.3 Concluding remarks   278

References   279
Index   297

Figures

1.1   Experimental auctions as a balance of control and context   *page* 15
5.1   Expected cost of sub-optimal bidding for $v_i = 3$, $N = 8$,
      and values/prices are drawn from a uniform distribution
      on [0, 10]   75
5.2   Expected cost of sub-optimal bidding for $v_i = 7$, $N = 8$,
      and values/prices are drawn from a uniform distribution on
      [0, 10]   76
5.3   Second price auction bids for five beef steaks across five
      bidding rounds   81
5.4   Bid functions and the determination of winner, loser, and
      market price   90
6.1   Distribution of fifth price auction bids for a non-genetically
      modified cookie in France   101
6.2   Hypothetical path model where six auction bids are
      represented by two latent factors   108
7.1   The three types of labels used for the vegetable oil   133
7.2   Distribution of round five auction bids by location   159
7.3   Effect of information on bids for irradiated pork   166
7.4   Average willingness to pay for "non-BST" milk in Iowa,
      Arkansas, Massachusetts, California (rural) and California
      (urban)   172
B7.1 Financial records inventory sheet   190
B7.2 Financial records bid sheet   190

Tables

1.1	Examples of experimental auctions in action	*page* 7
2.1	Payoffs from bidding strategies	22
2.2	Payoff from bidding true value instead of under- or over-bidding	23
2.3	Results of studies testing incentive compatible mechanisms in induced value experiments	31
4.1	Four experimental treatments	48
4.2	Treatments in a 2^3 design	49
4.3	Higher order effects in a 2^3 design	50
4.4	A comparison of two fractional factorial designs	51
4.5	Sample size correction table for 95% level of confidence	57
5.1	Some incentive compatible auctions	69
5.2	Summary of panel data categories in List and Shogren (1999)	83
5.3	Two-way fixed effects estimation results for bid equation	84
5.4	Second price auction bids for beef steak across five bidding rounds	87
5.5	Aggregate and individual models of the effect of posted prices on bidding behavior	88
6.1	Comparison of tobit to double hurdle model	99
6.2	Conditional mean and quantile regressions	103
7.1	Summary statistics of auction bids and the value of tenderness ($n = 116$)	119
7.2	Price and probability assumptions used in welfare calculations	120
7.3	Consumer welfare changes from a tenderness grading system (all units in $ per choice occasion; $n = 116$)	120
7.4	Subjective and objective risk and a comparison of naïve and informed option price (R^a) of five pathogens	127
7.5	Summary statistics of tests within each additional *salmonella* treatment	128
7.6	Bids on non-genetically modified food with differing tolerance levels	135

7.7   Comparison of bids for non-GM foods with and without GM
      tolerance levels   136
7.8   T-test on null hypothesis that consumers value foods with a
      1% tolerance the same as for a 5% tolerance   137
7.9   Market share simulations ($n = 119$)   140
7.10 Means of subjective evaluation scores of pork chop
      characteristics and auction bids by presentation format
      (scale = 1 to 100)   147
7.11 Ordinary least squares regressions: effect of pork chop
      characteristics on market prices and bids in three evaluation
      formats   148
7.12 Distribution of bids for farm records and characteristics of
      farmers in four bid ranges   153
7.13 Summary statistics of willingness to accept distribution by
      location and auction round   158
7.14 Effect of attitudes and nationality on willingness to accept:
      median regression estimates   160
7.15 Effect of information on relative safety assessments   166
7.16 Effect of new information   168
7.17 Frequency distribution of bids at trial 20   173
8.1   Fixed-effects estimation results of bid function   198
8.2   Summary of experimental design parameters   202
8.3   Summary statistics of the Becker-DeGroot-Marschak
      Mechanism   204
8.4   Summary statistics of the second price auction   205
8.5   Summary statistics of the random nth price auction   208
8.6   Descriptive statistics (all rounds)   211
8.7   Panel data estimation results (two-way)   212
8.8   On margin/off margin panel data estimation results
      (two-way)   214
8.9   Efficiency in the tournament and standard second price
      auction   215
8.10 The impact of arbitrage on preference reversal rates (%)   221
8.11 Random-effects estimates for treatment 1
      (Real arbitrage/real no-arbitrage)   222
8.12 Random-effects estimates for treatment 2
      (Real arbitrage/real no-arbitrage)   223
8.13 Random-effects estimates for treatment 3
      (Real arbitrage/hypothetical no-arbitrage)   224
8.14 Experimental design   226
8.15 Experimental results   228
8.16 Experimental results – across gifts   230

8.17 Selected characteristics of auction participants   234
8.18 Top two hypothetical and auction bids   235
8.19 Calibration functions   236
8.20 Summary of experimental design   240
8.21 Descriptive statistics (all rounds)   242
8.22 Panel data estimation results (7 outliers excluded)   242
8.23 Wald test results   243
8.24 Winners and price-setters in second price auction treatments   244
 9.1 Correlation coefficients between auction bids for Certified
      Angus Beef steaks across five bidding rounds ($n = 70$)   253
 9.2 Correlation coefficients between mean bids for five beef
      steaks across four auction institutions ($n = 5$)   255

1 Introduction

1.1 Introduction

Our choices reflect our values. People reveal their relative values when they choose to spend an extra hour at work rather than at the opera; purchase more groceries rather than extra MP3s or drop extra change into a jar promoting a charity at the check-out line rather than buying a candy bar. Economists characterize the *economic value* of these choices by determining the rate at which a person is willing to trade one good or resource for another. This rate is captured in a person's maximum *willingness to pay* to purchase a good or in their minimum *willingness to accept* to sell a good. Usually, these economic values are revealed within the context of an active exchange institution like a market or auction with numerous buyers and sellers. In such exchange institutions, buyers buy when their willingness to pay exceeds price and sellers sell when their willingness to accept falls below price.

But, how do people value new goods and services not currently bought and sold in the marketplace? These *non-market* goods and services include new private goods like cigarettes that have been genetically modified to possess less nicotine and diet cherry vanilla Coke with lime as well as public goods like cleaner air in Santiago, Chile or biodiversity in Madagascar. No exchange institution exists for buyers and sellers to make bids and offers, which would reveal people's relative values for these non-market goods. But there are policymakers and business managers who want information on the potential demand for these goods; they want to know if the perceived benefits from the products outweigh the costs to provide them.

Likewise, economists, psychologists, and marketers are also interested in eliciting people's values for both market and non-market goods. Economists elicit values to conduct applied cost-benefit analysis related to public good provision, and to estimate the welfare effects of technological innovation and public policy (see e.g., Boardman *et al.*, 2005). Psychologists and behavioral economists want to learn about people's values to understand the degree to which decisions are consistent with preferences and beliefs and to offer refinements to economic theory. This work focuses on how people's values can be influenced by the context of the decision and how people use rules of thumb to guide how they value goods (see Kahneman and Tversky, 2000). Marketing experts are interested in eliciting values to better understand consumer preferences, forecast new product success, and measure effectiveness of promotional activities, which in turn can help reduce the high failure rate of new products and the significant costs of advertising (see Wertenbroch and Skiera, 2002).

Over the last four decades, researchers have developed many *value elicitation* methods to tease out how people value various goods and services. These methods can be broadly categorized as *revealed* or *stated preference* methods (see Hanley *et al.*, 2006 for an overview). *Revealed preference* methods use existing market data to derive *implicit* values for a good, for example hedonic pricing, travel costs. Revealed preferences work when the good already exists, albeit indirectly, in the market. For example, while a natural wonder such as the Grand Canyon cannot be directly bought and sold, we can observe how far people drive and what they give up in terms of opportunity cost of time to visit the Canyon. By detecting systematic patterns from these observations, one can indirectly determine people's value for the park. Another example: the number of bathrooms in a house is not traded alone in the market; but by calculating the difference in the sales price of a two-bathroom home and the sales price of an otherwise identical one-bathroom home, we can indirectly determine people's values for an extra bathroom. The upside of revealed preference methods is that real choices are examined. The downside of revealed preference methods is that valuation is indirect and must be inferred from empirical patterns.

In contrast, *stated preference* methods use public opinion surveys or comparative choice trials that ask a person, directly or indirectly, to state his or her value for the new good or service. The upside of stated preference methods is that the researcher can create a hypothetical market where a person can, in theory, buy or sell any good or service. The stated preference method is flexible enough to construct alternative potential scenarios such that demand for the good can be understood given changes in market and non-market conditions. A well known downside of stated preference methods, regardless of how well the survey is designed and executed, is that people know they are valuing a hypothetical change in the good or service. The absence of market discipline, which takes the form of budget constraints and availability of substitutes in the real world, creates an environment conducive to questionable responses. Values elicited from hypothetical surveys have exhibited many inconsistencies such as a lack of responsiveness to the scale and scope of proposed benefits and a tendency for people to promise to pay significantly more than they actually do when asked to shell out the money, (see Diamond and Hausmann, 1994 and Hanemann, 1994 for a discussion of the pros and cons of contingent valuation).

Traditional approaches used to elicit valuations suffer from several shortcomings. Revealed preference methods are indirect and require several simplifying assumptions to translate observed behavior into valuations. At worst, stated preference methods are open to strategic manipulation by the participant. At best, the method does not provide incentives for respondents to invest sufficient cognitive effort when thinking about their valuation decisions. What is needed is an approach that combines the advantages of revealed and stated preference methods – *our world of experimental auctions*.

1.2   Why experimental auctions?

Many stated preference methods involve people hypothetically rating, ranking, or choosing between competing products or alternatives. The implicit assumption is that people perceive no gain or loss from stating their preferences strategically or that people answer such hypothetical questions truthfully. To the extent people believe their responses are *inconsequential*, that is researchers will not use their responses to formulate public policy or business strategy, one response is as good as another from an economic standpoint because all responses have the same effect on a person's level of utility. While people might try to answer a question sincerely, even if they believe their response to be inconsequential, standard economic models of individual decision making have nothing to say about inconsequential choices. Even under the maintained hypothesis of truthful responses, people have little incentive to expend cognitive effort on decisions involving hypothetical stated preferences making elicited values more "noisy" and systematically biased than they might otherwise be.

A more likely case is that people believe there is some chance that their responses are consequential and will be used by researchers to inform federal and business policy. In such cases, a person can benefit by offering non-truthful answers to survey questions in an attempt to influence the price, quality, and availability of future product offerings. When such incentives exist, mechanisms are needed to either align individuals' incentives with the researcher's or to impose some cost on people for offering responses that deviate from their true preferences. Over the past decade, evidence has accumulated indicating that people overstate the amount they are willing to pay when asked hypothetical valuation questions relative to when real money is on the line; stating values two to twenty times greater in hypothetical questions relative to non-hypothetical valuation questions (List and Gallet, 2001).

As a consequence, many applied economists have turned to experimental auctions to elicit consumer valuations for new goods and services (see Bohm, 1972; Brookshire and Coursey, 1987; Hoffman *et al.*, 1993; Shogren *et al.*, 1994; Lusk *et al.*, 2001a). The advantage of experimental auctions over other value elicitation methods is that they put people in an active market environment where they can incorporate market feedback and where there are real economic consequences to stating preferences that differ from what they actually want. This is not to say that people cannot misrepresent their valuations in an experimental auction, only that so-called incentive compatible mechanisms help impose a price on people if they choose to send "signals" to researchers by bidding in a manner that deviates from their real value. In addition, researchers can also control and vary the amount of market-like feedback provided to bidders (e.g., posted market clearing prices, prices of outside options) to examine how robust their bidding behavior is to exogenous contextual changes in the auction environment.

Experimental auctions also address the non-market valuation challenge – when an experimental auction is held, a market is created (albeit a stylized one). In experimental auctions, bids are revealed preferences obtained in a real market with real products and real money. Experimental auctions use real money and real goods to create a market where people's attention is focused on the valuation task. Experimental auctions have advantages over stated preference methods because an exchange mechanism (e.g., Vickrey's second price auction) is used which creates incentives for people to think about what they will actually pay for the good or service. Experimental auctions have advantages over revealed preference methods because valuations for a good are directly obtained.

Further, experimental auctions provide a convenient way to determine each person's willingness to pay. In an experimental auction, each person submits a bid that, in theory, is equal to their value for the good. This can be contrasted with most other value elicitation techniques, which rely on statistical models and assumptions about people's utility functions to generate probability statements about valuations. For example, "best practices" in contingent valuation requires the use of a so-called single-bounded dichotomous choice question wherein a person states (yes or no) whether they are willing to pay a given amount for a good. All that can be surmised from such responses is whether willingness to pay is greater than or less than the given dollar amount. As shown by Hanemann (1984), assumptions must be made about the form of a representative utility function and the distribution of errors in the random utility model for the yes/no responses to be meaningfully used.

Other stated preference methods such as conjoint analysis require similar assumptions to arrive at valuations (see Louviere et al., 2000). While heterogeneity can be incorporated in discrete choice models by investigating how willingness to pay varies by measured demographics, experience has shown that such measures typically explain only a small percentage of variation in valuations. In addition, advances in econometric techniques, such as random parameter models, mixed logit models, and hierarchical Bayes models, permit one to derive individual-level valuations from discrete choice responses (see Allenby and Rossi, 1999; Huber and Train, 2001). Such approaches, however, require assumptions about a functional form for the utility function and assumptions about the joint distribution of preferences. Our point is that relative to other value elicitation techniques, experimental auctions provide the richest description of heterogeneity in valuations across people and goods with minimal assumptions.

This is a key point given the increasing recognition that economists need to better understand the degree of heterogeneity in valuations. Heckman (2001, p. 674) stated in his Nobel Lecture that "[t]he most important discovery was the evidence on the pervasiveness of heterogeneity and diversity in economic life. When a full analysis was made of heterogeneity in response, a variety of candidate averages emerged to describe the 'average' person, and the long-standing edifice of the representative consumer was shown to lack empirical support." Identifying and understanding valuation heterogeneity is important for a number of reasons. First, market segmentation strategies rely on grouping individuals with similar preferences such that marketing efforts can be stylized for each segment. Experimental auctions can be used to understand how to group people based on revealed values. Second, to implement various models of price discrimination, businesses need accurate information on the distribution of valuations (see the vertical differentiation models such as that in Mussa and Rosen, 1978). Finally, properly characterizing heterogeneity is important to: determine, without bias, the welfare effects of public policy (see Graff Zivin, 2006; Giannakas and Fulton, 2002), identify whether firms practice anti-competitive behavior (see Berry *et al.*, 1995; Nevo, 2001), and properly test economic theory which is formulated to hold, with the fewest assumptions, at the individual level (see Heckman, 2001; Lou, 2002).

1.3   What is an experimental auction?

Auction-type mechanisms were originally designed to elicit people's values for monetary lotteries. The goal was to characterize individual preferences for risk taking or to investigate the empirical validity of expected utility theory (see Becker *et al.*, 1964). This early work was largely overlooked until three decades ago when a few researchers like Peter Bohm, Jeff Bennett, David Brookshire, Don Coursey, Jack Knetsch, and Bill Schulze began revisiting the idea of using experimental auction methods to elicit values for real goods, especially the demand for environmental protection (see Cummings *et al.*, 1986).

The approach developed out of the general experimental economics literature that had, for the most part, focused on *induced value* experiments in which people were given pre-assigned values for a fictitious good by the experimenter (see Smith, 1976, 1982 for discussions on induced value experiments in general and Coppinger *et al.*, 1980 for induced value experiments with auctions in particular). In an induced value experiment, a person is paid earnings equal to the difference between their assigned induced value and the market price, given that a purchase is made. Induced value experiments are a powerful tool to test theory because elicited values can be directly compared with the induced value benchmark. This high level of experimental control, however, comes at a cost. By definition, induced value experiments are abstract, focusing on the allocative efficiency of the auction institution itself; these auctions do not provide information on people's values for real-world goods and services.

In response, researchers started applying what they learned in induced value experiments to elicit people's *homegrown values*: those values that people bring into an experiment for real-world goods. Initial applications used experimental auction-type mechanisms to elicit values for items such as public TV, sucrose octa-acetate (a bitter liquid people bid to avoid tasting), and coffee mugs to study the difference between willingness-to-accept and willingness-to-pay measures of value and to determine people's values for public goods (see Bohm, 1972; Coursey, Hovis, and Schulze, 1987; Kahneman *et al.*, 1990). The work of Hoffman *et al.* (1993) and Menkhaus *et al.* (1992) on the demand for vacuum-packed meats was perhaps the first to use experimental auctions for marketing purposes.

Today, experimental auctions are used around the world by applied economists, psychologists, and marketers interested in valuing new products and technologies and in investigating theoretical models of individual decision making, auctions, and valuation. The reader can explore Table 1.1 to get a better idea for how experimental auctions have been used over the last three decades. Table 1.1 chronologically lists over 100 experimental auction studies. The list helps illustrate the varied uses and expanding growth of experimental auctions used to elicit valuations. These auctions have been used for a wide variety of products. Applications range from valuing food safety (i.e., specific pathogens, biotechnology, pesticides, traceability, and growth hormones), food attributes (e.g., meat tenderness, meat color, fat content, and packaging), a variety of foods (e.g., kiwis, apples, chocolates, potatoes, corn chips, cookies, milk, and sandwiches), and a variety of non-food, high-value goods ranging from sports cards to firm business records to used cars to gasoline to Christmas gifts.

Table 1.1 also shows that experimental auctions have been conducted for a number of non-mutually exclusive reasons: to *test theory*, including investigations into the willingness-to-pay/willingness-to-accept divergence, studies of preference reversals, tests of the commitment cost theory, and so on, to *study methods* for valuing public and private goods, including investigations of hypothetical bias, scope effects, the willingness-to-pay/willingness-to-accept divergence, studies comparing mechanisms, studies of procedural issues, and so on, and to *elicit homegrown preferences*, including preferences for risk and time, and the demand for new goods and services.

When experimental auctions are used to elicit homegrown values, the researcher aims to balance *control* and *context*. *Control* means the researcher has control over the environment such that no unmeasured external force drives choices. That is, confounding of cause and effect is eliminated. What

Table 1.1. *Examples of experimental auctions in action*

	Year	Author(s)	Product(s) auctioned	Study purpose(s)	Location	Publication
1	1964	Becker, DeGroot, and Marschak	Lotteries	Estimate risk preferences	USA	Behavioural Science
2	1972	Bohm	Public television show	Study methods for valuing public goods	Sweden	European Economic Review
3	1979	Grether and Plott	Lotteries	Study preference reversal phenomenon	USA	American Economic Review
4	1983	Bennett	Movie	Study contributions to a public good	Australia	Economic Analysis and Policy
5	1984	Bohm	Bus route	Study methods for valuing public goods	Sweden	Public Finance and the Quest for Efficiency
6	1986	Cummings, *et al.*	Sucrose octa-acetate (a bitter tasting liquid), public goods	Study methods for valuing public goods	USA	Valuing Environmental Goods: An Assessment of the CVM
7	1987	Brookshire and Coursey	Tree density in a park	Study methods for valuing public goods	USA	American Economic Review
8	1987	Brookshire *et al.*	Strawberries	Study external validity of experimental auctions	USA	Economic Inquiry
9	1987	Coursey *et al.*	Sucrose octa-acetate (a bitter tasting liquid)	Study WTP/WTA divergence	USA	Quarterly Journal of Economics
10	1988	Loewenstein	Delayed cash payment	Estimate time preferences	USA	Management Science
11	1989	Harless	Lotteries	Study WTP/WTA divergence	USA	Journal of Economic Behavior and Organization
12	1990	Kahneman, Knetsch, and Thaler	Coffee mugs	Study WTP/WTA divergence	USA	Journal of Political Economy
13	1990	Shogren	Protection and insurance against monetary loss	Study risk reduction mechanisms	USA	Journal of Risk and Uncertainty
14	1991	Crocker and Shogren	Lotteries	Study preference learning	USA	Environmental Policy and the Economy

(*cont.*)

Table 1.1. (*cont.*)

	Year	Author(s)	Product(s) auctioned	Study purpose(s)	Location	Publication
15	1992	Boyce et al.	Life of small pine tree	Study WTP/WTA divergence	USA	American Economic Review
16	1992	Kachelmeier and Shehata	Lotteries	Study WTP/WTA divergence; estimate risk preferences	China	American Economic Review
17	1992	Menkhaus et al.	Beef steaks	Estimate determinants of value for vacuum packaging	USA	Journal of Agricultural and Resource Economics
18	1993	Buhr et al.	Pork sandwich	Value growth hormones and marbling	USA	Journal of Agricultural and Resource Economics
19	1993	Hoffman et al.	Beef steaks	Study procedural issues; value vacuum packaging	USA	Marketing Science
20	1993	McClelland et al.	Insurance to avoid loss	Study risk preferences; study hypothetical bias	USA	Journal of Risk and Uncertainty
21	1994	Bohm	Used cars	Study preference reversal phenomenon	Sweden	Empirical Economics
22	1994	Fox et al.	Milk	Value growth hormones	USA	Journal of Dairy Science
23	1994	Shogren and Crocker	Protection and insurance against monetary loss	Study preferences for timing of risk reduction	USA	Economics Letters
24	1994	Shogren et al.	Candy bars, pork sandwiches	Study WTP/WTA divergence	USA	American Economic Review
25	1995	Fox et al.	Pork sandwiches	Value growth hormones	USA	Journal of Animal Science
26	1995	Hayes et al.	Pork sandwiches	Value food safety	USA	American Journal of Agricultural Economics
27	1996	Di Mauro and Maffioletti	Protection and insurance against monetary loss	Study preferences for ambiguity	Italy	Journal of Risk and Uncertainty
28	1996	Melton et al.	Pork chops	Value meat color, marbling, size, and tenderness	USA	American Journal of Agricultural Economics
29	1997	Bateman et al.	Gourmet chocolates, soft drink	Study WTP/WTA divergence	UK	Quarterly Journal of Economics

30	1997	Bohm et al.	30 liters of gasoline	Study procedural issues; compare mechanisms	Sweden	Economic Journal
31	1997	Frykblom	Atlas	Study hypothetical bias	Sweden	Journal of Environmental Economics and Management
32	1997	Kirby	Delayed cash payment	Estimate time preferences	USA	Journal of Experimental Psychology: General
33	1998	List and Shogren	Sports cards	Study hypothetical bias	USA	Journal of Economic Behavior and Organization
34	1998	List and Shogren	Various Christmas gifts	Estimate deadweight loss of Christmas	USA	American Economic Review
35	1998	List et al.	Sports cards	Study hypothetical bias	USA	Economics Letters
36	1998	Roosen et al.	Apples	Value pesticide use	USA	Journal of Agricultural and Resource Economics
37	1998	Rutström	Gourmet chocolates	Compare mechanisms	USA	International Journal of Game Theory
38	1998	Fox et al.	Pork sandwiches	Study hypothetical bias	USA	American Journal of Agricultural Economics
39	1999	List and Shogren	Candy bars, pork sandwiches	Study effect of price feedback on bids	USA	American Journal of Agricultural Economics
40	1999	Lucking-Reiley	Trading cards	Compare mechanisms in on-line auctions	USA	American Economic Review
41	2000	Frykblom and Shogren	Atlas	Study methods for valuing public goods	Sweden	Environmental and Resource Economics
42	2000	Horowitz and McConnell	Binoculars, coffee mugs, flashlights	Study hypothetical bias; study performance of mechanism	USA	Journal of Economic Behavior and Organization
43	2000	List and Lucking-Reiley	Sports cards	Compare mechanisms	USA	American Economic Review
44	2000	Shogren, List, and Hayes	Candy bars, mangos, pork sandwiches	Test for preference learning vs. experimental novelty	USA	American Journal of Agricultural Economics

(cont.)

9

Table 1.1. (*cont.*)

	Year	Author(s)	Product(s) auctioned	Study purpose(s)	Location	Publication
45	2001	Balistreri *et al.*	Lotteries	Study hypothetical bias	USA	Environmental and Resource Economics
46	2001	Knetch *et al.*	Coffee mugs	Study WTP/WTA divergence	Canada, Singapore	Experimental Economics
47	2001	List	Sports cards	Study methods for valuing public goods	USA	American Economic Review
48	2001	Lusk *et al.*	Beef steaks	Value tenderness	USA	American Journal of Agricultural Economics
49	2001	Lusk *et al.*	Corn chips	Value genetically modified food	USA	Journal of Agricultural and Resource Economics
50	2001	Shogren *et al.*	Candy bars, coffee mugs	Study WTP/WTA divergence	USA	Resource and Energy Economics
51	2002	Dickinson and Bailey	Beef sandwiches, pork sandwiches	Value traceability, food safety, production methods	USA	Journal of Agricultural and Resource Economics
52	2002	Fox *et al.*	Pork sandwiches	Study effect of information about irradiation	USA	Journal of Risk and Uncertainty
53	2002	Huck and Weizäcker	Contracts tied to other people's choices	Study people's ability to predict others' preferences	Germany	Journal of Economic Behavior and Organization
54	2002	Lange *et al.*	Champagne	Study performance of mechanism	France	Food Quality and Preference
55	2002	List	Sports cards	Study preference reversal phenomenon	USA	American Economic Review
56	2002	Masters and Sanogo	Infant foods	Estimate welfare effects of quality certification	Mali	American Journal of Agricultural Economics
57	2002	Noussair, Robin, and Ruffieux	Corn flakes	Study effects of labels on genetically modified food	France	Economics Letters
58	2002	Soler and Sanchez	Vegetables	Value organic and eco labels	Spain	British Food Journal
59	2002	Umberger *et al.*	Beef steaks	Value corn fed *vs.* grass fed beef	USA	Agribusiness

10

No.	Year	Authors	Goods	Purpose	Country	Journal
60	2002	Wertenbroch and Skiera	Cake, pen, soft drink	Study performance of mechanism	Germany, USA	Journal of Marketing Research
61	2003	Alfnes and Rickertsen	Beef steaks	Value growth hormones and country of origin	Norway	American Journal of Agricultural Economics
62	2003	Areily, Loewenstein, and Prelec	Annoying sounds, keyboard, wine	Test theory of coherent arbitrariness	USA	Quarterly Journal of Economics
63	2003	Cherry, Crocker, and Shogren	Monetary and wildlife lotteries	Study preference reversals	USA	Journal of Environmental Economics and Management
64	2003	Hong and Nishimura	Lotteries	Compare mechanisms; study mechanism performance	USA	Journal of Economic Behavior and Organization
65	2003	Huffman et al.	Corn chips, potatoes, vegetable oil	Value genetically modified food	USA	Journal of Agricultural and Resource Economics
66	2003	List	Sports cards	Study WTP/WTA divergence	USA	Quarterly Journal of Economics
67	2003	Loureiro, Umberger, and Hine	Cookies	Study procedural issues	USA	Applied Economics Letters
68	2003	Lusk	Coffee mug, lotteries	Test commitment cost theory	USA	American Journal of Agricultural Economics
69	2003	Stoneham, Chaudhri, and Strappazzon	Land conservation contracts	Value biodiversity and conservation; test-bed mechanism	Australia	Australian Journal of Agricultural and Resource Economics
70	2003	Umberger et al.	Beef steaks	Value country of origin	USA	Journal of Food Distribution Research
71	2004	Blondel and Javaheri	Apples, wine	Value organic food	France	Acta Horticulturae
72	2004	Carpenter, Holmes, and Matthews	Over 20 items including DVD players, gift certificates, and toys	Compare mechanisms in charity auctions	USA	IZA Discussion Paper
73	2004	Cummings, Holt, and Laury	Water permits	Value irrigation rights	USA	Journal of Policy Analysis and Modeling
74	2004	Feuz et al.	Beef steaks	Value tenderness and flavor	USA	Journal of Agricultural and Resource Economics

(cont.)

Table 1.1. (cont.)

	Year	Author(s)	Product(s) auctioned	Study purpose(s)	Location	Publication
75	2004	Hofler and List	Sports cards	Study hypothetical bias	USA	American Journal of Agricultural Economics
76	2004	Killinger et al.	Beef steaks	Value color, marbling, and origin	USA	Journal of Animal Science
77	2004	List	Sports cards	Study discrimination	USA	Quarterly Journal of Economics
78	2004	Lunander and Nilsson	Contracts for road painting	Study mechanism; test-bed mechanism	Sweden	Journal of Regulatory Economics
79	2004	Lusk et al.	Beef steaks	Value meat quality; compare mechanisms; test for endowment effects	USA	American Journal of Agricultural Economics
80	2004	Lusk et al.	Cookies	Study effect of information about biotechnology	France, UK, USA	European Review of Agricultural Economics
81	2004	Nalley et al.	Sweet potatoes	Value taste, origin, and health	USA	Mississippi State University
82	2004	Noussair et al.	Biscuits	Value genetically modified food; investigate effect of tolerance levels	France	Economic Journal
83	2004	Noussair et al.	Candy bars, cookies, orange juice	Study performance of mechanism	France	Food Quality and Preference
84	2004a	Rousu et al.	Corn chips, potatoes, vegetable oil	Study effect of genetically modified food tolerance limits	USA	Review of Agricultural Economics
85	2004b	Rousu et al.	Corn chips, potatoes, vegetable oil	Value conflicting information on genetically modified food	USA	Land Economics
86	2004	Rozan et al.	Apples, bread, potatoes	Value metal content; compare mechanisms	France	European Review of Agricultural Economics
87	2004	Umberger and Feuz	Beef steaks	Study performance of mechanism	USA	Review of Agricultural Economics

#	Year	Author	Good	Purpose	Country	Journal
88	2005	Ackert et al.	Mugs	Study WTP/WTA divergence	USA	Federal Reserve Bank of Atlanta
89	2005	Berg et al.	Lotteries	Estimate risk preferences; compare mechanisms	USA	Proceedings of the National Academy of Sciences
90	2005	Bernard	Chocolates	Study effect of price feedback on bids; value organic food	USA	Applied Economics Letters
91	2005	Bernard and Schulze	MP3 player	Study how people forecast future values	USA	Economics Bulletin
92	2005	Brown et al.	Chicken sandwich	Value food safety	Canada	Canadian Journal of Agricultural Economics
93	2005	Corrigan	Coffee mug	Test commitment cost theory	USA	Environmental and Resource Economics
94	2005	Dickinson and Bailey	Beef sandwiches, pork sandwiches	Value traceability, food safety, production methods	Canada, Japan, UK, USA	Journal of Agricultural and Applied Economics
95	2005	Ding et al.	Chinese food meals	Study performance of mechanism	USA	Journal of Marketing Research
96	2005	Hobbs et al.	Beef sandwiches, pork sandwiches	Value traceability, food safety, production methods	Canada	Canadian Journal of Agricultural Economics
97	2005	Hudson, Coble, and Lusk	Lotteries	Estimate risk preferences	USA	Agricultural Economics
98	2005	Jaeger and Harker	Kiwi fruit	Value new kiwi variety; value genetically modified food	New Zealand	Journal of the Science of Food and Agriculture
99	2005	Kassardjian et al.	Apples	Value genetically modified food	New Zealand	British Food Journal
100	2005	Lusk et al.	Cookies	Estimate welfare effects of biotechnology policies	France, UK, USA	Economics Letters
101	2005	Platter et al.	Beef steaks	Value meat color, marbling, size, and tenderness	USA	Journal of Animal Science
102	2005	Plott and Zeiler	Lotteries and mugs	Study WTP/WTA divergence	USA	American Economic Review

(cont.)

Table 1.1. (cont.)

	Year	Author(s)	Product(s) auctioned	Study purpose(s)	Location	Publication
103	2005	Rousu et al.	Cigarettes	Value genetically modified cigarettes with quality improvement	USA	Journal of Agricultural and Applied Economics
104	2006	Cherry and Shogren	Lotteries	Study preferences with market-like arbitrate	USA	Journal of Economic Psychology
105	2006	Corrigan and Rousu	Corn chips, salsa	Test for endowment effects	USA	American Journal of Agricultural Economics
106	2006	Corrigan and Rousu	Candy bars, coffee mugs	Study effect of price feedback on bids	USA	American Journal of Agricultural Economics
107	2006	Eigenraam et al.	Land conservation contracts	Value biodiversity and conservation; test-bed mechanism	Australia	Department of Primary Industries
108	2006	Hobbs, Sanderson, and Haghiri	Bison meat sandwich, beef sandwich	Value bison meat; value health information	Canada	Canadian Journal of Agricultural Economics
109	2006	Lusk et al.	Cookies	Value genetically modified food	France, UK, USA	Agricultural Economics
110	2006	Marcellino	Business records	Value farm records	USA	Purdue University
111	2006	Marette et al.	Fish	Value omega 3 fatty acid and metal content	France	Iowa State University
112	2006	Norwood and Lusk	Soft drinks	Test theory of excessive choice effect	USA	Oklahoma State University
113	2006	Shaw, Nayga, and Silva	Cookie	Value information on health risk	USA	Economics Bulletin

14

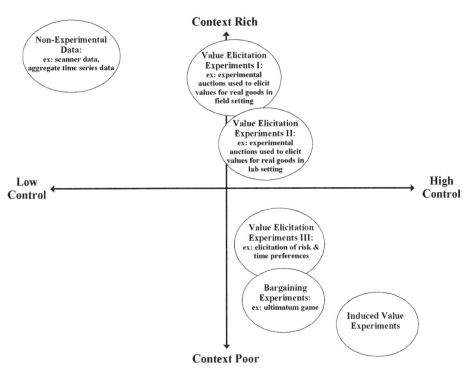

Figure 1.1   Experimental auctions as a balance of control and context

separates an *experimental* auction from other auctions is the attention given to control. *Context* implies that subjects have some contextual cues about why their decision might matter in a bigger world. Figure 1.1 shows several research methods that vary along the control/context spectrum. At one extreme are non-experimental data obtained from actual market transactions. Such data are valuable in the sense that they have high *face validity* (i.e., data are obviously useful in addressing the question at hand) and represent actual behavior of people in the markets our models attempt to emulate. The weakness of non-experimental data is that they come in aggregated form and, most problematic, it is a challenge to identify causality due to endogeneity and measurement error. At the other extreme are induced value experiments. Induced value experiments provide the control needed in non-experimental data: researchers control the market institution, the rules of exchange, the supply and demand schedules, and the level and extent of repetition and information. The problem, however, is that induced value experiments are abstract settings with little parallel to decisions in the wilds. They (purposefully) involve people making decisions devoid of natural context, that is buying and selling a redeemable token as opposed to a 1948 Gibson L-50 archtop guitar. Such an approach can create more powerful tests of treatment effects and some theoretical models. But to the extent that valuations, behavior, and constraints are context-specific, experimental data based on abstract monetary choices may bear little relation to actual choices in everyday life.

Recognizing the usefulness of both non-experimental data and induced value experiments, experimental auctions attempt to exploit the fruitful middle ground between total control and total context. In an experimental auction, researchers control factors manipulated across treatments, the exchange mechanism, study participants, and the level and extent of repetition and information. Unlike induced value experiments, in which values are controlled by the experimenter, individual preferences for goods and services are elicited in experimental auctions. Experimental auctions surrender some control relative to induced value experiments as the full range of outside factors like prices and availability of substitute/complementary goods can be beyond the researcher's control. Diminished control is traded off against a gain in context. People bid to buy real goods and products, and in some cases the auctions are held in a setting (e.g., a grocery store) where people regularly make decisions reflecting their valuations.

Although, experimental auctions come in several varieties, they frequently follow two basic strategies. In one approach people bid to upgrade from a typical good to a novel good, which is identical to the typical good except for the characteristic to be valued (e.g., bid to exchange a package of typical ground beef for a package of irradiated ground beef). In another approach, people bid simultaneously on these two (or more) competing goods and a random drawing determines which auction is binding (so that demand for a single unit can be elicited). In the first approach, the auction elicits the marginal value for the characteristic of the novel good (e.g., irradiation) relative to a pre-existing substitute. In the second approach, the auction elicits the total value for each good.

A key feature of experimental auctions is the type of mechanism used to determine the market price and auction winner(s). We are interested in so-called *incentive compatible* mechanisms in which a person has a dominant strategy to submit a bid exactly equal to his or her value for the good. Nobel laureate William Vickery formally launched the theoretical study of auctions by introducing a now classic mechanism – the second price auction. Although there is some evidence that people used the second price auction before Vickrey's formal demonstration (see Lucking-Reiley, 2000), it is still frequently referred to as the *Vickrey auction*. In a second price auction, the person with the highest bid wins the auction and pays a price equal to the second highest amount; the winner either exchanges their typical product for the novel product or obtains the good in the randomly selected auction, depending upon the chosen implementation method. All losing bidders either retain their typical product or obtain nothing.

In theory, each bid in this auction reflects a bidder's value or willingness to pay for the good(s). The beauty of a second price auction is that a person cannot be made better off by misrepresenting his or her actual value. A person's weakly dominant strategy (i.e., a strategy that yields at least as good an outcome as any other) is to bid his or her real value for the good. Chapter 2 discusses the incentive properties of the second price auction in more detail, as well as several other incentive-compatible mechanisms including, the BeckerDeGroot-Marschak mechanism, the English auction, Vickrey nth price auctions, and the random nth price auction. These auctions vary in terms of the level of market interaction and feedback, number of winners and the market price, but all yield the same result in theory.

1.4   Purpose of this book and boundaries of coverage

The purpose of this book is to present the basic elements of experimental auctions. We discuss issues one should think about when designing, implementing, and examining the data from an experimental auction. We take on this task because despite the appeal of experimental auctions to elicit valuations and their increasing use in the economic literature (see Table 1.1), there is no basic reference to help guide those interested in learning about the key ins and outs of experimental auctions. Several colleagues and students have expressed the desire to have a source that summarizes the extant literature. Further, there appears to be a need for a source to outline design features of experimental auctions such that practitioners can avoid critical inferential problems in their analysis. This book assimilates the current state of the knowledge on experimental auctions as they are used to elicit people's values for new goods, services, and other non-market goods. Our goal is for the chapters to guide practitioners interested in designing and using experimental auctions in applied economic, psychology, and marketing research. The book also serves as a pedagogical tool for graduate or upper-level undergraduate courses in economics, psychology, or marketing research, as well as an introduction to experimental auction methods for professional economists and marketing researchers.

We explore numerous questions that arise when thinking about how to design and implement experimental auctions to elicit people's economic values. After this introductory chapter, we present brief overview chapters on auction theory and value theory. In discussing the theory behind experimental auctions, we discuss how well neoclassical economic theory performs in practice by reviewing the induced value experiments that have been conducted with incentive compatible auctions.

These chapters set the stage for the primary contribution of the book: two chapters focus on specific experimental design issues, one examines statistical analysis of experimental auction data, and two further chapters detail numerous case studies. Each chapter contains material drawn from our experience of working with experimental auctions over the course of the past decade or so. We discuss key experimental design issues like choosing the elicitation environment (laboratory or field setting), determining the sample frame, demand reduction and wealth effects, effects of field substitutes, endowment effects, choosing between alternative auction mechanisms, shapes of payoff functions, price feedback, and treatment effects. The chapter on data analysis includes discussions primarily related to bid censoring and panel-data econometrics. The book contains several case studies that illustrate how experimental auctions are used in applied research and how research can be conducted to investigate the effect of context and auction design on valuations. The penultimate chapter discusses the validity of experimental auctions. The last chapter concludes with ten questions we believe to be worthy of future research.

What do we *not* cover? We do not focus on how to run induced value experimental auctions or experimental auctions that aim to test auction theory or test-bed auction designs in the laboratory prior to "real world" use. We purposefully restrict our discussion to experimental auctions designed for value elicitation. The theoretical study of auctions is a growing and vibrant area of research and many researchers have used the experimental approach to test propositions, such as the revenue equivalence theorem and efficiency criteria, using induced and homegrown value auctions (see Kagel, 1995; Kagel and Levin, 2002). The growth in auction theory has led to the creation of many innovative mechanisms for use in large-scale public auctions, such as those for spectrum waves. Researchers interested in studying the empirical performance of such auctions typically use laboratory induced-value experiments prior to full-scale implementation. Theory testing and test-bedding using induced value experiments are important areas of research, but are beyond the scope of our current task. We restrict our attention to the class of auction mechanisms considered incentive compatible and focus, almost exclusively, on the task of accurately eliciting people's values.

We hope our focused discussion throughout the book lends itself to a deeper understanding of the use of experimental auctions to elicit values, the subtle balance of context and control in experimental design, and perhaps the nature of economic value itself.

2 Incentive compatible auctions: theory and evidence

2.1 Introduction

Auctions have been used for centuries as a price-discovery mechanism (Lucking-Reiley, 2000). The theoretical study of auctions, however, is a relatively recent phenomenon. Starting with the pioneering work of William Vickrey in 1961, economists have developed a rich literature devoted to auction theory which is astounding in its results such as the revenue equivalence theorem and in its growing complexity. In addition to inventing and studying the properties of alternative auction mechanisms, theorists have addressed issues related to how bidding behavior is affected by numbers of bidders, information, value uncertainty, risk preferences, violations of expected utility theory, value interdependence, asymmetry, and multiple-unit demand. Good reference books and papers include: Klemperer (1999, 2004), Krishna (2002), Milgrom (2004), and McAfee and McMillan (1987). Such texts focus primarily on developing and espousing particular theoretical properties of auctions, with attention devoted to designing auctions for generating maximum possible revenue or efficiency (e.g., the ability of an auction to allocate units to the person or people with the highest value(s) for the auctioned good(s)). Students of experimental auctions should not by-pass this literature as it is important to understand such topics as revenue equivalence and efficiency.

Our book purposefully restricts the theoretical treatment of auctions to the question of incentive compatibility. An auction is said to be *incentive compatible* when it induces each bidder to submit a bid that sincerely reflects his or her value for the good. Auctions that elicit such *truthful* value statements focus the reader on the key issue at hand: eliciting values for use in cost/benefit analysis, marketing research, and testing the behavioral foundations of microeconomic theory.

A variety of auctions are considered *incentive compatible*, meaning each bidder has a weakly dominant strategy to submit a bid equal to their value. These auctions can be identified in that they *separate what people say from what they pay*. That is, an auction mechanism is incentive compatible if the market price paid by a person is independent from what he or she bids. The most famous incentive compatible auction is Vickrey's second price auction, in which the highest bidder pays the second-highest bidder's bid for the good or service. Other examples include the nth price auction (a second price auction being one example), the random nth price auction, the English auction, and the Becker-Degroot-Marschak (BDM) mechanism.

In what follows, we examine why such mechanisms are incentive compatible, at least under certain assumptions. We discuss cases where such mechanisms fail to provide incentives for truthful value revelation. The chapter concludes with the findings from several induced value experiments conducted to test whether the theoretical properties of the mechanisms are demand revealing in practice (also see Kagel, 1995).[1]

2.2   Theory of incentive compatible auctions

We begin by showing that Vickrey's second price auction is incentive compatible, first in a formal utility maximization framework, and then in a more intuitive, heuristic framework. For ease of exposition, we choose to illustrate the theory using the second price auction; but any of the other incentive compatible mechanisms could have been used in its stead. Showing that a mechanism, such as the second price auction, is incentive compatible is made easier by recognizing that the game participants play is characterized by a game theoretic prediction governed by a weakly dominant strategy, that is a strategy that yields a payoff that is at least as great as the payoff from all other strategies no matter what bidding strategies other rivals pursue. This insight allows us to focus on one single bidder's strategy while ignoring all other bidders.

Before going into the specifics, three key assumptions need to be made explicit. First, we focus on the case of independent private values – each individual's value is independently drawn from a known distribution, and while the distribution is common knowledge, each individual only knows their own particular realization from the distribution. Second, we assume one divisible unit is available for sale. Finally, we assume bidders have a smooth differentiable utility function and expected utility theory characterizes their valuations of risky outcomes.

Let v_i represent the value individual i places on a good. The person submits a bid, b_i, to obtain a good against N rival bidders, whose values are independently drawn from a known distribution. If the person wins the auction by submitting the highest bid, he or she derives utility from the difference between his or her value for the good and the market price, which in this case is the second highest bid, as given by $U_i(v_i - p)$, where p is the price and U is a utility

---

[1] In our discussion, we use the term incentive compatibility to refer to the theoretical properties of a mechanism, while the term demand revealing is used to refer to the empirical properties of a mechanism.

function increasing in income. If the bidder does not win the auction, his or her monetary value from bidding is normalized to zero. At the time the bid is submitted, the bidder does not know the second highest bid and thus does not know the price that will be paid. In effect, the price is a random variable. Suppose bidder i's expectation about the price is characterized by the cumulative distribution function $G_i(p)$ with support $[\underline{p_i}, \overline{p_i}]$ and the associated probability density function $g_i(p)$. The goal of the bidder is to submit a bid, b_i, to maximize expected utility, which is given by:

$$E[U_i] = \int_{\underline{p_i}}^{b_i} U_i(v_i - p)dG_i(p) + \int_{b_i}^{\overline{p_i}} U_i(0)$$

$$= \int_{\underline{p_i}}^{b_i} U_i(v_i - p)g_i(p)dp + \int_{b_i}^{\overline{p_i}} U_i(0). \tag{2.1}$$

The first integral is taken over all price levels less than his or her bid: cases in which the bidder wins the auction. The second integral is taken over all price levels greater than the bidder's bid: cases in which he or she loses the auction. Normalizing $U(0) = 0$, we find the optimal bid by taking the derivative of expression (2.1) with respect to b_i and setting the derivative equal to zero which yields:

$$\frac{\partial E[U_i]}{\partial b_i} = U_i(v_i - b_i)g_i(b_i) = 0. \tag{2.2}$$

Equation (2.2) is solved when $b_i = v_i$. The bidder's expected utility is maximized when he or she submits a bid equal to his or her value for the good. This is a general finding for the second price auction. The optimal strategy of "bidding one's value" does not depend on the bidder's risk preferences, the number of rival bidders, initial wealth levels, or any of the other bidders' bidding strategies. Interested readers can consult Milgrom and Weber's (1982) theorem 6 for a rigorous proof of the incentive compatibility of the second price auction.

There is a more intuitive way to illustrate the incentive properties of the second price auction. If a bidder submits a bid greater than his value, he runs the risk that the second highest bid will exceed his value, which would cause him to lose money; if he submits a bid less than his value, he runs the risk that someone could outbid him, causing him to miss out on a profitable opportunity. Over- and under-bidding one's value runs the risk of either paying too much or missing out on a good deal, which drives the bidder toward simply bidding his true value. By separating what a person pays from what they say, the second price auction induces sincere bidding in theory. We illustrate this intuition below.

Again, let v_i be a bidder's value for a good, b_i be their bid, p be the market price, and U_i be a strictly increasing utility function. By definition if $b_i > p$,

Table 2.1. *Payoffs from bidding strategies*

Realized price	Bidding strategy		
	Under-bid $(b_i < v_i)$	Over-bid $(b_i > v_i)$	Bid value $(b_i = v_i)$
$p > v_i > b_i$	0		
$v_i > p > b_i$	0		
$v_i > b_i > p$	$U_i(v_i - p) > 0$		
$p > b_i > v_i$		0	
$b_i > p > v_i$		$U_i(v_i - p) < 0$	
$b_i > v_i > p$		$U_i(v_i - p) > 0$	
$p > v_i = b_i$			0
$v_i = b > p$			$U_i(v_i - p) > 0$

then a bidder wins the auction and pays p. In contrast, if $b_i \leq p$, the bidder does not win the auction and pays nothing. Each bidder has three possible bidding strategies: bid less than true value ($b_i < v_i$), bid more than true value ($b_i > v_i$), or bid true value ($b_i = v_i$). Table 2.1 shows the possible payoff outcomes that could result from the three bidding strategies given various realizations of the market price, p.

First, assume the bidder underbids (i.e., $b_i < v_i$). Table 2.1 shows that three possible payoffs can be realized: (i) If $p > v_i > b_i$, the bidder loses the auction and earns 0; (ii) if $v_i > p > b_i$, the bidder again loses and earns 0; however, note that positive utility could have been experienced had they bid higher; and (iii) if $v_i > b_i > p$, the bidder wins the auction, pays p, and realizes $U_i(v_i - p) > 0$.

Assume now the bidder overbids (i.e., $b_i > v_i$). Again, three outcomes are possible: (i) If $p > b_i > v_i$, the bidder loses and earns 0; (ii) if $b_i > p > v_i$, the bidder wins the auction, but because $p > v_i$, realized utility is negative: $U_i(v_i - p) < 0$, the bidder would have been better off decreasing their bid; and (iii) if $b_i > v_i > p$, the bidder wins, pays p, and realizes $U_i(v_i - p) > 0$.

Finally, suppose the bidder pursues a truthful bidding strategy (i.e., $b_i = v_i$). Two outcomes are possible: (i) if $p > v_i = b_i$, the bidder loses and earns 0, or (ii) if $v_i = b_i > p$, the bidder wins, pays p, and realizes $U_i(v_i - p) > 0$.

The question is whether our bidder would have faired better if they had bid their true value rather than under- or over-bidding. Table 2.2 shows the outcomes by taking the difference between utility when the bidder bid their true value and the utility when they under- or over-bid. In most cases, the expected payoff is the same regardless of whether the bidder bids true value or under- or over-bid. In two cases, however, bidding true value generates a better outcome than under- or over-bidding. For under-bidding, the bidder could have won the auction and experienced positive utility if only a higher bid were offered. For over-bidding, the bidder could have prevented a loss yielding

Table 2.2. *Payoff from bidding true value instead of under- or over-bidding*

	Effect of bidding true value instead of ...	
Realized price	Under-bidding ($b_i < v_i$)	Over-bidding ($b_i > v_i$)
$p > v_i = b_i$ vs. $p > v_i > b_i$	$0 - 0 = 0$	
$v_i = b_i > p$ vs. $v_i > p > b_i$	$U_i(v_i - p) - 0 > 0$	
$v_i = b_i > p$ vs. $v_i > b_i > p$	$U_i(v_i - p) - U_i(v_i - p) = 0$	
$p > b_i = v_i$ vs. $p > b_i > v_i$		$0 - 0 = 0$
$p > b_i = v_i$ vs. $b_i > p > v_i$		$0 + U_i(v_i - p) > 0$
$b_i = v_i > p$ vs. $b_i > v_i > p$		$U_i(v_i - p) - U_i(v_i - p) = 0$

negative utility if only a lower bid were offered. The strategy of bidding one's true value never lowers utility and can increase utility relative to under- or over-bidding. Stated differently, a bidder can never generate a higher level of utility, but might generate less by offering bids that diverge from their valuation. Therefore, the weakly dominant strategy in the second price auction is to bid one's true value.

The key behind the incentives of the second price auctions and similar incentive compatible mechanisms is that the price paid by the bidder, p, is unaffected by their bid, b_i. To illustrate this point more forcefully, it is instructive to compare the bidding strategy in the second price auction to another mechanism in which the bid influences the price, such as the first price auction. In a first price auction, individual i submits a bid, b_i, to obtain a good against N rival bidders. The bidder wins the auction if they submit the highest bid and this winning bidder *pays a price equal to their own bid*. The optimal bidding strategy now depends on what the bidder believes other people will bid and how many other people participate in the auction. In a first price auction, a bidder weighs two competing factors: increasing one's bid increases the chance of winning, but it also implies lower utility because one must pay a higher bid. All bidders weigh these two competing factors when determining their best response to their rivals' best responses. As shown by Vickrey (1961) and others, if bidders are symmetric and risk neutral, with values drawn from a uniform distribution with support $[\underline{v}, \overline{v}]$, the closed form solution for a Nash equilibrium bid function, b_i^{NE}, is:

$$b_i^{NE} = \underline{v} + \frac{N-1}{N}(v_i - \underline{v}). \tag{2.3}$$

If $\underline{v} = 0$, the Nash equilibrium bid is $(N-1)/N$ times the bidder's value, v_i. In a first price auction, people do not have an incentive to reveal their true value. Rather they shave their bids downward based on the number of bidders in the auction. In a two person auction, for instance, a bidder would submit a bid equal to half their value, $b_i = 1/2v_i$. One might be tempted to draw the conclusion that a first price auction will provide a good approximation to true values if N is large; however, one must recognize the result in expression (2.3) also depends on the strong assumptions of a uniform distribution for values, risk neutrality, and symmetry. A violation of any of these assumptions can alter the Nash equilibrium bid function.

Of course the weakly dominant strategy of truthful value revelation in the second price auction rests on assumptions as well. These assumptions are significantly weaker than those required to arrive at a closed form solution for the first price auction. That said, one still should recognize that situations arise in which the second price auction and similar mechanisms are not incentive compatible. This is the topic of the next section.

2.2.1   Assumptions of incentive compatible auctions

Most theoretical work has examined how bidding strategies are affected by relaxing the assumption that bidders are expected utility maximizers or that bidders' values are *independent* (i.e., affiliated). We consider each assumption briefly in turn.

Several studies have investigated the implications of relaxing expected utility theory with particular focus on incentives of the BDM mechanism. In a BDM mechanism, a bidder submits a bid for a good. A random number or price is then drawn from a pre-specified distribution. If the bid is greater than the randomly drawn price, the bidder "wins" and purchases a unit of the good for an amount equal to the randomly drawn price. Focusing on the valuation of monetary lotteries, Holt (1986) and Karni and Safra (1987) showed that if the *independence axiom* of expected utility theory is relaxed, the optimal bid in a BDM mechanism need not equal the certainty equivalent of the lottery. Recall, according to the independence axiom, that a person's choices should not be unduly affected by unrelated information. Formally, if a person prefers lottery **A** to lottery **B**, that person also prefers the combination $\alpha\mathbf{A} + (1 - \alpha)\mathbf{C}$ to $\alpha\mathbf{B} + (1 - \alpha)\mathbf{C}$ for all $1 > \alpha > 0$ and **C**. Intuitively, the independence axiom says that a person's choice between two gambles depends only on the states of nature in which those gambles yield different results (see Machina, 1982). The independence axiom requires preferences for lotteries to be a linear function over the set of distribution functions. Stated differently, the axiom imposes the linear-in-probabilities property familiar to the expected utility paradigm.

Intuitively, when a bidder is determining what to bid on a lottery or risky prospect in a BDM mechanism, they are evaluating a compound lottery made up of the lottery itself and of randomness in realized price. When people do not weight probabilities linearly (e.g., they violate the independence axiom and thus expected utility theory), the value of the compound lottery can differ from the value of the underlying lottery of interest. Karni and Safra (1987) went on to prove that there is no mechanism for eliciting true values for lotteries that does not depend on the independence axiom. Popular variants of expected utility theory (e.g., rank-dependent utility theory in Quiggin (1982)) relax the independence assumption, implying that it is a difficult task to determine a bidder's value for a lottery once one foregoes the assumption of expected utility theory. Karni and Safra (1987) show this result pertains beyond the BDM to the second price auction, and by implication to all nth price auctions. Hong and Nishimura (2003) showed that these theoretical results go beyond academic curiosity. In an experimental study, they found that prices from English auctions for lotteries significantly exceeded prices from second price auctions, which according to the theoretical results of Neilson (1994), implies people exhibited non-expected utility preferences when bidding in the second price auction.

Still, direct tests of expected utility theory relative to competing theories suggest that expected utility may not be an unreasonable assumption. Hey and Orme (1994) and Harless and Camerer (1994) provide tests between the major competing theories. Both studies found that no single theory best described behavior and that there was significant heterogeneity in preference functions, at least for the college students used as subjects. Hey and Orme (1994) found expected utility theory provided the best fit to the experimental data with rank-dependent expected utility theory coming in second. Harless and Camerer (1994) investigated the trade off between parsimony and model fit and developed a menu of theories that could be used in this regard including mixed fanning, prospect theory, expected utility theory, and expected value. On a final note, these critiques relate to the valuation of random goods or those for which people are uncertain of the value.[2]

Now consider the question of *affiliated values*. Attention has focused on investigating bidding behavior when people have interdependent preferences. If the value to one bidder depends in part on information available to other bidders (i.e., values are affiliated), Milgrom and Weber (1982) and McAfee and McMillan (1987) show that the second price auction is neither incentive compatible nor efficient. Klemperer (1999) provides a straightforward illustration of the problem. Consider the general case in which a bidder's value for a good is given by $v_i = \alpha t_i + \beta \sum_{j \neq i} t_j$, where t is a signal received by each bidder. If $\beta = 0$, the model collapses to the case of private independent values. If $\alpha = \beta$,

---

[2] Horowitz (2005) suggests violations of expected utility theory could affect how people reveal values for non-random goods (i.e., those goods for which individuals are certain about the value). If people exhibit a certain type of non-expected utility preference function, as in Machina (1982), the optimal bid in a BDM mechanism or second price auction need not equal a bidder's value. Machina's preference function is characterized by people possessing a local utility function that depends on the particular probability distribution – e.g., $U_i(v_i|G)$. While Horowitz's results imply that the incentive compatibility of the BDM and second price auction are not universal, his results are not a condemnation of value elicitation for all non-expected utility models. For example, the BDM and nth price auctions are incentive compatible if individuals have rank-dependent expected utility or disappointment aversion (Gul 1991) preferences.

the model captures the idea of pure common values, that is everyone values the good identically. In reality, most auctions can be characterized by $\alpha > \beta$, where people combine their own signal of value with others' values given imperfect information about quality, resale value, or concerns related to social standing. Because individual i does not know others' signals, they do not know the precise value of the good to themselves. The bidder must form some expectation of the signal of all other bidders. Assuming bidders are risk neutral and signals are independently drawn from a uniform distribution on $[0, \bar{t}]$, Klemperer (1999) shows the optimal bid in a second price auction is:

$$b_i^* = \left(\alpha + \frac{N}{2} \beta \right) t_i. \tag{2.4}$$

A bidder will not bid his true value under affiliation; he could over- or under-bid depending on the number of bidders and the magnitude of β.

To get around the problem of affiliation, Dasgupta and Maskin (2000) proposed a generalization of the Vickrey auction in which each bidder submits a bid function contingent on other bidders' private values. In their *efficient auction*, the auctioneer takes these contingent bids and calculates each bidder's bid as a function of the bid functions, then determines the high bidder and the price, which is also a function of all bid functions other than the high bidder. Given affiliation, the key is that the auction once again separates what bidders pay from what they say, such that efficiency is achieved: the bidder with highest value wins the auction. Although some empirical support for Dasgupta and Maskin's efficient mechanism has been found (e.g., Margolis and Shogren, 2004), its practical implementation could prove difficult as it requires each bidder to submit bid functions over all possible preferences of rivals.

Perry and Reny (2002) suggest an alternative two-step bidding mechanism that requires each bidder to submit a bid for a good (or goods) in an initial round and then requires each bidder to submit a bid against each and every other bidder in a second round. Again, the mechanism separates what people say from what they pay. As noted by Perry and Reny (p. 1207), "[b]idder i's second-round bids against bidder j are submitted after i infers the entire vector of signals from the first-round bids. However, i's bids against j are independent of j's first-round bids. Consequently, j is unable to affect the price he pays for any unit."

Finally, we note that in deriving the incentive compatibility property of the second price auction, the utility function was defined only over income and goods consumed in the experiment. A person may not strictly bid true value if they have goals that extend beyond the immediate experimental context. For example, people may derive utility from sending a "signal" to researchers to influence future prices or offerings of a good or service that might later be purchased in the marketplace. Also, a person might derive utility from "looking good" to the researcher and this type of social desirability bias might manifest itself in bidding behavior. Bidders might just like to win for winning's sake – to be the top dog. However, virtually all experimental economic and marketing research methods are open to such criticism. The key point is that incentive compatible mechanisms, such as the second price auction, impose an immediate cost on people if they choose to send "signals" by bidding in a manner that deviates from their true value. The opportunity cost of non-optimal bidding is immediately obvious in the form of negative profits.

This section emphasizes that the class of auctions we consider in this book are incentive compatible given a set of assumptions. The reader will have to determine whether the assumptions underlying the theory of incentive compatibility holds for the good and context in which their auction is conducted. We considered three issues which might render an auction non-incentive compatible. First, if one believes bidders are not expected utility maximizers, standard auctions for goods with uncertain outcomes might not yield the desired bidding behavior. Thus far, the literature has yet to offer many solutions for how to truthfully elicit valuations in an auction context, when individuals have non-expected utility preferences. One suggestion offered by Tversky *et al.* (1990) is to have people bid on goods (or lotteries), but determine allocations based only on the ranking (and not the magnitude) of bids. Second, if one believes that bidders do not have independent private values, bidding behavior might not be in accordance to theory. Here several mechanisms exist, such as those suggested by Dasgupta and Maskin (2000) or Perry and Reny (2002), which can restore the incentive properties of the auctions. Third, people might not bid true value if they attempt to please the researcher with their bidding behavior or if they believe their response to be consequential beyond the immediate auction context. One way to better understand the robustness of the auction theory assumptions and concepts is to test them in an empirical setting. This is the topic of the next section.

2.3   Evidence from induced value auctions

The effectiveness of the incentive compatibility properties of nth price auctions, the BDM, and the English auction depends on several key assumptions. The open question is whether these mechanisms are empirically demand revealing. Several experimental studies have investigated this issue for a variety of mechanisms using *induced values*: values assigned to participants by the experimenter. The idea is that people gain value by selling the "good" won in the auction back to the monitor; profits equal market price minus the induced value. Studies vary in the procedures implemented, but the general approach is as follows. First, people are recruited to participate in an experimental session in which they participate in several bidding rounds. At the beginning of each round, each person is assigned an *induced value* for one unit of a fictitious commodity – "a unit." In some applications, people are informed about the distribution from which the values were drawn; in others, they are not told. People are told that winning bidder(s) will earn an amount equal to the difference between their assigned induced value and the market price. The winning bidder(s) and market price depend on the particular auction mechanisms under inquiry. For instance, the highest bidder pays the second highest bid in the second price auction, the last remaining bidder pays the last rejected bid in an English auction, and people with bids higher than a randomly drawn price pay the random price in the BDM. Bidders that do not win the auction earn $0 for that round. The process is repeated for several rounds (the literature reports applications using as few as five rounds and some applications have used as many 45 rounds) and partic- ipants are paid what they earn either over all rounds played or over one or more randomly selected rounds.

The advantage of induced value studies is that the experimenter assigns (i.e., induces) values to each bidder. By investigating whether each bidder then offers bids equal to the induced value, one can explicitly test whether an auction mech- anism is demand revealing. These induced value experiments directly measure bidding behavior. By understanding which auctions work poorly or successfully under these conditions, one can have more confidence in a particular auction used to reveal homegrown values, which is the focus of this book.

Coppinger *et al.* (1980) were the first to investigate bidding behavior in the second price and English auctions in an induced value experiment. They tested the isomorphism between Dutch and first-price auctions and between the English and second price auctions, and they investigated efficiency and revenue generation of the mechanisms. Their results directly pertain to the demand revealing nature of the English and second price auctions. They were unable to reject the hypothesis that the observed market prices in the English and second price auctions differed from theoretical predictions (e.g., the second highest induced value). They also found that individual bidding behavior tended to improve relative to the theoretical prediction with experience. Finally, they found that the English auction was most efficient (about 97% efficient) followed by the second price auction (about 96% efficient). First price and Dutch auctions lagged these two mechanisms with efficiency at 90% and 78%. A similar study by Cox *et al.* (1982) found that the second price auction behaved according to theory (in terms of observed prices) when there were six or nine bidders but not when there were three.

Following these initial studies, Kagel *et al.* (1987) and Kagel and Levin (1993) investigated the demand revealing properties of the English and second price auctions. Their framework differed from the earlier studies in at least one important way. Whereas Coppinger *et al.* (1980) prohibited people from bidding more than their induced value, Kagel *et al.* (1987) did not constrain bidding behavior. The results from these studies suggested the second price auction was not demand revealing, rather people tended to over-bid in second price auctions. For example, Kagel *et al.* (1987) found that in 80% of auctions investigated, the market price exceeded the second highest induced value in the second price auction. This finding contrasted sharply with the English auction in which 76% of bidding behavior was characterized by the truth-telling strategy.

Despite these findings, Kagel (1995) contended that it is surprising that deviations from the truthful bidding strategy were not *larger* than what was observed, given the lack of transparency of truthful bidding when such a strategy is not revealed, and that (p. 513), "the dominant bidding strategy does have some drawing power in explaining behavior . . . Thus, what we are seeing in the second-price auction is relatively stable and modest (in terms of expected cost) bidding above valuations, rather than a complete collapse of the theory."

The influence of the findings from Kagel *et al.* (1987) and their on-going work cannot be understated. Their findings have instilled a commonly held view among economists that the second price auction is not demand revealing and that the typical result from such auctions is over-bidding relative to valuations. For example, in a recent paper Bernard (2005) indicates, "One of the more commonly known and used results of auction theory is the equivalence of the second-price and English auction mechanisms . . . Despite the theoretical equivalence of the two auctions, experimental studies have shown consistently that only the latter matches predictions. Instead, many studies . . . have found a strong tendency for subjects in a second-price auction to submit bids great than their values."

Unfortunately, this view does not consider more recent papers that focused on individual bidding behavior, in which the hypothesis of truthful bidding in the second price auction cannot be rejected (e.g., Noussair, Robin, and Ruffieux, 2004; Shogren *et al.*, 2001a; Parkhurst, Shogren, and Dickinson, 2004; Lusk and Rousu, 2006). These papers typically estimate the parameters (α and β) of the following bid function: $bid = \alpha + \beta$ (*induced value*) and test the joint hypothesis that $\alpha = 0$ and $\beta = 1$.

In many ways, this analysis is more convincing than earlier studies as it relates to whether the market price is as expected and whether *all* bids are as expected. Even if one looks at individual bidding behavior and does not address the estimated bid functions, it becomes evident that over-bidding, at the individual bidder level, is not necessarily the norm in second price auctions. For example, Shogren *et al.* (2001a) found that of 280 second price auction bids, about 56% were exactly equal to induced values, 33% were less than induced values, and only 11% were over-bids; further 65% all bids were within $0.10 of induced values. Similarly, Lusk and Rousu (2006) found that about 38% of subjects in their induced value study bid exactly true value after only two rounds of learning (68% bid within two tokens of their induced value) while only 33% over-bid. Further, although Hong and Nishimura (2003) were, in some circumstances, able to reject the equality of market prices and the second highest bid, they observed *under-bidding* in the second price auction. Noussair *et al.* (2004) also observed significant *under-bidding* in the second price auction in initial bidding rounds. At this point it is unknown exactly why the more recent results of Hong and Nishimura (2003), Shogren *et al.* (2001a), Parkhurst *et al.* (2004), and others differ from the earlier results in Kagel *et al.* (1987), Kagel and Levin (1993), and Harstad (2000), although differences in instructions, experimental methods, and methods of data analysis certainly play a role. What is clear is that the view that over-bidding in the second price auction is a universally pervasive phenomenon can be rejected.

In addition to these studies focused on the second price and English auctions, other incentive compatible mechanisms have been investigated as well. Table 2.3 provides a list of studies that have tested incentive compatible mechanisms in induced value studies. Irwin *et al.* (1998) was the first to study the BDM mechanism in an induced value setting in both willingness-to-pay and willingness-to-accept settings. They found that, after five practice rounds, 62% of willingness to pay bids and 67% of willingness to accept bids were approximately equal to true value. They could not reject the hypothesis that bids equaled induced values for either type of valuation. In the willingness-to-pay treatment, they found that accuracy improved with learning: individuals bid $0.03 closer to true value, on average, each additional round. Noussair *et al.* (2004) found that bids in the BDM were significantly different than true values in all five rounds of their study; however, while the average bid was 40% less than true values in round 1, it was only 6% less than true values by round 5.

Shogren *et al.* (2001a), Parkhurst *et al.* (2004), and Lusk and Rousu (2006) investigated the performance of the random *n*th price auction. The general results from these studies are that the random *n*th price auction is demand revealing in aggregate, but that it performs better for off-margin subjects (i.e., those with relatively low valuations) than for on-margin subjects (i.e., those with relatively high valuations). These studies also showed the second price auction tended to be demand revealing all along the demand curve, but that it performs relatively better for high-value individuals. Lusk and Rousu (2006) also investigated the random *n*th price auction in addition to the second price auction and the BDM mechanism. Although they could not reject the hypothesis of truthful bidding with the BDM, they found that the second price and random *n*th price auctions were more accurate at truthfully revealing values than the BDM.

In summary, performance of incentive compatible mechanisms in induced value studies reveals equivocal support for demand revealing nature of the mechanisms. In the few studies that have investigated the English auction, its performance has been nothing short of stellar; it generates almost 100%

Table 2.3. *Results of studies testing incentive compatible mechanisms in induced value experiments*

Author(s)	Year	Mechanism	Unit of Analysis[a]	Reject Incentive Compatibility?	Explanation
Coppinger et al.	1980	Second price	MP	No	
Coppinger et al.	1980	Second price	IB	Yes and No	Rejected in early bidding rounds, but not in late bidding rounds
Coppinger et al.	1980	English	MP	No	
Cox et al.	1982	Second price	MP	Yes and No	Rejected in auctions with only 3 bidders; but not in auctions with 6 or 9 bidders
Kagel et al.	1987	Second price	MP	Yes	Rejected in favor of over-bidding
Kagel et al.	1987	English	MP	No	
Kagel and Levin	1993	Second price	IB	Yes	Rejected in favor of over-bidding
Irwin et al.	1998	BDM	IB	No	
Harstad	2000	Second price	IB	Yes	Rejected in favor of over-bidding
Harstad	2000	English	IB	Yes and No	Rejected in fixed effects model, but not in pooled model
Shogren et al.	2001a	Second price	IB	Yes and No	Rejected for off-margin bidders in fixed effects model, but not rejected for off-margin bidders in random effects model or for on-margin or entire sample of bidders
Shogren et al.	2001a	Random nth price	IB	Yes and No	Rejected for on-margin bidders, but not for entire sample or off-margin bidders

(*cont.*)

Table 2.3. (cont.)

Author(s)	Year	Mechanism	Unit of Analysis[a]	Reject Incentive Compatibility?	Explanation
Hong and Nishimura	2003	English	MP	No	
Hong and Nishimura	2003	Second price	MP	Yes and No	Result depends on type of test conducted
Parkhurst et al.	2004	Second price	IB	No	Not rejected for on- or off-margin bidders or for negative or positive valuations
Parkhurst et al.	2004	Random nth price	IB	No	Not rejected for on- or off-margin bidders or for negative or positive valuations
Noussair et al.	2004	Second price	IB	Yes and No	Rejected in favor of under-bidding in early rounds, but not rejected after round three
Noussair et al.	2004	BDM	IB	Yes	Rejected in favor of under-bidding
Lusk and Rousu	2006	Second price	IB	No	
Lusk and Rousu	2006	BDM	IB	No	
Lusk and Rousu	2006	Random nth price	IB	No	

[a] MP indicates analyses that focused on market prices, IB indicates analyses that focused on individual bids

efficiency and generates prices very close to the predicted outcome. The performance of the second price auction is mixed. Some studies suggest over-bidding to be a problem with the mechanism, but others do not observe such behavior. Evidence exists to suggest that repeated experience with the mechanism helps improve performance. The BDM mechanism has only received scant attention, but evidence suggests it is reasonably demand revealing after a period of learning, though perhaps less so than the second price or random nth price auctions. The random nth price auction appears to perform well for relatively low-value individuals, but does not always accurately reveal relatively high bids.

One interpretation of these results is that the mechanisms are too inaccurate to be used to elicit homegrown values that are the focus of this book. We are more optimistic. Participants in the induced value studies identified in Table 2.3 were not informed of the dominant strategy in these auctions (Shogren *et al.* (2001a) is one exception). Participants either had to infer this strategy from raw intuition, reasoning, or from trial and error. Considering that many of the studies in Table 2.3 only used five to 10 bidding rounds, any feedback from trial and error is weak. What induced values studies have shown is that incentive compatible mechanisms can reasonably approximate truthful bidding (better than ad-hoc or random bidding strategies) even when it is likely that experimental participants do not explicitly realize the dominant strategy of truthful bidding. What one need recognize is that when incentive compatible auctions are used to elicit homegrown values, people are explicitly told the weakly dominant strategy and are provided with reasoning as to why they should follow it when bidding. Although some experimentation is likely to take place in experimental auctions, it is hard to imagine that people would regularly act against their own self-interest and not offer bids equal to their values.[3] This argument is best summarized by Kagel (1995 p. 513), ". . . there is little doubt that if presented with Vickrey's argument [of incentive compatibility], or clear enough examples embodying that argument, subjects would follow the dominant strategy."

---

[3] In the context of a bargaining game, Lusk and Hudson (2004) showed that explicitly revealing the theoretic Nash equilibrium to players served to push outcomes closer to the predicted outcome compared to when subjects had to act using their own reasoning and intuition.

3   Value theory

3.1   Introduction

For auction markets to be useful in understanding demand for new products, services, or technologies, we assume people *have* an economic value, v_i, for the good or service up for auction. This value can be positive, negative, or zero, but the assumption is that a value does exist. We now discuss exactly what we mean by the idea of economic value and how it is derived from a utility theoretic framework.

This chapter discusses the economic concepts of willingness to pay (WTP) and willingness to accept (WTA), which are the values that are elicited in an auction. The chapter lays the foundation for how to interpret a person's value using the benchmark model of rational individual decision making characterized in neoclassical economics.[1] The chapter first considers how to derive WTP and WTA for the case when the quality of a good is known with certainty. Valuation measures are then derived for the case of uncertainty, where a person attaches probabilities to whether a good possesses particular levels of quality. For uncertain quality, we start by discussing the expected utility model, and then we consider a few non-expected utility models. The last part of this chapter considers how to derive WTP and WTA in a dynamic setting when people have the ability to delay their decision to buy or sell. Later in the book, in Chapter 9, we extend our discussion to include some of the findings from behavioral economics and psychology.

3.2   Valuation under certainty

We begin by focusing on a consumer's valuation for a good of known quality. A person's value for a good can be viewed from two perspectives: his willingness

---

[1] Recent work in behavioral economics and psychology has led some to question the descriptive validity of the neoclassical view due to experiential evidence suggesting that expected utility fails in certain situations and that valuations often appear contextual and malleable. One difficulty with such critiques is that formal models of decision making and welfare have not been fully developed to incorporate such behaviors. One exception is with regard to decision making under uncertainty, wherein a number of alternative theories have been proposed. A few of these models are discussed in this chapter.

to pay (WTP) to purchase the good or his willingness to accept (WTA) compensation to sell the good. The appropriate value measure to use in an auction depends on whether the person owns the perceived property rights to the good. If a person does not own the rights to the good, WTP is the appropriate measure of value. If a person owns the rights, WTA is the appropriate measure of value. The neoclassical model suggests WTP and WTA should be approximately equivalent if (1) the value of the good is small relative to income, (2) close substitutes exist for the good, and (3) there is no uncertainty about a person's preference for the good (Haneman, 1991).

3.2.1   Willingness to pay

Suppose we are interested in eliciting WTP to improve the quality of an existing good, say improving the gas mileage of a car from 18 miles/gallon to 25 miles/gallon, holding all other factors constant. Heuristically, WTP is the amount a person will pay that makes them *indifferent* to improving the quality of the good or keeping the status quo quality. More formally, consider a consumer's utility maximization problem subject to a budget constraint, in which the level of a good's quality (q) is fixed exogenously. Let $u(X, q)$ represent the consumer's utility function. The consumer chooses the level of market goods, X, that maximize utility subject to the budget constraint $XP = y$; where P is a vector of associated market prices for the market goods and y is income. Traditional Marshallian demand curves resulting from the maximization decision are given by $X_m(P, y, q)$. Plugging these demand curves back into the original utility function yields the indirect utility function, $v(P, y, q)$. This indirect utility function shows the maximum utility that can be gained given market prices, income, and q. Now assume a consumer considers an improvement in the quality of an existing product from quality level q_0 to q_1. The value the consumer has for this improvement is derived by determining the magnitude of WTP such that the following equality holds:

$$v(P, y - WTP, q_1) = v(P, y, q_0).$$

Thus, WTP is the amount of money that, when subtracted from a person's income, makes them indifferent to improving the quality of the non-market good from q_0 to q_1.

Conceptually, one can equivalently consider the consumer's dual expenditure minimization problem subject to a given level of utility, that is minimize XP subject to the constraint $U = (X, q)$. The consumer chooses the level of consumption of the market goods that minimizes expenditures, producing the Hicksian demand curves, $X_h(P, U, q)$, where U is the level of utility. The associated indirect expenditure function is, $m(P, U, q)$. The expenditure function shows the minimum level of expenditure required for a person to obtain utility level U, given market prices and q. The estimated value the consumer places on the change in the good's quality from q_0 to q_1 is:

$$WTP = m(P, U_0, q_0) - m(P, U_0, q_1).$$

All else being equal, it takes a higher level of expenditure to achieve utility level U_0 if a person is restricted to consume low quality, q_0, instead of high quality, q_1. Viewed in this way, we can see that WTP is the difference in the level of expenditure with and without high quality required to generate a fixed utility level, U_0. There is no difference conceptually or empirically whether WTP is viewed as a utility maximization problem or expenditure minimization problem.

An equivalent way to conceptualize WTP is to assume a consumer chooses both the level of quality, q, and the consumption of market goods, X. Here q is endogenous. Demand functions, $X_m(P, g, y)$ and $q_m(P, g, y)$, result from the utility maximization problem, where g is the price of q. The dual to this problem is to minimize expenditures on X and q subject to a given level of utility. The resulting Hicksian demand for quality is $q_h(P, g, U)$. This inverse compensated demand function for quality, $g(q_h, P, U)$ can be viewed as the WTP curve. The function identifies the price a person will pay for a given level of quality, q, given levels of P and U. The WTP for a change in quality from q_0 to q_1 is $\int_{q_0}^{q_1} g(q_h, P, U_0)dq$. Viewing WTP from this perspective makes clear that WTP for quality changes in one good depends on market prices, P, of market goods.

Our discussion has focused on the final consumer. But researchers are often interested in estimating a firm's WTP for a new product or service. Although WTP is almost always discussed within the context of consumer utility maximization, this concept can also be extended to producers. Consider a firm's profit maximization decision subject to a given production function. The producer chooses the level of inputs, W, to use, but the level of one input, q, is fixed exogenously. Here q can be thought of as the level of some service provided, a new technology, or the quality of some input. Given a vector of input prices, R, and a vector of output prices, P, the firm chooses the optimal level of inputs, which yields the indirect restricted profit function, $\pi(P, R, q)$. This indirect profit function shows the maximum profit that can be obtained given input and output prices, and a fixed level of q. Now assume the firm considers improving the quality of an existing input from q_0 to q_1. The WTP, or shadow price, for the change is: $WTP = \pi(P, R, q_1) - \pi(P, R, q_0)$. Here WTP represents the maximum amount of profit a firm would be willing to forgo to have q_1 rather than q_0.

3.2.2   Willingness to accept

Suppose now the person owns the good up for auction such that the appropriate measure of value is WTA. Consider the case in which a person considers how much compensation they would accept for a reduction in the quality of a good they own from q_1 to q_0. Here WTA is the compensation required to make a person indifferent to the reduction in quality and the status quo. From the utility maximization perspective, a consumer maximizes, $u(X, q)$, subject to the budget constraint, $XP = y$, which yields the indirect utility function $v(P, y, q)$. The value the consumer places on the quality degradation is given by the magnitude of WTA such that the following equality holds:

$$v(P, y + WTA, q_0) = v(P, y, q_1).$$

Thus, WTA is the amount of money, that when added to income, makes a person indifferent to having q_1 or q_0. From the perspective of the expenditure minimization problem, WTA is given by:

$$m(P, U_1, q_0) - m(P, U_1, q_1),$$

where $m(P, U, q)$ is the indirect expenditure function. One can also derive a WTA function from a utility maximization problem in which q is endogenous. Here the inverse demand for quality is $g(q_h, P, U)$; and the WTA for a change in quality from q_1 to q_0 is $\int_{q_0}^{q_1} g(q_h, P, U_1)dq$.

3.3   Valuation under uncertainty

The WTP and WTA measures of value were derived under the assumption that people knew exactly how quality would change. In reality, this is not always the case; people frequently evaluate alternatives where the exact quality is unknown *a priori*. For example, every day people consume food with some positive risk that they will get sick from a food-borne pathogen. Risk is defined by the combination of two elements: the *probabilities* (or chances) that good or bad outcome occurs, and the *outcomes* or *consequences* realized when the event does occur.

Suppose a person is asked to consider a change in a product that could produce one of two quality outcomes: q_0 or q_1. For food safety, a technological change might produce "good quality" such as better health, but might produce "low quality" by making a person ill. For example, although irradiation is a technology that can be used to kill food-borne pathogens, reducing the short-term chance of food poisoning, some people believe the technology might also increase the chance of developing illnesses like cancer in the long term. As before, assume the person knows with certainty the utility they derive from a high or low quality good: they derive $U(y, q_1)$ if a "good" outcome occurs and high quality is realized; they derive $U(y, q_0)$ if a "bad" outcome occurs and low quality is realized, where $U(y, q_1) > U(y, q_0)$ for all levels of income y, and U is increasing in y.

Despite knowledge of the utility derived from high and low quality, the person does not know with certainty whether a good will be of low or high quality until after consuming the product. Assume the product is of high quality with probability p and low quality with probability $(1 - p)$. Expected utility from consuming the good is:

$$EU = pU(y, q_1) + (1 - p)U(y, q_0).$$

Now suppose a person is offered the opportunity to choose between purchasing a good with the uncertain outcome given above and a new product of high quality with certainty, producing utility of $U(y, q_1)$ with probability one. The most a person would be willing to pay to obtain the new good is given by the *ex ante* WTP that produces the following equality:

$$U(y - WTP, q_1) = pU(y, q_1) + (1 - p)U(y, q_0).$$

WTP is amount of money that makes a person indifferent between having the high quality good for sure and playing the gamble of consuming the risky good. If the risk reduction did not completely eliminate the chance of a bad outcome, then the most a person would be willing to pay for an increase in the probability of a good outcome from p_0 to p_1 is:

$$p_1 U(y - WTP, q_1) + (1 - p_1)U(y - WTP, q_0)$$
$$= p_0 U(y, q_1) + (1 - p_0)U(y, q_0).$$

Now, consider the case in which a person owns a high quality product, in which they derive $U(y, q_1)$. Suppose the person is asked to sell this product for one with uncertain quality, yielding expected utility $pU(y, q_1) + (1 - p)U(y, q_0)$. The minimum compensation one will accept to give up the certain product for the risky one is:

$$U(y, q_1) = pU(y + WTA, q_1) + (1 - p)U(y + WTA, q_0).$$

WTA is the level of compensation that makes a person indifferent between the high quality product with certainty without WTA and the gamble of a low quality product with the extra income WTA. If the person is offered the chance to be paid to decrease the probability of a good outcome from p_1 to p_0, the minimum compensation required to accept this change is:

$$p_1 U(y, q_1) + (1 - p_1)U(y, q_0)$$
$$= p_0 U(y + WTA, q_1) + (1 - p_0)U(y + WTA, q_0).$$

In the preceeding, it was assumed that when provided with new information on the probability of a good outcome, people took the information at face value; however, in reality it is not always true. The probabilities of good and bad states are subjective and people use various updating rules to incorporate new information. To illustrate, consider again the expected utility obtained from consuming a product:

$$EU = \tilde{p}U(y, q_1) + (1 - \tilde{p})U(y, q_0),$$

where $\tilde{p}$ represents prior beliefs of a good outcome, which is a function of all accumulated information obtained by the decision maker. Suppose a new "signal" is received concerning the probability of observing a good outcome: p'. Examples include public information from the government, firm advertising, word of mouth, or previous experience consuming the product. If a Bayesian perspective is taken when considering the new information, then prior beliefs will be updated based on this new information. Following Viscusi (1989) and Hayes et $al.$ (1995) and assuming a general beta distribution, a person's belief in the likelihood of a good outcome after receiving the new information is $\hat{p} = \frac{\alpha\tilde{p} + \beta p'}{\alpha + \beta}$, where α is the weight assigned to prior beliefs and β is the weight put on the new information. Substituting this expression into the expected utility formula yields:

$$EU = \left(\frac{\alpha\tilde{p} + \beta p'}{\alpha + \beta}\right) U(y, q_1) + \left(1 - \frac{\alpha\tilde{p} + \beta p'}{\alpha + \beta}\right) U(y, q_0).$$

The person's WTP to obtain q_1 for sure is now written as:

$$U(y - WTP, q_1) = \left(\frac{\alpha\tilde{p} + \beta p'}{\alpha + \beta}\right) U(y, q_1) + \left(1 - \frac{\alpha\tilde{p} + \beta p'}{\alpha + \beta}\right) U(y, q_0).$$

Totally differentiating this expression with respect to WTP and p', and rearranging terms indicates that:

$$\frac{dWTP}{dp'} = \frac{\beta}{\alpha + \beta} \left(\frac{U(y, q_0) - U(y, q_1)}{dU(y, q_1)/dy}\right) \leq 0. \tag{3.1}$$

Equation (3.1) shows that WTP to obtain q_1 is decreasing in p'. If a person learns there is a higher likelihood of receiving the high quality outcome from consuming the good, they will pay less to obtain a good that is high quality with certainty. But as equation (3.1) shows, WTP is conditioned by how the person weighs the new information relative to their prior information. For example, if $\beta = 0$ the person ignores the new information and WTP is unchanged. Incidentally, the right-hand side of the equality in equation (3.1) is the same for WTA. WTA to consume the good with an uncertain outcome falls once one learns there is a greater likelihood q_1 will be obtained and the magnitude of the change is conditional on the relative magnitudes of α and β.

It is also useful to consider how people value changes in a continuous set of risky outcomes as opposed to the simple dichotomous good/bad outcomes just discussed. Suppose a person evaluates the desirability of consuming a new good, and the outcome of this consumption is risky. Let $\tilde{Z}$ be a random variable representing the risky outcome with variance σ^2 and mean $E[\tilde{Z}] = \bar{Z}$. Define *CE* as the certainty equivalent, which is the amount of money that makes the person indifferent between consuming the good with outcome $\tilde{Z}$ and receiving the certain amount non-random money *CE*. *CE* represents the person's monetary value of consuming the good, that is a person's WTP for the good. The definition of the certainty equivalent implies the following equality:

$$E[U(y + \tilde{Z})] = U(y + CE) \tag{3.2}$$

where, as before, y is income or wealth. Pratt (1964) shows by taking a Taylor series expansion around y on both sides of equation (3.2) and rearranging terms that the certainty equivalent is approximately equal to:

$$WTP = CE \approx \bar{Z} - \frac{1}{2}\sigma^2 \left(-\frac{U''(y)}{U'(y)} \right) \tag{3.3}$$

where $r(y) = -U''(y)/U'(y)$ is the Pratt-Arrow measure of absolute risk aversion and an increase in $r(y)$ is associated with an increase in risk aversion.

Recalling that *CE* represents the individual's monetary value for the good, or an individual's WTP for the good, equation (3.3) implies that the value of the good to the individual is *decreasing* in the variance, σ^2, and in the measure of risk aversion, $r(y)$. Because σ^2 represents the perceived risk in consuming the good, increases in perceived risk are associated with decreases in WTP. That is, if there is a higher chance that consuming the good will yield a bad outcome (i.e., σ^2 increases), the good becomes less valuable and WTP falls. Increases in risk aversion $r(w)$ are also associated with reductions in WTP to obtain the good. In summary, equation (3.3) implies that WTP to obtain a risky good, as measured by certainty equivalent, is influenced by risk preferences, perceptions of the risk in consuming the good, and the expected value of consuming the good. The preceding discussion focused on WTP to obtain a risky good; however, interest often lies in one's WTP to avoid a risky good – a concept referred to as the risk premium. Formally, the risk premium is the difference between the *CE* and the expected value of the lottery, that is, risk premium $= \bar{Z} - CE$. From equation 3.3, it is straightforward to see that WTP to avoid a risky outcome (i.e., the risk premium) is increasing in perceived risk, σ^2, and in the level of risk aversion, $r(w)$.

These findings imply that to fully understand the determinants of auctions bids obtained from an experiment, measures of risk preferences and risk perceptions are needed. There are several methods available to elicit these constructs. In the context of food safety, Hayes et al. (1995) directly asked people about their perceived likelihood of becoming ill from eating a pork sandwich and investigated how auction bids varied across such stated perceived risk. Hayes et al. (1995) asked people to respond to the following question, "What do you think is the chance of becoming ill from (pathogen name), given that you eat an average amount of typical products in the United States over a year? Answer: _____chance out of 1 million people." Stating an exact probability, especially for a low-probability event, can be a difficult task for people. An alternative approach is to use psychometric scales. For example, Pennings *et al.* (2002) measured risk perceptions by asking people questions like, "I think eating beef is risky" on a scale of 1 (strongly disagree) to 9 (strongly agree). Lusk and Coble (2005) took a similar approach to measure risk perceptions by asking questions like, "The side-effects from genetic modification in food production are largely unknown" on a scale of 1 (strongly disagree) to 9 (strongly agree).

Measuring risk preferences can be more involved. One approach is to use economic experiments to estimate Pratt-Arrow coefficients of risk aversion. For example, Holt and Laury (2002) introduced an approach that has been used in many subsequent studies (e.g., Lusk and Coble, 2005). Their approach asks people to make ten choices between two lotteries that have uncertain monetary outcomes. Choices are used to identify people's Pratt-Arrow coefficients of relative risk aversion. Another approach might involve asking people to state their certainty equivalent for monetary lotteries as in Becker *et al.* (1964), which can be used to construct a utility function for each person. A less precise, but easy-to-implement approach is to use psychometric scales to estimate risk preferences. For example, Pennings *et al.* (2002) measured risk preferences by asking people questions like, "I am willing to accept the risk of eating beef" on a scale of 1 (strongly disagree) to 9 (strongly agree).

3.3.1   Non-expected utility behavior

Expected utility theory is the traditional model of decision making under risk. If there are n states of nature or monetary outcomes, the expected utility model is then:

$$V_{EUT} = \sum_{i=1}^{n} p_i U(y, x_i) \tag{3.4}$$

where V_{EUT} is the expected utility of a lottery, p_i is the probability of receiving monetary outcome x_i, and $U(\bullet)$ is a strictly increasing utility function. Expected utility theory reduces to expected value maximization if $U(x) = x$. WTP for an n-outcome lottery is given by:

$$U(y - WTP) = V_{EUT}.$$

While expected utility theory has historically guided many economists' advice about behavior, not everyone agrees with this perspective. When the outcome is potentially very bad but not likely to happen, our experience tells us little about how to deal with such low-probability threats. Numerous experimental studies show that people commonly overestimate the chance that they will suffer from a risk with low odds and high damage. People use *heuristics*, or rules of thumb, to deal with risk (e.g., see Kahneman and Tversky, 2000; Tversky and Fox, 1995). People choose to think about probabilities and outcomes separately or in sequence, rather than in combination as predicted by expected utility theory. Economists and psychologists continue to test whether notions of expected utility or alternative models of behavior better explain how people make choices under risk and uncertainty.

Two recent models that attempt to capture this non-expected utility behavior include rank-dependent expected utility theory (Quiggin) and cumulative prospect theory (Kahneman and Tversky, 1979; Tversky and Kahneman, 1992). In these models, a person does not necessarily weight probabilities linearly. A probability weighting function, $w(p)$, is used to transform probabilities into weights. The probability weighting function is a strictly increasing function with bounds at zero and one.

First, consider the rank-dependent expected utility model, which is:

$$V_{RD-EUT} = \sum_{i=1}^{n} \pi_i U(y, x_i), \tag{3.5}$$

where $\pi_i = w\left(\sum_{k=i}^{n} p_k\right) - w\left(\sum_{k=i+1}^{n} p_k\right)$ for $i \leqslant n-1$, $\pi_n = w(p_n)$, and $x_1 \leq \ldots \leq x_n$. Various forms have been proposed for the weighting function: two common forms are $w(z) = z^\gamma$ and $w(z) = z^\gamma / [z^\gamma + (1-z)^\gamma]^{1/\gamma}$, where γ is a parameter indicating the shape of the weighting function. Equation (3.5) models behavior under risk as ranking the outcomes in order of preference and then distorting the decumulative probabilities through a probability weighting function. To illustrate, consider a lottery with a p_1 chance of x_1 and p_2 chance of x_2 (where $x_1 < x_2$), then the rank-dependent expected utility of the lottery is $(1 - w(p_2))U(y, x_1) + w(p_2)U(y, x_2)$. Rank-dependent theory collapses to expected utility theory if $w(p) = p$ or if $\gamma = 1$. People's valuations under rank-dependent expected utility theory are similar to that in expected utility theory for a 100% reduction in risk. WTP to obtain an n-outcome lottery is:

$$U(y - WTP) = \sum_{i=1}^{n} \pi_i U(y, x_i).$$

WTA to give up an n-outcome lottery is:

$$U(y) = \sum_{i=1}^{n} \pi_i U(y + WTA, x_i).$$

Cumulative prospect theory is similar to rank-dependent theory except prospect theory permits different probability weighting functions and utility functions for gains and losses relative to some reference point (Tversky and Kahneman 1992). For the sake of convenience, assume the reference point is zero and $x_1 \leq \ldots \leq x_r \leq 0 \leq x_{r+1} \ldots \leq x_n$. The utility of a lottery in cumulative prospect theory is:

$$V_{CPT} = \sum_{i=1}^{r} \pi_i^{-} U^{-}(x_i) + \sum_{j=1}^{n} \pi_j^{+} U^{+}(x_j), \tag{3.6}$$

where the decision weights for losses, π_i^{-}, and gains, π_i^{+}, are separately defined in a manner similar to that above and where $U^{-}(x)$ and $U^{+}(x)$ are the utility functions for losses and gains, respectively. Cumulative prospect theory reduces to rank-dependent expected utility if $w^{-}(p) = 1 - w^{+}(p)$ for all p and $U^{-}(x) = U^{+}(x)$ for all x. In cumulative prospect theory, valuation measures, WTP and WTA, depend on the initial reference point and whether a lottery is perceived as a gain, in which the formulas $w^{+}(p)$ and $U^{+}(x)$ apply or as a loss in which the formulas $w^{-}(p)$ and $U^{-}(x)$ apply.

3.4 Valuation in a dynamic environment with uncertainty, limited information, and irreversibility

A person's value for a good has been treated as static in that WTP remains constant throughout time so long as prices, income, risk preferences, and the degree of uncertainty remained constant. Recent work by Zhao and Kling (2001, 2004) illustrates that WTP for a good *today* may depend on expectations about the ability to gain additional information in the future and the ability to reverse the buy/sell decision. They define "commitment costs" as the difference between the expected value of a good in the future and what one is willing to pay for a good today; it is the cost of forgoing the opportunity to learn more about the value of the good if a purchase is made today.

Understanding commitment costs is potentially important for experimental auction practitioners. First, if one is to understand the determinants of WTP and WTA, then one should understand commitment costs. Second, an experimental design itself might have an influence on commitment costs and thus elicited WTP/WTA. One might be tempted to suggest that experiments should be designed to eliminate commitment costs, but further reflection would indicate that people face commitment costs in everyday purchasing decisions. New goods are routinely encountered in grocery stores, for example, and we must weigh the benefits of gathering more information about the new good against the costs of giving up the enjoyment of consuming the new good today. Ideally, a laboratory experiment would not interject or alleviate commitment costs that would not be present in the decision task one is attempting to model.

The concept of dynamic WTP is best illustrated by example. Suppose a person is presented with an opportunity (perhaps in an experimental auction) to purchase an item that is relatively unfamiliar to them, say a bottle of wine. Suppose that the person is not a wine connoisseur, but has a close friend who claims to be an expert. What is the person's WTP for the bottle of wine today? If the person buys the bottle of wine today, they give up the opportunity to ask their friend how much the bottle might really be worth. WTP for the bottle of wine today is probably less than what the individual expects the wine to be worth. We might expect WTP for the wine bottle today to be influenced by a number of factors including: how thirsty the individual is, how much of an expert they believe their friend to be, whether there is a return policy at the wine store, and whether the same bottle of wine will be available for sale tomorrow. We can state the following formula:

$$\text{WTP today} = \text{expected value} - \text{commitment costs}$$

Zhao and Kling (2001, 2004) show that commitment costs are decreasing and thus WTP increasing when people: 1) are less uncertain about a good's value, 2) expect less information to be gathered about the good in the future, 3) are more impatient, 4) expect that reversing the transaction is easier, and 5) have more freedom in choosing when to make the purchase decision.

The story is just the opposite if one considers a person's WTA to sell an item they own. From the preceding example, suppose a person inherits a bottle of wine. How much is the individual willing to accept to sell the bottle? If they have a close friend who is a wine connoisseur, their WTA today might be relatively high prior to seeking the friend's advice on the bottle's value. In general, WTA for a good today is the expected value of the good plus commitment costs associated with the selling decision. Zhao and Kling (2001, 2004) show that commitment costs are decreasing and thus WTA decreasing when people: 1) are less uncertain about a good's value, 2) expect less information to be gathered about the good in the future, 3) are more impatient, 4) expect that reversing the transaction is easier, and 5) have more freedom in choosing when to make the purchase decision.

This discussion implies that variations in WTP/WTA across people are likely to be partially attributable to the amount of information one has about the good, the ease of reversing the transaction later, the difficulty in delaying the decision, and the availability of similar substitutes outside the laboratory.

3.5   Summary

This chapter provided background on theoretical models that are useful in interpreting the values elicited in experimental auctions and in identifying determinants affecting valuations. We began by discussing the benchmark neoclassical model, where there is no uncertainty. A person's willingness-to-pay (WTP) for a quality improvement can be derived by determining the dollar amount that when subtracted from maximized utility given that quality is constrained to be high quality is exactly equal to maximized utility when the quality is constrained to be low quality. A person's willingness-to-accept (WTA) degradation in quality can be derived by determining the dollar amount that, when added to maximized utility when quality is constrained to be low quality is exactly equal to maximized utility when the quality is constrained to be high quality. Deriving WTP and WTA in this fashion illustrates that valuations are affected by income, prices, and elasticity of substitution between the auctioned good and substitute/complementary goods.

This chapter also showed how to derive valuations when there is uncertainty regarding the quality of a good. If one is interested in a person's total value for a risky good, WTP can be viewed as the certainty equivalent of a lottery; if one is interested in how much a person will pay to avoid a risk, WTP can be viewed as the risk premium of a lottery. More precisely, WTP to obtain a risky good is the amount of money that makes a person indifferent between having a high quality good with certainty (less WTP) and playing the gamble of consuming a risky good where quality might be high or low. The amount of money that must be given to a person that would make them indifferent to consume a risky good with uncertain quality and a good that is high quality for certain is WTA. The theoretical models discussed in this chapter show that people's values for risky prospects depend on the probabilities (or chances) that a good or bad event occurs, the way people weight those probabilities, the extent to which people hold on to their prior beliefs, the outcomes or consequences realized when an event does occur, and people's preferences for the outcomes, that is, risk preferences.

The final portion of this chapter discussed valuations in dynamic environments with uncertainty, limited information, and irreversibility. In such environments, WTP and WTA can be viewed as option values that depend on the amount of information expected to be gathered about the good in the future, the degree of uncertainty about a good's value, the ease in reversing and delaying the transaction, and the degree of impatience.

4   Conducting experimental auctions: some preliminaries

4.1   Introduction

In this chapter, we address some broad issues worth considering before starting off on the path of choosing specific auction parameters. Perhaps the most important initial step in any project is to define the study objectives. What are the goals of the analysis? What are the testable hypotheses? Who is the intended audience? Answering these questions will necessarily dictate many of the resulting design choices. A study that aims to test a particular behavioral or economic theory might require a significantly different design than one that aims to estimate the welfare effects of a new technology or to inform new product design. For example, a common complaint of experimental studies is that students are frequently used as subjects. The veracity of this criticism, however, depends on the nature and type of study. A theory is a generalization that should hold for everyone, *including students*. As stated by Noussair, Plott, and Riezman (1995, p. 462):

Since the world's international economies are vastly more complicated than the economies created for this study, of what relevance are laboratory-generated data? The answer is that laboratory experiments are not attempts to simulate field situations, as the question of the skeptic seems to presume. Laboratory research deals with the general theories and the general principles that are supposed to apply to all economies, the economies found in the field as well as those created in the laboratory. The laboratory economies are very simple and are special cases of the broad class of (often complex) economies to which the general theories are supposed to be of relevance. If the general theory does not work successfully to explain behavior in the simple and special cases of the laboratory, it is not general. When a model is found not working, opportunities exist to modify the theory to account for the data or to reject the theory. Thus, the laboratory provides an arena in which competing notions and theories about the nature of human (and market) capacities can be joined with the data.

Using a student sample in a laboratory auction for a study designed to test a theory or behavioral phenomenon is likely to be of little concern. The same is not necessarily true, however, for a study designed to extrapolate the value of a particular good to a population.

Although it might appear trivially obvious that one should define a study's objectives, this critical step can be overlooked. In addition to defining the objectives, several other preliminaries relating to implementing experimental auctions should be considered. This chapter considers the issues of experimental design, sample size, and study setting. Experimental design primarily concerns itself with collecting data such that the effect one is interested in measuring is actually what is measured and is not confounded with other effects. Another key purpose of experimental design is to collect data in such a way as to minimize the standard error of estimated effects. In addition to investigating *how to* collect data via experimental design, this chapter also discusses *how many* participants should be enrolled in a study. Here again, determination of sample size depends on the purpose of the study. If the purpose is to estimate a population statistic using a random sample of individuals from the population, the idea is to minimize the sampling error. If the purpose is to test for means between two treatments, the idea is to maximize the power of the test. In both cases, a key factor influencing the appropriate number of participants is the anticipated variability in valuations across people; the more diverse the opinion, the larger the sample size required. Finally, this chapter considers *where* an auction should be conducted; the laboratory or the field.

4.2   Experimental design

A primary advantage of data collected in economic experiments versus data collected from naturally occurring markets is the ability to control treatment variables and isolate the effects of changes in key variables of interest. Properly identifying the effect of a change in a treatment variable on some outcome variable (e.g., the bid) means careful thought must be given to experimental design. In auctions designed to elicit homegrown values, there are a variety of variables that can affect auction bids. To the extent possible, one should control all these variables, either by holding the variable constant at some fixed level or by systematically varying the variable between different levels to investigate the effect of the variable on auction bids.

For example, suppose one were interested in eliciting values for a new product and wanted to determine the effect of two treatment variables on bids: product information and package size. For the time being, assume all other variables potentially affecting auction bids are held at some constant level and the effects of those variables are independent of product information and package size. Assume product information is varied between two levels, *high* and *low*, and package size is varied between two levels, *small* and *large*. Table 4.1 shows there are four possible treatments created by combining all levels of product information with package size.

Table 4.1. *Four experimental treatments*

Package size	Product information	
	High	Low
Small	A	B
Large	C	D

Table 4.1 shows a *full factorial design*, where all possible combinations of variables and levels of variables are considered. In this case, the full factorial consists of four distinct treatments (A, B, C, and D). This design allows one to test the linear effects of information and package size on auction bids (e.g., the effect of moving from high to low information and the effect of moving from small to large package size), and any interaction effects that might exist (e.g., the effect of information on auction bids conditional on package size). The point of experimental design is to identify the effects of interest. Suppose data were only obtained from treatments A and D; if so, it would be impossible to determine whether a change in auction bids from treatment A to D was due to package size or information. The treatment effects are *confounded*. If one only wanted to conduct two treatments and avoid confounding the design, one could carry out treatments A and C while holding product information at *low*. Such an experiment would identify the effect of package size on bids.

This example of confounded treatment effects is trivially obvious and few practitioners would fall prey to such a mistake. But real world experiments are seldom as simple. There are many variables of interest in addition to product information and package size. To illustrate, consider the addition of another explicit treatment variable, product color, which is varied between two levels: *red* and *blue*. Now there are $2^3 = 8$ possible treatments in the full factorial design as shown in Table 4.2. Suppose resources are too scarce to collect data from all eight treatments. How can one obtain a smaller number of treatments and still estimate the effects of interest? One method involves creating *fractional factorial designs* that uses portions of the treatments from the full factorial by making assumptions about higher-order effects.

Probably the most common fractional factorial is a *main-effects only* design – a design where all linear (or main) effects are separately identifiable (Louviere *et al.*, 2000). Table 4.2 illustrates a full factorial and a main-effects design taken there from. One can identify the linear effects of information, package size, and product color by only collecting data associated with treatments F2 (high, small, blue), F3 (high, large, red), F5 (low, small, red), and F8 (low, large, blue) from the full factorial. Data only need be collected on four treatments instead of eight so long as one assumes no interaction effects exist. But how is this possible? The

Table 4.2. *Treatments in a 2^3 design*

	Variables		
Treatment	Information	Size	Color
Full factorial design			
F1	High	Small	Red
F2	High	Small	Blue
F3	High	Large	Red
F4	High	Large	Blue
F5	Low	Small	Red
F6	Low	Small	Blue
F7	Low	Large	Red
F8	Low	Large	Blue
Main-effects only design			
F2	High	Small	Blue
F3	High	Large	Red
F5	Low	Small	Red
F8	Low	Large	Blue

answer is that an assumption is made about higher order, interaction effects. To illustrate, Table 4.3 shows the interaction (or higher order) effects between each of the variables in the design, in which each level within an attribute is either coded -1 or $+1$. Table 4.3 shows that in the main-effects fractional factorial design, information $(x1)$ is exactly the same as the interaction between size and color $(x2*x3)$. In the terminology of experimental design, these two effects are *aliased*. In a similar fashion, we can see that $x2 = x1*x2$, $x3 = x1*x2$, and $x1*x2*x3 = 1$. If data were collected from the fractional factorial design in Table 4.3, the interaction effects between each of the attributes must be zero for the linear effects to be estimated without bias. Unlike the fractional factorial design, in the full factorial design, the main effects are not aliased with any of the interaction effects, meaning these effects can be separately identified.

One question that might arise is that if one must assume that interaction effects are zero, how can one determine if a main-effects design is "good"? At a basic level, experimental design is about two issues: avoiding bias and improving efficiency. Avoiding bias has already been discussed in the sense that bias is avoided by removing confounds between attributes. That means the second criterion, *efficiency*, is used as a judge of the quality of a fractional factorial design. In linear models, such as an ordinary least squares regression, the efficiency of an estimate is proportional to the inverse of the information matrix: $(X'X)^{-1}$. If $(X'X)^{-1}$ is "smaller," this means there is a greater chance of rejecting the null hypothesis that estimated coefficients are equal to zero. In general, a "smaller" information matrix will be obtained when a design is

Table 4.3. *Higher order effects in a 2^3 design*

			Variables				
Treatment	Information (x1)	Size (x2)	Color (x3)	x1*x2	x1*x3	x2*x3	x1*x2*x3
Full factorial design							
F1	High (−1)	Small (−1)	Red (−1)	1	1	1	−1
F2	High (−1)	Small (−1)	Blue (1)	1	−1	−1	1
F3	High (−1)	Large (1)	Red (−1)	−1	1	−1	1
F4	High (−1)	Large (1)	Blue (1)	−1	−1	1	−1
F5	Low (1)	Small (−1)	Red (−1)	−1	−1	1	1
F6	Low (1)	Small (−1)	Blue (1)	−1	1	−1	−1
F7	Low (1)	Large (1)	Red (−1)	1	−1	−1	−1
F8	Low (1)	Large (1)	Blue (1)	1	1	1	1
Main-effects only fractional factorial							
F2	High (−1)	Small (−1)	Blue (1)	1	−1	−1	1
F3	High (−1)	Large (1)	Red (−1)	−1	1	−1	1
F5	Low (1)	Small (−1)	Red (−1)	−1	−1	1	1
F8	Low (1)	Large (1)	Blue (1)	1	1	1	1

orthogonal and *balanced*. An orthogonal design is one in which each of the variables or attributes are uncorrelated with one another. A balanced design is one in which each level of one variable occurs with each level of other variables a proportional number of times. For example, in the main effects design shown in Table 4.3, the level High under product information appears with the levels Small one time, Large one time, Red one time, and Blue one time. Similarly, the level Low under product information appears with the levels Small one time, Large one time, Red one time, and Blue one time. The main effects design in Table 4.3 is perfectly balanced and the variables information, size, and color are orthogonal (uncorrelated).

To illustrate the advantages of balance and orthogonality, consider the two fractional factorial designs shown in Table 4.4. The first fractional factorial design is the same as that shown in Table 4.3. In the first fractional factorial design, the correlation between each variable is zero (i.e., the design is orthogonal). By contrast, consider the second design in Table 4.4 in which F2 from the full factorial is replaced with F6. In this non-orthogonal design, x1 is now correlated with x2 and x3. The information matrices for both designs are reported in Table 4.4. As can be seen, the diagonals of the information matrix for the orthogonal design (the elements that would be used to calculate the standard error of the estimates) are much smaller than in the non-orthogonal design. One way to determine the overall "size" of the information matrix is to take its determinant (in the terminology of the experimental design literature,

Table 4.4. *A comparison of two fractional factorial designs*

Orthogonal fraction profiles in design				Correlation matrix				$(X'X)^{-1}$			$\frac{1}{|(X'X)^{-1}|}$
	x1	x2	x3		x1	x2	x3	x1	x2	x3	
F2	−1	−1	1	x1	1			0.25	0	0	
F3	−1	1	−1	x2	0	1		0	0.25	0	64
F5	1	−1	−1	x3	0	0	1	0	0	0.25	
F8	1	1	1								

Non-orthogonal fraction profiles in design				Correlation matrix				$(X'X)^{-1}$			
	x1	x2	x3		x1	x2	x3	x1	x2	x3	
F6	1	−1	1	x1	1			0.5	0.25	−0.3	
F3	−1	1	−1	x2	−0.6	1		0.25	0.38	−0.1	32
F5	1	−1	−1	x3	0.58	0	1	−0.3	−0.1	0.38	
F8	1	1	1								

inverse of the determinant of the information matrix is referred to as the D-optimality of the design). As can be seen in Table 4.4, for the orthogonal design the "size" of the information matrix is much smaller than in the non-orthogonal design; the orthogonal design is roughly twice as efficient as the non-orthogonal design.

It is relatively straightforward to find fractional factorial designs for a wide range of experiments. Addelman (1962) and Louviere *et al.* (2000) report tables providing orthogonal main effects designs for a number of full-factorials. Further, several statistical software packages have routines to generate experimental designs. For example, SAS can generate main-effects designs for any full factorial using the procedure PROC FACTEX. If one is unable to reasonably assume zero interaction effects, there are fractional factorial designs that permit estimation of higher-order effects. For example, a two-way interaction effects design can be created such that all linear and interaction effects are not confounded with each other.

Once one has settled on the experimental design, and thus the treatments to be conducted, it is important to consider replicating the treatments to reduce experimental error, which arises when two identically treated experimental units fail to yield identical results. This raises the question of how to define the experimental unit. Technically, an experimental unit is the smallest unit of experimental material to which a treatment can be allocated independent of all other units. In the case of experimental auctions, the unit is often a single individual. One must determine how people should be assigned to the treatments and how many replications (e.g., how many subjects) to conduct (we discuss the number of subjects in Section 4.3). Instead of a person, the experimental unit may be an auction session if, for example, the price generated by the auction is the statistic of interest. If so, the question is how many experimental sessions should be conducted for each treatment. In either case, it is important to realize there can be session-specific effects which implicitly serve as separate treatment variables. For example, in Table 4.1, if data were obtained from only one session in each of treatments A, B, C, and D, one could not be certain that the difference in auction bids between sessions A and C was truly due to package size or whether it was due to session-specific effects. An easy-to-implement and powerful approach to assign experimental units to treatments is *randomization* – each unit is randomly assigned to a treatment.

In addition to explicit design variables, there are other extraneous variables that might influence auction bids. For example, the time of the day or the day of the week that the experiment is conducted has been shown to influence bids (see Hoffman *et al.*, 1993). The influence of such factors might result from the dynamics of individual preference (e.g., people are hungrier closer to meal time) or to differences across people that result in selection effects (e.g., only people without a job will show up at sessions during the day). One way to hold constant such factors is to conduct all experimental treatments at the same time and day with people randomly assigned to a treatment. All too often university professors are apt to assign all students in a class to a single treatment or perhaps to assign all early arrivals to an experiment to a single treatment. One can see how such practices can lead to confounding influences if, for example, one class is made up of seniors taught in the evening and the other class is made up of juniors taught in the morning or if early arrivals have different attitudes and preferences than late arrivals. Logistically, it may not be feasible to carry out all treatments at the same time, and if so, one might consider making time, day, classification, etc. explicit treatment variables if the effects are anticipated to be large.

There will, of course, be some variables that are difficult or impossible to hold constant across subjects in an experiment. Many times these are subject-specific variables such as knowledge or income; we cannot reasonably vary a person's income from $20,000 to $100,000 and investigate the effect of this change on auction bids. There are a couple of approaches that might be followed to control for such variables. First, one can use a *within-subject design*, where a single person is assigned to more than one treatment. For example, in Table 4.1, a person might first participate in treatment C and then in treatment D. Because the individuals' age, income, gender, etc. are unchanged (i.e., held constant), the difference in behavior should be due to the treatment effect of interest, product information in this case. A word of caution: within-subject designs can create order effects due to learning or fatigue. A change in behavior from treatment

C to D may be because a person was tired of putting cognitive effort into their bidding decisions or because they learned more about the mechanics of the auction. A common method to alleviate such concerns is to use what is called an ABA design. People first participate in treatment A, then treatment B, and then treatment A again. Differences in behavior between the two A treatments can be investigated to determine whether learning or fatigue is a problem. Further, ABA experiments can be used in combination with their mirror image, BAB experiments, to average out the order effects. A second word of caution in within-subject experiments is demand reduction. If a subject makes a purchase in treatment A, they will move down their demand curve and will bid less for a second unit in treatment B. Chapter 5 provides more discussion on the effects of demand reduction and provides suggestions for dealing with the problem. The most straightforward way to handle the potential problem is to only make one of the treatments binding, by randomly picking one of the treatments after the experiment is complete.

A final method to control for other confounding variables is the one familiar to most economists: randomly recruit a large sample of participants and use ex-post regression analysis to determine the *ceteris paribus* treatment effects. Data can be collected from people after the experiment on income, age, education, etc., and regression equations can be estimated in which the auction bids are regressed against these demographic variables and dummy variables for treatment effects. The estimated coefficients on the treatment dummy variables indicate the effect of the experimental treatment effect holding constant the effect of demographics. More information on regression analysis with auction bids is included in Chapter 6.

In our motivating example, we assumed all other variables besides product information, package size, and color were held constant at some fixed level. Subsequent discussion mentioned a variety of ways to practice control in experiments. Control is a multifaceted issue. For example, in Chapter 3 on value theory, we saw that auction bids can depend on the price of substitute goods. If subjects are uninformed about the price of an important substitute, much of the variation in auction bids may be due to heterogeneity in individuals' perceptions about the price of the substitute and not any pertinent treatment effect, *per se* (e.g., see the discussion in Harrison *et al.*, 2004). In such a case, the researcher has lost control over their experiment in the sense that a potentially sizable portion of the variation in auction bids is now unexplainable. A straightforward way to handle this problem is to inform subjects of the price of the substitute good outside the laboratory such that all participants have a common expectation or perhaps to offer the substitute good for sale at a fixed price in the experiment.

Other factors also have the potential to affect auction bids and the key is to determine the factors most salient and hold them fixed at some constant level in the experiment. Unless the effects of these variables on auction bids interact with the effects of the key treatment variables of interest, it is not important at what level the variables are held (e.g., high or low, red or yellow, yes or no, etc.), simply that they are held constant. In many ways, the choice of what variables to explicitly consider in a design, which to hold constant, and which to vary, is as much an art as a science. Theory can provide a guide regarding factors expected to influence bids, but even here guidance is limited. For example, it was just argued that, based on theory, the price of substitute goods is expected to influence auction bids; however, many questions remain. Which substitute goods should be considered? How many? In this section between-subject designs, where the same person takes part in several treatments, were suggested as a way to hold constant many factors. Later in the book we discuss how endowing subjects with a good and having them bid to "upgrade" to a substitute can also hold constant many potentially compounding factors. Sill, there are likely to be significant differences across researchers as to the importance of a particular factor in a particular study.

One researcher's gain of control can be another's loss of context. Some researchers argue that it is these *confounding factors* (e.g., uncontrolled body language sent in face-to-face bargaining) that provide the rich economic context that motivates real-world behavior. They point out that striving for complete control is self-defeating because it creates an economic environment that is too sterile, too abstract, too unreal, with no parallel in the real world, and generates subjects who are motivated by salient payoffs, but unmotivated by the context in which these payoffs are earned. The inspiration is that economic theory should be robust enough to explain actions in real world social interactions that have copious contextual cues that occur simultaneously. In response, advocates of more control point out that too much context makes the experiment too much like an open-ended case study or descriptive naturalist observations. Experiments based on too many confounding factors and misidentified motivation yield no universal patterns based on first principles, which creates little ability to generalize beyond the specific case. One might even argue this approach is non-experimental. The recommendation is that when examining such contextual issues one should note whether the method permits the conclusions that the author has made. A causal inference may have been made when the design does not allow such inference.

This section outlined many basics of experimental design. There are many good reference books on the topic that can provide more depth and insight. For examples, see Kirk (1994) for a detailed text on experimental design from the perspective of a psychologist, Montgomery (2000) for a general text written by an engineer, Friedman and Sunder (1994) for a discussion on experimental design in relation to experimental economics, and Louviere, Hensher, and Swait (2000) for discussions on experimental design in relation to stated choice surveys.

4.3   Sample size determination

An initial step that must be taken when beginning an experiment is to determine the needed sample size. This choice will depend on a variety of factors including the study objectives and budget constraints. Although providing a detailed discussion on the statistics surrounding sample size calculation is beyond the scope of this book, a brief introduction on the subject is provided to assist practitioners designing experimental auctions. For further information on the topics of sampling and sample size, see Kraemer and Thiemann (1987), Levy and Lemeshow (1991), Groves (1987), or Kupper and Hafner (1989).

In general, an experimental auction will be conducted for one of two non-mutually exclusive purposes. The first purpose is to identify whether there are differences in valuations between treatments or goods. The second is to provide an estimate of the mean WTP/WTA for a good in the population. The necessary sample size, required to accomplish these two objectives differ. If the study is being conducted to make inferences about treatment effects and the distribution of a valuation in the population, the most logical action is to take the larger of the two sample size calculations.

First consider the objective of determining the sample size required to compare means from two independent samples of identical sizes. Such a situation might arise, for example, if one were interested in comparing auction bids from one experimental treatment to another, in which the treatments might differ in terms of the information given to subjects or in the auction mechanisms used to elicit bids. Alternatively, one might be interested in comparing bids for two different goods; a conventional good and an improved counterpart. In such cases, suppose the null hypothesis that there is no treatment effect, i.e., the mean from treatment 1 (μ_1) is equal to the mean from treatment 2 (μ_2), is compared against the alternative hypothesis that $\mu_1 \neq \mu_2$. In such cases, choice of sample size depends on four factors:

- σ, the expected standard deviation of auction bids pooled across treatments,
- Δ, the critical effect size that identifies the minimum difference between means in treatments 1 and 2 that would be considered "important",
- α, the significance level that represents the likelihood of rejecting the null hypothesis if it were true, where z_α represents the z-statistic at α, e.g., $z_{0.05} = 1.96$, and
- β, the power of the test that represents the probability of rejecting the null (probability of obtaining a significant result), where z_β represents the $100*\beta$th percentile of the normal distribution, e.g., $z_{0.80} = 0.84$.

For a large population, the minimum per-group sample size is:

$$\frac{2(z_\alpha + z_\beta)^2 \sigma^2}{\Delta^2}.$$

To explore the formula a bit further, consider an example in which one is interested in determining whether consumers value a new product X over a conventional counterpart Y. To investigate this issue, one set of consumers might bid on product X in one treatment and another set of consumers might bid on product Y in another treatment. Assume that the minimum difference between bids for X and Y that would be economically profitable to the firm is $0.50 and the expected standard deviation is $1. The minimum sample size for a 95% test of significance with 80% power is 63 subjects per treatment. If the power of the test were increased to 90% (e.g., $z_{0.90} = 1.28$), the required sample size is 84 subjects per treatment. If the experiment were conducted such that the same people were to bid on products X and Y, i.e., there are paired responses, the above formula is still relevant, except it is reduced by a factor of 2. For a test with power of 90%, only 42 subjects would be required. The above formula, while convenient, does not provide insight into how σ or Δ should be determined. The standard deviation could be based on bids from other similar studies, but Δ will be study and context specific. Nevertheless, if there is uncertainty about these values, the prudent step is to use a higher than expected value of σ and a lower than expected value of Δ, both of which would serve to increase the required sample size.

Although testing for significance between treatment effects is the primary focus of many studies, other studies might be interested in estimating the distribution of a valuation in the population. For example, as in Hayes et al. (1995), one might be interested in estimating the value of increased food safety that could be broadly applied in a cost-benefit analysis. Assume interest is in determining the mean valuation, μ, of a random sample from a population. To determine the required sample size for such applications, the following information must be determined:

- σ, the expected standard deviation of bids in the population,
- δ, the desired level of precision in units of the mean, e.g., the estimated mean is within plus or minus of the true mean, μ, and
- α, the significance level that represents the confidence one can place on the estimated mean falling within $\pm\delta$ of μ, where z_α represents the z-statistic at α, e.g., $z_{0.05} = 1.96$.

The minimum sample size required to achieve the stated level of precision is:

$$n = \frac{\sigma^2 z_\alpha^2}{\delta^2}.$$

Although this measure is frequently used to determine the minimum sample size, Kupper and Hafter (1989) showed that the formula tends to *underestimate* the required sample size. They provide a table to relate the calculated n above to the appropriate required sample size, n^*. The correction table for $\alpha = 0.05$ and tolerance probabilities of 0.80, 0.90, and 0.95 is provided in Table 4.5.

Table 4.5. *Sample size correction table for 95% level of confidence*

	Corrected sample size n^*		
Calculated sample size, n	Tolerance probability 0.80	Tolerance probability 0.90	Tolerance probability 0.95
5	10	11	12
10	16	18	19
15	22	24	26
20	27	30	32
25	33	36	38
30	39	42	44
35	44	48	50
40	50	53	56
45	55	59	62
50	60	65	68
55	66	70	74
60	71	76	80
65	77	81	85
70	82	87	91
75	87	92	97
80	93	98	102
85	98	103	108
90	103	109	114
95	109	114	119
100	114	120	125

Source: Kupper and Haftner (1989).

The tolerance probability, t, indicates the desired level of precision relative to the mean, e.g., $t = 1 - \delta/\mu$. As an example, consider the case in which one is interested in estimating the mean value for a product in the US population, where it is assumed that the true mean is \$10, the expected standard deviation is \$3, and the desired level of precision is 90%, e.g., $t = 0.90$ and $\delta = \$1$. For $\alpha = 0.05$, $n \approx 36$, and $n^* \approx 49$. In this example, if 49 independent bids were collected from a random sample of people, one could be 95% confident the estimated mean bid would be within $\pm$ \$1 (or within $\pm$ 10%) of the true mean bid.

4.4   Experiment setting and context: field versus laboratory

An important consideration when conducting an auction is *where* to hold the value elicitation experiment. The vast majority of economic experiments take place in a laboratory or classroom setting. Recent experimental work has begun to move from the lab to the field to elicit values (e.g., Bohm, 1994; List and

Shogren, 1998; Shogren *et al.*, 1999; List, 2001; Lusk *et al.*, 2001a; Lusk and Fox, 2003; see the review by Harrison and List, 2004).[1]

There are advantages and disadvantages to field and laboratory experiments. The primary advantage of conducting experiments in a laboratory setting is more control. In a laboratory, an experiment can be constructed in such a way as to minimize confounding factors such that the effects of interest can be isolated. When dealing with the elicitation of homegrown values, our focus, one must recognize that while laboratory permits control over many aspects of a design, one has to contend with "outside" market influences. For example, a rational person would never bid more for a good in a laboratory auction than the price of the good in the market outside the lab (plus some transaction costs). The laboratory, however, gives a researcher control over both the content and sequencing of price and non-price information provided to subjects.

Moving the valuation setting to more familiar territory such as a grocery store or a mall might be advantageous for a number of reasons. First, subjects self-select into the market, and as such, sample-selection biases are of less concern as the population of interest is directly intercepted. Second, in a field setting, subjects are able to bring all their learned knowledge to bear on the task at hand. To the extent that individuals develop heuristics to make purchase decisions in the marketplace, conducting an experiment in a field setting allows individuals to use such heuristics. Many times, field experiments provide interesting tests of the effect of market experience on behavior. The effect of market experience on behavior is non-trivial and has important economic consequences (e.g., see Crocker *et al.*, 1998 and List, 2003).

Finally, in many instances field valuation can reduce the costs of experimental work. This cost reduction is potentially achievable because compensatory fees must often be paid to subjects to attend a laboratory session, but such fees are unnecessary in the field. Because the magnitude of compensatory fees has

---

[1] Harrison and List (2004) came up with a nomenclature to categorize experiments done with the general population: a) artefactual field experiments that take place in a laboratory setting, but use "real" people as subjects as opposed to a convenience sample of students, b) framed field experiments are similar to laboratory experiments except they occur within the field context (in either the commodity, task, or information set that the subjects use), and c) natural field experiments that are similar to framed field experiments except that subjects do not know they are taking part in an experiment. To illustrate, consider an experiment aimed at determining the value a person places on a new food product. A typical laboratory experiment would involve student subjects bidding on the new good in a classroom or laboratory. With an artefactual field experiment, one would randomly recruit people representative of the market of interest and would elicit auction bids for the new good in a classroom or laboratory. A framed experiment would involve the experimenter moving to the place where individuals actually make the purchase decision (e.g., grocery store, mall, internet, etc.). Then subjects would bid in an auction for the new good in the environment that matches that where subjects would consider purchasing such a good. A natural field experiment would be similar to the framed experiment except that subjects would not know they were participating in a research project. An example of a natural field experiment might be the auction of a good on e-bay.

been shown to influence bids (e.g., Rutström, 1998), field valuation offers the potential to omit this bias. A variety of methods have been used to attract participants to participate in a field auction including offering a free unit of a "traditional" good and eliciting bids to exchange the endowed good for a "new" counterpart (e.g., Lusk *et al.*, 2001a) and offering coupons to the retail establishment in which the elicitation task is taking place (e.g., Lusk *et al.*, 2006a). In a natural experiment, no inducement is needed; subjects select into the market because they are interested in purchasing the good.

Lusk and Fox (2003) directly tested whether auction bids elicited in a laboratory setting were equal to those elicited in a retail setting. After controlling for zero bidders, they found that bids were significantly higher in the store setting than in the lab; about 30% higher after controlling for other exogenous factors. They suggest this difference may be due to value uncertainty and impatience. Zhao and Kling (2001) illustrate that in a dynamic context that willingness-to-pay should increase when consumers are more certain about a good's value, more impatient about consuming the good, and expect less information can be gathered about a good's value in the future. In the retail setting, individuals enter the store ready to make a purchase and are more impatient than someone sitting in a laboratory. Further, the store setting has more information about substitute prices for goods, which should make subjects more certain about a good's relative value and decrease the chance that more information will be gathered later, which would serve to increase willingness-to-pay.

Another key study was conducted by Shogren *et al.* (1999), who compared the similarity of lab valuation choices to field retail store choices for risk reduction. They also compared choices made in hypothetical surveys. All subjects came from the same small college town and made choices between typical chicken breasts versus chicken breasts irradiated to reduce the risk of foodborne pathogens. The results from both the survey and experimental market (note: the experimental market was not an auction market, it consisted of participants making non-hypothetical choices) suggested significantly higher levels of acceptability of irradiated chicken than in the retail setting at an equal or discounted price for irradiated chicken. However, consumer choices were more similar across market settings when irradiated chicken was sold at a premium over regular chicken. They observed that in a mail survey and a lab experiment, both of which included information about irradiation, 80% of participants preferred irradiated to non-irradiated chicken breasts when they were offered at the same price; however, only about 45% of shoppers in the retail setting bought irradiated chicken when it was priced the same as non-irradiated. In contrast, when the irradiated product was offered at a higher price, the survey and experimental results predicted market share in a subsequent retail trial remarkably well. In all three settings (survey, experimental market, and store), about 33%

of people bought the irradiated chicken when it was priced at a 10% premium over regular chicken.

While differences in choices across institutions were observed in Shogren *et al.* (1999), each of the three decision settings involved unique features and incentives that were absent from the other two settings. Retail purchases involved payment of real money for real products within an environment in which thousands of products competed for the consumer's dollar. Any attempt to collect consumer information in a retail setting was liable to interfere with the realism of the market itself. The goal of the retail setting was to establish the most realistic baseline possible against which one could judge the lab or survey. In contrast, while the experiments also required exchange of real money for real goods, the participants knew they were being monitored and the range of alternative purchases was limited. The survey involved hypothetical decisions, information about irradiation, and people knew that they would not be held accountable for choices they made. Perfectly simulating a retail experience in the lab or a survey so as to control every nuance is unattainable. Rather the goal should be to compare lab and survey choices relative to a real world baseline. The research program that emerges for future work is to explore how comprehensive the lab or survey environments must be to come closer to replicate an actual market outcome.

An important consideration in the decision of whether to carry out valuation in the lab or field regards how consumers view their participation in the experiment. Levitt and List (2005) proposed a model of individual decision making to explain how responses from laboratory experiments might diverge from the "real world." Their model assumes people derive utility from wealth and moralistic concerns. Levitt and List (2005) posit that the weight a person attaches to the latter of these concerns depends on the extent to which one's actions are scrutinized or "watched." This idea revisits the classic Hawthorne effect. Experimenters examining job performance made changes in the workplace of the Hawthorne plant of the Western Electric Company in Chicago that made people feel important and thus improved their performance. In any survey situation, people know their actions are being scrutinized, and as such, they could have incentive to provide more pro-social and moralistic answers as compared to what they might do in a naturally occurring marketplace.

The contribution of studies such as Lusk *et al.* (2001a), List (2001), Bohm (1994), and others, in which the valuation setting was moved to the field, but where the researchers retained control over certain key design parameters, is that they represent an effort to bridge the gap between the uncontrolled, yet realistic retail setting and the highly controlled, yet abstract lab setting. Practitioners now choose where to conduct their experiments along the continuum ranging from laboratory auctions with students to natural field auctions with naturally occurring participants.

4.5   Conclusions

This chapter introduced and discussed some preliminary issues associated with the design of experimental auctions. The chapter covered inter-related issues associated with control over the experiment (e.g., experimental design), context (e.g., field versus the laboratory), and the number of participants (e.g., sample size). The purpose of experimental design is to collect data in a way so as to identify all the "effects" one is interested in. Experimental design involves identifying the variables most likely to influence auction bids and combining the levels of these "important" variables to create treatments. There is no magic bullet for determining what variables are "important" and should be included as an experimental control.

We offered up several pieces of advice. Researchers should hold constant as many factors as possible either through implementing between-subject designs, randomization, eliciting bids to upgrade from an endowed good, using ex-post regression analysis, or creating instructions and procedures to create common expectation among participants. Another key purpose of experimental design regards the efficiency of estimates. The more efficient an experimental design, the fewer observations necessary to reject a hypothesis. Lusk and Norwood (2005) show that, provided an experimental design does not confound two effects, large sample sizes can compensate for poor experimental design.

In addition to concerns with efficiency, the chapter also discussed sample size from a sampling standpoint. Because every person in the population does not participate in an experimental auction, the mean auction bid from a sample of recruited experimental auction participants will consist of some level sampling error. This chapter illustrated how to determine the level of sampling error for a given sample size. The section on sample size also discussed how to determine the minimum sample size required to test the null hypothesis of equality between two treatments given assumptions about the power of the statistical test. The chapter concluded with a discussion regarding the setting (field versus lab) of the valuation experiment. In general, laboratory auctions permit more control over the decision environment, but this comes at the loss of context and realism. When designing experimental auctions practitioners must weigh the importance of a number of competing factors including control, context, and sample size and make judgment calls regarding the importance of each factor relevant to the study objective.

5   Conducting experimental auctions

5.1   Introduction

Researchers have explored and debated many issues on the proper design and conduct of experimental auctions used to elicit values for lotteries, new goods, services, and technologies. This chapter examines six essential design issues in detail – training and practice; endowment of a good versus full bidding; choosing an auction mechanism; multiple good valuation, demand reduction and field substitutes; learning and affiliation in repeated bidding rounds and negative values. For each issue, we discuss the choices available to the practitioner, outlining the pros and cons that have emerged from theoretical and empirical literature. The goal of this chapter is to make readers aware of the relevant issues so that informed and justifiable choices can be made when designing an experimental auction.

Some obvious "best practices" have emerged that should be followed in conducting auctions. For example, practitioners should initially conduct a qualitative study prior to designing an experiment such that they can learn about individuals' decision-making processes and explore how people think about the good and experimental procedures in question. Focus groups in conjunction with pre-tests of the experiment will help ensure that the study's objectives are properly met. Once a design has been settled on, it is critical that subjects properly understand the auction in which they participate and that every effort is made to ensure against misperceptions. Aside from these issues, the practitioner has some judgment calls to make. Thinking through these issues when deciding what choices to make will also introduce a new set of concerns and challenges into the literature.

5.2   Training and practice

With the advent of technologies such as e-bay, more people participate in auctions today than in recent history. The procedures employed in experimental auctions, however, are still unfamiliar to most participants. Even when people have experience participating in e-bay auctions the researcher should take care to ensure that people do not attempt to use the optimal strategies from those auctions, in which truthful bidding is not necessarily the dominant strategy.

We believe it is critical that prior to conducting the main auction, people should: (a) receive training on the incentive compatible mechanism; (b) participate in real-money practice rounds with another good; and (c) be assured of anonymity. Without such safeguards there is little reason to believe that elicited bids will correspond to individuals' values. For example, Brown (2005) used a BDM mechanism to elicit values for several goods without using any practice rounds. The contribution of Brown's study was the use of a "verbal protocol," in which people say aloud what is going through their mind as they formulate their bids. Brown (2005) found that most subjects mentioned the item's value to others, the expected market price, or the opportunity for making a profit when formulating their bids. These findings indicate that people have misperceptions about the incentives in the auctions. Such findings would likely induce some to question the ability of auctions to elicit true values at all. For example, in a study comparing bids from second and ninth price auctions, Knetsch, Tang, and Thaler (2001) concluded (at p. 265), "Contrary to common understanding, a Vickrey auction may not be demand or value revealing . . ." This conclusion is premature. Plott and Zeiler (2005) provide evidence that misperceptions play an important role in individuals' bidding and that these can be removed with careful experimental design that includes training and experience.

Without any training or experience, people will probably resort to heuristics they have learned by participating in other markets, such as buy low and sell high. They must be brought to the realization that such strategies are not the best response in incentive compatible auctions. This can be partially accomplished through good explanations of the properties of mechanisms, but experience with the mechanism is critical as well. Real-money practice rounds (with a non-focal good) permit people to learn first hand the perils of bidding sub-optimally.

Prior to conducting an auction, we recommend that nine steps are implemented.

Step 1. Carefully explain the mechanics of the auction. This means creating written instructions that have been tested on a control group to eliminate any confusing statements and other misunderstandings. One might find it helpful to use terms that discourage participants from engaging in behaviors that deviate from truthful value revelation. For example, using words like "buyer" or "seller" rather than "winner" might serve to mitigate "auction fever."

Step 2: Provide concrete numerical examples. To avoid confounding influences, examples can be contextualized with a fictitious good or different good than the one of interest. Candy bars can provide a useful reference good both to use as an example and for practice rounds. A numerical example for the second price auction might go something like the following. Suppose there were five people participating in an auction like the one described. Suppose that these people were bidding to obtain a Snickers bar. Participant #1 bid $0.00 for the Snickers bar, participant #2 bid $0.10, participant #3 bid $0.25, participant #4 bid $0.40, and participant #5 bid $0.50. Participant #5 would win the auction because they bid the highest amount and they would pay $0.40, which was the second highest bid. Participants #1, #2, #3, and #4 would not pay anything and would not receive the Snickers bar. Examples might also be followed with a disclaimer that the monetary values are used for illustrative purposes and are not meant to convey what the goods should or might be worth to participants.

Step 3: Clearly explain why it is in each person's best interest to bid truthfully. Despite the incentives inherent in mechanisms such as the second price auction, these incentives are probably not obvious to people that have never used the auction. The incentive structure of most auctions is easily conveyed to people. A variant on the following would serve to explain the incentives: *In this auction, the best strategy is to bid exactly what it is worth to you to obtain the good.* When you submit your bid, you do not know what the price will be. If you bid more than the candy bar is worth to you, you may end up having to buy the good at a price that is more than you really want to pay. By contrast, if you bid less than the candy bar is really worth to you, you may end up not winning the auction even though you could have bought the candy bar at a price you were actually willing to pay. Your best strategy is to bid exactly what each candy bar is worth to you. Numerical examples, could further illustrate the advantages to truthful bidding. Suppose your value for a Snickers bar is $0.50. If you decide to offer a bid less than your value, say $0.40, you may not win the auction if the market price is $0.45. This means that by under-bidding you have given up the opportunity to buy a Snickers bar for only $0.45 when it was worth $0.50 to you. By contrast, suppose you decide to bid $0.60, which is more than the Snickers bar is worth to you, and you end up winning the auction. If the market price is $0.55, you would have to buy a Snickers bar for $0.05 more than it is really worth to you.

Step 4: Use a simple quiz to test individuals' knowledge of the mechanism. Asking people to answer questions about the mechanics of the auction encourages people to think through the auction mechanism and allows the researcher to correct any misperceptions that might exist. For example, one could re-pose a Snickers bar auction scenario and ask people to indicate the winning bidder(s) and the market price. It might be indicated that Participant #1 bid $0.01 for the Snickers bar, participant #2 bid $0.17, participant #3 bid $0.05, participant #4 bid $0.52, and participant #5 bid $0.37. Then people can be asked questions such as: Who would win this auction? How much would the winner pay?

Step 5: Allow questions that pertain to the mechanics of the auction. To avoid creating confusion between experimental treatments, researchers may wish to avoid some types of question. A formal protocol can be developed for responding to potential questions.

Step 6: Conduct several rounds of real-money practice auctions with a non-focal good. Although good written and verbal instructions are key, there is no substitute for actual experience with the mechanisms. People should have the opportunity to participate in several real-money auctions. A number of possibilities exist to help ensure that behavior from the practice auctions does not confound valuations for the good of interest. One possibility is to auction a good that is unrelated to that which is the primary focus of the investigation. Again, candy bars may serve as a useful practice good. Experience can be gained by conducting a series of auctions for different candy bars (e.g., Snickers, Milky Way, etc.) or by repeating auctions for the same candy bar. Another possibility is to auction generic lotteries. For example, people could bid to obtain a 50% chance of winning $1 and a 50% chance of winning $0 (as determined via a coin flip). Another option is to use an induced value auction to teach people about the mechanism.

Step 7: Impose anonymity. If people are not sure their identities are confidential, they could submit bids to look good to other participants or to please the experimenter. A lack of anonymity could cause people to offer bids related to how others might value the good (e.g., a "fair" market price). The assignment of ID numbers and individualized pay-outs at the end of the experimental session can be used to impose anonymity. Some experimental labs add an additional layer of anonymity by using individualized keys and mail boxes in which people receive their recruitment fee and experimental earnings (minus the price of any purchased items) and any goods they might have purchased during the experiment. The practice auctions can be carried out with or without anonymity. Relaxing the anonymity restriction during some portion of the practice can improve understanding as people can ask questions during the auction and the experimental monitor can use bids to further explain the properties of the auction.

Step 9: Once a person has been trained in the auction mechanism, one can run the real-money auction for the focal good.

5.3   Endowment versus full bidding

A beneficial feature of experimental auctions is that they hold everything constant except for one specific characteristic of the good to be valued. This is accomplished by comparing values for two goods that differ only by the characteristic of interest. In their food safety experiments, for example, Hayes *et al.* (1995), held constant $(n - 1)$ characteristics of a sandwich, and then varied the probability of food-borne illness to elicit values for more or less health risk. There are two ways to implement this idea in an auction: the endowment approach and the full bidding approach. The *endowment approach* has people bidding on "upgrading/downgrading" from one endowed good to another good. The *full bidding* approach has people bidding on both goods simultaneously. Consider the pros and cons of each approach.

The endowment method involves giving subjects one good, X, and eliciting bids to exchange X for another good, Y. Bids from the endowment approach directly reflect the value difference between X and Y. An advantage of the endowment method is that it mitigates outside-market influences. Suppose good X is a typical good sold in the market and Y is a new good to be valued. Consumers can buy X at market price $P outside the experiment, but Y is only available in the experiment.

Assume a consumer's true values for X and Y are V_X and V_Y. Using the endowment method, one directly elicits $V_Y - V_X, which is not confounded with outside lab opportunities (assuming opportunities for resale of Y in the field are limited).

The full bidding approach involves subjects bidding simultaneously to obtain one of two goods, X or Y. To avoid demand reduction effects, only one of the goods is randomly selected and sold; this determination is made after both bids have been submitted. Now, if the full bidding method is used with an incentive compatible auction, a rational consumer's bid for X is: min(V_X, $P + c$), where c is the perceived transaction cost of purchasing X in the field rather than in the lab. A consumer will bid their true value, V_X, in the experiment only if it is less than the price for which they can buy the good in a grocery store or vending machine – the bid for X is censored at the market price plus some transactions cost. By contrast, because Y is only available in the lab, the consumer's bid for Y is unbounded and should be equal to V_Y. So, using the full bidding method, the difference in bids might be $V_Y - $P - c$ which is *not* the measure of real interest: $V_Y - V_X.

Corrigan (2005) provides a similar discussion related to option values. If values are uncertain in that people expect to gather more information in future about the value of the good, then a person's WTP today contains an option value associated with the value of the future information (see section 3.4). If so, comparing bids for two goods in the full value bidding method entails comparing an individual's expected value for the two goods *and* the option values for both goods. There is a confound between the compensating variations for the goods and the option values. If one is only interested in comparing the value participants place on an attribute (i.e., the compensating variation), and not the option values associated with future information, the endowment method presents a straightforward way to eliminate comparisons of option values and focuses attention on comparisons of valuations between two goods. With the endowment methods, participants know they will leave the experiment with one of two goods, either X or Y, thus the opportunity for future learning about both goods is eliminated.

In addition to controlling for the problem of field substitutes and option values, the endowment method has several other advantages. The endowment method is useful because it can be used with a consumption requirement as in Shogren *et al.* (1994). When a consumption requirement is imposed, people must consume the good they possess at the end of the auction. Winners of the auction consume the auctioned good; losers of the auction consume the endowed good. Several reasons exist as to why one might want to use a consumption requirement. First, it increases attentiveness and encourages participants to put cognitive effort into their bidding decisions. The requirement encourages subjects not to submit $0 bids for both products as they might in the full bidding method. Second, the consumption requirement ensures that the value elicited corresponds to the value of the person who is bidding. Without a consumption requirement, a subject might bid on a good to give to a peer or spouse and formulate their bid based on their expectation of someone else's value. Further support for the endowment approach is given by Hoffman *et al.* (1993), who contended that the most useful and reliable estimates from experimental auctions are *differences* in willingness to pay (WTP) between two goods. The endowment approach directly elicits this difference. As illustrated by Lusk *et al.* (2001a), the endowment approach can be helpful in attracting participants in a field setting such as a grocery store. Rather than paying subjects to attend a laboratory setting, which has been shown to influence valuations (Rutström, 1998), subjects can be given a lower quality good for participation and WTP for a higher quality good can be elicited. Such an approach removes the effects of high participation fees.

The endowment approach has some disadvantages relative to the full bidding method. Tversky and Kahneman (1979) suggest that valuations may be reference-dependent. One manifestation of reference-dependent valuation is that people might place greater value on a good if they possess it than if they do not – an effect that is thought to arise from loss aversion, where losses are valued more highly than gains. If the reference-dependent preferences exist, then value estimates for a novel product or attribute depend on the subject's initial reference point: whether they initially possess the good.

Another problem with the endowment method is that the endowment itself might send an implicit quality signal to participants. If a person is endowed with a good and is asked to bid to exchange their endowed good for another, it might create the impression that the endowed good is in some way inferior to the auctioned good. The latter concern could be assuaged by initially asking which good people prefer and endowing them with the lesser preferred good as in Lusk *et al.* (2001a).

Two studies have investigated whether the endowment method generates these biases. Lusk *et al.* (2004a) compared differences in bids between goods using the full bidding method to bids to exchange an endowed good for another good using the endowment method. Results were mixed. For the random nth price auction, they found results consonant with the loss-aversion hypothesis; people provided an endowment were willing to pay less to upgrade to another good as compared to people without such an endowment. For the second price auction, however, the opposite result was obtained. For BDM and English mechanisms, they found that there was not a statistically significant difference in bid differences in the full bidding method and bids in the endowment method. Lusk *et al.* (2004a) speculate that differences in dynamics of the auction mechanisms might be one explanation for divergent findings. In their study, the English and BDM were single-round auctions, whereas the second and random nth were multiple-round auctions. In the multiple-round auctions, they found that the endowment effect become more pronounced in later auction rounds.

Corrigan and Rousu (2006a) addressed the endowment issue from a slightly different angle. They compared the difference in bids for one unit and two units of the same good to bids to upgrade from one endowed unit of a good to a second unit of the same good. They found that bids for the second unit of the good were significantly higher under the endowment method as compared to the full bidding method. In their experiment, subjects never had to give up an endowed good to obtain another, which means loss-aversion can be ruled out as an explanation for the results. Corrigan and Rousu (2006a) attributed the difference in bids to upgrade from one endowed unit to two and the difference in bids to obtain one and two units to the effect of "reciprocal obligation," in which subjects may want to "repay" or be kind to the experimenter for providing the initial endowment. They conclude researchers should use the full bidding method instead of the endowment approach. To the extent one believes that "reciprocal obligation" may be problematic in the endowment approach, however, the problem might be mitigated by charging people for their endowment, perhaps by reducing their show-up fee accordingly, such that the endowment is not seen as a windfall gain for which they should reciprocate.

The decision on whether to endow subjects with a good and have them bid to exchange their endowment for an alternative, or whether to have subjects bid full value for several goods depends on several factors. The full bidding method is more preferable the more one believes: (a) few outside options exist for the auction goods; (b) there are few opportunities for learning more about the value of the auctioned goods in the future; (c) the endowment effect and loss aversion are pervasive phenomena; (d) the endowment will cause subjects to reciprocate in subsequent bidding; and (e) actual consumption of the product is not an important part of the measured value.

Table 5.1. *Some incentive compatible auctions*

Elicitation mechanism	Participant procedure	Market price	Rule	Number of winners
English	Sequentially offer ascending bids	Last offered bid	Highest bidder pays market price	1
2nd Price	Simultaneously submit sealed bids	Second highest bid	Highest bidder pays market price	1
nth Price	Simultaneously submit sealed bids	nth highest bid	$n - 1$ highest bidders pay market price	$n - 1$
BDM	Simultaneously submit sealed bids	Randomly drawn price	People pay market price if bid exceeds randomly drawn price	individually determined
Random nth price	Simultaneously submit sealed bids	Randomly drawn (nth) bid	$n - 1$ highest bidders pay market price	$n - 1$
Collective auction	Simultaneously submit sealed bids	Mean bid	Each individual pays market price (subject to unanimity rule) if sum of bids exceeds sum of costs	none or all

5.4   Choosing an auction mechanism

Another key design issue is the choice of auction mechanism. Several auction mechanisms are incentive compatible. Table 5.1 gives a flavor of the varied types of mechanisms between which a practitioner can choose. For now, we only consider mechanisms that elicit demand for a single unit; we briefly discuss auctions that elicit multiple-unit demand later in the chapter. Consider briefly each auction mechanism in Table 5.1. In an English auction, people offer ascending bids until only one participant remains. This person wins the auction and purchases the auctioned good at the last offered bid amount. In practice, the English auction is implemented by using a "clock" that starts at a low price and increases at regular time intervals. People signal their willingness to stay in the auction at each price, perhaps by holding up a sign with their participant identification number.

In a second price auction, subjects submit sealed bids; the high bidder wins the auction and pays the second highest bid amount for an item. The second price auction can be generalized to any nth price auction in which subjects submit sealed bids for a good and the $(n - 1)$ highest bidders win the auction and pay the nth highest bid amount. Another popular value elicitation mechanism is the Becker-Degroot-Marschak (BDM) mechanism. The BDM is not an auction *per se* as subjects do not bid against one another in a market environment, but the structure is nonetheless similar. With the BDM, a person submits a bid and purchases the good if their bid is greater than a randomly drawn price.

Shogren *et al.* (2001a) formally introduced the random nth price auction to combine features of the second price auction, which encourages competition amongst bidders, and the BDM mechanism, in which there is a relatively high chance any bidder can win. In a random nth price auction, subjects submit sealed bids for a good, one bid is randomly drawn from the sample, and all bidders that bid higher than the randomly drawn bid win the auction and pay an amount equal to the randomly drawn bid.

Originally introduced by Smith (1980) to value public goods, one could also use a collective auction. Here, sealed bids are submitted and summed. If the sum of bids is greater than the sum of the cost of provision (a cost that is unknown to the subjects when bidding), each person pays a price equal to the mean bid amount so long as all people agree to proceed with the purchase via an anonymous vote.

Which mechanisms should be chosen for a given application? There is no straightforward answer. From a purely theoretical basis, it should not matter; all auctions should yield bids equal to true values. Auction theory relies on many assumptions, some more tenuous than others. The choice of auction mechanism comes down to pragmatic considerations and to properties of auctions that have been determined through empirical research. We now review some of the studies investigating the empirical properties of the auction mechanisms to aid the selection decision.

Evidence exists that subjects over-bid in second price auctions in induced value experiments (Kagel *et al.*, 1987); but this finding is far from universal (Shogren *et al.*, 2001a). In an induced value experiment, Noussair, Robin, and Ruffieux (2004a) found that the second price auction was demand revealing and generated more accurate bids, as measured by the absolute difference between bids and values, than the BDM.

In another induced value experiment, Shogren *et al.* (2001a) used a within-subject experimental design to compare bidding behavior in the random nth price and second price auction, where participants were informed of the weakly dominant strategy in both mechanisms. Overall, their results showed that the second price auction worked better on-margin (i.e., for people with valuations near the market price), but the random nth price auction worked better off-margin (i.e., for people with valuations far from the market price). The two auctions did not perform differently when data for on-margin and off-margin bidders were pooled. A regression of induced values on bids generated estimated lines that were flatter than the perfect-revelation line, with positive intercepts and slopes below one. In the case of the random nth price auction for on-margin bidders, this flattening was significant. This behavior could represent a tendency for bidders who do not fully understand the random nth price mechanism to offer bids near the middle of the range. This pattern can arise if the parameter estimates are biased by the classic attenuation of least squares (Greene 2000, p. 437) which occurs when an independent variable is measured with error. If the mean error is zero and no correlation exists between induced value and the error with which it is measured, the slope coefficient is biased down and the constant term biased up. In the present context, this would mean the induced value is transformed inside the subject by some noisy and unobserved process, for example, a belief that the experience of redeeming tokens will be occasion for social display or embarrassment.

Whereas Noussair *et al.* (2004a) compared the second price auction to the BDM and Shogren *et al.* (2001a) compared the second price auction to the random nth, Lusk and Rousu (2006) carried out a comparison of all three mechanisms (the second price auction, random nth price auction, and BDM mechanism) in an induced value experiment. Their analysis focused on comparing accuracy of the mechanisms by investigating the squared/absolute difference between bids and induced values. They found that, on average, the second price and random nth price auctions were significantly more accurate than the BDM. Consistent with Shogren *et al.* (2001a), they found a tendency for the random nth price auction to have a lower mean squared deviation for off-margin bids than the second price auction, whereas the second price auction had a lower mean squared deviation at high induced values than the random nth price auction.

Overall, these studies suggest that choice of auction mechanisms might depend on whether one is interested in more accurately estimating the upper or lower end of the demand curve. The second price auction is likely to generate more accurate bidding for high value bidders; the random nth is likely to generate more accurate bidding for low value bidders.

In addition to comparisons of mechanisms in induced-value experiments, several studies have compared homegrown values across auction mechanisms. Lusk *et al.* (2004a) found in initial bidding rounds, the second price, random nth price, English, and BDM all generated similar mean bids for beef steaks. After several rounds of bidding, however, the second price auction generated higher bids than the other mechanisms, and the random nth tended to generate lower bids than the other mechanisms. Rutström (1998) found that the English auction and the BDM mechanism generated similar mean bids for chocolates, but the second price auction generated bids in excess of either of the other mechanisms. In a field experiment where trading cards were auctioned on the internet, Lucking-Reiley (1999) found that the second price and English auctions generated similar levels of revenue.

In addition to the empirical findings, other pragmatic factors can come into play when considering which mechanism to use for a given application. Most people are somewhat familiar with the English auction, and as such, experimental procedures for this auction should be relatively easy to convey to subjects. The English auction is also an "open" auction in that every subject knows the bids of every other subject. This can be an advantage in the sense that subjects can quickly incorporate market information into their valuations, but this feature can also be a disadvantage if participants are unduly influenced by other bidders or if bid affiliation (discussed in a later section) is a major concern.

The second price auction is relatively easy to explain to subjects and to implement. Nevertheless, evidence suggests subjects might over-bid in this auction and there is potential for low-valued subjects to "misbehave" in multiple bidding rounds. The BDM mechanism is the only one that can be used on an individual basis that does not require a group of subjects (although the mechanism can be used in a group setting by randomly drawing a price for the entire group). The mechanism has proved useful for eliciting values in field settings such as grocery stores (Lusk et al., 2001a; Rousu et al., 2005). The strength of the BDM is also its weakness. Because people participate individually with the BDM, no active market is present. Shogren (2005) contends that an active market environment is important in inducing economic rationality at the margin or at the individual level if arbitrage has enough power. Shogren et al. (2001b) observed that certain anomalies, for example the WTP/WTA disparity, are still present with the BDM, but disappear in active market environments such as the second or random nth price auctions. If a BDM mechanism is implemented, there are several factors a researcher must consider. For example, what distribution should be used for the random price generator and how should this be conveyed to participants? It is desirable to use a price range greater than the range of potential values so that bids are not censored, but care must also be given that the range is not so large that participants with reasonable valuations have little chance of winning.

An advantage of the random nth price auction is that it potentially keeps bidders with relatively low values engaged in the auction. It also provides a relatively high degree of market feedback if used over multiple bidding rounds with posted prices. The random nth price auction can be a challenge to explain to some participants and can be difficult to manage for the experimental monitor.

One factor to consider when choosing an auction mechanism relates to the shape of the payoff function and the expected cost from bidding suboptimally (Lusk et al., 2006a). Harrison (1989) originally suggested using such an approach to explain "misbehavior" in first price auctions. Although his suggestion to evaluate behavior in terms of expected payoff was heavily debated and has some limitations (see Cox et al., 1992), we believe that investigating individuals' expected payoffs should be one of several criteria practitioners might consider when selecting between competing auctions. Consider the formalities now.

Although a person has an incentive to submit a bid, b_i, equal to their value, v_i, in the auctions we are considering, each mechanism differs in the expected monetary loss from bidding $b_i \neq v_i$. Some findings on the relative accuracy of mechanisms are probably related to payoff function shape. A risk neutral, expected profit maximizing person derives expected benefits from submitting the bid, b_i:

$$E[\pi_i] = (v_i - E[\text{Price}|(\text{winning}|b_i)])(\text{ Probability of winning}|b_i)$$
$$(5.1)$$

where E is the expectations operator and π_i is individual i's benefit or payoff from submitting b_i in an auction. A person expects to earn the difference between their value for the good and the expected price paid conditional on winning the auction, which is conditional on b_i. This expected payoff is multiplied by the probability that a person wins the auction given b_i. As shown in Lusk *et al.* (2006a), the payoff function for a BDM mechanism in which the price, p, is drawn from a known distribution with a cumulative distribution function $F(p)$ and probability density function $f(p)$ is:

$$E\left[\pi_i^{BDM}\right] = \left[v_i - \int_{-\infty}^{b_i} \frac{f(p)}{F(b_i)} p\,dp\right] F(b_i),$$
$$(5.2)$$

This function is maximized at $b_i = v_i$. If the price is drawn from a uniform distribution on $[0, T]$, the BDM payoff function is: $[v_i - 0.5b_i](b_i/T)$.

Using order statistics, Lusk *et al.* (2006a) show that the payoff function for any kth price auction with N bidders whose values are independently drawn from a distribution with cdf given by $F(v)$ and pdf given by $f(v)$ is:

$$E\left[\pi_i^{kthprice}\right]$$
$$= \left[v_i - \int_{-\infty}^{b_i} \frac{\frac{(N-1)!}{(N-k)!(k-2)!}(F(v))^{N-k}[1-F(v)]^{k-2}f(v)}{\int_{-\infty}^{b_i}\frac{(N-1)!}{(N-k)!(k-2)!}(F(x))^{N-k}[1-F(x)]^{k-2}f(x)x\,dx}v\,dv\right]$$
$$\times \sum_{r=N-k+1}^{N-1} \frac{(N-1)!}{r!(N-1-r)!}F(b_i)^r[1-F(b_i)]^{N-1-r} \qquad (5.3)$$

assuming all bidders except individual i bid truthfully (i.e., $b_j = v_j$ for all $j \neq i$). While F represents the distribution of random prices in the BDM, which is an endogenous choice to the researcher, it represents the distribution of bidders' values in a kth price auction, which is exogenous to the researcher.

The payoff function for a second price auction (i.e., $k = 2$) is a simplified version of equation 5.3:

$$E\left[\pi_i^{2ndprice}\right] = \left[v_i - \int_{-\infty}^{b_i} (N-1)\left[\frac{F(v)}{F(b_i)}\right]^{(N-2)}\left[\frac{f(v)}{F(b_i)}\right] vdx\right](F(b_i))^{N-1}.$$

(5.4)

If bidders' values are uniformly distributed on $[0, T]$, the payoff function for the second price auction is: $(v_i - b_i(N-1)/N)*(b_i/T)^\wedge(N-1)$.

Conceptually, a random nth price auction is similar to the BDM, with two key differences. First, rather than bidding against a random price generator as in a BDM, in a random nth price auction a person bids against N other bidders, whose values/bids are distributed according to F. Second, unlike the BDM, in the random nth price auction one of the N bidders' values is drawn at random and that bid is set as the price. From the perspective of bidder i, there is a $(N-1)/N$ chance another individual's bid will be drawn as the price, in which case the payoff function is simply the BDM. There is a $1/N$ chance that individual i's bid will be chosen as the random nth bid, in which case the individual i's payoff is zero. The payoff function for individual i bidding b_i in a random nth price auction with N bidders is:

$$E\left[\pi_i^{randomnth}\right] = \frac{N-1}{N}\left[v_i - \int_{-\infty}^{b_i} \frac{f(v)}{F(b_i)}vdp\right]F(b_i).$$ (5.5)

Equation (5.5) is $(N-1)/N$ times the payoff function of the BDM.

The expected cost of deviating from optimal bidding can be compared across mechanisms. Lusk *et al.* (2006a) compared payoff functions for several kth price auctions to the BDM for a wide range of true values and value/price distributions. They suggest that mechanisms that impose a higher cost on subjects from submitting a bid different from value are more preferred. They define the expected cost of sub-optimal bidding for a mechanism as $E[\pi_i|b_i = v_i] - E[\pi_i|b_i \neq v_i]$, a statistic which is zero if a truthful bid is submitted and increasingly positive as b_i moves farther from v_i.

We now illustrate how equations (5.3) to (5.5) can be used to choose between auction mechanisms. Suppose, for argument's sake, one was choosing between a second price auction, a third price auction, and the BDM mechanism. Assume values/prices are drawn from a uniform distribution on $[0, 10]$ and there are $N = 8$ bidders. Figures 5.1 and 5.2 show the expected cost of sub-optimal bidding for each mechanism for people with true values equal to $v_i = 3$ and $v_i = 7$, respectively. For a relatively low value bidder ($v_i = 3$), Figure 5.1 shows that the BDM punishes sub-optimal bidding more than the second or third price auctions. In contrast, Figure 5.2 generally shows that the second and third price auctions impose higher costs for sub-optimal bidding than the BDM for

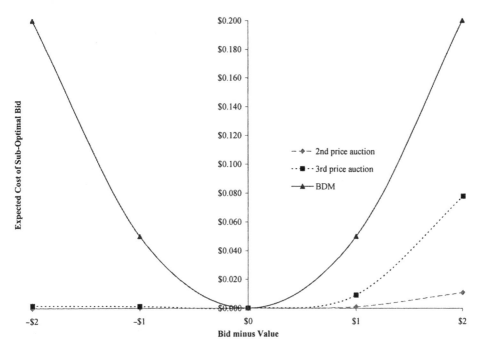

Figure 5.1 Expected cost of sub-optimal bidding for $v_i = 3$, $N = 8$, and values/prices are drawn from a uniform distribution on [0, 10]

a relatively high value bidder ($v_i = 7$). If a person with true value of $7 bids $8 instead of $7, their expected loss in profits is $0.13, $0.07, and $0.05 for the third price, second price, and BDM mechanisms, respectively. Figures 5.1 and 5.2 both show that in the second and third price auctions, it is more costly to overbid than to underbid, but that the costs of deviation are symmetric for the BDM. These findings rest on the assumption of a uniform distribution and eight bidders, which is likely to vary in each study. The expected costs of sub-optimal bidding can be calculated for a wide variety of mechanisms, distributions, participant numbers, and values given the preceding equations.

Whether the equations are actually used to calculate the expected cost of submitting bids that differ from true values, the general ideas presented are important to consider. For example, does an auction mechanism and do auction instructions convey that each person has a chance of winning? If an individual believes they are not likely to win, they have little incentive to bid truthfully. The figures also suggest that mechanisms differ by the type of individual that is given the greatest incentive for truthful bidding. While the BDM imposes higher costs for non-truthful than the second price auction for low-value participants, the opposite is true for higher-value people. Practitioners might consider which type of person is of most interest. The figures also show that while the BDM imposes equal costs for under- and over-bidding, the second price auction

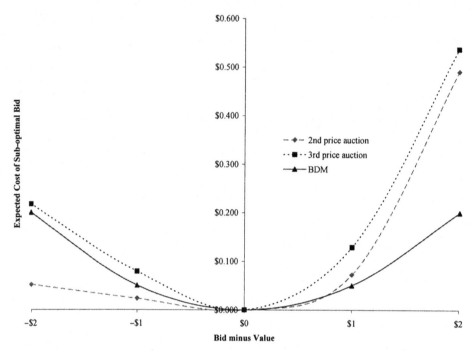

Figure 5.2 Expected cost of sub-optimal bidding for $v_i = 7$, $N = 8$, and values/prices are drawn from a uniform distribution on [0, 10]

imposes higher costs for over-bidding than under-bidding. (It is also true that a kth price auction with $k = N - 1$, e.g, an seventh price auction with eight people, would impose higher costs for under-bidding than for over-bidding.) Practitioners might consider whether, for their particular application, people are more likely to use heuristics to over- or under-bid and use a mechanism that counters such behavior.

5.5   Multiple good valuation, demand reduction, and field substitutes

In experimental auctions, practitioners often want to obtain bids on several goods with slightly different quality attributes from the same set of subjects. The motivation for such a procedure is clear: there are relatively high fixed costs associated with recruiting subjects and conducting experimental sessions. More data can be gathered for little additional cost by obtaining valuations for multiple goods from each person. Practitioners are also interest in comparing bids for a conventional good to several altered counterparts.

Despite the need for multiple good valuation, several factors should be considered if values are elicited for several goods concurrently. The critical issue is demand reduction or diminishing marginal utility. A closely held tenet of economic theory is that of diminishing marginal utility; the extra utility obtained from an additional unit of a good falls as more units are consumed. If two substitute goods are simultaneously auctioned, there is a chance a person could end up purchasing two goods, which would be similar to obtaining two units of a good. To illustrate, consider the data reported in Corrigan and Rousu (2006a). They found that when subjects bid for only one jar of salsa, the average bid was $0.65, but when subjects bid to purchase two jars of salsa, the average bid was $1.13. Demand for the second jar of salsa was effectively $0.17 (or 26%) lower than the first unit. Intuitively, we might expect a person bidding in an auction in which they might win two units of a good to reduce their bid for each good if they expect they might win both.

In the previous section, we showed the payoff function associated with the BDM mechanism. Reconsider this auction payoff function for the case where prices are drawn from a uniform distribution on [0, T]:

$$E[\pi] = [v - 0.5b]\frac{b}{T}. \tag{5.6}$$

Now consider an experiment in which a person bids simultaneously for two substitutable goods in two concurrent BDM mechanisms both using a uniform random price generator on [0, T]. Let d represent the money-metric discount a person receives from having two units of a good versus only one that results from demand reduction or diminishing marginal utility. A person's payoff function for bidding on two goods (A and B) simultaneously is:

$$E[\pi] = [v^A - 0.5b^A]\frac{b^A}{T} + [v^B - 0.5b^B]\frac{b^B}{T} - d\frac{b^A}{T}\frac{b^B}{T}, \tag{5.7}$$

where b^A and v^A represent the bid and value for good A, respectively, and b^B and v^B represent the bid and value for good B, respectively. The last term, $d\frac{b^A}{T}\frac{b^B}{T}$, represents the discount from diminishing marginal utility, d, multiplied by the probability of winning both goods given bids b^A and b^B. Differentiating the equation with respect to b^A and b^B and setting equal to zero, the payoff is maximized when $b^A = v^A - d(b^B/T)$ and $b^B = v^B - d(b^A/T)$. Instead of bidding true value, a person offers a bid equal to his value for the good less the diminishing marginal utility discount factor times the probability of winning the other auctioned good. After a bit of algebra, we see the optimal bid for good A is:

$$b^{A*} = \frac{T(v^A T - v^B d)}{T^2 - d^2}. \tag{5.8}$$

The payoff function is *not* maximized at $b^A = v^A$ as in a single good valuation unless A and B are completely unrelated in consumption, that is, $d = 0$. The differences in bids are contaminated by demand reduction. Further algebraic manipulation yields the insight that at optimum $b^{A*} - b^{B*} = (v^A - v^B)/(1 - d/T)$. The difference in bids for goods A and B is *not* equal to the difference in value between goods A and B. In most instances, $T > d$, and as such, differences in bids between goods will tend to be greater than differences in valuations.

This problem is exacerbated if subjects bid on multiple goods in several bidding rounds and have the possibility of winning goods in each bidding round. To further illustrate, consider an application in which a subject bids on two unrelated goods, but in which they must submit bids on each good in each bidding round. Consider a participant who wins a unit of good A in round 1, but does not win a unit of good B. Now, demand for good A will decline by d in the second round, but demand for good B will be unchanged. In round 2, the value of good A versus good B has changed due to a movement down the good A demand curve; not necessarily due to an inherent difference in the value of the goods. If d is sufficiently large, a person that prefers good A in round 1 could become a good B preferring individual in round 2. The inferential problem of demand reduction grows more complex if one allows goods A and B to be related in consumption within any round. The key issue here is that research results might be an artifact of poor experimental design instead of a reflection of true preferences that would be displayed in the marketplace.

This raises the question of how to handle demand reduction and diminishing marginal utility. First, demand reduction is not a problem *per se*; it is an essential feature of consumer preference. The problem lies in drawing correct inferences when demand reduction exists. If one wants to determine how demand falls as multiple units are purchased, there are multiple-unit variants of the Vickrey auction that are incentive compatible (see Vickrey, 1961; List and Lucking-Reiley, 2000). For example, suppose 10 units of a good were offered for sale. A multiple-unit Vickrey auction would entail each individual submitting up to 10 bids for each unit, with the top 10 bids winning the auction and all 10 units being sold at the 11th highest bid amount. See Brookshire *et al.* (1987) for an application of such an auction in a food marketing context.

The more traditional case is in estimating a person's value for one unit of a good (or a unit each of a few differentiated goods). One solution is to conduct an auction for a single unit of a single good in a single bidding round. This solution is overly restrictive because it eliminates within-subject valuation comparisons and does not allow the researcher to easily investigate the value of multiple product attributes. A straightforward way to mitigate the demand reduction problem is to use random drawings to determine a binding bidding round and/or a binding good. For example, Hayes *et al.* (1995) had subjects participate in twenty bidding rounds, in which only one of these rounds was drawn as binding; Lusk *et al.* (2004a) auctioned five different types of beef steaks and randomly drew only one of the steak types as binding after all bids were submitted. Assuming a subject's expected utility is linear in probabilities, randomly drawing a binding auction should produce the same results as conducting several single auctions. Roosen *et al.* (1998) provides evidence to suggest that individuals' behavior in these sorts of applications is consistent with this assumption.

One might be tempted to think of demand reduction as an issue that relates only to the goods being auctioned in the experiment. But one should also recognize there are field or "outside the experiment" substitutes for the goods auctioned inside a laboratory experiment. Chapter 3 showed that a person's WTP or WTA for a good depends on the price of substitute goods; this includes goods in the experiment and goods outside the experiment. Empirical evidence shows that bids are influenced by the price of field substitutes. For example, Corrigan (2005) showed that bids for coffee mugs were significantly influenced by perceptions of perceived costs of purchasing the item in the future and the perceived ability to sell the item in the future. People who believed it relatively costly to delay their decision bid more in the auction.

In an induced value experiment, Cherry *et al.* (2004) showed that bids in a second price auction were influenced by the price of an outside option that was a perfect substitute for the auctioned good; lower prices for the outside option were associated with lower bids in the auction. Cherry *et al.* (2004) used a 2×3 treatment design to test for bid reduction in the presence of an outside option. The treatment conditions involved real or hypothetical payments, and three uniform outside option prices; $2, $4 or $6. All other design features were the same across treatments: ten bidders in each of ten rounds participating in a second price auction. In each round, the monitor assigned each bidder a unique induced value for the good.

Bidders were given a bid slip that informed the bidder of their resale value and allowed the bidder to indicate, if they lost the auction, whether they wanted to buy the good in the secondary outside option market. At the end of each round, the monitor collected bid slips, calculated profits for each bidder, recorded the individual results on the bid slip, and returned the slips to the bidders so they could follow the results of their actions. Profits equaled the difference between the resale value and the price the bidder paid for the good, either in the auction or in the secondary market. If a bidder did not purchase the good, his profit was zero for that round. In the real payments sessions, total profits for all ten sessions were paid to bidders in cash at the end of the experiment. Only the winner saw the two highest bids.

The results from Cherry *et al.* (2004) show bid reduction existed due to the outside option, as measured by the percentage of total bids per round relative to the baseline demand. Both the real and hypothetical auction elicited about 76% and 77% percent of baseline demand. Bid reduction was consistent with comparative static predictions: as the outside option price got cheaper, auction bids decreased. Comparing observed behavior in round ten of the real auctions, for instance, shows that as outside price increased from $2 to $4 to $6, total bids increased from $25.2 to $34.4 to $48.6. Overall, the evidence suggested bidders considered the outside option when formulating their bid strategies, and changed their bids accordingly. Results also indicate that although bid reduction existed, bidders who reduced bids did not necessarily bid *exactly* the price of the outside option. Statistical tests found both real and hypothetical bidding schedules were significantly above the choked demand curve. Finally, while bidding was subject to hypothetical bias, bid shaving due to the outside option was equally likely to occur in real and hypothetical auctions.

These findings suggest that practitioners need to think about: (a) controlling for the prices and availability of field substitutes; or (b) making this feature an integral part of the experimental design. A simple method of control is to provide subjects with a common expectation about the price of outside options. For example, Lusk *et al.* (2004a) explicitly informed subjects of the price of one of their steaks in the local grocery store. Harrison, Harstad, and Rutström (2004) discuss methods for dealing with bids that may be truncated at the stated field price if such a procedure is implemented. Another method of control is to ask people what they believe to be the price and availability of outside options and to use this information in subsequent regression analysis to help explain bidding behavior. This approach was partially implemented by Corrigan (2005). The task of directly incorporating field substitutes into the research design is more complicated, but one option might entail offering a menu of potential substitutes at a posted price while auctioning another good of interest. Varying the price of these substitutes in repeated auctions would provide insight into the degree of substitutability between goods.

5.6   Learning and affiliation in repeated bidding rounds

A common practice among early studies using experimental auctions was to carry out several repeated bidding rounds for the same good, with prices posted at the conclusion of each round, and with one of the rounds randomly selected as binding. In one recent example, Lusk *et al.* (2004a) carried out an experiment in which people bid to obtain one of five beef steaks (to be selected at random) in five bidding rounds and the second highest price for each steak was posted after each round. Figure 5.3 shows the average bid for each beef steak across the five bidding rounds. Bidding behavior matches the prototypical result in WTP auctions: bids tend to increase over the first few bidding rounds and then tend to stabilize after a few rounds of bidding.

We now consider why bids respond in such a manner and whether conducting repeated rounds is a useful feature of experimental auction design. The initial practice of using repeated rounds with price feedback in homegrown value auctions originated from induced value experiments. In a variety of contexts and in different experiments, induced value studies showed it took several rounds

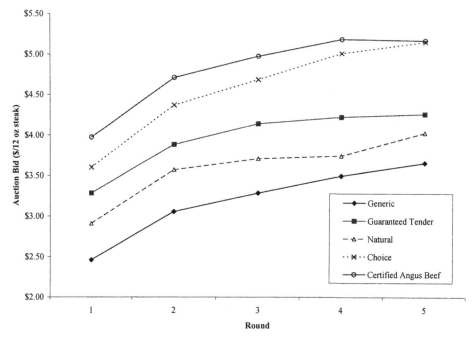

Figure 5.3 Second price auction bids for five beef steaks across five bidding rounds

for behavior to conform to the predictions of economic theory. These findings implied that repeated rounds allow subjects to learn and gain experience with the mechanism. Repeated rounds allow people to learn the weakly dominant strategy by being punished for sub-optimal bidding.

Despite these advantages, the use of multiple bidding rounds with price feedback has its critics (see Harrison *et al.*, 2004). In auction theory, bidders are typically characterized as either having independent private values or as sharing a single common value. But values may be affiliated: a condition in which a high value for one bidder implies a greater likelihood of high values for other bidders. Since the study of Milgrom and Webber (1982), the theoretical effects of bidder affiliation have been well understood. Assuming risk neutrality, affiliation results in a break-down of the revenue equivalence principle between auctions. Milgrom and Webber (1982) show that when values are affiliated, providing information about the value of the good increases revenue for the seller. The concern is that if values are or become affiliated, mechanisms such as the second price auction are no longer incentive compatible.[1]

---

[1] For example, Klemperer shows for the case of the uniform distribution that if a person's value, v_i, is given by $v_i = \alpha t_i + \beta \sum_{i \neq j} t_j$, where t_j is the "signal" received by individual j and α and β are the respective weights assigned to person i's signal versus all other individuals' signals, that the optimal bid in a second price auction is $b_i^* = (\alpha + (n/2)\beta)t_i$, where n is the number of bidders. A person only bids true value if $\beta = 0$, i.e., values are independent.

Based on this theoretical literature, Harrison *et al.* (2004) argue that values *become* affiliated because posted prices serve to signal relative quality or the price/availability of outside options. People take the posted prices as signals of what the good should be worth to themselves, causing values to become inter-related or affiliated. That auction bids tend to increase each bidding round in homegrown value auctions provides *prima facie* evidence of bidder affiliation. But such a phenomenon could also be related to learning about the mechanism. People can be unfamiliar with the types of auctions we are considering. In auctions and in everyday bargaining experiences, people have probably developed heuristics such as "buy low" that they might follow even if told that optimal strategy is to bid true value. Repeated rounds with price feedback can force people to abandon such heuristics, but it might also cause affiliation as prices send signals of unknown characteristics of the good.

The difficulty in determining the veracity of the criticism of price feedback is that true values are not known in homegrown value experiments and it is impossible to know whether people are bidding true value or whether values are affiliated. It is also a challenge to separate learning effects from affiliation effects. A few studies have tackled the issue of affiliation directly in homegrown value auctions. List and Shogren (1999) found that repeated auction rounds with price feedback caused a slight increase in bids for unfamiliar goods. They used panel data from published and unpublished experimental auctions that used repeated trials of the second price auction for familiar and unfamiliar products such as food products that varied in safety (e.g., sandwiches with a risk of food-borne diseases or produced with growth hormones). All the experiments followed a common experimental design. The instructions said why it was in a bidder's best interest to tell the truth when bidding in the second price auction. Each experiment used a repeated round design, in which only one round was chosen at random as the binding auction. The second-highest price was publicly posted after each round. The posted price provided subjects with market price information generated by the group interaction that would otherwise be unavailable in one-shot experiments.

Table 5.2 summarizes the six categories of data collected: categories 1 and 2 represent *naïve* willingness to pay (WTP) bids and willingness to accept (WTA) offers for unfamiliar products without non-price information about the product; categories 3 and 4 represent *informed* WTP bids and WTA offers for unfamiliar goods with non-price information; and categories 5 and 6 represent *ex ante* WTP bids and WTA offers for a familiar good (Snickers or Milky Way candy bars).

List and Shogren (1999) estimated the following model for each of the six categories of panel data:

$$B_{it} = \alpha_i + \beta P_{i,t-1} + \varphi_t + \varepsilon_{it}$$

Table 5.2. *Summary of panel data categories in List and Shogren (1999)*

Data category	Information	Measure of value	Treatments	Trials	Total observations
1. *Naïve*	Price only	WTP	32	9	288
2. *Naïve*	Price only	WTA	5	9	45
3. *Informed*	Price & non-price	WTP	32	10	320
4. *Informed*	Price & non-price	WTA	5	10	50
5. *Ex ante familiar*	*Ex ante* knowledge & price	WTP	23	4	92
6. *Ex ante familiar*	*Ex ante* knowledge & price	WTA	5	4	20

where B_{it} denotes median bid or offer in experiment i and trial/round t; $P_{i,t-1}$ denotes the posted price in experiment i for trial $t - 1$, α_i represents a fixed/random experiment effect, φ_t is a trial fixed/random effect, and ε_{it} represents the contemporaneous error term. The median bid was used to proxy for bidding behavior to avoid extreme outliers and overweighting random patterns of bidding behavior in the last few trials of experiments. Auction or experiment effects, α_i, control for characteristics that vary from auction to auction but are invariant over trials of the same auction, for example, unique characteristics of auctioned goods, the lab environment, and nuances of monitors and subjects. Trial effects, φ_t, capture variables invariant across auctions, and controls for trends in subject behavior and market experience.

Table 5.3 summarizes the regression results. The results in the top panel of Table 5.3 suggest that a posted price effect does exist for unfamiliar products, although the size of the effect is very small. Estimated coefficients (column 1) indicate posted prices affect the behavior of the median *naïve* WTP bidders facing unfamiliar goods. A dime increase in the posted second price increased the median willingness to pay by about a penny. Parameter estimates (column 3) for the *naïve* WTA measures for unfamiliar goods are similar but even less severe in economic significance; if the posted price falls by one dollar the median offer falls by about half a cent. Absent information about the product, naïve bidders seem to rely on the signal sent by the posted second-price from round t when updating their bids, or offers, in round $t + 1$.

Is the tendency for prices to lead naïve bidders to increase bids economically significant given that the unfamiliar products, sandwiches, would retail for about $4? If the posted price increased by one dollar between trial two and ten, the implied increase in the median naïve WTP bid is about eight cents or about 2% of value. Large price spikes were rare in the WTP naïve markets. The average

Table 5.3. *Two-way fixed effects estimation results for bid equation*

| | Ex Ante Unfamiliar | | | | Ex Ante Familiar | |
| | WTP | | WTA | | | |
Variable	Naïve	Informed	Naïve	Informed	WTP	WTA
Constant	0.54*	0.67*	1.39*	1.29*	0.34*	0.36
	(0.05)[a]	(0.03)	(0.05)	(0.23)	(0.03)	(0.32)
$Price_{t-1}$	0.08*	−0.002	0.004*	−0.001	−0.04	−0.47
	(0.03)	(0.02)	(0.001)	(0.001)	(0.06)	(0.89)
R^2	0.73	0.89	0.89	0.62	0.93	0.58
Adj. R^2	0.69	0.87	0.84	0.45	0.90	0.20
$F(\alpha_i = 0)$	7.88	57.02	23.36	6.18	14.82	2.84
(d.f.)	(31, 255)	(31, 287)	(4, 39)	(4, 44)	(22, 68)	(4, 14)
$F(\varphi_t = 0)$	3.50	2.27	5.25	2.42	3.03	0.50
(d.f.)	(8, 246)	(9, 277)	(8, 30)	(9, 34)	(3, 64)	(3, 10)
Hausman	25.84	2.80	29.22	0.82	30.10	0.72
(d.f.)	(1)	(1)	(1)	(1)	(1)	(1)
N	288	320	45	50	92	20

Note: Dependent variable is median bid in trial t.
[a] Standard errors in parentheses under coefficient estimates.
* Significant at the .01 level.

posted price increased to $1.59 (s.d. = 1.28) in the late trial from $1.21 (s.d. = 0.76) in the early trial, which results in a point estimate increase of $0.03 in the median bid (= $0.38 × 0.08), which is less than 1% of value. If we build a 95% confidence interval around the estimated coefficient, $\beta = 0.08$, we see that the lower and upper bounds of the price effect are $0.01 and $0.05, translating into about 0.02% and 1.3% of value. This price effect seems relatively modest. About five cents of the change in median bids is caused by posted prices, implying a small percentage of overall variability is attributable to price changes.

In the WTA naïve regression, the average posted price falls to $9 (s.d. = 7.21) in trial ten from $8 (s.d. = 125) in trial two. With the small regression coefficient estimate and the relatively large standard error for the WTA bids, the argument made for naïve WTP holds for WTA as well. The price-induced decreases are within the margin of error surrounding the average bid, suggesting an exaggerated fear of onerous quantitative bias for the goods considered herein.

Table 5.3 shows that the price effect disappears when the subject is given non-price information or is more familiar with the product. Bidders seem to use price and non-price information as substitutes when formulating their measure of value. Results indicate that posted prices affect neither the median informed-WTP bid nor the median informed-WTA offer at any conventional level of significance (columns 2 and 4). This suggests that informed bidders treat the written word as a substitute for market signals. Bids and offers for the familiar candy bars reinforce this observation; posted prices do not affect WTP bids or WTA offers (columns 5 and 6) at conventional significance levels. In general, the more a bidder knows about the good before entering the lab, the less the posted second price affects his or her behavior. List and Shogren (1999) concluded that the ultimate effect of repeated rounds and price-posting was to improve learning about the mechanism.

Alfnes and Rickertsen (2003) also found that posted prices caused small increases bids. They also showed that the trend in bid increases was similar across all goods investigated in their study leading them to conclude that learning about the mechanisms is primarily responsible for the increase in bids over bidding rounds.

Shogren et al. (2001b) also provide support for multiple-round bidding with price feedback showing that the procedure yields valuations more consistent with neoclassical economic theory. Neoclassical theory suggests that the WTP and WTA measures of value should be similar under certain assumptions; other studies have shown significant divergence between the two measures. Consistent with these studies, Shogren et al. (2001b) showed that WTA was 1.5 to 2 times WTP in the first rounds of bidding; but, the two measures converged over repeated rounds for auction mechanisms that used active markets with price feedback. We describe this study in more detail in Chapter 9.

Harrison, Harstad, and Rutström (2004) re-analyzed the data in Hoffman et al. (1993) and showed that controlling for price feedback in regression analysis reversed one of the main conclusions of the original study regarding the relative value of vacuum packaging. They found that bids for beef steaks were affected by prices in previous rounds and they argued that such an effect was due to affiliation. While also consistent with standard notions of Bayesian updating on beliefs, this finding led them to argue against using repeated round auctions. But before one accepts this conclusion, recognize that Hoffman et al.'s (1993) experimental design made every round binding. The finding that prices in previous rounds affected subsequent behavior is not surprising as it is due to movement down the demand curve as people purchase additional steaks and demand curve shifts as people learn the price of a substitute good. Because of this feature of Hoffman et al.'s experimental design, repeated rounds are likely to have generated a much larger effect on behavior. Homegrown value studies after Hoffman et al. (1993) have selected only one round to be binding circumventing the confounding influences on bids.

One can also think about this issue from a slightly different angle by comparing bidding behavior across mechanisms that use different levels of price feedback. For example, Lusk *et al.* (2004a) and Rutström (1998) both found that the BDM mechanism and English auctions generated statistically equivalent results. This finding is fascinating because the English auction permits the greatest possible amount of market feedback as every person can see exactly what every one else is doing (and has the greatest potential for bidder affiliation), whereas the BDM permits no feedback about other individuals' values (and has no bidder affiliation). Two mechanisms which span the spectrum in terms of potential of bidder affiliation seem to generate very similar results in single-round auctions. These results seem to suggest that changes in bids across bidding rounds are unlikely to be due to affiliation.

We now consider some new findings on this question. The difficulty with many previous studies investigating bidding behavior over repeated rounds is that affiliation is defined as a positive relationship between posted prices in a previous period and bids in the current period. Such an effect could also result from learning about the mechanism. For example, suppose a person, based on previous buying behavior in other contexts, takes a strategy of under-stating their true valuation in a misunderstood attempt to garner additional surplus. Posting a high price will cause such a person to re-evaluate this strategy and force them to increase their bid and the higher the price the more pronounced the departure from the heuristic. A positive relationship between posted prices and bids need not imply affiliation. We take a different approach to investigate whether the practice of posting prices in repeated round auctions causes affiliation. Recalling a primary argument against price feedback is that people use posted prices to partially infer the quality of the good, we investigate whether *relative* valuations for qualities of a good are affected by posted prices.

Looking at Figure 5.3 yields some insight into this issue. While bids for each steak type tend to increase across rounds, the differences between steak bids remain reasonably constant as the lines are roughly parallel. Relative preferences for quality do not seem to be changing with the price information, which implies people are not using posted prices to signal unknown quality or availability. The data in Table 5.4 provide more formal support for this observation. Parametric and non-parametric tests reject the hypothesis that mean bids for each steak are unchanged over the five bidding rounds. When investigating the differences between each steak's bid and the average bid for all steaks, however, we cannot reject the hypothesis of uniform bids across rounds. While the mean bid for the generic steak increased about $1.20 from round one to round five (an increase which is statistically significant), people bid $0.79 less for the generic steak than the mean for all steaks in round one and this statistic only increased one cent to $0.80 by round five (not statistically different).

To delve even further into the issue, Table 5.5 reports regression results similar to those in List and Shogren (1999), Alfnes and Rickertson (2003), and Harrison *et al.* (2004), in which bids are regressed against dummy variables for

Table 5.4. *Second price auction bids for beef steak across five bidding rounds*

Steak	1	2	3	4	5	ANOVA[a]	Rank-Sum[a]
	Round					Test for equality of bids across rounds	
Absolute bids							
($/12 oz steak)							
Generic	$2.46	$3.06	$3.29	$3.50	$3.66	0.07	0.05
Guaranteed tender	$3.29	$3.88	$4.14	$4.22	$4.26	0.26	0.05
Natural	$2.91	$3.57	$3.71	$3.74	$4.03	0.23	0.15
Choice	$3.60	$4.37	$4.68	$5.01	$5.15	0.01	0.00
Certified Angus Beef	$3.97	$4.71	$4.97	$5.18	$5.17	0.09	0.04
Overall mean	$3.25	$3.92	$4.16	$4.33	$4.45	0.05	0.03
Differences from							
overall mean							
Generic	−$0.79	−$0.86	−$0.66	−$0.68	−$0.80	0.99	0.96
Guaranteed tender	$0.04	−$0.04	$0.07	−$0.07	−$0.19	0.76	0.99
Natural	−$0.34	−$0.35	−$0.42	−$0.31	−$0.43	0.89	0.86
Choice	$0.36	$0.45	$0.85	$0.82	$0.70	0.14	0.37
Certified Angus Beef	$0.73	$0.79	$1.02	$0.84	$0.72	0.95	0.81

[a] p-values associated with the hypothesis that the mean bids (central tendencies in the case of the Rank-Sum test) for each steak are equal across all five bidding rounds.

each steak type, dummy variables for each round, and the lagged price posted in the previous round. When aggregate models are estimated, as in previous studies, we find posted prices affect both absolute and relative bids.[2] Results indicate a $1 price increase in a previous round increased bids in the subsequent round by about $0.30; similarly a $1 increase in the price of a steak relative to the mean price for all steaks in a previous round increased bids for the steak by about $0.30 over the mean for all steaks in the subsequent round. At first blush, these results are largely consistent with previous findings. The problem with the aggregate models is that they are mis-specified. F-tests reveal strong interactions between all the variables in Table 5.5 and individual dummy variables, that is, we reject the hypothesis that all people have the same coefficients for each variable in Table 5.5 at the 0.05 level of significance.

Because the thirty-five people in our sample submitted twenty-five bids (each person bid for five steaks in five bidding rounds), we are able to estimate individual-level models. Table 5.5 reports the average coefficients from these thirty-five models. Overall, results are similar to the aggregate models *except* the lagged price effects are not statistically significant at any standard level of

---

[2] The aggregate models are ordinary least squares regressions including fixed effects for each individual; less than 4% of the bids were zero and as such using a censored model instead of the OLS has virtually no effect on results.

Table 5.5. *Aggregate and individual models of the effect of posted prices on bidding behavior*

Variable	Dependent variable is absolute bid level		Dependent variable is bid differences from overall mean	
	Pooled model with fixed effects[a]	Average parameters from individual-level models[b]	Pooled model with fixed effects[c]	Average parameters from individual-level models[d]
Intercept	5.550*[e]	5.571*	0.509*	0.886*
	(0.258)[f]	(0.911)	(0.258)	(0.170)
Generic[g]	−1.057*	−1.694*	–	–
	(0.252)	(0.294)		
Guaranteed Tender[g]	−0.591*	−1.098*	−0.589*	−1.115*
	(0.161)	(0.251)	(0.152)	(0.254)
Natural[g]	−0.894*	−1.430*	−0.891*	−1.447*
	(0.179)	(0.318)	(0.169)	(0.330)
Choice[g]	−0.100	−0.168	−0.099	−0.169
	(0.123)	(0.101)	(0.179)	(0.103)
Round 2[h]	−0.535*	−0.699*	0.025	0.001
	(0.103)	(0.171)	(0.106)	(0.145)
Round 3[h]	−0.293*	−0.390*	0.023	0.014
	(0.103)	(0.120)	(0.106)	(0.020)
Round 4[h]	−0.121	−0.195*	0.014	−0.005
	(0.103)	(0.068)	(0.106)	(0.075)
Lagged price[i]	0.295*	−0.034	0.297*	−0.044
	(0.114)	(0.113)	(0.111)	(0.122)
R^2	0.79	0.95	0.30	0.85

[a] Number of observations = 700; fixed effects for each individual were estimated but are not reported in the table.
[b] A regression with 20 observations was estimated for each of the 35 people in the sample.
[c] Number of observations = 560; fixed effects for each individual were estimated but are not reported in the table.
[d] A regression with 16 observations was estimated for each of the 35 people in the sample.
[e] One asterisk (*) indicates statistical significance at the 0.05 level or lower.
[f] Numbers in parentheses are standard errors.
[g] Estimated effects relative to the Certified Angus Beef Steak.
[h] Estimated effects relative to round 5.
[i] In the models with bid differences as the dependent variable, the lagged price difference is included as the regressor.

significance. Estimates from individual-level models indicate no relationship between posted prices and either absolute or relative bids. If we investigate the individual-level models estimated with the absolute bid as the dependent variable, we find that although we are able to reject the hypothesis that bids for all five types of beef were equal for thirty out of thirty-five people at the 0.05 level of significance, only one person exhibited a statistically significant lagged price coefficient, and this was negative. Regarding the round dummies in the individual-level models, we reject the hypothesis all round effects are equal to zero for fourteen out of thirty-five people for the absolute bid models, but we could not reject the hypothesis of no round effects for any person in the bid difference models. These results suggest that prior findings on affiliation may be due to model misspecification resulting from inadequate attention to modeling individual heterogeneity.

These findings do not rule out the possibility that values might become affiliated from posted prices. An additional point needs to be made clear. If the argument is that values are affiliated when people walk into the experiment and that the posting of prices accentuates the affiliation process, the act of only conducting one bidding round, as suggested by Harrison *et al.* (2004) or Corrigan and Rousu (2006b), does not solve the problem. When valuations are inter-related the mechanisms we have considered herein are not incentive compatible. Auction mechanisms like those developed by Dasgupta and Maskin (2000) or Perry and Reny would be required to address this issue. With the Dasgupta and Maskin mechanism, people submit a bid *function* relating their bid to other individuals' bids.

Margolis and Shogren (2004) showed this mechanism has some promise in eliciting values in induced-value laboratory experiments; however, they suggest the complicated nature of the mechanisms might require multiple bidding rounds and experience to achieve its full theoretical potential. They used a five-step design to explain the two-person efficient auction.

Step 1: The resale value (i.e., private value) was explained to the subjects. Here each bidder did not immediately know his or her exact resale value since it depended on two factors: (a) his or her own private information *PvtInfo(You)* and (b) private information received by the other bidder, *PvtInfo(Other bidder)*. A person's own private information was randomly determined by drawing a value from a uniform distribution on [0, 20] in one dollar increments. The other bidder's private information was similarly determined. A person's resale value was the sum of their private information and half the other bidder's information: Resale Value(You) = $PvtInfo(You) + [0.5 \times $PvtInfo(Other bidder)].

Step 2: Bids. Each bidder submitted two bids once they received their private information. The other bidder did the same. In particular, each person submitted one bid conditional on the other bidder having drawn the value of $1 (Bid-Low(You)) and a second bid given that the other bidder drew the value of $20

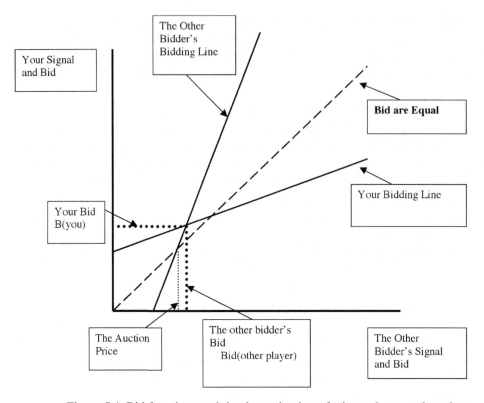

Figure 5.4 Bid functions and the determination of winner, loser, and market price

(Bid-High(You)). These two bids were combined to create a bidding line (see Figure 5.4).

Step 3: Auction winner. The winner of the auction is determined by the intersection of the two bidding lines relative to the **bids are equal** line in Figure 5.4. Consider two bidders: A and B. If Figure 5.4 is drawn from A's perspective, A will win because the two bidding lines intersect above the **bids are equal** line.

Step 4: Auction price. The price is also determined by the **bids are equal** line. For an auction winner, the price is set by where the other player's bidding line intersects the **bids are equal** line.

Step 5: Payoffs. For an auction winner, the payoff for that round is simply: Resale Value(You) − Auction price. For auction losers, the payoff was $0.

Margolis and Shogren (2004) found, based on regression estimates of private values regressed on bids, that behavior in their experiment was not perfectly described by the optimal bidding strategy. The bidding behavior, however, was systematic. In almost every treatment, the coefficient on private value was *below* one. Overall, this suggests bidders did not respond as strongly as they should to their private signals; rather, they offer bids that were about what the average subject offered. While this behavior might indicate that bidders lack confidence in their understanding of the auction and preferred to avoid behavior that appeared extreme, it is consistent with findings in other auctions of flatter bidding than the perfect-revelation line. Overall, the results from this initial exploration suggest this relatively complicated auction designed with inexperienced bidders and no feedback can work to alleviate concerns with affiliation. Future work in which bidders gain experience through many trials and are provided more information on payoffs through computer implementation, is likely to generate greater efficiency levels for the experimental auction.

If the argument is that values are somehow *not* affiliated when people walk into an experiment, and that posting prices causes affiliation, conducting only one bidding round, as suggested by Harrison *et al.* (2004) has some merit. But even if people do not react to posted prices, evidence suggests bidding behavior changes across rounds; an effect most likely due to learning. If only one bidding round is conducted, training people with the mechanism is extremely important. One approach is to follow the steps outlined in Plott and Zeiler (2005) to avoid subject misperceptions. These steps include a significant about of discussion about the mechanism and numerous practice bidding rounds with lotteries.

Even if bidders' values become affiliated over multiple bidding rounds, there are several interesting areas of investigation that need more attention. For example, in everyday shopping experiences, people respond to price information and other cues from friends, family, and advertising. Affiliation may be a common feature of individuals' valuations even when the context has nothing to do with experimental auctions. It is also worth thinking about why and how values become affiliated. For example, Lusk *et al.* (2006) conducted fifth price auctions in several US and European locations, in which they elicited the minimum amount of compensation subjects demanded to consume a genetically modified food. These values were elicited over ten bidding rounds, with one of the rounds randomly selected as binding. As is common in WTA auctions, they found median bids were relatively high in the first bidding round and trended downward as the experiment progressed. The trend in bids, however, differed significantly from location to location and from individual to individual. The aggregate behavior implies something about the relative importance of market prices and individuals' concern for biotechnology. Subjects, on average, demanded less compensation to consume a genetically modified food when they were informed of the market price potentially indicating that a portion of acceptance/rejection of biotechnology is a function of their perception of *market acceptance*.

That some subjects responded differently than others illustrates that affiliation has several potential mediating factors. Responses to posted prices can have meaningful interpretation beyond theoretical concerns with affiliation. The key is to set up the experiment so effects of interest can be properly controlled to ensure that there are no confounding factors. One approach in this regard is to use surrogate or confederate bidders to control the market price while investigating changes in bidding behavior (see Corrigan and Rousu (2006b)). Another approach is to employ a "menu" of nth price auctions – second price, third price, fourth price, etc., and investigate how bidding behavior responds to changes in the magnitude of the price induced by a change in the mechanism.

The jury is still out regarding the appropriateness of using repeated rounds with price feedback. When price feedback is used, care should be taken through econometric analysis or experimental design to ensure that price feedback, in and of itself, is not confounding results. More work is needed to uncover the conditions under which valuations might become affiliated and the process by which people learn in experimental auctions given alternative market circumstances and information.

5.7   Negative values

Many practitioners will be interested in estimating demand for goods for which people have different perceptions of quality and risk. One person may view genetically modified food as a good thing due to reduced pesticide and herbicide use; another person might see the same product as a "Frankenfood." Buhr *et al.* (1993) examined consumer preferences for pork that was leaner due to the use of a genetically engineered growth enhancer. As they demonstrated, many consumers found caloric content more important than concern over biotechnology. But a non-trivial portion of the population had serious concerns about biotechnology. Fox *et al.* (1998) reported survey results with a serious split in the population: nearly 80% of respondents preferred irradiated food to non-irradiated food but 20% had the opposite preference.

If an auction is conducted for a good of ambiguous quality, there is a strong chance that some portion of the population will have a negative value for the good – one would have to pay them to consume the good. But typically auctions do not permit people to bid negative values. Bids are truncated at zero. This practice serves to inflate statistics such as the mean and median bid if consumers place negative values on the good. Two studies have explored the issue of negative values in experimental auctions. Dickinson and Bailey (2002) found that about 5 to 10% of subjects bid a negative amount to exchange a regular ham sandwich for a sandwich that had been screened to ensure food safety; this is despite the *a priori* expectation that improved food safety would be considered a universal "good."

In an induced value study, Parkhurst *et al.* (2004) could not reject the hypothesis that people with negative (and positive) values bid induced values. They found that the second price and random nth price auctions were demand revealing for people with both positive and negative values. Their study followed standard procedures in induced value experiments, except they use three sets of positive and negative induced values as the treatments and subjects were assigned a new induced value in each round.

Their results suggest neither the second price nor the random nth price auction performed without fault. Bidding in the second price auction was precise but biased; the highest positive-value bidders tended to overstate their values, whereas the lowest negative-value bidders tended to understate their values. In contrast, bidding in the random nth price auction was demand revealing across all induced values, but it was imprecise; the variance was relatively large and some bidders submitted very negative bids, seemingly strategically. The average negative-value bidder tended to understate values in the second price auction, irrespective of positive or negative induced value, and to overstate values in the random nth price auction.

What if these results transfer to non-induced lab auctions? For Dickinson and Bailey's (2002) second price auction on meat characteristics, the findings suggest their results are an upper bound on consumers' actual valuation of the auction items (as they noted). Though negative bids were relatively rare, actual consumer negative reaction to some types of information they examined would be understated, based on the findings of Parkhurst *et al.* (2004). In contrast, had Dickinson and Bailey (2002) used a random nth price auction, their results might have been more demand revealing but more noisy, making it difficult to attach any statistical significance to important *changes* in bids across individual auctioned items – a key objective of their study. The choice of auction can attenuate or exaggerate subjects' negative reactions to a new good.

An outside observer using such lab data should note the risk of underestimating the negative reaction to new goods in the marketplace (e.g., consumer picketing or boycotts). That Parkhurst *et al.* (2004) found insincere bidding by people with large positive values and a tendency for people with large negative values to underbid relative to their values suggest that a homegrown value study with a second price auction might cause one to overstate the extent of public support and acceptance for a product and understate the extent of opposition. However, people in the lower tail of the value distribution are most likely to boycott and protest undesirable products. Kalaitzandonakes and Bijman (2003) argue, with respect to genetically modified food, it is the extreme consumers not the average consumer that drives the market acceptance of controversial products.

The potential for negative values is important for policy analysis. While it could be argued that people will not have a negative value for a good that they could freely dispose, for example, a genetically modified food can be thrown away by someone, policy issues arise in which interest lies in determining the welfare effects of moving from one state of the world to another. Consider the welfare effects of a policy requiring all food to be irradiated to reduce the risks of food-borne pathogens. If such a policy were implemented, people would have no choice but to consume irradiated food. The only way to fully measure the welfare change is to measure the negative values for irradiated food that might exist among some segment of the population.

In practice, the potential for negative values can be handled in experimental auctions in two ways. The easiest way to account for such values is to allow people to bid any amount, positive or negative, in experimental auctions. If such a procedure is implemented, care might be taken to ensure that people do not bid negative values for strategic reasons. This might be accomplished by following the suggestions in section 5.2 to ensure that people understand the auction mechanism. Another approach taken by Buhr *et al.* (1993), Fox *et al.* (1998), and Lusk *et al.* (2001a) is to elicit a preference ranking between goods prior to the auction. Subjects are then separated, endowed with the good they indicate as least preferable, and are asked to bid to exchange the endowed good for one of the more preferred goods.

5.8   Conclusions

This chapter considered six design issues in conducting an experimental auction: training and practice; endowment of a product versus full bidding; choosing an auction mechanism; multiple good valuation, demand reduction and field substitutes; learning and affiliation in repeated bidding rounds; and negative values. Our goal in this chapter was to raise critical issues so the reader is aware that his or her choices of experimental auction design can and do affect the values elicited. Even if preferences for new goods are robust to the path taken to elicit them, experience shows that values can be context-specific. The key is to understand whether these revealed values respond to the context in predictable ways as predicted by economic theory (e.g., lower values given lower priced outside options) or whether these values react to uncontrolled contextual cues not addressed or appreciated by the experimenter (e.g., negative values). Given the nascent nature of the field of experimental auctions, the list of design issues considered in this chapter is not comprehensive. Future research will identify additional strengthens and weaknesses of these six features and most likely will raise concerns about other design issues. Being aware of the potential pros and cons of the topics discussed herein should help the reader look for additional challenges and opportunities when conducting experimental auctions.

6 Data analysis

6.1 Introduction

We now examine several methods commonly used to examine bidding behavior in experimental auctions. We focus attention on econometric models and other techniques that have direct applicability for auction data and are likely to receive less coverage in introductory econometrics and statistical texts. The chapter does not cover elementary statistical analysis such as ANOVA and ordinary least squares regression since numerous sources already exist for interested readers (e.g., see Greene, 2000).

6.2 Censored regressions with auction bids

One strength of experimental auctions is that they provide continuous measures of individuals' valuations; one drawback is that these bids are often censored. Censoring occurs when bids are transformed to a single value when they exceed or fall below a particular threshold. A common form of censoring occurs in auctions where people are not permitted to bid below zero. Participants transform negative bids to $0.00. It is helpful to contrast censoring with truncation. Censored data are observed but their observed values take on restricted values, that is, $0.00. In contrast, if a dependent variable is truncated, observations will be unobserved in particular ranges.

To make concrete these ideas, consider a latent, unobserved variable y^* that can take on any value on the real line, but where y is the variable actually observed. For example, y might represent observed auction bids censored from below at zero in auctions that do not permit negative bidding. In contrast, if the good being auctioned is readily available outside the lab setting, bids might be censored from above at the market price of the field substitute. As another example, y might represent the difference between auction bids in two treatments or bidding rounds, for example $WTP_2 - WTP_1$. If a person's bid is positive in treatment/round 1, but zero in the subsequent treatment/round, then the calculated bid difference may be less than the true difference. For such censored observations, all that is known is that the true value difference falls in the range [WTP$_2$ − WTP$_1$, ∞). Similarly, if a person's bid was zero in treatment/round 1 but positive thereafter, then the calculated bid difference may be less negative than the true difference. For such censored observations, the true bid difference falls in the range of (−∞, WTP$_2$ − WTP$_1$]. The point is that the observed value y is not a direct corollary to true underlying value or value difference, y*.

Let y* = Xβ + ε, where X represents a matrix of explanatory variables hypothesized to influence bids such as attitudes, risk preferences, demographics, or treatment identifiers, β is a conformable vector of coefficients, and ε is an error term assumed normally distributed with mean zero and variance σ². One of four forms of censoring can occur, each of which is discussed in turn.

Left censored observations (Censoring from below). An observation is *left censored* if y = t$_L$ when y* ≤ t$_L$, where t$_L$ is the point of censorship. For auction data t$_L$ = 0 when people are not permitted to bid negative values. In general, the contribution of left censored observations to the likelihood function is Φ((t$_L$ − Xβ)/σ), where Φ is the cumulative standard normal distribution function. If t$_L$ = 0, the contribution of left censored observations to the overall likelihood function simplifies to 1 − Φ(Xβ).

Right censored observations (Censoring from above). An observation is *right censored* if y = t$_R$ when y* ≥ t$_R$, where t$_R$ is the point of censorship. If a familiar, pre-existing good is auctioned in a lab setting, t$_R$ might represent the price of the good outside the lab as people would not rationally bid above the price for which they can easily buy the good when the session is over. An auction bid would represent true values (y*) at values below t$_R$, but will only represent a lower bound when bids equal t$_R$. The contribution of right censored observations to the likelihood function is 1 − Φ((t$_R$ − Xβ)/σ).

Interval censored observations. An observation is *interval censored* if all that is known is t$_{I1}$ < y* < t$_{I2}$. This situation can arise, for example, if auction bids are elicited in intervals. Sometimes people are asked to indicate their bid by checking one of the following intervals, $0 to $0.99, $1.00 to $1.99, $2.00 to $2.99, etc. The contribution of interval censored observations to the likelihood function is:

$$\Phi((t_{I2} − X\beta)/\sigma) − \Phi(t_{I1} − X\beta)/\sigma).$$

Uncensored observations. The ideal situation is when y = y* meaning bids are uncensored. Uncensored observations are modeled as φ((y − Xβ)/σ), which is an ordinary least squares regression with φ representing the standard normal density function.

Likelihood function. Taken together, for a sample of N individuals, the likelihood function is:

$$LF = \prod_{i=1}^{N} \left(\frac{1}{\sigma} \phi \left(\frac{y_i - X_i\beta}{\sigma} \right) \right)^{UC_i} \Phi \left(\frac{t_L - X_i\beta}{\sigma} \right)^{LC_i} \Phi \left(\frac{t_R - X_i\beta}{\sigma} \right)^{RC_i}$$

$$\times \left(\Phi \left(\frac{t_{I2} - X_i\beta}{\sigma} \right) - \Phi \left(\frac{t_{I1} - X_i\beta}{\sigma} \right) \right)^{IC_i} \tag{6.1}$$

where UC_i, LC_i, RC_i, and IC_i are indicator (dummy) variables representing uncensored, left censored, right censored, and interval censored observations. If there are no interval censored observations in the sample, for example, that particular portion of the likelihood function is omitted.

Maximization of the likelihood function in (6.1) yields coefficient estimates, β, that represent the marginal effect of X on y^*; however, these are not the marginal effect of X on observed data, y. Which marginal effect is of interest will of course depend on the purpose of the study. For example, consider the case where auction bids are censored from above at the market price of a field substitute. In such a case, interest often lies not in the censored distribution of bids, y, but in the uncensored distribution, y^*, because it is the uncensored bids that represent indicate maximum willingness to pay, a statistic that is needed, for example, if firms or policy analysts want to investigate how demand will change if price is increased beyond current market prices. Of course, there are other situations where we might expect bids to always be censored (e.g., if there is a policy mandating a price ceiling) in which interest lies in the censored bid distribution, y. Calculating the marginal effect of X on y is a bit more complicated as can be most easily illustrated with the Tobit model.

Tobit model. Although it might not be obvious, the left-censored Tobit model is a restricted version of the model outlined in equation (6.1) with $RC_i = 0$ and $IC_i = 0$ for all i. In the usual case of censoring from below at zero, the likelihood function for the tobit becomes:

$$LF = \prod_{i=1}^{N} \left(\frac{1}{\sigma} \phi \left(\frac{y_i - X_i\beta}{\sigma} \right) \right)^{UC_i} \Phi \left(\frac{-X_i\beta}{\sigma} \right)^{LC_i}. \tag{6.2}$$

Again, the estimated coefficients resulting from the maximization of (6.2) represent the marginal effects of X on y^*, but do not represent the marginal effect of X on observed data, y. When data is always censored, one might be more interested in obtaining the mean of y and marginal effects of X on y. As shown by Greene (2000), the censored mean and censored marginal effects are given by:

$$E[y_i|X_i] = \Phi \left(\frac{X_i\beta}{\sigma} \right) \left(X_i\beta + \sigma \frac{\phi((X_i\beta)/\sigma)}{\Phi((X_i\beta)/\sigma)} \right) \tag{6.3}$$

and

$$\frac{\partial E[y_i | X_i]}{\partial X_i} = \beta \Phi \left(\frac{X_i \beta}{\sigma} \right) \tag{6.4}$$

McDonald and Mofitt (1980) provide useful results showing how the marginal effects can be decomposed into two components: the effect of X on y* given that y > 0 and the effect of X on the probability that y > 0. Cragg (1971) provides another useful insight by suggesting it may be overly restrictive to assume equality of coefficients in the uncensored and censored portions of the likelihood function. For example, a particular independent variable, such as age, might be expected to have a positive effect on the probability a person bids zero, but a negative effect on observed bids. Even in situations in which the anticipated signs of the two effects are equivalent, the relative magnitudes might differ. In its basic form, Cragg's double hurdle model can be estimated in a two step process by first estimating a binomial probit model to investigate the determinants of X on the probability that y > 0 followed secondly by a truncated regression model where X is regressed on positive values of y = y*. These two models can be estimated separately or jointly. The joint likelihood function for the double hurdle model comprised of the probit and truncated regression is:

$$LF = \prod_{i=1}^{N} \Phi(-X_i \beta_1)^{(1-t_i)}$$

$$\times \left(\Phi(X_i \beta_1) \left[\frac{1}{\sigma} \phi \left(\frac{y_i - X_i \beta_2}{\sigma} \right) \middle/ \Phi \left(\frac{X_i \beta_2}{\sigma} \right) \right] \right)^{t_i}, \tag{6.5}$$

where $t_i = 1$ when y > 0 and $t_i = 0$ when y = 0. This specification has two separate coefficients β_1 and β_2 corresponding to the first and second hurdles.

When the same set of independent variables are used in the first and second hurdles as in equation (6.5), Lin and Schmidt (1984) show the tobit model is a restricted version of the double hurdle model, in which $\beta_1 = \beta_2/\sigma$. The appropriateness of the tobit versus the double hurdle can be tested with a likelihood ratio test. The likelihood ratio statistic is calculated as:

$$LR = -2[\ln LF_{Tobit} - \ln LF_{Probit} - \ln LF_{Truncated\ Regression}], \tag{6.6}$$

where LF represents the maximized log likelihood function values for the model type indicated in the subscript, each of which is estimated independently. The null hypothesis is that the tobit model is the appropriate specification, i.e., $\beta_1 = \beta_2/\sigma$. If the calculated likelihood ratio statistic exceeds the critical chi-squared value with number of degrees of freedom equal to the number of variables in X, the tobit is rejected in favor of the double hurdle model.

Table 6.1. *Comparison of tobit to double hurdle model*

Variable	Definition	Ordinary least squares[a]	Tobit[a]	Double Hurdle Model Hurdle 1: probit[b]	Hurdle 2: Truncated regression[c]
Constant	Model intercept	−0.097 (0.147)[d]	−0.280 (0.209)	1.236 (1.139)	0.150 (0.152)
Gender	1 if female; 0 if male	−0.020 (0.050)	−0.032 (0.073)	−0.099 (0.292)	0.001 (0.060)
Age	Age in years	0.012*[e] (0.007)	0.160 (0.010)	0.060 (0.054)	0.006 (0.008)
Shop	1 if previously shopped in store; 0 otherwise	−0.035 (0.052)	−0.038 (0.075)	0.005 (0.317)	−0.063 (0.058)
Income	Monthly disposable income (in 100s of dollars)	0.023* (0.013)	0.034* (0.019)	0.137* (0.083)	0.011 (0.015)
In-Store	1 if valuation took place in store; 0 if in laboratory	0.062 (0.057)	0.051 (0.083)	−0.172 (0.326)	0.168** (0.070)
Hypothetical	1 if valuation was hypothetical; 0 otherwise	0.361*** (0.059)	0.450*** (0.083)	1.254*** (0.423)	0.307*** (0.619)
σ		0.223	0.314*** (0.027)		0.194*** (0.019)
Number of observations		119	119	119	78
Log likelihood at maximum		9.796	−54.601	−67.819	25.083

[a] Dependent variable is the bid for cookie C from the study reported in Lusk and Fox (2003).
[b] Dependent variable takes the value of 1 if cookie bid was positive; 0 otherwise.
[c] Dependent variable includes only positive cookie bids.
[d] Numbers in parentheses are standard errors.
[e] One (*), two (**), and three (***) asterisks represent 0.10, 0.05, and 0.01 levels of statistical significance, respectively.

Example. We illustrate these concepts by considering the auction data collected by Lusk and Fox (2003). The data consists of bids obtained from a Becker-Degroot-Marshack mechanism for three unique cookies in a field and laboratory setting. Lusk and Fox (2003) were primarily interested in testing whether the value elicitation setting (store versus lab) had an influence on bids. Table 6.1 reports regression results corresponding to bid data from one cookie (cookie C in Lusk and Fox (2003), which is Oatmeal Scotchie flavor). There were a total of 119 bids collected, but 41 of these bids were zero. The first column of Table 6.1 reports ordinary least squares estimates, and in doing so, ignores the censored nature of the data. The second column reports tobit estimates accounting for censoring at zero. The tobit estimates tend to track closely with the OLS estimates. The last two columns in Table 6.1 report the double hurdle model, which consists of probit and truncated regression estimates.

The data in Table 6.1 can be used to test the appropriateness of the tobit specification. Using the likelihood ratio test described above, the calculated likelihood ratio statistic is $-2[-54.601 + 67.819 - 25.083] = 23.73$, which can be compared against the 95% critical chi-square value with seven degrees of freedom, which is 14.07. These calculations indicate that the tobit model is rejected in favor of the double hurdle model. As shown in Table 6.1, model specification is not inconsequential. It is only in the last column that one finds that the value elicitation setting has a significant effect on bidding behavior. Conditional on bids being positive, the results indicate bids were higher in the field setting than in the laboratory setting.

6.3   Quantile regression with auction bids

In a typical regression context, one is interested in estimating a conditional mean function, that is, the expected auction bid given the particular treatment and a person's age, income, attitudes, and so on. If the distribution of auction bids is symmetric, say normally distributed, traditional regression procedures are likely to provide reliable information. But auction data can be highly skewed. When data are skewed, a few outliers can have a pronounced influence on the mean, making the mean a less useful summary statistic.

Consider the auction data in Figure 6.1. These data come from an experiment with French consumers bidding in a fifth price WTA auction; the consumers offered bids for the amount of money they demanded to exchange an endowed non-genetically modified cookie for a cookie containing genetically modified ingredients in the presence of a consumption requirement (see Lusk *et al.*, 2006). Figure 6.1 shows the data are highly skewed; there are many "low" bids and many "high" bids, but few in between. To further illustrate the skewed nature of the data, consider that the mean auction bid was $7.20, whereas the median bid was only $1.96. Clearly, only investigating the conditional mean can ignore other important information. Results of a conditional mean regression are sensitive to outliers, in this case the three observations in excess of $30. The effects of a co-variate, say education, might differ for people with low bids and people with high bids. Additionally, one may be interested in the effect of a particular treatment variable (e.g., information) at different parts of the bid distribution. If people with high bids are those most likely to start a violent protest, a firm might like to know how an advertising campaign affects the "extreme" consumers, not the average one.

As a complement to the traditional ordinary least squares analysis, one can consider estimating quantile regressions. In a quantile regression, a conditional

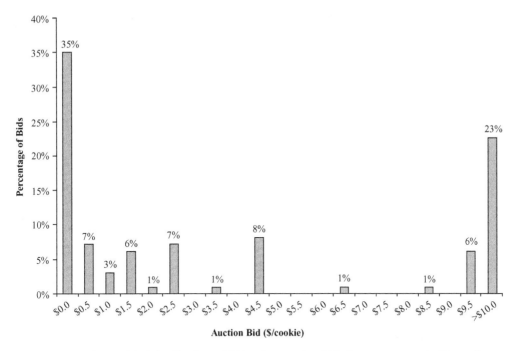

Figure 6.1   Distribution of fifth price auction bids for a non-genetically modified cookie in France

quantile function is estimated as opposed to a conditional mean function. For example, for the 50% quantile, a conditional median function is estimated; estimated parameters illustrate the effect of independent variables on the median bid. Quantile regression was pioneered by the work of Koener and Bassett (1978).

For background, consider the mechanics of a traditional conditional mean regression. Parameters are estimated in a traditional regression by choosing the parameters, β, that minimize the sum of squared errors: minimize $\sum (y_i - X_i\beta)^2$, where y is the dependent variable and X is a vector of independent variables. In a quantile regression the sum of squared errors is replaced with the objective function:

$$\text{minimize} \sum_{i=1}^{N} \rho_\theta (y_i - X_i\beta), \tag{6.7}$$

where θ is the quantile and ρ is a weighted absolute value function (also known as "check" function) defined as follows:

$$\rho_\theta(y_i - X_i\beta) = \begin{cases} \theta(y_i - X_i\beta), & \text{if } y_i - X_i\beta > 0 \\ (\theta - 1)(y_i - X_i\beta), & \text{if } y_i - X_i\beta \leq 0. \end{cases} \tag{6.8}$$

If $\theta = 0.5$, the estimation is a median regression and the problem reduces to:

$$\text{minimize } 0.5 \sum_{i=1}^{N} |y_i - X_i\beta| = \text{minimize } \sum_{i=1}^{N} |y_i - X_i\beta|. \qquad (6.9)$$

Minimizing the sum of absolute errors generates coefficient estimates of a conditional median function. Standard errors can be obtained for quantile regression estimates via bootstrapping procedures.

A final issue that should be discussed is the issue of censoring. As discussed in a previous section, censoring with auction bids is likely to be a problem. This is clearly illustrated in Figure 6.1, with 35% of the bid less than $0.50 (roughly 6% of the bids are exactly equal to zero). Powell (1984) showed how to handle censoring in linear conditional quantile models. Suppose that bids are censored from below at t_L. The optimization problem becomes:

$$\text{minimize } \sum_{i=1}^{N} \rho_\theta(y_i - \max(t_L, X_i\beta)). \qquad (6.10)$$

Buschinsky (1994) suggests a practical method to estimate equation (6.10). The estimator can be employed by first estimating equation (6.7) for the full sample of observations. Observations with predicted values $(X_i\beta)$ below t_L are deleted. Equation (6.7) is re-estimated on the trimmed sample. This process is repeated until there are no predicted values less than t_L for two successive iterations.

To illustrate the additional information that can be obtained by performing quantile regressions, again consider the auction data in Figure 6.1. Ignoring the problem of censoring, Table 6.2 presents results for a mean regression, and quantile regressions for the 20%, 50%, and 80% quantiles, where the dependent variable is the WTA auction bid to give up a non-genetically modified food and instead consume a genetically modified food. In every regression, an increase in subjective knowledge of genetically modified food and an increase in the perceived risk of genetically modified food increased the amount of money demanded (e.g., the auction bid) to consume a genetically modified food. The magnitudes of the estimated effects of these variables differed substantially across regressions. A one-unit increase in subjective knowledge was associated with a $1.92 increase in the expected mean but only a $1.04 increase in the expected median bid. Increasing subjective knowledge had an even larger effect at the 80% quantile: $2.72. Education did not significantly affect the mean bid; but it had a significant impact on the expected median. The median auction bid for people with a college degree was $2.13 higher than the median auction bid for people without a college degree, holding all other variables constant.

Table 6.2. *Conditional mean and quantile regressions*

Variable	Mean	Regressions		
		20% quantile	50% quantile	80% quantile
Intercept	7.512	0.805	−1.304	11.599
	(9.574)[a]	(1.339)	(2.539)	(11.415)
Subjective knowledge of facts and issues concerning genetic modification in food production (1 = not at all knowledgeable and 9 = extremely knowledgeable)	1.917* (1.018)	0.257** (0.118)	1.035** (0.269)	2.717** (1.269)
Level of trust in information about genetic modification in food production from government food regulatory agencies (1 = strongly distrust; 9 = strongly trust)	−0.332 (0.663)	0.936 (0.093)	0.016 (0.177)	0.307 (0.614)
Perception of the risk and benefit of genetic modification in food production (1 = risky; 9 = beneficial)	−1.565** (0.732	−0.276** (0.100)	−1.051** (0.192)	−3.363** (0.625)
Age in years	−0.080 (0.128)	−0.022 (0.020)	0.042 (0.034)	−0.101 (0.132)
Education: 1 if obtained university undergraduate degree or higher; 0 otherwise	1.374 (2.973)	0.137 (0.465)	2.126** (0.778)	4.264 (3.152)
Income: 1 if household income is greater than $50,000/year; 0 otherwise	−1.488 (4.863)	−0.114 (0.690)	−0.436 (1.246)	−2.173 (4.203)
Quantile/Mean	$7.198	$0.098	$1.960	$13.720

Note: Dependent variable is round five willingness to accept bid to consume a genetically modified cookie among French consumers; data comes from the study reported by Lusk *et al.* (2006c). Number of observations in each regression = 97.
One (*) and two (**) asterisks represent 0.10 and 0.05 levels of statistical significance, respectively.
[a] Numbers in parentheses standard errors.

6.4   Panel data regression with auction bids

In most experimental auctions, each person submits multiple bids. Bidders might submit several bids on the same good across several bidding rounds. He or she might submit bids for several different goods in a single bidding round. Experimental auctions are frequently conducted in sessions, with five to 20 people assigned to a session, and numerous bids are obtained from a single session. All this is to say that most experimental auction studies collect *panel data*, data that is multidimensional, in which repeated observations are obtained from the same individual, good, or session. In general, an auction can consist of several dimensions. For example, the ith individual might submit a bid on the jth good in the rth round in the tth experimental session. In principle, any number of dimensions can be accounted for with panel data regression. We begin with a single dimension and then move to more complicated cases.

6.4.1   One-way fixed and random effects models

Consider a two-dimensional panel data set. For example, suppose N people submit bids on J goods. The ith individual's bid for the jth good can be written as:

$$bid_{ij} = \alpha_i + \lambda_j + \beta X_{ij} + \varepsilon_{ij}, \qquad (6.11)$$

where X is a matrix made up of independent variables expected to influence bids *not including* a constant term, β is a conformable vector of parameters, α_i represent individual-specific effects, and λ_j represent good-specific effects.

We first consider a model in which we assume $\lambda_j = 0$ for all j. This implies the absence of good-specific effects and generates the following one-way panel data model:

$$bid_{ij} = \alpha_i + \beta X_{ij} + \varepsilon_{ij}. \qquad (6.12)$$

Now, if $\alpha_i = \alpha$ for all i, a conventional regression model is produced and ordinary least squares is the appropriate method to estimate the model parameters. In practice, however, individual-specific effects can be expected to exist. There are two general methods to incorporate individual-specific effects, α_i, into the model. The first approach is a *fixed-effects* model, where α_i are estimated as individual-specific constant terms. If there are N individuals, a fixed-effects model generates N separate constant terms – one for each person. This model assumes all behavioral differences across people can be captured by differing intercepts. Most software packages have routines to estimate fixed-effects models, but they can easily be constructed by hand by creating a dummy variable for each individual.

An F-test of the hypothesis that $\alpha_i = \alpha$ for all i provides an indication of whether individual-specific, fixed effects are present in the data. The second common approach is the *random-effects* model, where α_i are individual-specific errors. This produces an error components model, where the overall error in the model is $\alpha_i + \varepsilon_{ij}$. In a random effects model, the constant is treated as a random variable and is modeled as $\alpha_i = \bar{\alpha} + \sigma u_i$, where $\bar{\alpha}$ is the population mean intercept, σ is the population standard deviation of the intercept, and u_i is an unobserved random term that is typically assumed to be distributed normal with zero mean and unit standard deviation. A variety of methods exist to estimate random effects models and most econometric software packages have canned routines to estimate such models. A test of the hypothesis that $\sigma = 0$ provides an indication as to whether random effects exist in the data.

Whether the fixed-effects or random-effect specification is appropriate for a given data set depends on one's view of the data generating process, practical considerations (e.g., if N is large the fixed-effects specification may use too many degrees of freedom), whether one is interested in the effect in the

observed sample (e.g., if α_i represent different goods instead of different people, the fixed-effects approach seems to make more sense in this context), and
perhaps on statistical tests. A statistical test used to test the appropriateness
of the random-effects specification is the Hausman test for fixed- or random-
effects. The approach tests whether the individual-specific error term is uncorrelated with the included regressors. If so, the random effects specification is
preferred, otherwise the fixed-effects or ordinary least squares specification is
more appropriate (see Greene 2000 for more detail).

6.4.2   Two-way fixed and random effects models

Although we predicated our discussion on the idea the data were multidimensional, the last section only considered a single dimension. We now return
to equation (6.11), which shows that bids are affected both by individual-specific
effects, α_i and good-specific effects, λ_j. Again, this model can be estimated via
fixed- or random-effects specifications. In the one-way fixed-effects specification, no overall constant term was estimated; rather a separate constant was
estimated for each individual. In typical two-way fixed-effects specifications,
an overall constant, η, is included in the model as in expression (6.13):

$$bid_{ij} = \eta + \alpha_i + \lambda_j + \beta X_{ij} + \varepsilon_{ij}, \qquad (6.13)$$

such that α_i and λ_j are estimated as contrasts relative to a particular person and
a particular good, whose coefficients have been omitted. One can use F-tests of
the hypothesis that $\alpha_i = \alpha$ and/or $\lambda_j = \lambda$ to test for the presence of individual- and
good-specific effects. In a random-effect specification, α_i and λ_j are treated as
random disturbances. The disturbances can be modeled as independent normal
or as bivariate normal.

6.4.3   An individual-specific model

We have assumed thus far that difference across people can be captured by
differences in constant terms or intercepts. It is possible, however, that people
differ in every regressor, not just the constant. Equation (6.14) posits just such
a model:

$$bid_{ij} = \beta_i X_{ij} + \varepsilon_{ij}, \qquad (6.14)$$

where now β_i includes a constant term, and as is evidenced by the i subscript,
the entire vector is individual-specific. The primary weakness of such a model
is that it requires sufficient degrees of freedom such that (6.14) can be estimated
for each person.

   In section 5.6, we considered a problem that fit directly in this framework.
In that data set thirty-five people submitted twenty-five bids (each person bid

for five steaks in five bidding rounds). Table 5.5 shows an important difference in a key variable of interest (the lagged-price effect) depending on whether a single constant is estimated for each individual or whether the entire parameter vector is permitted to be individual specific. An F-test was able to reject the hypothesis that $\beta_i = \beta$ for the models reported in Table 5.5.

6.4.4   A random coefficients model

As in the other panel data models, there is a direct random-effects counterpart to the fixed-effects model in (6.14). Instead of estimating β_i for each individual, one can estimate the joint distribution of parameters in the population. This approach is advantageous in the sense that it can be estimated with fewer observations on each person. The parameter vector is specified as:

$$\beta_i = \beta + \Delta Z_i + \Gamma v_i, \tag{6.15}$$

where β is a vector of the means of the random parameters, Z_i is a set of individual invariant variables such as gender, age, treatment variables, etc. that affect the mean of the random parameters via the coefficient matrix Δ, v_i is a vector of random standard normal deviates, Γ is unrestricted lower triangle matrix of parameters to be estimated where $\Omega = \Gamma'\Gamma$ represents the variance-covariance matrix associated with the random parameters. To summarize, this model estimates the joint distribution of parameters in the population, allowing for the calculation of the mean parameters, potentially conditional on other variables Z, and the variation and co-variation in parameters. Greene (2004) shows how such a model can be estimated via simulation methods.

6.5   Other types of data analysis with auction bids

There are also a variety of other data analytic methods one might consider when attempting to glean insight and make use of auction bids. The material presented in this sub-section most readily lends itself to the types of analysis carried out by marketing researchers: factor analysis, cluster analysis, and market share simulations. We do not claim to offer an exhaustive treatment of the subjects. Our goal is to introduce additional ideas and thoughts on alternative tools that may be useful in examining auction bids.

6.5.1   Factor analysis

Factor analysis is one of the most widely used quantitative tools in the social sciences. Factor analysis refers to a variety of statistical techniques which aim to represent a larger set of observable variables in terms of a smaller set of constructed variables – or factors. The purpose of factor analysis is often variable reduction: rather than using say twenty variables in a subsequent analysis, a researcher may want to use a smaller number, say two or three, which capture most of the variation in the larger set of twenty. Of primary interest to auction practitioners is exploratory factor analysis. Exploratory factor analysis explores a set of theoretical constructs or dimensions which explain the observed data. In applications where people submit bids for several related goods, exploratory factor analysis can be a useful tool in identifying whether there are common dimensions of preference or some theoretical constructs that explain bids for some goods, but not others. Identifying these underlying, latent constructs (or factors) would help identify which goods people view similarly and might aid marketing researchers in identifying new goods that could be strong competitors in existing markets and new goods with few competitors.

Consider an example to make concrete these ideas. Suppose people bid simultaneously on six beef steaks in an experimental auction: a generic steak that has no quality label or distinction, a guaranteed tender steak, a "natural" steak produced from animals that were not given any antibiotics or growth hormones, a "traceable" steak that could be traced back to the farm of production, a USDA Choice steak, and a Certified Angus Beef (CAB) steak. Such a procedure would yield six bids from each person: one bid per steak. The aim is to use factor analysis to identify common dimensions or factors that can explain the correlations in bidding behavior. The input to the factor analysis would be a matrix of the correlation coefficients (or the covariance matrix) between bids for the six steaks. Figure 6.2 offers one hypothesis to explain the pattern of bidding behavior.

Figure 6.2 hypothesizes that two underlying latent factors might "cause" the observed bidding behavior: a factor representing preferences for food safety and a factor representing preferences for taste. The model hypothesizes that bids for the natural, traceable, and generic steaks are related to the first factor, while bids for the generic, guaranteed tender, USDA Choice, and CAB steaks are related to the second factor. The path coefficients, b_{ij}, identify the relationship between the hypothetical, latent factor and the observed auction bids. One might expect that bids for the natural and traceable steaks are positively related to the first factor, food safety preferences, but that the generic steak might be negatively related to this factor: $b_{11} > 0$, $b_{12} > 0$, and $b_{13} < 0$. Similarly, taste preferences might be expected to positively influence bids for guaranteed tender, Choice, and CAB, but might negatively influence bids for generic.

Figure 6.2 only represents one possible model that might explain bidding behavior. The purpose of exploratory factor analysis is to identify how many "important" factors exist and to estimate the relationships (e.g., the path coefficients b_{ij}) between the latent factors and the observed data. In exploratory factor analysis, the analyst examines the data to *explore* how many "important" factors might exist. Exploratory factor analysis is an ad hoc method which relies on ex-post rationalizations to name and define the resulting factors. Other

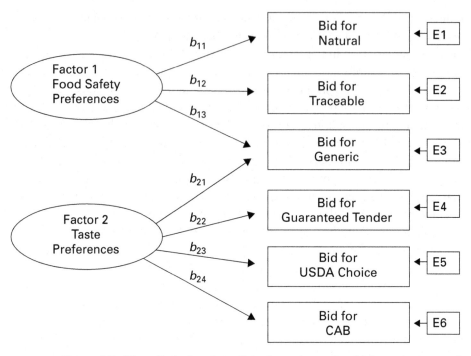

Figure 6.2   Hypothetical path model where six auction bids are represented by two latent factors

approaches such as confirmatory factor analysis allow the analyst to test statistically whether a particular theoretical model, such as that in Figure 6.2, is consistent with the observed data.

The exact methods for carrying out factor analysis, which involves methods for determining how to select the appropriate number of factors, how to estimate the path coefficients, how to interpret the path coefficients, and so on is a subject too vast for this book. There are many good references available and many common statistical packages such as SAS and SPSS support factor analysis. For good introductory reference guides on the subject see Hatcher (1994), Kline (2002), or Kim and Mueller (1978).

6.5.2   Cluster analysis

Whereas factor analysis is a method used to identify relationships between *variables*, or auctioned goods, cluster analysis is a method for organizing *people* into similar response categories based on their bidding behavior. When people submit multiple bids on several goods, cluster analysis might be used to identify groups of people with similar bidding behavior. Such knowledge can be useful for marketing researchers interested in creating market segments. Many companies use segmentation strategies to cluster people with similar purchasing behavior, and then tailor their marketing approaches to each segment.

Numerous methods are used to create clusters. A common approach is k-means clustering which creates clusters to minimize the variability within clusters and maximize the variability between clusters. Cluster analysis is a completely ad hoc procedure. Cluster analysis identifies structures in data, based on inputs given by the analyst, such as the number of clusters, without explaining why such structures exist. The analyst decides to determine whether the identified data structures, or clusters, are economically and operationally meaningful.

Again it is instructive to consider an example. Suppose people simultaneously bid on six beef steaks in an experimental auction: a generic steak that had no quality label or distinction, a guaranteed tender steak, a "natural" steak produced from animals that were not given any antibiotics or growth hormones, a "traceable" steak that could be traced back to the farm of production, a USDA Choice steak, and a Certified Angus Beef (CAB) steak. Cluster analysis could be carried out based on individuals' bids for the six steaks. Suppose through comparing and testing several cluster structures one determined that four clusters best represent the data. There might be a "price sensitive" cluster in which all people in that cluster uniformly offered low bids on all steaks. There might exist a "taste preferring" cluster wherein people submitted relatively high bids for CAB and Choice steaks but low bids on other steaks. There might be a "safety conscious" cluster which contains people who submitted high bids on the natural and traceable steaks, but low bids on the others. Finally, there might be a "steak lover" cluster that contains people who submitted relatively uniform and high bids for all steaks. Additional data analysis could be conducted to determine whether cluster membership differs by observables such as age, gender, income, and so on. Again, cluster analysis groups *people* that exhibit similar bidding behavior; factor analysis groups *variables* that exhibit similar correlations. Further, while quantile regressions permit an investigation of the conditional distribution of bids for a single good, cluster analysis can group people based on their bidding behavior for multiple goods.

As with factor analysis, we refrain from delving into the rather complex and voluminous issues of how to carry out cluster analysis. Instead, we offer the idea that cluster analysis may be a useful tool in examining auction data (additional references include Kaufman and Rousseeuw (2005), Aldenderfer and Blashfield (1984), or Romesburg (2004)).

6.5.3   Market share simulation

In marketing, the goal of preference elicitation is to determine the potential success of a new product or investigate the effect of changes in price, quality, and the like. The unit of measurement that is of most interest, especially to managers, is market share. While it may not be initially apparent, bids from experimental auctions readily lend themselves to market share simulations. In discussing how auction bids can be used to predict market share, it is helpful to draw comparisons with conjoint analysis, a preference elicitation method commonly used to carry out market share simulations. In conjoint analysis, people are asked to rate, rank, or choose between a series of goods described by a set of attributes. These responses are used to estimate an attribute-based utility function, which is in turn used to simulate market shares.

Although experimental auctions do not provide a utility level for competing goods, they do provide a measure of the monetary value of a good which, when coupled with a price and the assumption of linear marginal utility, can provide a money-metric measure of the utility. Suppose people submit bids for J goods in an experimental auction. The money-metric utility individual i derives from good j can be written as:

$$U_{ij} = WTP_{ij} - p_j, \tag{6.16}$$

where WTP_{ij} is the bid for good j and p_j is the price of good j. This approach calculates the utility of each of the J auction goods, and as such, the approach can only be used to simulate the market share of the J goods for which values were elicited in the auction.

An alternative approach is to estimate a willingness to pay *function* for each individual where WTP depends on the attributes of a good and possibly attribute interactions. Suppose a good can be described with N attributes, each with L levels. There are L^N possible goods that could be created either for use in an auction or later in a market share simulation. For example, people might be asked to consider various descriptions of orange juice described by the attributes of brand, package size, and sweetness, where each attribute is varied at several levels (e.g., brand might be varied between the levels of Tropicana, Minute Maid, and Florida's Natural).

An experimental design could be constructed in which people submit bids on a smaller set of goods, but where one can identify the linear (main) effects of each of the attribute levels and possibly two-way interaction effects. Using this data, a WTP function can be estimated for each individual where WTP is a function of the attributes and attribute levels. For example, Melton et al. (1996) used this approach to estimate a WTP function for pork where the value of pork depended on color, marbling, and size. There were 125 possible combinations of attributes and attribute-levels in their application, but they were able to estimate all effects of interest by only auctioning eight goods. Once a WTP function is estimated, equation (6.16) can be used to calculate the utility of any of the L^N descriptions of the good. Thus, one can calculate the utility of L^N possible goods even if only a sub-set were auctioned.

Once the money metric-utility is calculated, there are several ways to use these values to determine market share. First, one must identify the choice-set that describes the goods to be considered in the simulation. This choice set can contain the number of goods in the auction, J, a subset of the auctioned goods, or when a *WTP* function is estimated, any arbitrarily large set of goods. Once the initial choice set has been constructed, interest lies in calculating the market share of the jth good given a set of K goods. In the conjoint literature, a common approach is to use the "first choice" or "highest utility" rule in which each person is assumed to choose the product producing the highest utility from a choice set. If equation (6.16) is less than zero for all K goods, it is assumed that the person would have not bought any of the goods, that is, no choice would be made. Under the first choice rule, the market share of a particular good j is calculated by dividing the number of people predicted to choose the product (i.e., the number of people having the highest utility for good j) by the total number of people in the simulation.

A second approach is to use the Bradley-Terry-Luce model or the so-called *share of preference* model. With this approach, the market share of good j is calculated by dividing the utility of good j by the sum of utilities for all K goods in the simulated market as shown in (6.17):

$$Market\ Share_{ij} = \frac{U_{ij}}{\sum\limits_{k=1}^{K} U_{ik}}. \tag{6.17}$$

The final market share estimate is calculated by averaging each person's estimated share.

A final model frequently used in market share simulations is the logit model. Market shares are calculated by dividing the logit value for one product by the sum for all other products in the simulation. Using the logit formula, the market share of good j for individual i is given by:

$$Market\ Share_{ij} = \frac{e^{\lambda U_{ij}}}{\sum\limits_{k=1}^{K} e^{\lambda U_{ik}}}, \tag{6.18}$$

where λ is a scale parameter. As the scale parameter approaches infinity, the model approximates the first choice or maximum utility rule. As the scale parameter approaches zero, estimated market shares become uniform for all K goods. In most conjoint applications, λ is chosen to force estimated shares to match current market conditions before more advanced simulations are run. Again, these individual shares are averaged across respondents to arrive at a final market share estimate.

Our discussion has focused on experiments in which people submitted bids to obtain a good outright. When such information is obtained, a market-share model can predict some consumers will not buy the good if the price of each good exceeds the bid for each good. This is realistic in that not all consumers make a purchase every chance they have and that price discounts encourage additional consumers to make a purchase. If it can be assumed all people make a purchase, one can also use bids from auctions where people bid to exchange an endowed good for several substitute goods to calculate market share. A market share model based on bids from an endow-and-upgrade approach is essentially a model of utility and price *differences*. For example, assume people were endowed with good A and bid to exchange A for goods B and C. Under the first choice or highest utility rule, a person would be expected to choose good B if ($WTP_{AB} - p_B + p_A$) was greater than zero and was greater than ($WTP_{AC} - p_C + p_A$), where WTP_{Aj} is the auction bid to exchange good A for good *j*, and p_j is the price of good *j*. Good A would be expected to be chosen if both ($WTP_{AB} - p_B + p_A$) and ($WTP_{AC} - p_C + p_A$) are less than zero.

Once market share has been calculated under a base-line condition, any number of alternative scenarios can be considered. For example, one might be interested in determining the market share of a new product and how shares of existing products will fall once the new product is introduced. As another example, own- and cross-price elasticities of demand can be calculated by investigating how market shares change when prices are altered.

6.6   Conclusions

This chapter discussed several data analytic methods useful for investigating bidding behavior and drawing inferences from auction bids. Some of the most interesting and useful types of data analysis are the simplest. A great deal can be learned simply by plotting the distribution of bids and comparing bid distributions across goods and/or treatments. Similarly, simple comparisons of statistics such as the mean, median, and standard deviation can reveal important insights. This chapter considered more advanced methods frequently used in examining auction data. Since auction bids can be censored from below at zero or from above at a field price, we covered censored regression models, for example, the Tobit model. Because auction data are frequently skewed, practitioners may be interested in the effects of a co-variate, say a treatment dummy variable, on other portions of the bid distribution than the mean. Quantile regressions permit just such an investigation. We have also considered panel-data regressions because multiple auction bids are often submitted by the same person. Finally, we offered some thoughts on other data analytic methods that might have use in examining auction data, but have yet to be applied to such a context: factor analysis, cluster analysis, and market share simulations.

7   Valuation case studies*

7.1   Introduction

We now present nine case studies to illustrate experimental auctions at work in practical applications. This chapter presents case studies showing how we have used experimental auction methods to estimate the value of new or non-market goods and how those values are used in welfare analysis and to estimate the success of new products. These case studies are grouped into three broad categories: informing policy, marketing, and valuing controversial goods. In the policy case studies, we consider experimental auctions designed to address a grading system for beef tenderness, behavior toward food safety, and the acceptable tolerance levels for genetically modified food. For the marketing case studies, we present auctions designed to evaluate the market share for branded beef products, value characteristics of pork, and value financial records. The last set of case studies focus on controversial goods, where we estimated demand for genetically modified food, the impact of information on preferences for irradiated foods, and the demand for products of ambiguous quality like fresh meat produced with growth hormones.

7.2   Informing Policy I: beef tenderness grading system

Since the 1900s, the United States federal government has set and maintained grades and standards for many agricultural products. In theory, grades and standards improve market efficiency by reducing problems associated with information asymmetry, that is, consumers and producers know the type/quality of the goods they are buying and selling. Federal grading of agricultural products was authorized by the US Congress through the Agricultural Marketing Act of 1946. The beef quality grading system has evolved since its earliest inception; today the US beef quality grading system is primarily based on the attribute

---

* This chapter draws on research conducted jointly with our colleagues over the last decade including Dermot Hayes, John Fox, Matt Rousu, Wally Huffman, Bryan Melton, Abe Tegene, S. Y. Shin, Jim Kliebenstein, Ted Schroeder, Lisa House, Carlotta Valli, Sara Jaeger, Melissa Moore, Burt Morrow, and Bruce Traill.

of *marbling* – the amount of intra-muscular fat content in a steak. Steaks with higher levels of intra-muscular fat receive higher quality grades and have a higher market price. The highest quality grade is USDA Prime, followed by USDA Choice, USDA Select, and USDA Standard.

Although the current quality grading system transmits information through the marketing channel, many observers contend the grading system is ineffective. The problem is the system says nothing about *tenderness*, which has been shown in taste panels to be one of the most important palatability attributes in beef. Marbling and tenderness levels are only weakly correlated. Thus, consumers cannot readily use quality grade as a signal of tenderness. Some beef industry experts argue the current US beef quality grading system should be augmented with a tenderness grading system. Determining the potential value of such a grading system is a natural application of the experimental auction method.

7.2.1   Analytical framework

In an application such as this, it is useful to present an analytical model that is the basis to construct the auction and interpret the results. Assume a person consumes one unit of steak within a given time period. Consumer i derives utility from consuming steak brand j:

$$U_{ij} = \alpha_{ij} + \phi_{ij} VT_i - p_j, \tag{7.1}$$

where α_{ij} is the fixed amount individual i is willing to pay for brand j independent of the steak's tenderness level. This value can be derived from other perceived palatability attributes such as juiciness or from utilitarian value, say from stew meat. Let VT_i be the monetary value a person places on tenderness, ϕ_{ij} is the probability that steak option j is tender, and p_j is the price of steak brand j. A consumer is willing to pay $\alpha_{ij} + VT_i$ for a guaranteed tender steak, and only α_{ij} for a guaranteed tough steak. At present there is currently no grading system such that steaks can be labeled as to their tenderness. Consumers make their own subjective assessment about ϕ_{ij}, which we label as $\tilde{\phi}_{ij}$. If there are J steak brands, consumers choose the brand that generates the highest utility. If no steak generates positive utility, the consumer chooses not to buy and receives the utility of zero. Consumer surplus is given by:

$$CS_i^{NG} = \max\{U_{i1}, U_{i2}, \ldots, U_{iJ}, 0\} \tag{7.2}$$
$$= \max\{\alpha_{i1} + \tilde{\phi}_{i1} VT_i - p_1, \alpha_{i2} + \tilde{\phi}_{i2} VT_i - p_2, \ldots, \alpha_{iJ}$$
$$+ \tilde{\phi}_{iJ} VT_i - p_J, 0\}. \tag{7.3}$$

If a grading system is introduced, the subjective probabilities, $\tilde{\phi}_{ij}$, are replaced with objective probabilities. Consider a basic tenderness grading system that requires retailers to report the average objective probability of tenderness for steak type j: ϕ_j^A. Note the i subscript and the $\sim$ have been dropped because we assume all consumers now use the same objective probability when assessing steak brand j. The superscript A denotes a grading system in which tenderness levels are reported at their pre-existing average levels. Now, consumer surplus is:

$$CS_i^A = \max \left\{ \alpha_{i1} + \phi_1^A VT_i - p_1, \alpha_{i2} + \phi_2^A VT_i - p_2, \ldots, \alpha_{iJ} \right.$$
$$\left. + \phi_J^A VT_i - p_J, 0 \right\}. \tag{7.4}$$

More complicated grading systems can be introduced. One can use a grading system that categorizes steaks into either *high* (H) or *low* (L) tenderness grades. For each steak brand j there are two products, H and L, with the only difference being the probability the steak is tender. Let ϕ_j^H and ϕ_j^L denote the objective probabilities of tenderness for the high and low categories for brand j. Under such a system (denoted 2G for two grades), consumer surplus is given by:

$$CS_i^{2G} = \max \left\{ \alpha_{i1} + \phi_1^H VT_i - p_1^H, \alpha_{i1} + \phi_1^L VT_i - p_1^L, \ldots, \alpha_{iJ} \right.$$
$$\left. + \phi_J^H VT_i - p_J^H, \alpha_{iJ} + \phi_J^L VT_i - p_J^L, 0 \right\}. \tag{7.5}$$

In this grading system, consumers choose between $J \times 2$ steak products because each brand is offered at two tenderness levels or grades: high and low. This scheme can be generalized to any number of grades, for example, high, medium, and low.

We assess the welfare effects of introducing a grading system by calculating changes in consumer surplus. The change in consumer surplus from introducing the simple average label is:

$$\Delta CS_i^{A-NG} = CS_i^A - CS_i^{NG}, \tag{7.6}$$

and the change in consumer surplus from introducing a grading system with two grades is:

$$\Delta CS_i^{2G-NG} = CS_i^{2G} - CS_i^{NG}. \tag{7.7}$$

Total changes in consumer welfare are obtained by summing equations (7.6) or (7.7) across all N consumers. The average change in consumer surplus is total surplus divided by N.

7.2.2   Linking the theoretical model to auction bids

Now consider how the changes in consumer surplus can be calculated using experimental auctions. A person's willingness to pay (*WTP*), which is his auction bid in an incentive compatible auction, for steak brand j is:

$$WTP_{ij} = \alpha_{ij} + \phi_{ij}VT_i. \tag{7.8}$$

We need a way to estimate α_{ij} and VT_i separately. One way is to elicit bids for steak brand j (e.g., WTP_{ij}) and individuals' subjective probabilities of tenderness for steak brand j. Equation (7.8) could be directly estimated via conventional regression procedures in which the estimated constant would represent α_{ij}, the value of brand j independent of tenderness, and the coefficient on the estimated probability would represent VT_i. This approach would only provide an estimate of the average α_{ij} and VT_i in the sample. One of the primary advantages of using experimental auctions is that they provide individual-level valuations. It is more helpful to estimate α_{ij} and VT_i for *each person* in the sample.

To obtain individual valuation estimates, consider the difference in bids a person places on brand 1 versus brand k, written as:

$$WTP_{ik} - WTP_{i1} = (\alpha_{ik} - \alpha_{i1}) + (\tilde{\phi}_{ik} - \tilde{\phi}_{i1})VT_i. \tag{7.9}$$

Equation (7.9) shows that the difference in bids between two steaks results from differences in non-tenderness preferences for 1 versus k, $(\alpha_{il} - \alpha_{ik})$, and differences in the perception of probability of tenderness between the two brands. Now, we uniquely identify the value of tenderness, VT, by introducing a steak brand guaranteed to be tender (while remaining identical in all other characteristics to another steak brand j). To illustrate, suppose a person was asked to bid on steak brand 1 with no assurance of tenderness (people bid WTP_{i1} and used $\tilde{\phi}_{i1}$ to derive their valuation). Further, people also bid on steak brand 2 that is identical to brand 1 except it is guaranteed to be tender (people bid WTP_{i2} and set $\phi_{i2} = 1$ to derive their valuation). The difference in bids between these two steaks is:

$$WTP_{i2} - WTP_{i1} = (\alpha_{i2} - \alpha_{i1}) + (1 - \tilde{\phi}_{i1})VT_i. \tag{7.10}$$

If brands 1 and 2 are identical except for the tenderness guarantee, as is assumed in this case, then $(\alpha_{i2} - \alpha_{i1}) = 0$. The value of tenderness for each person is:

$$VT_i = (WTP_{i2} - WTP_{i1})/(1 - \tilde{\phi}_{i1}). \tag{7.11}$$

Now, since VT_i can be calculated for each person, α_{ij} can be calculated for each person and brand by substituting (7.11) into (7.8) and solving for α_{ij}, given a person's stated belief, $\tilde{\phi}_{ij}$, for example:

$$\alpha_{ij} = WTP_{ij} - \tilde{\phi}_{ij}[(WTP_{i2} - WTP_{i1})/(1 - \tilde{\phi}_{i1})].$$

Once individual-specific values for α_{ij} and VT_i are calculated, the utility derived from a steak of any tenderness level is determined through equation (7.1).

7.2.3 Data and methods

We take data from the study by Lusk *et al.* (2004a). In their study, people were randomly recruited from the general population of a university town to participate in the experiment. The experiment was held in the meat laboratory at the local university. Upon arrival at the experiment, subjects were provided an information sheet that described five different types (e.g., brands) of beef steaks. The information sheet and all experimental instructions are provided in the Appendix to this chapter. After reading the information sheet, subjects were asked to complete a short survey. The survey contained some key questions needed to implement the model. Participants were asked to indicate the likelihood that the generic steak, the USDA Choice steak, and the Certified Angus Beef (CAB) steak were tender. In the case of the generic steak, the question was, "If you were to purchase a *generic* steak, what is the likelihood that this steak would be tender? For example, a 0% chance would mean there is NO chance the *generic* steak would actually be tender; whereas, a 100% chance would mean that the *generic* steak would be tender for certain." We did not ask the tenderness question for the natural steak as it only makes up a very small portion of total sales at present, and we did not intend to include it in the calculations of consumer surplus.

After completing the survey, subjects were asked to bid to obtain *one* of five steak types: a generic steak, a guaranteed tender steak, a "natural" steak, a USDA Choice Steak, and a CAB steak. Depending on the session, one of four auction mechanisms was used: the second price auction, the random nth price auction, the English auction, or the BDM. The Appendix provides the details on each of the mechanisms.

A few points about the design are noteworthy. First, although subjects bid on five steaks, only one of the bid was selected as binding. This ensures that demand for a single steak was elicited and that there were no problems with demand reduction. Second, although we could have endowed subjects with a generic steak and elicited bids to upgrade to the other types, we needed total bids for steaks to solve for all the parameters described in the previous section; subjects were given a show-up fee, but were not endowed with a steak. Third, a non-hypothetical practice auction was conducted with candy bars to illustrate the procedures prior to the steak auctions. Because steak is a perishable good, we implemented procedures to safeguard valuations. The auctions were held in a meat lab, so we kept the steaks refrigerated, yet visible to the bidders. We allowed people the opportunity to pick up their steaks at a future date if they were not immediately going home.

We pooled bids from all four auction mechanisms. For the second and nth price auctions, which were repeated round auctions, we use the bids from the initial bidding round. We do this for two reasons. First, this case study is meant to illustrate how auction bids can be used and pooling the data helps ease the exposition. Second, all mechanisms are theoretically demand revealing and each has its own advantages and disadvantages. A literature exists that shows that composite forecasts from various models or people generally outperform a single forecast (e.g., Clemen, 1989). We believe it is reasonable to expect that estimates of WTP (e.g., forecast of true WTP in the population), from several mechanisms might outperform estimates from any single mechanism.

7.2.4   Results

In total, 119 subjects took part in the auctions; three people did not provide usable observations on the likelihood the generic steak was tender and were dropped. Table 7.1 contains summary statistics on the bid distributions for each of the five steaks and the subjective probabilities of tenderness for the generic, Choice, and CAB steaks. On average, subjects were willing to pay $2.14 to obtain a 12 oz generic steak, which was $0.81, $1.65, and $2.21 less than the average bids for the guaranteed tender, Choice, and CAB steaks. The subjective probabilities of tenderness varied, but averaged 46%, 79%, and 82%, for the generic, Choice, and CAB steaks.

The estimated value of tenderness, VT_i, was calculated for each person and summary statistics are also reported in Table 7.1. This figure was calculated by assuming the generic steak and the guaranteed tender steak were identical except for the guarantee of tenderness in the latter; this assumption along with equation (7.11) gives the value for VT_i. The value of tenderness ranges from a low of $0.00 to a high of $8.00, with a mean of $1.54. The last three rows of Table 7.1 show the value of the generic, Choice, and CAB, net the value of tenderness. On average, the value that consumers derived from a generic steak that is not a result of tenderness is $1.41; whereas the value that consumers derived from the CAB steak that is not a result of tenderness is $3.06. This implies that CAB steaks have other quality attributes that consumers desire above and beyond tenderness.

We investigated the consumer welfare effects of three different tenderness grading systems. As a baseline, we calculate consumer surplus under the present situation, in which only subjective probabilities are used to evaluate steak tenderness. In the second scenario, we calculate consumer surplus under the situation in which steaks are labeled with the average probability of tenderness, which we set at the average levels shown in Table 7.1. The difference between the baseline scenario and the second scenario is that in the former each person uses their own subjective probability whereas in the latter scenario all consumers

Table 7.1. *Summary statistics of auction bids and the value of tenderness*
(n = 116)

Variable	Minimum	25th Percentile	Mean	Median	75th Percentile	Maximum
WTP for generic steak ($/12 oz steak)	$0.00	$1.00	$2.14	$2.00	$3.21	$6.75
WTP for guaranteed tender steak ($/12 oz steak)	$0.00	$1.75	$2.95	$3.00	$4.00	$12.00
WTP for natural steak ($/12 oz steak)	$0.00	$1.00	$2.59	$2.50	$4.00	$10.00
WTP for choice steak ($/12 oz steak)	$0.00	$2.06	$3.79	$3.75	$5.00	$13.00
WTP for CAB steak ($/12 oz steak)	$0.00	$2.60	$4.35	$4.00	$5.50	$15.00
Probability generic steak is tender ($\tilde{\phi}_{generic}$)	5%	30%	46%	50%	50%	95%
Probability choice steak is tender ($\tilde{\phi}_{Choice}$)	25%	70%	79%	80%	90%	100%
Probability CAB steak is tender ($\tilde{\phi}_{generic}$)	30%	75%	82%	85%	90%	100%
Value of tenderness (VT) ($/12 oz steak)	$0.00	$0.00	$1.54	$1.22	$2.04	$8.00
$\alpha_{generic} = \alpha_{guaranteedtender}$ ($/12 oz steak)	−$4.00	$0.00	$1.41	$1.50	$2.76	$5.52
α_{Choice} ($/12 oz steak)	−$3.20	$1.03	$2.55	$2.59	$4.06	$7.09
α_{CAB} ($/12 oz steak)	−$3.20	$1.25	$3.06	$2.91	$4.52	$13.04

use a common belief about the tenderness of each steak. In the third scenario, consumer surplus is calculated when a tenderness grading system is implemented with two grades: high (with a probability of tenderness equal to 85%) and low (with a probability of tenderness equal to 15%). A fourth scenario investigates a three-grade system that uses the previous high and low grades, but with an additional medium tenderness grade with a probability set to 50%. Table 7.2 reports the price assumptions used to calculate the welfare effects. Prices were set to correspond to changes in tenderness. For example, in the baseline scenarios, the price of generic was set at $2.50 and the price of Choice was set at $3.50. When assigning a price for the "high" tenderness grade, the generic price was increased $0.50 and the price of Choice was increased $0.25; this was done because there is a much larger difference between the generic probability of tenderness between the baseline and "high" scenarios (43% versus 85%) than for Choice (only 75% versus 85%). In other applications, practitioners might consider constructing supply functions rather than assuming exogenous prices. Exogenous prices are used in this case study for ease of exposition and to illustrate the points at hand.

Table 7.2. *Price and probability assumptions used in welfare calculations*

Variable	Prices ($/12 oz steak)
Prices with no grade and simple average labeling	
Generic ($\tilde{\phi}_{generic}$ or $\phi_{generic} = 47\%$)	$2.50
Choice ($\tilde{\phi}_{Choice}$ or $\phi_{Choice} = 79\%$)	$3.50
CAB ($\tilde{\phi}_{CAB}$ or $\phi_{CAB} = 83\%$)	$4.00
Prices with two or three grades	
Generic (High; $\phi = 85\%$)	$3.00
Choice (High; $\phi = 85\%$)	$3.75
CAB (High; $\phi = 85\%$)	$4.25
Generic (Medium; $\phi = 50\%$)	$2.55
Choice (Medium; $\phi = 50\%$)	$3.00
CAB (Medium; $\phi = 50\%$)	$3.50
Generic (Low; $\phi = 15\%$)	$2.00
Choice (Low; $\phi = 15\%$)	$2.50
CAB (Low; $\phi = 15\%$)	$3.00

Table 7.3. *Consumer welfare changes from a tenderness grading system (all units in $ per choice occasion; n = 116)*

Variable	Minimum	25th Percentile	Mean	75th Percentile	Maximum
ΔCS^{A-NG}	−$0.593	−$0.019	−$0.010	$0.000	$1.645
ΔCS^{2G-NG}	−$0.679	$0.000	$0.172	$0.438	$1.525
ΔCS^{3G-NG}	−$0.679	$0.000	$0.179	$0.438	$1.525
ΔCS^{3G-2G}	$0.000	$0.000	$0.006	$0.000	$0.125

Table 7.3 shows the estimates of changes in consumer surplus. Recall the welfare calculation permits people to opt out of purchasing a steak at all if none provide positive surplus. This means the units of the welfare measures are in dollars per choice occasion, that is, each time a person considers purchasing a steak whether they actually consummate the purchase. The number of shopping trips a person makes in a year might be considered the number of purchase occasions. Results indicate that moving from no tenderness grading to the single average grade actually results in a decline in consumer surplus (about $0.01/choice occasion). This occurs because as shown in Table 7.1, the median probabilities of tenderness exceed the means for all three steaks; implementing the single average label implies a decrease in the perceived level of tenderness for more than half the consumers. The next two rows in Table 7.3

show the effect of implementing a two- and three-grade tenderness grading system. The two-grade tenderness grading system increases consumer surplus $0.173 per choice occasion on average; whereas the three-grade tenderness system increases consumer surplus about $0.179 per choice occasion relative to no grading system. The increase in consumer surplus arises due to the increased availability of choice and heterogeneity in preferences.

7.2.5   Conclusions

With a grading system in place, consumers who are unconcerned about tenderness can find lower-priced steaks that fit their needs; whereas "tenderness-lovers" can find what they desire. The consumer welfare improvement moving from two to three grades is minimal; however, the aggregate effects of moving from no-grading to a two-grade system are substantial. Assuming each US household makes one trip to the grocery store each week, the aggregate increase in consumer welfare from a two-grade tenderness label would be estimated at: 105,000,000 (number of households in the US) × 52 (number of purchase occasions per household, per year) × $0.173 (welfare gain per choice occasion) = $944.58 million per year under the stated price assumptions. One can draw broader conclusions about the total welfare effects of a tenderness grading system by comparing these estimated benefits against the costs of implementing and maintaining such a grading system.

7.3   Informing Policy II: valuing safer food

Dr. Susan Alpert, the leader of the US Food Safety Initiative has made the case for food safety (US FDA 1999, pg. 1), "Bacteria are smarter than people. We will never totally eliminate them from the food supply." Well-publicized outbreaks of cholera, *Salmonella, Listeria monocytogenes*, and *E. Coli 0157: H7* have made people aware that food-borne diseases make a lot of us sick every year; an estimated 76 million illnesses annually in the United States alone, with over 300,000 hospitalizations and 5,000 deaths, imposing an estimated cost in the tens of billions (Crutchfield *et al.*, 1997; Mead *et al.*, 1999).[1] One estimate suggests one out of three consumers in industrialized nations suffer from known and newly recognized food-borne diseases each year (WHO, 2000). Gro Harlem Brundtland, the Director-General of the World Health Organization, noted that globally: "[h]undreds of millions of people around the world fall sick as a result of consuming contaminated food and water . . . [C]hildren under five still suffer

---

[1] For example, Buzby *et al.* (1996) estimate that for six bacterial pathogens, the costs of human illness are estimated to be $9.3–$12.9 billion annually. Of these costs, $2.9–$6.7 billion is attributed to food-borne bacteria.

an estimated 1.5 billion annual episodes of diarrhea which result in more than three million premature deaths" (Brundtland, 2001).

Van Ravenswaay (1988) emphasized that the key economic question in food safety research is to determine individual willingness to pay for reduced risk. She argues that "we know nothing about the demand for food safety . . ." and that more research is needed to develop methods to evaluate willingness to pay values. In response, Hayes *et al.* (1995) developed an experimental auction to elicit the value for safer food. Their experimental markets elicited both option price (i.e., WTP) and compensation (i.e., WTA) measures of value for five food-borne pathogens. They also constructed six treatments to evaluate how subjects responded to changes in the risk of illness for a given pathogen, *Salmonella*, to explore if pathogen-specific values act as surrogate measures of general food safety preferences. We now review their objectives, experimental design, and findings for policy.

7.3.1   Study objectives

The experimental auction had four objectives. First, Hayes *et al.* (1995) explored whether people overestimate the per-meal risk of food-borne illness. Such overestimation of low probability risks is common, and violates the independence axiom of expected utility theory (Machina, 1982). Hayes *et al.* (1995) elicited each participant's subjective probability of becoming ill from each of the five major food-borne pathogens: *Campylobacter, Salmonella, Staphylococcus aureus, Trichinella spiralis*, and *Clostridium perfringens*. They asked each subject's subjective probability:

What do you think is the chance of becoming ill from (pathogen name), given that you eat an average amount of typical products in the United States over one year? Answer: – chance out of 1 million people.

Second, they measured the *ex ante* economic value of reducing health risks posed by the pathogens. They estimated either the option price (R) for a lower probability of illness on a per meal basis, or the compensation demanded (C) for a greater probability of illness. Let a person's state-dependent preferences be defined by a utility function, U(M,H), where M is monetary wealth and H reflects the person's health state (H = 0 if sick; H = 1 if healthy), $U_S(M) \equiv U(M, 0)$ and $U_H(M) \equiv U(M, 1)$, where $U_H(M) > U_S(M)$. Assume $U_i' > 0$ and $U_i'' < 0$ ($i = S, H$), where primes denote first- or second-order derivatives. If a person has a probability p_i of getting sick from pathogen i and $(1 - p_i)$ chance of remaining healthy, their expected utility is:

$$EU_i = p_i U_S(M) + (1 - p_i)U_H(M) \quad i = 1, 2, \ldots 5.$$

The maximum the person will pay to eliminate the probability of illness is R_i:

$$U_H(M - R_i) = EU_i \quad i = 1, 2, \ldots 5.$$

The minimum compensation, C_i, they would accept to increase the chance of illness from pathogen i, is:

$$U_H(M) = p_i U_S(M + C_i) + (1 - p_i)U_H(M + C_i) \quad i = 1, 2, \ldots 5.$$

Third, Hayes *et al.* (1995) examined how people respond to increases in the probability of illness holding constant the illness *severity* for *Salmonella*. They created an environment to help ensure that people would believe the chances by conducting the experiments in a building where animals are slaughtered and processed, new food products are continually being made and tested, and large numbers of bacterial plate counts are conducted on a daily basis. The building adjoins a meat irradiation facility where pathogens on meat can be eliminated via high-energy gamma rays. From a Bayesian perspective, a person's risk perception is represented by a general beta distribution $\hat{p}_i = \frac{\alpha_i p_i + \beta_i q}{\alpha_i + \beta_i}$, where q represents the new information on the chance of illness for *Salmonella*, and α_i and β_i are the weights he or she assigns to his or her prior beliefs, p_i, and the new information. If the chance of illness supplied by the new information is less than his or her prior belief ($q < p_i$), the perceived risk will exceed the new information ($\hat{p}_i > q$); the chance of illness will be overestimated. If $q > p_i$, the opposite occurs, $\hat{p}_i < q$. The question is how bidding behavior is affected by changes in the probability of illness. Totally differentiating the above equation and rearranging yields:

$$\frac{dR_i}{dq} = \left(\frac{\beta_i}{\alpha_i + \beta_i}\right)\left(\frac{U_H - U_S}{U_{H'}}\right) > 0 \quad \text{and} \quad \frac{d^2 R_i}{dq^2} = 0.$$

The option price increases as the probability of illness increases, but it is conditioned by the person's relative weight on the new information and his or her prior beliefs. If the new information is not trusted ($\beta_i = 0$), the option price remains unchanged. If priors receive some weight, option price increases as the chances increase.

The fourth purpose of the research conducted by Hayes *et al.* (1995) was to examine whether bids for specific pathogens acted as *surrogate* measures for general food safety preferences. Surrogate bidding occurs when prior beliefs on odds seem to motivate bidding more than the new information on the objective odds, that is, illness option prices are relatively flat across the probabilities of illness. They tested for surrogate bidding by comparing the value estimates from each pathogen treatment with the value estimate from a treatment that combines all the pathogens. The objective risk of the combined pathogens is a 1 in 46,585 chance of illness per meal from at least one of the pathogens.

7.3.2   The experiment

Hayes *et al.* (1995) examined these four objectives using an experimental auction designed in a ten-step process. Step 1 elicited each person's prior experience with food poisoning, the opportunity cost of illness, and the frequency he or she ate red meat, poultry, and fish. Information on age, gender, and number of children was also elicited. Since food would be auctioned and eaten, each subject signed a consent form agreeing to participate in the experiment.

Step 2 introduced the value measure used in the experiment. A treatment used either the option price or the compensation measure, not both. Step 3 explained the nature of the second price auction mechanism. Step 4 ran the auction for a familiar market good. Each subject was given a $3 capital allocation and was asked to write a bid on a recording card indicating his or her option price (or compensation) to upgrade a small piece of candy to a large candy bar over five trials. The goal was to provide experience with the auction before moving to the more exotic food safety stage. Step 5 introduced the food safety auction. Each subject was given a warm, breaded meat sandwich wrapped in paper, which they were required to eat at the end of the experiment. In the option price treatments, this "test product" had a typical chance of being contaminated by the pathogen. No objective probabilities or outcomes were provided. *Typical* here implied the sandwich was purchased from a local source. One "stringently controlled" sandwich for which the objective risk was a 1 in 100 million chance of suffering from the pathogen in question from eating the sandwich was displayed in a glass container. In the compensation treatments, all subjects were given the stringently controlled sandwich and bid to be paid to eat a "typical" sandwich.

Step 6 began the auction, which lasted a total of twenty trials. Each respondent was given a $15 endowment. They then bid over ten initial rounds. Multiple rounds were used to provide people the opportunity to reflect on their bids given the revealed information on the market price – the second-highest bid. The option price bids were the subjects' values to upgrade their test product for the stringently screened sandwich. The compensation bids were the value to exchange their stringently screened sandwich for the test product. For each trial, the only additional information that was provided was the winner's identification number and the market price (the second-highest bid) in each round. Because only the name of the pathogen was known, this procedure allowed us to explore how subjective risk influenced the value of risk reduction, given repeated market participation and the subsequent impact of new information on the reigning market price.

Step 7 introduced new information after the tenth round on the two key elements that define risk: the objective probability and health severity of the pathogen. Each subject received only one pathogen description, not all five. For example, the information given in the treatment for *campylobacter* was as follows:

- *Test product*: *If you eat this food, there is a 1 in 125,143 chance that you will become ill from campylobacter.*
- *Stringently screened*: *This food has been subjected to stringent screening for Campylobacter. There is a 1 in 100,000,000 chance of getting Campylobacteriosis from consuming this food.*
- *Symptoms are those of an intestinal disease with acute diarrhea and severe abdominal pains. Diarrhea is preceded by brief fever and malaise. The actual individual chance of infection of campylobacteriosis is 1 in 114 annually. Of those individuals who get sick, 1 individual out of 1,000 will die annually. The average cost for medical expenses and productivity losses from a mild case of campylobacteriosis is $230.*

Step 8 elicited *informed* bids over ten additional rounds. In all, each subject made twenty bids: ten uninformed and ten informed. Step 9 determined which of the twenty trials would be randomly selected as binding. We used one binding trial to control for wealth effects. Step 10 required all subjects to eat their sandwich to reinforce the non-hypothetical nature of the experimental auction. In the option price treatments, only the winner of the binding trial ate the stringently controlled sandwich. In the compensation treatments, all but the lowest bidder ate the stringently controlled sandwich. Each subject was required to eat the sandwich (either a test product or the stringently screened sandwich) before receiving money. Each subject signed a second agreement of understanding before eating the food.

Subjects were recruited from several non-intersecting undergraduate classes at Iowa State University by announcing the chance to participate in an experiment providing an approximate stipend of $18 and a "free lunch". Fifteen participants and two alternates were chosen from each class and were asked to appear at a specified date and time at an on-campus taste-testing room with modern kitchen facilities. The taste-testing room is regularly used to measure reactions to experimental products developed at a nearby facility. A total of 230 subjects participated in the experiment.

For each treatment, subjects were given an identification number and asked not to communicate with each other. Each subject was given a set of instructions, with the only differences across treatment being the name of the pathogen and the trial 11 description of the probability and severity of illness. After reading the instructions, the subjects answered a set of questions to determine their understanding of the experimental auction market. After the monitor answered all relevant questions, the experiment began.

7.3.3   Results

Four main results emerged. First, subjects underestimated the objective risk of food-borne pathogens. As shown in Table 7.4, the average subject overestimated the likelihood of only one of the five pathogens – *Clostridium*, the lowest probability pathogen. More than 96% of the subjects underestimated the risk of *Salmonella*, the most common and familiar of all pathogens. For *Campylobacter*, with the highest probability of illness, nearly 94% underestimated the risk. One explanation is that people sometimes do not understand the nature of food-borne illness since it displays symptoms similar to those of the flu.

Second, value measures across food-borne pathogens were not robust to changes in the relative probabilities and severity, suggesting that people place more weight on their own prior perceptions than on new information on the odds of illness. Given market participation and full information, one can make the case that the bids in trials 17 to 20 are the most useful for policy. The bids reflect information obtained after the bidding process had stabilized with market experience. The bids suggest the typical participant was willing to pay between $0.42 and $0.86 per meal to reduce the objective probability of food-borne illness caused by the presence of each pathogen to a 1 in 100 million chance. Table 7.4 also compares the mean naïve bids of trials 7 to 10 with the mean informed bids of trials 17 to 20. The t-test and signed-rank test indicate that the option price differences between naïve and informed bids for *Salmonella* and *Clostridium perfringens* were statistically significant at the 1% level. The mean differences for *Campylobacter* and *Staphylococcus aureus* were significant at the 5% level, and the mean differences for *Trichinella spiralis* were significant at the 10% level. Overall, full information and repeated exposure to the auction market impacted average option price values.

Third, marginal willingness to pay decreased as probabilities increased, suggesting people put more weight on their prior beliefs even as new information suggested greater chances of illness (see Table 7.5). The additional *Salmonella* treatments that varied only the probability of illness shed some light on the original experiments. Results indicate that, given the small sample sizes, attempts to rank the pathogens by using the compensation or option price trials would be meaningless. The intra-group variability (as measured by the range of the *salmonella* results) is greater than the variability of responses among pathogens. Any differences among the pathogens in the first ten trials therefore can be attributed to the different participant groups we used. These results indicate that participants overestimated the smallest odds (1 in 1.37 million), underestimated the largest odds (1 in 13.7), and reacted to the presence of risk as much as to the actual level of risk. These results are inconsistent with the argument that option price increases linearly with increases in perceived risk. Instead, the explicit Bayesian updating process appears not to be linear. Instead

Table 7.4. *Subjective and objective risk and a comparison of naïve and informed option price (R^a) of five pathogens*

Treatment	Annual probability of illness		Naive and informal option price ($)	Comparison of naive and informal option prices ($)			
				$H_0 : R_{7-20} = R_{7-10}$ $H_1 : R_{17-20} \neq R_{7-10}$			
	Objective	Subjective	Mean[b]	Mean[d]		t-test[e]	S-R test[f]
Campylobacter	1/114	1/910	$R_{17-20} = 0.86$ $(0.38)^c$ $R_{7-10} = 0.71$ (0.43)	$R_{iff} = 0.15$ $(0.30)^c$		2.33*	24*
Salmonella	1/125	1/194	$R_{17-20} = 0.55$ (0.25) $R_{7-10} = 0.44$ (0.23)	$R_{Diff} = 0.11$ (0.10)		4.13**	39**
Staphylococcus aureus	1/159	1/2,681	$R_{17-20} = 0.84$ (0.33) $R_{7-10} = 0.92$ (0.32)	$R_{Diff} = -0.08$ (0.12)	−2.14*	−21*
Trichinella spiralis	1/2,400	1/5,665	$R_{17-20} = 0.81$ (0.55) $R_{7-10} = 0.69$ (0.46)	$R_{Diff} = 0.12$ (0.25)		1.59	19
Clostridium perfringens	1/24,000	1/287	$R_{17-20} = 0.42$ (0.33) $R_{7-10} = 0.58$ (0.41)	$R_{Diff} = -0.16$ (0.27)	−2.25*	−26**

Note: Sample sizes: *Campylobacter* (R = 15), *Salmonella* (R = 15), *Stapylococcus aureus* (R = 12), *Trichinella spiralis* (R = 13), *Clostridium perfringens* (R = 13).
[a] R_{17-20} = Mean informed option price for trials 17 through 20.
  R_{7-10} = Mean naive option price for trials 7 through 10.
[b] Mean option price in dollars of trials 17 through 20 and mean of trials 7 through 10.
[c] Sample standard deviations are in parentheses.
[d] Difference between the mean of trials 17 through 20 and the mean of trials 7 through 10.
[e] For the t-statistics, * (**) denotes rejection of H_0 at the 0.05 (0.01) significance level for the two-tail t-test.
[f] The critical values are shown and * (**) denotes rejection of H_0 at the 0.05 (0.01) significance level for the Wilcoxon signed-rank test.

Table 7.5. *Summary statistics of tests within each additional* salmonella *treatment*

		Difference (Mean of trials 17th–20th – 7th–10th)		
		H_0: $R^a_{17-20th} = R_{7-10th}$ H_1: $R_{17-20th} \neq R_{7-10th}$		
Treatment Probability (of illness)	Mean[b]	Mean[c]	t-test[d]	Signed-rank test[e]
1/13.7	$R_{17-20} = 1.42$ $(0.57)^f$ $R_{7-10} = 0.54$ (0.30)	$R_{Diff} = 0.88$ $(0.36)^c$	9.04**	52.5**
1/137	$R_{17-20} = 1.76$ (0.80) $R_{7-10} = 0.88$ (0.45)	$R_{Diff} = 0.88$ (0.57)	5.84**	45.5**
1/1,370	$R_{17-20} = 0.50$ (0.21) $R_{7-10} = 0.52$ (0.20)	$R_{Diff} = -0.02$ (0.09)	−0.84	−11.5
1/13,700	$R_{17-20} = 0.92$ (0.30) $R_{7-10} = 0.67$ (0.23)	$R_{Diff} = 0.25$ (0.12)	8.15**	52.5**
1/137,000	$R_{17-20} = 0.55$ (0.25) $R_{7-10} = 0.44$ (0.23)	$R_{Diff} = 0.11$ (0.10)	4.13**	39.0**
1/1,370,000	$R_{17-20} = 0.02$ (0.06) $R_{7-10} = 1.32$ (0.95)	$R_{Diff} = -1.30$ (0.93)	−5.42**	−45.5**

Note: The sample sizes are as follows: 1/13.7 (n = 14), 1/137 (n = 14), 1/1,370 (n = 15), 1/13,700 (n = 15), 1/137,000 (n = 15), 1/1,370,000 (n = 15).
[a] R = Option price in dollars.
[b] Mean of trials 17 through 20 and mean of trials 7 through 10.
[c] Difference between the mean of trials 17 through 20 and mean of trials 7 through 10.
[d] The t-statistics are shown and ** denotes rejection of H_0 at the 0.01 significance level for the two-tail t-test.
[e] The critical values are shown and ** denotes rejection of H_0 at the 0.01 significance level for the Wilcoxon signed-rank test.
[f] Sample standard deviations are in parentheses.

the observation that subjects respond to the log of the probability and not the actual probability suggests that the weight they place on the new information is affected by the new information. The average subject placed increasingly less weight on the new information the greater the chance of illness.

Fourth, the evidence does not contradict the view that individual values for specific pathogens might act as surrogates for general food safety preferences. The information provided in trial 11 on the probability of suffering from at least one of the five pathogens was the sum of individual pathogen odds, 1 in 46,585. If surrogate bidding exists, the values elicited for the combination of pathogens would not be significantly different from the values elicited for each individual pathogen. The average bid at trial 10 was $0.73, and the average bid at trial 20 was $0.78. The results do not reflect the increase in probability of illness, again suggesting that consumers responded to the presence of pathogens in food rather than to the levels of individual pathogens.

7.3.4   Conclusions

In conclusion, the general policy implications suggest the average subject in our experimental environment was willing to pay approximately $0.70 per meal for safer food. The *Salmonella* treatments under alternative probability levels indicate that the average subject would pay approximately $0.30 per meal to reduce risk of food-borne pathogens by a factor of 10. If one could transfer these values to the US population, the value of food safety could be at least three times the largest previously available estimates. But one should also recognize these values represent upper bounds on value. The La Chatelier principle suggests these current option price bids represent a measure of the upper end of the distribution of food safety preferences, the experimental auctions should be constructed such that people participate in daily auctions over a week or more and be provided more substitution possibilities.

7.4   Informing Policy III: tolerance for genetically modified food

Genetically modified products have triggered visions of a new Green Revolution and Frankenfood. Many consumers around the globe say they are reluctant to accept new food products they perceive as risky, which includes products that involve some form of genetic modification. Genetically modified (GM) foods remain controversial. Several experimental auctions have been used to examine the willingness to pay for GM foods. Using potatoes, vegetable oil, and tortilla chips, US consumers from the Midwest discounted GM-labeled foods by an average of 14%, and the discount could be higher (or lower), depending on the information the consumer received (Rousu *et al.*, 2004a). Lusk *et al.* (2001b), using fifty students from the Midwestern United States, found that most subjects in an experiment were not willing to pay to upgrade a bag of GM chips to a bag of non-GM chips. Noussair *et al.* (2004c) conducted experimental auctions using ninety-seven consumers in France and found that consumers valued biscuits with a 1% and a 0.1% tolerance level differently. They reported that consumers did not view 0.1% GM or 1.0% GM content as preferable to a GM-free product.

A complete GM ban has been politically infeasible. In response, environmental and consumer groups have successfully lobbied for labeling of GM foods in many countries. Labels now exist in the European Union (EU) and other countries, including Australia, Brazil, China, Japan, Korea, and New Zealand. A one key issue in the GM labeling debate is *tolerance* – the acceptable percentage of GM impurity in a product before it must be labeled as GM or before it cannot use a non-GM label. Countries have accepted *positive tolerance standards* because a zero tolerance standard is prohibitively costly, and a perfect segregation system can never be guaranteed. The EU revised its mandatory GM-labeling policy in January 2000 to contain a positive tolerance level: all foods have to be labeled as GM if any ingredient in the product is at least 1% GM. The European Parliament recently voted to reduce the threshold to 0.5% (Food Traceability Report). Australia also has defined a 1% tolerance for GM-impurity. Other countries have also defined tolerance levels that must be met before GM labeling is required. Japan tolerates up to 5% impurity before a GM label is needed. Korea allows a 3% tolerance of GM material, and Brazil allows a 4% tolerance. Thailand has different tolerance levels for different products: 5% for soybeans and 3% for corn (Shipman, 2001).

The US does not currently require labeling of GM foods and has not defined a positive tolerance standard. Legislation to require mandatory labeling in the US was introduced in the 2000 session of Congress in the House (HR 3377) and Senate (S 2080). Although neither bill passed, the bills suggest the mix of policy choices being considered by some US legislators. Information from experimental auctions can help provide an indication of the effects of the options available to policy makers.

7.4.1   Experiment

We now examine the experimental auctions used by Rousu *et al.* (2004b) to address how US consumers react to a positive tolerance standard for GM ingredients. They designed an experimental auction using three GM products to test two hypotheses: (a) mean bids for the GM-free products equal the mean bids for the GM-threshold products, set either at 1% or 5% and (b) mean bids for the 1% GM product equal the mean bids for the 5% GM product. In their experiment, participants were randomly assigned to a treatment that differed in terms of the tolerance level. Consumers bid on three food products that had different tolerance levels. In one trial, all consumers bid on foods with a non-GM label, certified to be completely free of GM material, and in the other trial consumers bid on foods with a non-GM label, indicating that a certain percentage of genetically modified material, either 1% or 5%, was tolerated. These specific tolerance levels are of particular importance because they match the current European and Japanese standards and would be the likely tolerance choices should a standard be enacted.

Consider the four key elements in their experimental design: the GM food, the auction mechanism, the experimental sessions, and the specific steps in the experiment. First, they anticipated consumers might react differently to GM content for foods of different types. Believing that one food item was unlikely to reveal enough information, three items were selected: a 32-ounce bottle of vegetable oil made from canola, a 16-ounce bag of tortilla chips made from yellow corn, and a five pound bag of russet potatoes. Second, a random nth price auction was used to engage both the on- and off-the-margin bidders.

Third, all auctions were conducted in Des Moines, Iowa. Participants in the auctions were consumers contacted by the Iowa State University (ISU) Statistics Laboratory. The Statistics Laboratory used a sample of randomly selected telephone numbers to solicit participants. An employee of the ISU Statistics Laboratory called each number to make sure that it was a residence and then asked to speak to a person in the household who was 18 years of age or older. They were told that "Iowa State University was looking for people who were willing to participate in a group session in Des Moines that related to how people select food and household products." Three sessions were held, each consisting of thirteen to sixteen adult consumers drawn from households in the Des Moines, Iowa, area. The total sample size was forty-four consumers. The three sessions were held on the same day, and potential participants were informed that the sessions would last about ninety minutes. Participants were also told that at the end of the session they would receive $40 in cash for their time. The Statistics Laboratory followed up by sending willing participants a letter containing more information, including a map and instructions on when and where the meeting would be held, directions for getting there, and a telephone number to contact for more information. After accounting for unusable numbers, the response rate was approximately 19 percent.

Fourth, the experiment had nine specific steps. In *Step 1* each consumer signed a consent form, was given $40 for participating, and was assigned an ID number to preserve the participant's anonymity. The participants then read brief instructions and completed a pre-valuation questionnaire. The questionnaire was purposefully given to consumers before the experiment to elicit demographic information and to capture the consumer's prior perception of GM foods. The survey also asked several risk perception questions to ensure consumers would not focus exclusively on GM foods in the opening questionnaire.

In *Step 2* participants were given detailed instructions (both oral and written) about how the random nth price auction works. A short quiz was given to ensure everyone understood how the auction worked. In *Step 3* the random nth price auction was introduced by conducting an auction in which the consumers bid on one brand-name candy bar. Each consumer examined the candy bar, submitted a bid, and the auction was run for real.

In *Step 4* the second practice round of bidding was run, and consumers bid separately on three different items: the same brand-name candy bar, a deck of playing cards, and a box of pens. Participants knew only one of the two rounds would be chosen at random to be binding, which prevented anyone from taking home more than one unit of any product. Selecting a random binding round eliminates the threat of a person reducing his bids because he could buy more than one unit. The consumers first examined the three products and then submitted their bids. In *Step 5* the binding round and the binding nth prices were revealed to the consumers. All bid prices were written on the blackboard, and the nth price was circled for each of the three products. Participants could see the items they won and the market-clearing price. The participants were told that the exchange of money for goods was in another room nearby and would take place after the entire experiment was completed.

After Step 5 the GM-food products were introduced for the next two rounds of bidding. The two bidding rounds were differentiated by the food label – either a non-GM label certified to be GM-free or a non-GM label that indicated the tolerance of GM material. Figure 7.1 shows the three types of labels used for the vegetable oil product; the other product labels were constructed similarly. These labels were on the front of the package and large enough for participants to easily read them. In one round (which could be round one or two depending on the experimental treatment), participants bid on the three food products each with the certified non-GM food label. In the other round, participants bid on the same three food products with the 1% or 5% GM tolerance level. Consumers knew that only one round would be chosen as the binding round that determined auction winners.

In *Step 6* consumers submitted sealed bids for the vegetable oil, tortilla chips, and potatoes, either with the certified non-GM label or the GM-tolerant label. Each consumer bid on each good separately. The monitor collected the bids and then told the participants that they would now look at another group of food items. In *Step 7* consumers examined the same three food products, each with a different label from round 1. Again they examined the products and submitted their bids. Consumers bid on food products with only two types of labels, the GM-free and the GM-tolerant label. Consumers either saw the 1 or 5% tolerant labels but not both. In *Step 8* the monitor selected the binding round and determined the random nth prices for the three goods and notified the winners. A participant might purchase a bottle of vegetable oil and a bag

Vegetable Oil

Net weight 32 fl. oz.

This product is made without
genetic engineering *

* This product is certified to BE FREE OF ANY
GM-material.

Vegetable Oil

Net weight 32 fl. oz.

This product is made without
genetic engineering *

* Subject to a 1 percent tolerance, that is up to
1 percent of any ingredient could be genetically
engineered.

Vegetable Oil

Net weight 32 fl. oz.

This product is made without
genetic engineering *

* Subject to a 5 percent tolerance, that is up to
5 percent of any ingredient could be genetically
engineered.

Figure 7.1   The three types of labels used for the vegetable oil

of potatoes, for example, but there was no chance they would win two bottles of vegetable oil. The assumption here is that vegetable oil, potatoes, and chips are unrelated in consumption. In *Step 9* each consumer completed a brief post-auction questionnaire, and the monitors dismissed the participants who did not win. The monitors and the winners then exchanged money for goods, and the auction ended.

Rousu *et al.* (2004b) used several design features that differed from previous studies. First, subjects submitted only one bid per product. They stepped back from the protocol of using multiple repeated trials and posted market-clearing prices to avoid any question of creating affiliated values that can affect the demand-revealing nature of a laboratory auction. Second, subjects were not endowed with any food item and were not asked to "upgrade" to another food item; rather participants were paid $40 and then they bid on different foods in only two trials. This avoids the risk that an in-kind endowment effect distorts the participant's bidding behavior, but introduces the potential for bids for goods to be influenced by the price of oil, potatoes, and chips outside the experiment. Third, each consumer bid on three food items assumed to be unrelated in consumption, such that if he or she did not have positive demand for one or two products, information on their tastes for genetic modification was obtained on the second and (or) third products. Finally, as did Lusk *et al.* (2004a) they used adult consumers over eighteen years of age who were chosen using a random digital dialing method.

7.4.2   Results

The demographic characteristics of the sample, while not perfectly matching the population demographic characteristics for this region as reported by the US Census Bureau, were similar and provided a sufficient representation for the initial probe into labeling and information for GM products. This is particularly true recognizing that adults, rather than students, are likely to better reflect a typical household of consumers. Using a national random sample of grocery store shoppers, Katsaras *et al.* (2001) showed that the share of college-age (eighteen to twenty-four years) shoppers falls far below their share in the population – 8.5% of shoppers versus 12.8% in the US Census of Population. College students obtain a large share of their food from school cafeterias and a small share from grocery stores and supermarkets compared to older shoppers (Carlson *et al.* 1998). Although our participants are slightly skewed toward women, Katsara *et al.* (2001) show that women make up a disproportional share of grocery shoppers – 83% of shoppers versus 52% in the US Census of Population.

Two primary results emerge. First, consumers bid less for the products having GM-tolerance levels relative to the GM-free benchmark. Table 7.6 shows the

Table 7.6. *Bids on non-genetically modified food with differing tolerance levels*

A. Mean bids – all participants

Food type	N	Mean Bid	Std. Dev.	Median	Minimum	Maximum
Oil	44	0.99	0.92	0.75	0	3.50
Oil – Tolerance	44	0.92	0.76	0.75	0	2.50
Chips	44	1.13	0.99	0.82	0	5.00
Chips – Tolerance	44	0.99	0.80	0.75	0	3.49
Potatoes	44	0.95	0.71	0.89	0	3.00
Potatoes – Tolerance	44	0.86	0.67	0.84	0	3.00

B. Mean bids when participants bid on food with a 5 percent tolerance level

Oil	28	0.94	0.81	0.75	0	3.00
Oil – Tolerance	28	0.88	0.71	0.68	0	2.50
Chips	28	0.99	0.77	0.75	0	3.00
Chips – Tolerance	28	0.90	0.69	0.73	0	2.00
Potatoes	28	0.83	0.64	0.75	0	3.00
Potatoes – Tolerance	28	0.76	0.65	0.75	0	3.00

C. Mean bids when participants bid on food with a 1 percent tolerance level

Oil	16	1.06	1.12	0.75	0	3.50
Oil – Tolerance	16	0.97	0.85	0.88	0	2.39
Chips	16	1.38	1.28	1.13	0	5.00
Chips – Tolerance	16	1.13	0.98	0.77	0	3.49
Potatoes	16	1.15	0.81	1.00	0	3.00
Potatoes – Tolerance	16	1.03	0.69	0.99	0	2.00

mean and median bids by food type. Twenty-eight participants bid in the 5% tolerance treatments; sixteen participants bid in the 1% treatment. Overall, the average consumer bid less on the food product with the GM-tolerance labels relative to the GM-free products. Consumers, on average, bid seven cents less on the GM-tolerant oil, fourteen cents less on the tortilla chips, and nine cents less on the potatoes. Consumers, on average, discounted the foods with the GM tolerance by an average of seven to thirteen percent. In comparison, Rousu *et al.* (2004a) observe that consumers discounted food that had a GM label without a tolerance level by an average of fourteen percent. Pooling all observations, Table 7.7 shows we can reject the null hypothesis that bidding behavior over GM-tolerance labels is identical to that for the GM-free benchmark for the tortilla chips and the potatoes but not for the vegetable oil. The significant discount for the GM-tolerant food is consistent with Viscusi *et al.* (1987) which indicate a *reference risk effect*. In their study, consumers initially purchased a given product when told that it injured fifteen out of 10,000 people who used

Table 7.7. *Comparison of bids for non-GM foods with and without GM tolerance levels*

A. T-test for null hypothesis of no difference in bids for non-GM and GM-tolerant foods – all observations (N = 44)

	Bid non-GM	Bid w/Tolerance	Difference	T-Test statistic
Oil	0.99	0.92	0.07	1.24
Chips	1.13	0.99	0.14	2.44**
Potatoes	0.95	0.86	0.09	1.70*

B. T-test for null hypothesis of no difference in bids for non-GM and GM-tolerant foods – 5 percent tolerance.

Oil	0.94	0.88	0.06	1.05
Chips	0.99	0.90	0.09	1.51
Potatoes	0.83	0.76	0.07	1.33

C. T-test for null hypothesis of no differences in bids for non-GM and GM-tolerant foods – 1 percent tolerance

Oil	1.06	0.97	0.09	0.71
Chips	1.38	1.13	0.25	1.93*
Potatoes	1.15	1.03	0.12	1.08

* Significant at 10 percent level
** Significant at 5 percent level

the product, but over two-thirds of the consumers were unwilling to purchase the same product when the chance of injury increased to sixteen out of 10,000. Such findings could explain why consumers placed such a large discount on the GM-tolerant food.

Second, no statistically significant difference existed for consumers' discount of the 5% GM products and 1% GM food. Table 7.7 shows that at the 5% significance level we cannot reject the null hypothesis that bid differences are different between the two GM-tolerance levels.

7.4.3   Conclusions

The findings in this case study support the view that if a GM-tolerance policy is implemented in the US, consumers might not place a greater value on a 1% GM tolerance level relative to a 5% GM tolerance level. Because of the higher segregation and handling cost of a 1% tolerance level compared to a 5% level, society may be better off implementing a higher tolerance level, if it is in fact optimal to implement a mandatory label at all (see Lusk *et al.*, 2005). Consumers value GM-free products, but if GM contamination does exist, we

Table 7.8. *T-test on null hypothesis that consumers value foods with a 1% tolerance the same as for a 5% tolerance*

	Non-GM premium – 5%	Non-GM premium – 1%	Difference	T-Test statistic
Oil	0.06	0.09	−0.03	−0.20
Chips	0.09	0.25	−0.16	−1.33
Potatoes	0.07	0.12	−0.05	−0.47

find no evidence that consumers prefer a 1% GM-tolerant food relative to a 5% GM-tolerant food (see Table 7.8).

This result is consistent with the notion of surrogate bidding or scope effects. Such bidding occurs when consumers reveal nearly the same willingness to pay to avoid varying levels of contamination relative to an uncontaminated product. Surrogate bidding has been shown to exist in other experimental food markets as shown in the previous case study. Hayes *et al.* (1995) used experimental auctions to show when consumers bid to reduce risk by eliminating a cluster of food-borne pathogens they were indistinguishable from bids to reduce specific pathogens. Similar results have been obtained from surveys (e.g., Hammitt and Graham, 1999).

While the present sample is small, which indicates that one should not generalize the findings too broadly, the results do not contradict the policy proposal that if the US decides to allow a tolerance of GM material in food products, the 5% tolerance would be better socially than the 1% tolerance. Consumers do not value a product with 1% impurity significantly higher than with 5% impurity, and it is less expensive for food producers and distributors to comply with a higher tolerance level. Findings suggest consumers are willing to pay a large premium to avoid GM contamination in an uncontaminated product. The premium did not vary, however, by the amount of GM-contamination in each product. An interesting extension of this work, however, would be to examine whether consumers view 10% (or 20%) impurity differently from 1 or 5% levels. Also, it would be interesting to see if the results generalize to other products by examining the marginal willingness to avoid small amounts of contamination.

7.5   Marketing I: forecasting market share of a new product

Economists and marketers are interested in determining how interrelated demands change after a price change or in forecasting the market share of a new product. Bids from experimental auctions can be readily used to make such predictions. Write the utility derived from purchasing brand j as:

$$U_{ij} = WTP_{ij} - p_j, \tag{7.12}$$

where WTP_{ij} is the maximum willingness to pay for brand j (i.e., the bid for j in an incentive compatible auction) and p_j is the price of good j. There are several ways of utilizing this utility function to determine market share. One common approach is to use the "first choice" or "highest utility" rule in which each person is assumed to choose the product producing the highest utility from a choice set with J brands. Assume individual i chooses brand j if $U_{ij} > U_{ik}$ for all $k \neq j$. Let I_{ij} be an indicator variable that takes the value of 1 if individual i chooses brand j and 0 otherwise. Further, let w_i be the number of units individual i purchases once a choice between brands has been made. Now, in a sample of N individuals choosing between J goods, the market share of brand j (MS_j) is:

$$MS_j = \frac{\sum_{i=1}^{N} I_{ij} w_i}{\sum_{k=1}^{J} \sum_{i=1}^{N} I_{ik} w_i}. \tag{7.13}$$

Because of the term w_i in the summation, the percentage of people predicted to choose a particular brand need not match the market share if, for example, "heavy users" are more likely to prefer one brand than another. Market share will also differ from the frequency of individual choices because some consumers may choose not to purchase at all if prices and values are such that equation (7.12) is negative for all brands; such people would be excluded in the calculation in (7.13). Note expression (7.13) generates the market share of consumption. To get value shares, the prices of the various brands need to enter (7.13).

Before proceeding, it is worthwhile to discuss the relative merits of calculating market share with auction bids in the manner described by (7.13). One drawback to this approach is that w_i is assumed to be exogenous and not affected by prices or available brands. One could estimate a two-part model. First, the effects of aggregate prices and available substitutes on w_i could be determined in a traditional demand framework, and second, equation (7.13) could be used to calculate market share based on estimated w_i (see Phaneuf et al., 1998, 2000 for more discussion on this and other approaches in a slightly different context). Despite this drawback, calculating market share in this manner is appealing relative to estimates based on the multinomial logit (MNL) model. The MNL is typically estimated using either hypothetical stated choices or time-series data on actual market shares (e.g., see Louviere et al., 2000). The MNL suffers from the well known independence of irrelevant alternatives problem, which has a number of unfortunate consequences such as (a) forcing the ratio of the market shares of any two goods to remain constant regardless of prices or available brands; and (b) forcing equality of cross-price elasticities across all brands. Equation (7.13) does not rest on the independence of irrelevant alternatives assumption, and it does not impose the aforementioned restrictions on substitution patterns. Further, the MNL and other such models often assume homogeneity in preferences across people. Although a variety of econometric models have been proposed to undercover heterogeneity in choice and market share data, auction bids provide direct, continuous measures of value for each person for each good, which is the most one can ask for when attempting to identify heterogeneous preferences.

7.5.1   Data and methods

To illustrate how market share can be calculated using auction bids, we return to the data collected by Lusk *et al.* (2004a) that was described in the case earlier in section 7.2. All experimental instructions are provided in the Appendix to this chapter. Recall that subjects were asked to bid to obtain *one* of five steak types: a generic steak, a guaranteed tender steak, a "natural" steak, a USDA Choice Steak, and a CAB steak. Subjects bid in one of four types of auctions, the data from which are pooled for sake of exposition. The data set consists of data from 119 subjects that submitted bids on five steaks, yielding a data set containing 595 bids. Summary statistics for the bid data are in Table 7.1. People completed a short survey that asked how often steak was purchased each month such that the parameter w_i could be defined. On average, people indicated they purchased about 4lbs of steak each month.

  This data was used to simulate market share under several scenarios. As a base-line scenario, we assumed people were presented with a choice between a 12 oz generic steak at $2.50, a 12 oz Choice steak at $3.50, a 12 oz CAB steak at $4.00, and no purchase. Each person in the data set was then assumed to choose the option that generated the highest utility – that is, the largest difference between the auction bid and price. This information along with the frequency of purchase for each person was then plugged into equation (7.13) to calculate market share for the base-line scenario. A second scenario was considered that was the same as that described above except the price of CAB was increased $0.50. This scenario permits an investigation in the own- and cross-price responsiveness. We then investigated how the introduction of a new "natural" steak would affect market structure. Scenario three was the same as the first except now consumers were able to choose a 12 oz natural steak at $3.50 in addition to the other four choices described above.

7.5.2   Results

Table 7.9 contains the results of the market share simulations. In the base-line scenario, about 14% of subjects were predicted to choose the generic steak, whereas 27% and 29% of consumers were predicted to choose the Choice and CAB steak. At the price levels used in the simulation, about 30% were not

Table 7.9. *Market share simulations (n = 119)*

		Scenarios	
Steak Type	Baseline[a]	Price of CAB increased $0.50[b]	Natural Steak introduced[c]
Percent of people choosing			
Generic	14.29%	15.97%	14.29%
Choice	26.89%	34.45%	24.37%
CAB	28.57%	15.97%	26.89%
Natural	0.00%	0.00%	4.20%
None	30.25%	33.61%	30.25%
Market share			
Generic	19.41%	22.14%	19.41%
Choice	47.26%	62.01%	46.37%
CAB	33.33%	15.86%	32.15%
Natural	0.00%	0.00%	2.07%
Change in market share from baseline			
Generic		2.73%	0.00%
Choice		14.75%	−0.89%
CAB		−17.47%	−1.18%
Natural		0.00%	2.07%

[a] In baseline scenario, the prices of generic, choice, and CAB are $2.50, $3.50, and $4.00 per 12 oz steak; the natural steak was not available.
[b] This scenario is the same as the baseline except the price of CAB is $4.50 instead of $4.00 per 12 oz steak.
[c] This scenario is the same as the baseline except the natural steak is introduced at a price of $3.50 per 12 oz steak.

expected to choose a steak at all; the prices of all steaks exceeded the bids for all steaks for 30% of bidders in the sample. It is not unrealistic to suppose a similar phenomenon occurs on routine shopping trips as consumers only buy if the price is right. In terms of market share in the baseline scenario, almost half the share went to Choice steak, a third went to CAB, and the remainder to generic. The second column of Table 7.9 illustrates the effect of a $0.50 CAB price increase. As expected, demand for CAB fell when the price increased; market share of CAB declined about 17%, indicating an own-price elasticitiy of $(-17.47/15.86)/(0.5/4) = -8.81$. The Choice steak experienced a much larger increase in market share due to the CAB price increase than did generic, indicating Choice and CAB are stronger substitutes. The cross-price elasticities of Choice and generic with respect to CAB are 1.90 and 0.98, respectively. The last column of Table 7.9 shows the effects of introducing a new steak to this market: a natural steak produced without growth hormones or antibiotics. When this steak is introduced, only about 4% of the people are predicted to choose it, and the steak only generates about a 2% market share. The natural steak primarily takes market share away from the CAB steak. Further, the introduction of the natural steak did not affect demand for the generic steak at all. In addition to the results shown in Table 7.9, any number of scenarios could be described and simulated. For example, the effect of introducing a guaranteed tender steak could be investigated or one could investigate the effect of increasing the natural steak price by $0.50. The point is that once auction bids have been collected on a number of goods, a variety of market impact scenarios can be investigated.

7.6   Marketing II: preferences for fresh food with multiple quality attributes

Consumers' purchases are conditioned by their utility, household production functions, and resource constraints. Similar, but not identical, goods will frequently be valued differently by consumers. Fresh food products typically exhibit these qualitative differences that may result in different lots being valued differently. Although several packages of pork chops may be available at a particular price per pound, consumers typically select among them based on some perceived or expected qualitative difference. Information about how consumers make these selections is useful in both pork production and marketing. Producers are understandably reluctant to make the genetic and management changes that can alter pork quality characteristics if changes in quality cannot be related to enhanced value (Melton et al., 1994). Similarly, advertising that focuses on pork characteristics of uncertain importance or value to consumers may have unexpected long-term effects on the demand for the product.

Melton et al. (1996a) and (1996b) examined consumer perceptions and willingness to pay for quality differences in fresh pork chops using information obtained from an experimental auction. They considered the marketing of pork as fresh meat in the form of pork chops (the loin). Chops account for nearly twenty percent of the weight of a pork carcass and nearly half of its value. Their experimental design accounted for the potentially important effects of both appearance and taste on consumers' perceptions and their willingness to pay for pork chops. They addressed two questions relevant to producing and marketing quality differentiated products such as fresh pork. First, what do alternative attributes contribute to the value or price of the overall product? Second, how does the presentation format affect consumer perceptions and willingness to pay for the product and/or its attributes?

7.6.1   Experimental design

Melton *et al.*'s (1996a) and (1996b) experiment focused on pork chop attributes of two broadly defined types: (1) visual attributes that a consumer can perceive by looking at a chop and (2) attributes that consumers can discern only after tasting the product. No *a priori* assumptions were made regarding possible interactions and interrelationships among the attribute types. Visual attributes include color, marbling (intra-muscular fat), size, and bone and can be objectively scored independently of the consumer. Taste attributes include tenderness, juiciness, and flavor and tend to be highly subjective. Different consumers will perceive a bite of the same chop differently depending on their individual preferences for flavor, juiciness, tenderness, and past experiences. Repeated trials for taste attributes were difficult because a chop (the experimental treatment) is destroyed (eaten) in the process of conducting the trial. Melton *et al.* (1996a and 1996b) designed the experiment to ascertain consumer preferences for pork attributes based on visual attributes as experimental treatments. They concentrated the experimental design on the attributes of chop color, marbling, and size which are largely determined by genetics and pre-slaughter production practices.

When the experiments were designed, the auction literature provided little guidance regarding the maximum number of alternatives that could be successfully evaluated in a reasonable amount of time – especially when those alternatives exhibit only subtle differences in attributes. A trip to local supermarkets revealed that six to eight packages of each meat cut are typically on display at one time. Because consumers can apparently make choices among them, they concluded it was reasonable to expect consumers in an experimental auction to be able to evaluate eight chops in the experiment.

The experiment focused on three attributes of pork chops (color, marbling and size). To simplify the consumer's decision problem each attribute was indexed on a scale of 1 to 5, resulting in a large overall consumer decision problem involving a full factorial design consisting of $5^3 = 125$ combinations of attributes and attribute levels. The problem of experimental design was then reduced to one of selecting eight treatments (chops) that best represented the 125 possible combinations of the three attributes in question using three replications of twelve consumers each. The biology of pork production helped to limit the number of possible treatments. Many combinations, especially those representing extremes of the attributes infrequently occur in nature (i.e., either 1 or 5 of one attribute with either 1 or 5 of another attribute). The extremes of each attribute were initially ignored to reduce the number of combinations to a maximum of twenty-seven ($3^3 = 27$). Size effects were treated as independent of either color or marbling so that nine combinations of marbling and color encompassed the three sizes.

A second-order central-composite response design was used by defining the central point of the response surface to be a 3-3-3 (C-M-S) chop (Cochrane and Cox, 1957). Four additional treatments (chops) were selected from the perimeter of the nine combinations that define the basic color-marbling response surface (2-2-3, 2-4-3, 4-2-3, and 4-4-3) and two from the central point (3-3-2 and 3-3-4) to reflect size differences in a total of seven treatment chops. To explore the extremes in a limited way, an eighth and final chop was then selected from the extremes of the color-marbling response surface (1-1-3, 5-1-3, and 5-5-3) to be partially replicated, changed between the three replications of the trial. Finally, as a point of reference and to reflect the potential availability of alternatives in the consumers' purchase decisions, a USDA Choice T-bone steak and bone-in chicken breast were added to the trial.

The subjects were primary shoppers of meat consuming households. A random telephone survey of local consumers was conducted to learn about their meat purchase and consumption patterns. Demographic questions regarding employment and profession, household size and income, age, sex, and education were included in this survey. From the survey responses, a stratified random sample of thirty-six consumers was drawn to match the characteristics of primary shoppers in local market in terms of meat consumption, gender, income, age, and education. The thirty-six consumers were then randomly assigned to the three replications by income strata using confidential identification numbers to maintain the desired overall household income distribution within each replication.

Three presentation formats were defined: (1) p = photographs of the chops provided consumers two dimensional information on visual attributes comparable to the information presented in advertising, (2) a = visual appearance of fresh chops provided consumers information on visual attributes under conditions comparable to a supermarket purchase, and (3) t = consumers tasting freshly cooked chops provided them with information on attributes similar to in-home consumption of chops. Each experimental subject made bids under each format: p, a, and then t. Consider the details of each format. High quality professional color photographs of ten pork chops, one chop per photograph, representing each of the defined treatments were secured from the National Pork Producers Council (NPPC). Also similar quality photographs were obtained for the T-bone steak and skinless chicken breast. Photographs of the experimental chops were re-randomized and placed on a large poster board (two rows by four chops each), followed by the photographs of the T-bone steak and chicken breast. The poster board was covered to prevent premature viewing.

The actual chops were obtained from two commercial slaughter plants and the university meat laboratory in the week prior to the trial. Carcasses at each facility were inspected to identify those that would yield chops corresponding to the pre-defined treatments. Rib sections of the loins were purchased that would provide at least twelve chops of each treatment (i.e., all twelve chops needed for each treatment were from the same carcass). Two days before the trial excess back-fat was removed to a common 1/8–1/4 inch depth, corresponding to current retail marketing standards, and the loins were cut into chops of 3/4 to one inch thickness. The chops were individually vacuum wrapped, marked for identification, and stored in the meat cooler. Despite the extensive search, loins corresponding to two of the extreme treatments (5-5-3 and 5-1-3) could not be located due to their low frequency in nature. The fresh products used for visual and taste assessments of attributes were limited to the 1-1-3 chop in each replication. On the morning of the trial, two chops of each treatment were removed from their vacuum packaging, placed on a yellow Styrofoam tray, and wrapped with clear plastic in a manner similar to local retail marketing standards. The eight packages representing the alternative treatments were marked for identification and were randomly placed in a commercial chest-type retail cooler at 45°F in two rows of four chops each. To these we added the T-bone steak and skinless chicken breast purchased at retail on the morning of the trial. The cooler was covered to avoid incidental and premature viewing. Both photographs and fresh chops were coded for experimental identification so consumers could not discern the independently determined level of treatment variables represented by the chop (i.e., its level of color, marbling, or size). Furthermore, they could not associate the photographs with the fresh product by treatment identification code.

The multi-unit auction was conducted in five phases. *Phase I*: the consumers were re-surveyed to update information on frequency of pork chop consumption and current stock of pork chops. *Phase II*: consumers learned about how the auction worked by a pre-auction of eight candy bars. A second price Vickrey auction format was employed.

Phase III: consumers were shown photographs of the chops and asked to evaluate the chops' attributes of color, marbling, size, bone, and overall appearance using a scale from "Strongly Dislike" to "Strongly Like." Consumers were then provided reference prices for the beef T-bone ($5.00 per pound) and the chicken breast ($3.00 per pound) and asked to simultaneously submit hypothetical bids for each of the eight chops represented by the photographs. These bids were described as hypothetical because consumers were aware no purchase would occur (in that phase).

Phase IV: consumers were shown the actual chops, including the beef T-bone and chicken breast, and were asked to evaluate their appearance using forms identical to those used in Phase III. The reference prices for the beef T-bone and chicken breast were the same as in phase three, and the consumers were asked to submit eight simultaneous bids in a second-price auction. Consumers were told the market price (second high bid) and the identification number of the highest bidder for each of the eight pork chops. Consumers were given the opportunity to increase their bid for any of the eight chops and the bidding was continued in this manner until no one wanted to increase their bid for any chop.

Phase V: consumers were escorted to another room where they tasted a sample (approximately 3/4 inch cube) of a professionally prepared chop broiled to 71°C internal temperature from ribs adjacent to the eight fresh chops viewed in phase four. Participants were asked to evaluate each chop tasted for flavor, juiciness, tenderness, and overall eatability using a scale comparable to their previous visual evaluations. After completing the taste test, consumers then returned to the original auction room and were allowed to re-inspect the fresh chops using, if desired, their taste evaluation forms as added information. Consumers were then asked to re-bid for fresh chops. As in Phase IV, the auction ended when no one wished to increase his/her bid for any chop. Each of the eight chops was sold to the highest bidder in packages of two at the second-highest bid per pound for that chop. The chops not purchased by the high bidder were then sold to the second highest bidder at the third highest price bid for that chop, which became the new market price. Note: consumers were kept unaware of any subsequent phase of the experiment to enhance the validity and independence of data collected within each phase. Anonymous consumer identification numbers were changed between Phases IV and V to further enhance the independence of data collected.

7.6.2   Results and discussion

Melton *et al.* (1996) first examined the correlation of consumers' appraisals of chop attributes between the photograph (p) and visual appraisal conditions (a). To evaluate the consistency of consumers' evaluations across presentation formats, a strongly cardinal index was constructed from the experimental data by scoring subjective evaluations on a standardized scale from 0 to 100. Consumers are expected to consistently order the visual attributes of pork, whether evaluating chops based on fresh product or photographs of the product. The photographed chop with the greatest visual appeal should signal the most preferred chop; the most preferred chop should signal the preferred photograph to be used in advertising. The results, however, show the format of chop presentation matters. They found significant variability in consumers' evaluations and low correlations among consumers' appraisals of visual attributes. Attributes of pork reflected in photographs seemed to be poorly correlated with information obtained from viewing the fresh product. Although photographs used in advertising may affect overall demand for the product, the results suggest that they may be ineffective as a means of educating consumers about subtle differences in visual attributes that exist in fresh pork.

Consumers' evaluations of the photographs of pork chops and the fresh chops tended to indicate a general preference for large pork chops having small amounts of marbling and light to pale white color (Table 7.10). But after tasting cooked samples, consumers exhibited a preference for chops having greater marbling and to some degree for uncooked chops having darker color and smaller size than those chosen based on photographs. Rankings after taste-testing tended to contradict consumers' preferences obtained from visual appraisals. As a result, the correlations of overall chop eatability, as measured on a scale, with overall chop appearance rankings were negative for photographs and small, but positive, for fresh product.

Melton *et al.* (1996) also examined price differences associated with subjective evaluations. They considered both bids (one per consumer per chop) and market prices (one per replication per chop). The bids provide an indication of each consumer's willingness to pay for a fixed supply, whether or not a sale is actually consummated at that price. The experimental market price approximates the competitive market price that could be observed in a non-experimental setting in that a number of consumers have been "priced" out of the market and are unobserved. Table 7.11 reports the results of several ordinary least squares regressions that summarize the effect of color, marbling, size, and presentation format on market prices and individual bids. Overall, results tended to follow the pattern of overall preference ratings. Focusing on market prices, results indicate higher prices for lower marbled and larger cuts in the photo evaluation, but higher prices were observed for higher marbled cuts in the taste evaluation. Individual bids exhibit a similar pattern: higher bids are offered for larger, less marbled, and lighter color chops when evaluated visually. After tasting, however, consumers tended to bid more for more marbling whereas color and size had very little effect on bids.

Although appearance is an important consideration in consumers' fresh pork purchases, repeat purchases are likely to be most affected by taste-assessed attributes. Our results suggest that first-time purchasers of pork chops may inadvertently be selecting, based on appearance, what becomes their least preferred tasting pork quality, or at least a product that is likely to be judged as less desirable. We cannot easily identify the source of these apparently inconsistent and contradictory preferences. However, we suggest that the observed preferences for less marbling and lighter color in fresh pork appearance may be a result of the growing health concern for reduced dietary fat intake and the "Other White Meat®" advertising campaign that promotes pork that looks good but tastes bad. Such strategies seem unlikely to sustain long-term market success.

Consumers may be over-reacting to the "low fat" health concerns when making visual appraisals. Actual fat differences between marbling score 2 and marbling score 4 are small (about 2%), but taste differences appear to be much greater. This inconsistency suggests that consumers may not be well informed about the taste-health tradeoffs of intra-muscular (i.e., marbling) as opposed

Table 7.10. *Means of subjective evaluation scores of pork chop characteristics and auction bids by presentation format* (*Scale = 1 to 100*)

Chop (C-M-S)	Photo					Appearance					Taste			
	Color score	Marb. score	Size score	Overall score	Bid	Color score	Marb. score	Size score	Overall score	Bid	Juiciness score	Tender score	Eatability score	Bid
2-2-3	37.5	50.3	58.6	46.3	$1.97	41.0	54.5	60.9	56.5	$1.94	32.2	30.4	35.2	$1.49
2-4-3	40.0	41.5	58.6	48.4	$2.03	50.8	40.7	48.6	50.5	$1.95	55.6	60.7	61.0	$2.10
3-3-2	48.1	36.8	28.8	28.8	$1.72	41.0	52.6	29.7	35.7	$1.62	40.8	53.6	48.9	$1.88
3-3-3	58.9	52.7	53.3	53.4	$2.22	41.9	41.1	52.1	42.6	$1.69	42.8	37.0	40.1	$1.59
3-3-4	53.4	61.0	68.5	59.8	$2.17	55.5	48.8	60.4	54.2	$1.95	40.6	44.3	44.3	$1.66
4-2-3	65.1	66.5	47.1	63.7	$2.36	37.2	48.0	36.9	39.0	$1.79	42.3	36.9	42.5	$1.71
4-4-3	51.3	41.2	41.7	35.4	$1.94	37.3	29.1	42.3	38.8	$1.76	61.9	58.8	57.8	$2.10
1-1-3	35.1	38.6	52.8	47.1	$2.13	51.4	66.6	64.0	62.5	$2.08	39.9	40.9	44.2	$1.71
5-1-3	51.2	62.4	39.6	50.9	$1.97									
5-5-3	40.3	11.7	18.1	15.2	$1.53									

Table 7.11. *Ordinary least squares regressions: effect of pork chop characteristics on market prices and bids in three evaluation formats*

Independent variables	Market price is dependent variable			Bid is dependent variable[a]		
	Photo	Appearance	Taste	Photo	Appearance	Taste
Constant	0.737	1.189	0.988	0.331	0.776	0.959
	$(3.50)^b$	(5.11)	(7.33)	(0.73)	(1.52)	(1.86)
Replication 1[c]	0.095	0.040	−0.034	0.131	0.006	−0.129
	(2.26)	(−1.40)	(−1.36)	(2.44)	(0.10)	(−2.17)
Replication 2[c]	−0.061	−0.060	0.021	0.123	0.355	0.157
	(−1.44)	(−1.40)	(0.84)	(2.20)	(5.76)	(2.53)
Replication 3[c]	−0.034	0.020	0.013	−0.254	−0.361	−0.027
Color	0.005	−0.008	−0.026	−0.004	−0.065	−0.029
(scale of 1 to 5)	(0.18)	(−0.23)	(−1.26)	(−0.13)	(−1.78)	(−0.78)
Marbling	−0.063	−0.060	0.058	−0.043	0.005	0.138
(scale of 1 to 5)	(−2.08)	(−1.69)	(2.82)	(−1.48)	(0.14)	(3.74)
Size	0.082	−0.004	−0.033	0.079	0.106	−0.002
(area in sq in)	(2.84)	(−0.13)	(−1.91)	(2.85)	(3.52)	(−0.06)
R^2	0.47	0.25	0.46	0.39	0.50	0.37
Sample Size	24	24	24	264	264	264

[a] Bid regressions also included nineteen other variables related to socio-economic and demographic characteristics as well as pork consumption patterns.
[b] Numbers in parentheses are t-statistics.
[c] These dummy variables are effects coded: the estimated effects across the three replications sum to zero and are estimated relative to the mean replication effect.

to extra-muscular (subcutaneous) fat content. More definitive information on dietary fat content and its role in consumers' taste evaluations of fresh meat products may be needed before consumers can form reasonable and consistent expectations of taste attributes based on visual appraisal. In fresh products such as pork chops, grades and standards are used for this purpose. Revision of the current grades and standards of pork marketing may be one step to remedying this problem. Labeling of pork and other fresh meat products with fat percentages, as opposed to grades, would be one alternative.

The Other White Meat® advertising campaign funded by the National Pork Producers Council may have increased pork demand by adding new consumers. At the same time, it may have also contributed to the documented preference inconsistently by suggesting to consumers that lighter colored pork is a "better" product. The experimental results, however, indicate that consumers judged a light colored chop as having low eating quality. Coupled with the possible interaction of chop color with marbling (i.e., marbling is less apparent in lighter meat), the National Pork Producers Council may inadvertently be promoting their least tasty product. Although the Other White Meat® campaign may have been successful in getting consumers to see pork as a good alternative to poultry (i.e., poultry and pork may now be closer substitutes than beef and pork), continued promotion of an "inferior product" may lead to the long-run loss of any short-run gains in market share that the pork industry has achieved.

7.6.3   Conclusions

Melton *et al.*'s (1996) experimental auction was designed to evaluate consumer perceptions and willingness to pay decisions for fresh pork chops that differ in selected attributes: color, marbling, and size. They found that consumers attached value to the attributes of color, marbling and size in fresh pork; appearance and taste effect consumer purchase decisions differently; consumers did not consistently prefer white chops over dark red chops, but instead varied their preference depending upon presentation format. The results showed evaluations based on taste were positively related to visual evaluations of the fresh chop, but consumer evaluations of chops based on photographic format were shown to be unreliable sources of market information.

7.7   Marketing III: the value of farm financial records[2]

For almost a century, agricultural economists have attempted to demonstrate to farmers the benefits of keeping financial records and have advocated sound accounting practices, e.g., Pond (1931) and Arnold (1931). Since 1914, Land Grant Universities have encouraged better farm record keeping by forming farm management associations. With the dwindling size of the farm population and better technology and education, some farmers have questioned the value of using public resources to support the maintenance of farm records. Today only the University of Illinois, Kansas State University, and Cornell University still maintain farm management associations with modern record keeping capabilities. Nevertheless, evidence exists that farmers' record keeping may be sub-optimal. For example, 57% of farm loan applicants in Kentucky did not keep separate records for their farm and household, with only a meager 3% using a computerized accounting system (Idbendahl *et al.* 2002). Another study found that 29% of New York dairy farmers never formulate financial budgets (Gloy and LaDue, 2003). Several studies have attempted to link record keeping with profitability and performance, but evidence is mixed and is plagued with problems of endogeneity.

---

[2] We would like to thank Christine Wilson and Dana Marcellino for permitting use of the information used in this case study.

Although the academic literature is replete with examples exposing the merits of farm record keeping and investigating the link between record keeping and financial performance, very little is known regarding the value farmers place on their financial information and the determinants of such value. Such information is needed as public institutions determine the quantity and quality of resources to devote to encouraging and supporting maintenance of farm records.

7.7.1   Data and methods

Because this research is interested in valuing a good, e.g., farm records, which is owned by the study participants in question, a willingness to accept (WTA) auction was conducted. That is, we sought to measure the minimum amount of money that must be paid to a farmer so that they would be willing to permanently give up their financial records. Several preliminary focus groups and pre-tests were conducted to determine a person's reaction to the auction mechanism and to determine how to characterize records which could vary greatly in terms of quantity and quality. It was learned that a non-trivial number of people were unwilling to bid to give up their records. This led us to modify the auction format so that people could check a box on their bid-sheet indicating if they did not want to participate in the auction.

Participants in the primary portion of the study came from two main sources. First, thirty-five people were recruited from a "Top Farmer Crop Workshop" held at Purdue University; the audience was a group of competitive, commercial producers. Participation in the experiment was part of an optional luncheon session. Second, thirty-seven people were recruited by Purdue University extension educators to attend one of five sessions in various regions of Indiana. An average of seven farmers came to each session, which took place at a local restaurant or at the county building. To encourage farmer participation, the farmers were given a free lunch.

Data collection proceeded in three stages. Participants first completed a written survey, then participated in a WTA auction to give up an endowed candy bar, and bids in the non-hypothetical financial records auction were collected. The survey collected information on the people, their farms, and their farm records. Once respondents completed the survey, they read instructions for the second price candy bar auction. The candy bar auction was used to introduce the mechanism to participants so as to increase understanding. Each participant was endowed with a Snickers candy bar and subjects bid, in a second price auction, to sell their candy bar back to the monitor. The lowest bidder won the auction and was paid the second lowest bid amount for their Snickers bar.

After the candy bar auction, participants were informed of the chance to sell their financial records in a second price auction similar to the one they had previously participated in. The farmers then completed an inventory sheet identifying the type and quality of records they possessed. For example, subjects were asked whether they maintained a balance sheet, statement of cash flows, income statement, statement of owner's equity, checkbook register, tax records, etc. For each item listed, farmers were asked if they prepared the item listed, for how many of the past five years had they prepared the item, and if the item's form was handwritten or electronic.

After the participants filled out the financial records inventory sheet, they were requested to decide on an amount, e.g., a bid, for which they were willing to sell all the documents listed on their inventory. Because the bid consists of the price at which participants were willing to sell several different types of financial information, the participants were asked to indicate, in percentage terms, the amount that reflected their value for the balance sheet, statement of cash flows, income statement, statement of owner's equity, etc.

Several key points were emphasized to the participants. They were informed that bids would be collected at several locations over a time period of several days. The lowest bidder across all locations would be contacted later to be informed if they had won. It was also stressed that the auction was not hypothetical; the winner would receive real money for his/her financial records. The instructions emphasized that the winner was expected to give all originals and copies of the records listed on their individual financial records inventory sheet. The monitor made it clear that the farmer with the lowest bid would receive in cash the overall second lowest bid price, but he/she would forfeit his records. A tax audit was the only exception to the winner of the auction regaining the right to view his/her records. As in the candy bar auction, it was explained, in detail, why the best strategy was to submit a bid exactly equal to the amount that would make the person indifferent between money and their records. It was explained that no bid was too small or too high. The participants were also told that if there was no amount of money they were willing to accept for their financial records, they could select that option on the bid sheet. An opt-out option was offered to discourage participants from writing down an artificially high bid price in "protest" and to discourage participants from leaving the bid sheet blank. Instructions are included in Appendix.

7.7.2   Results

Of the 72 participants in the study, 53 submitted positive bids, 18 people checked the box on the bid sheet indicating that there was no amount of money they would accept for their records, and one person did not complete their bid sheet. Of those people submitting bids, the range was from $100 to $2,500,000, with the average bid being $145,657 and the median being $25,575.

Because of the wide dispersion of auction bids, farmers were placed in one of four categories: bids between $0 and $14,999, between $15,000 and $75,499, and $75,000 and greater, and farmers who did not submit a bid. Table 7.12 shows the means for several record, farm, and farmer characteristics segregated by the four bid categories. Results indicate those people submitting the lowest bids spent the least amount of time, on average, preparing their records. The hypothesis that the mean time spent preparing records is the same for each of the four bid categories can be rejected at the $p = 0.01$ level according to an ANOVA test. Time spent examining records was roughly increasing in the amount bid for financial records, but the means were not statistically different across category. Table 7.12 shows a pronounced difference in the value of farm records across farm size. Farmers in the lowest bid category ($0 to $14,999) had gross farm sales 4.26 times lower ($1,015,000 vs. $238,160), on average, than farmers in the highest bid category ($75,000 and greater).

The results in Table 7.12 provide some insight into the characteristics of people choosing not to bid in the auction. Such people tended to be the least educated, the oldest, and while having relatively large farms in terms of acreage, their gross sales were relatively low (i.e., they were low performing as exhibited by relatively small gross sales per acre).

Each person's bid included their value for six potential types of records (balance sheet, statements of cash flows, income statement, statements of owner's equity, checkbook register, and tax records). After submitting their bid, farmers indicated, of the total bid amount, the percentage value attributable to each record type. By multiplying the percentages by the bid, a value for each record type can be found. For those 51 farmers who submitted a bid, results indicate that tax records, on average, were the most valuable record type with a calculated value of $39,755, followed by the balance sheet, which was worth $30,747. On average, the two least valuable types of records were the statement of cash flows and the checkbook register.

7.7.3   Conclusions

This case study illustrated how experimental auctions can be used to elicit the values for an extremely high-valued good: business records. Results indicate that, for the sample of farmers considered, farm records were extremely valuable. On average, people bid $145,657 to give up their farm financial records. Results also suggest wide diversity in valuations with bids ranging from $100 to $2,500,000. Some of this diversity is explained by the characteristics of the records and farmers: farmers who owned large terms tended to value their records more as did farmers who spent more time preparing their records.

This case study also demonstrates some challenges in implementing experimental auctions for high-valued goods. For this study, the theoretical construct of interest was willingness to accept. We were interested in the value people placed on the records they owned. The study indicated that a quarter of the

Table 7.12. *Distribution of bids for farm records and characteristics of farmers in four bid ranges*

Bid Category	Number of bids	Average time preparing records (hours/week)	Average time analyzing records (hours/week)	Average gross farm sales (thousands of dollars)	Average acreage	Average education level[a]	Average age
$75,000 and greater	15	19.00	10	1,015.00	2,533	4.27	43.87
$15,000–$75,499	17	21.47	9.12	1,050.00	2,571	3.76	43.47
$0–14,999	19	8.95	6.32	238.16	689	4.16	50.95
No submitted bid	18	13.33	8.61	633.33	2,311	3.50	52.11
P-value[b]		0.01	0.56	0.01	0.01	0.41	0.10

[a] 1 = high school credit, 2 = high school graduate, 3 = college credit, 4 = college graduate, 5 = graduate credit, 6 = graduate degree.
[b] P-value from an ANOVA test of the hypothesis that the mean value of the variable in the column is the same for all bid ranges.

bidders were not willing to sell their records. Such a finding is difficult to reconcile in that there is likely some amount of money that would make a person indifferent to having their records and not having them. What the result likely implies is that some people either do not understand the mechanism or are "protesting" the auction as conducted. That low-performing, older, and less-educated farmers were less likely to submit a bid is consistent with this hypothesis.

This case study illustrates that experimental auction methods need not be limited to low-valued goods or food. Despite the relatively high frequency of no-bidders, bidding behavior conformed to *a priori* expectations, i.e., farms with higher gross sales valued their records more highly, suggesting a reasonable degree of validity. This case study also demonstrated how experimental auctions can be used to value a relatively complex good comprised of many sub-components and offered one method for separately valuing each sub-component.

7.8   Controversial goods I: demand for genetically modified food in three countries

The use of biotechnology in food production is one of the most controversial issues in modern agriculture. On one side of the debate are life science companies and US agricultural producers, who point to the benefits of GM crops such as a) reduced production costs resulting in lower food prices for consumers; b) reduced use of pesticides and herbicides resulting in greater biodiversity and fewer health and environmental problems; and c) the ability to better feed a world with an ever-growing population by increasing production at home and creating new crops that can grow in arid climates.

On the other side are consumer and environmental activist groups. They argue that a) use of GM crops can create "super weeds" and "super bugs" that will wreak havoc on natural habitats when insects develop resistance and when GM crops cross-pollinate with native vegetation; b) the long-term health consequences of humans eating GM crops are unknown; c) some consumers are allergic to new genes introduced into foods; and d) the benefits from introduction of biotechnology are unfairly distributed across the marketing channel, primarily being concentrated with large multinational agribusiness firms.

Interestingly, the two largest economies in the world, the US and the European Union (EU) have taken different stances on the issue. In the US, almost 90% of soybean acres and over half of corn acres were planted with GM seeds in 2005 (USDA NASS). Further, no mandatory labeling laws presently exist in the US. In contrast, the EU has upheld a moratorium on accepting GM crops since 1998 and imposes mandatory labels on all products containing GM ingredients.

Virtually all major food retailers in the EU have stopped carrying GM products, essentially banning GM food from the European market.

The EU contends that differences in consumer concerns for food safety across the Atlantic justify the precautionary policies regarding GM food. But it is not readily apparent that EU consumers *are* more concerned about GM foods than are US consumers. US agricultural producer groups argue that the more restrictive labeling policies, moratoriums on approving new GM crops, and grocery store bans on GM food are simply a way for the EU to protect domestic agricultural producers from international competition. The US recently filed a complaint with the World Trade Organization over the EU's stance on GM foods. Nevertheless, EU consumers might truly have different preferences for GM foods than consumers in the US. If so, the interesting issue is why these differences exist and how these differences should be addressed in international trade negotiations.

Although some studies have compared EU and US consumer preferences for GM food, the analysis has relied on hypothetical surveys that asked simple scale questions or elicited hypothetical choices (e.g., Gaskell *et al.*). To fully document whether differences exist, what is needed is a study involving real financial incentives and economic commitments.

7.8.1   Experiment

We draw from the data reported in Lusk *et al.* (2004a, 2005, and 2006). In their studies, an experimental market was constructed and they elicited the minimum amount of compensation randomly recruited female shoppers demanded to consume a GM rather than a non-GM food. Experimental sessions were held with over 160 individuals in three diverse US locations: Jacksonville, FL, Long Beach, CA, and Lubbock, TX; and with over 200 individuals in two EU locations: Reading, England and Grenoble, France.

In each of the five locations, market research companies were hired to randomly recruit individuals for participation in a "food preference study" by offering $50 to attend a one-hour research session. Several sessions were held in each location and about twenty people were assigned to a session. The US locations were selected to provide diversity in geography, population, and culture. The selected EU locations are roughly similar to Lubbock, TX in that they were towns of relatively similar population, are located in agricultural areas, and possess relatively large universities. Recruitment was restricted to females because we were interested in food preferences and females are, overwhelmingly, the primary grocery shoppers in most households (see Katsara *et al.*, 2001). Limiting the sample to females creates a more homogeneous sample across the geographic locations allowing for a stronger test of the location effect. Age restrictions were implemented to ensure that a disproportionate number of students or retirees, with relatively low opportunity costs of time, would not dominate the sample. Subjects were originally contacted by phone and offered $50 to participate in the study. Several experimental sessions were conducted in each city.

Once subjects arrived at a research session, they were assigned a random number, were read a brief informational statement about GM foods, and were asked to complete a survey that contained questions about knowledge of, and attitudes toward, GM foods. After describing the auction mechanism and conducting non-hypothetical practice auctions with candy bars, subjects were endowed with a non-GM cookie and were asked to bid, in an incentive compatible fifth price auction, the minimum amount they had to be paid to exchange their non-GM food for a GM food, with full knowledge that consumption of the food was required at the end of the auction. The survey and experimental instructions were originally written in US English. The survey and instructions were then translated into French (and adjusted for differences between US and British English). The survey and instructions were back-translated into US English. The original survey and the back-translated surveys were compared for discrepancies and appropriate changes were made.

Several design features of the auctions reported in Lusk *et al.* (2004a, 2005, and 2006) are worthy of more comment. First, because both GM and non-GM products are available for sale in the US, whereas only non-GM food is available in the EU, they chose to use the "endow and upgrade approach" with a consumption requirement which allows them to control for the differences in price and availability of GM goods outside the experiment. Second, chocolate chip cookies (referred to as biscuits in the EU) were chosen as the unit of analysis because the good is widely consumed in the US and EU and forcing consumption of this product was practical in a lab setting. This wouldn't have been possible with a variety of other goods (e.g., vegetable oil or raw potatoes), and we were able to readily obtain comparable GM and non-GM cookies. Third, as opposed to many applications using auctions to elicit homegrown values, they elicited consumer willingness-to-accept (WTA) compensation to consume a GM food rather than willingness-to-pay (WTP) to consume a non-GM food. This approach was taken because, historically, consumers have been "endowed" with non-GM foods and with the advent of biotechnology, consumers are now being asked what it will take to accept GM foods. Further, given the desire to use a consumption requirement, it was believed that had subjects been endowed with a GM food and bid to "upgrade" to a non-GM food, a large frequency of people might object and withdraw from the experiment. The WTA approach also avoids a problem frequently observed in WTP auctions, where many zero bids are present. In a WTA setting, zero bidding is less problematic as a subject would not bid zero in a WTA auction unless they truly placed no value on the traded good or attribute.

Fourth, the fifth price auction was used for several reasons: a) it is theoretically incentive compatible; b) the market price is endogenously determined and subjects could incorporate feedback from the market with this mechanism; and c) it should engage both people with high and low values as a non-trivial number of people will "win" the auction. Finally, the experiment involved people bidding to exchange their endowed non-GM cookie for a GM cookie over ten bidding rounds with the market price being posted at the end of each round (one round was randomly selected at the end as binding). Given that most participants would be unfamiliar with GM food, it was felt that repeated rounds were needed to promote learning about the mechanism and the good. This approach also permitted an investigation into the effect of information on valuations by comparing naïve bids in the first five bidding rounds to bids in last five rounds, where different information shocks were introduced (see Lusk *et al.*, 2004a).

The experimental auction proceeded as follows:

Step 1. Participants were given a free chocolate chip cookie (referred to as a biscuit in the EU). The cookie was in a transparent package containing a label that clearly indicated the cookie contained no GM ingredients.

Step 2. Participants were shown an otherwise identical cookie that was labelled as being made with GM ingredients.

Step 3. Subjects wrote on a bid sheet the least amount of money they were willing to accept to exchange their cookie for the cookie containing GM ingredients.

Step 4. Once all bids were recorded, the monitor collected the bid sheets.

Step 5. The ID numbers of the four lowest bidders were posted in front of the room along with the fifth lowest bid amount (the market price).

Step 6. Steps 3 through 5 were repeated for nine additional rounds.

Step 7. At the completion of the tenth round, a random number was drawn to determine the binding round.

Step 8. Once the binding round was determined, the four winning bidders were paid the fifth lowest bid amount to exchange their cookie for the cookie made with GM ingredients. All other participants kept their cookie made without GM ingredients.

Step 9. All subjects ate the cookie they possessed at the end of Step 8.

7.8.2   Results

Table 7.13 reports the summary statistics of the bids in rounds 1 and 5. The median bid varies greatly by location. In round 5, the median bid from England is over twice that in any of the US locations and the median bid in France is

Table 7.13. *Summary statistics of willingness to accept distribution by location and auction round*

Willingness-to-accept statistic	Location				
	Lubbock TX, USA	Long Beach CA, USA	Jack'ville FL, USA	Reading England	Grenoble France
Round 1					
Low bid	$0.00	$0.00	$0.00	$0.00	$0.00
20% quantile	$0.03	$0.10	$0.05	$0.16	$0.10
Median bid	$0.23	$0.50	$0.12	$0.71	$1.57
80% quantile	$1.00	$5.00	$0.50	$4.74	$9.80
High bid[a]	$100.00	$100.00	$2.00	$158.00	$98.00
Average	$2.44	$5.23	$0.33	$4.82	$8.51
Standard deviation	$11.91	$16.44	$0.43	$17.53	$17.08
Round 5					
Low bid	$0.00	$0.00	$0.00	$0.00	$0.00
20% quantile	$0.00	$0.05	$0.02	$0.11	$0.10
Median bid	$0.10	$0.20	$0.05	$0.40	$1.96
80% quantile	$0.50	$1.00	$0.15	$1.58	$11.76
High bid[a]	$100.00	$100.00	$2.00	$158.00	$98.00
Average	$2.13	$4.03	$0.19	$3.58	$6.95
Standard deviation	$11.84	$16.52	$0.41	$17.67	$13.32

[a] One observation in Florida and two observations in France were in excess of $10,000 and were removed from the analysis.

almost ten times that in any US location. The non-parametric Mann-Whitney and Kolmogorov-Smirnov test both indicate that bid distributions in the two EU locations are significantly different than in any of the US locations. The test results also reject the equality of bidding behavior between France and England and between California and the other two US locations, suggesting strong within-continent heterogeneity as well. In every location, the mean is much larger than the median, suggesting the data are highly skewed and are affected by a few outliers. Data in Table 7.13 show that median WTA bids fell from round 1 to round 5 in all locations except France and the mean bid fell across bidding rounds in all locations.

Histograms showing the distributions of round 5 bids are reported in Figure 7.2 along with plots of exponential distributions fit to the data in each location. A much higher frequency of people bid $0 to $0.25 in the three US locations than in the EU locations. The percentage of consumers that bid exactly zero in round five was 23%, 11%, 13%, 3%, and 6% in Lubbock, Long Beach, Jacksonville, Reading, and Grenoble. In all locations, there were a few people that bid more than $5 to exchange cookies; however, this percentage was much

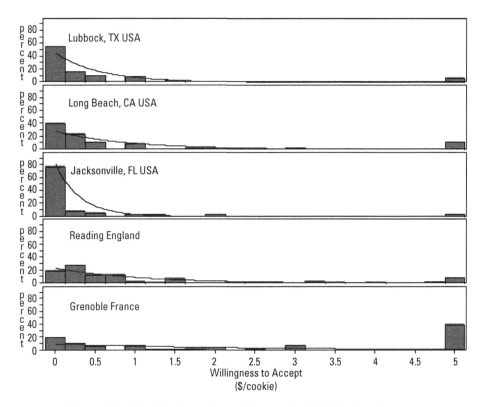

Figure 7.2   Distribution of round five auction bids by location

higher in France than in any of the other locations. In France, more than 30% of people bid more than $5 as compared to only about 8% in England and 2% to 5% in the US locations. The take home message from the data in Table 7.13 and Figure 7.2 is that consumers in the European locations demanded significantly greater levels of compensation to consume the GM cookie than did the US consumers.

Having established that bid distributions are different across location, the interesting question is why such differences might exist. In the survey people filled out before the auction, they were asked a variety of questions that related to factors hypothesized to influence consumer acceptance of GM foods including: subjective and objective knowledge of biotechnology, level of trust in information about biotechnology from the government and activist groups, perceptions of the benefits and risks of biotechnology, and general attitudes toward the environment, food, and technology. To determine how these variables affect WTA, quantile regression methods were used (Koenker and Hallock, 2001; Koenker and Bassett, 1978). As shown in previous tables and figures, there are a few "large" outliers. As is well known, such outliers have a pronounced influence in typical conditional mean (e.g., ordinary least squares) regressions. The median

Table 7.14. *Effect of attitudes and nationality on willingness to accept: median regression estimates*

Variable	Variable definition	Estimates
Constant		2.443**
		(0.328)
Age	Age in years	−0.013**
		(0.004)
Education	1 if obtained university undergraduate degree or higher; 0 otherwise	−0.014
		(0.082)
Income	1 if household income is greater than $50,000/year; 0 otherwise	0.003
		(0.076)
Homemaker	1 if full time homemaker; 0 otherwise	−0.004
		(0.109)
Child	1 if children under the age of 16 living at home; 0 otherwise	−0.153**
		(0.078)
Subjective knowledge	Knowledge of facts and issues concerning genetic modification in food production (1 = not at all knowledgeable; 9 = extremely knowledgeable)	0.035 (0.025)
Objective knowledge 1	Response to True/False Question: Ordinary fruit does not contain genes, but genetically modified fruit does (1 = correct answer; 0 = incorrect answer or don't know)	0.117 (0.074)
Objective knowledge 2	Response to True/False Question: It is impossible to transfer animal genes to plants (1 = correct answer; 0 = incorrect answer or don't know)	−0.031 (0.078)
Government trust	Level of trust in information about genetic modification in food production from government agencies such as the USDA and FDA (1 = strongly distrust; 9 = strongly trust)	−0.021 (0.018)
Activist trust	Level of trust in information about genetic modification in food production from activist groups such as Greenpeace (1 = strongly distrust; 9 = strongly trust)	0.037** (0.017)
Risk/benefit	In general I believe the use of genetic modification in food production is (1 = risky; 9 = beneficial)	−0.086** (0.021)
Environment 1	When humans interfere with nature, it often produces disastrous consequences (1 = strongly disagree; 9 = strongly agree)	−0.013 (0.019)
Environment 2	Mankind is severely abusing the environment (1 = strongly disagree; 9 = strongly agree)	0.020 (0.017)
New food	I don't trust new foods (1 = strongly disagree; 9 = strongly agree)	0.037** (0.017)
Food quality	Quality is decisive for me in purchasing foods (1 = strongly disagree; 9 = strongly agree)	−0.019 (0.022)
Natural food	I usually aim to eat natural food (1 = strongly disagree; 9 = strongly agree)	0.025 (0.019)

Table 7.14. (*cont*).

Variable	Variable definition	Estimates
Technology 1	The degree of civilization of a people can be measured from the degree of its technological development (1 = strongly disagree; 9 = strongly agree)[a]	−0.032* (0.018)
Technology 2	In this country we are probably better off than ever, thanks to the tremendous progress in technology (1 = strongly disagree; 9 = strongly agree)[a]	0.022 (0.021)
Lubbock, TX[b]	1 if resident of Lubbock, TX USA; 0 otherwise	−1.456** (0.123)
Long Beach, CA[b]	1 if resident of Long Beach, CA USA; 0 otherwise	−1.466** (0.142)
Jacksonville, FL[b]	1 if resident of Jacksonville, FL USA; 0 otherwise	−1.515** (0.153)
Reading, England[b]	1 if resident of Reading England; 0 otherwise	−1.321** (0.130)

Note: dependent variable is round five willingness to accept bid.
Number of observations = 346.
One (*) and two (**) asterisks represent 0.10 and 0.05 levels of statistical significance, respectively.
[a] Numbers in parentheses are standard errors estimated via bootstrapping.
[b] Locational dummy variables relative to Grenoble, France.

is much less influenced by outliers. As such, Table 7.14 reports the results of a median regression. In a median regression, parameters are chosen to minimize the sum of *absolute* errors, which can be contrasted with OLS parameter estimates which result from minimizing the sum of *squared* errors.

Reported coefficients can be interpreted as the impact of a one-unit change in the covariate on median WTA holding other covariates constant. For example, results indicate that a one-year increase in age is associated with a $0.013 decline in median WTA. The only other demographic variable to significantly influence median WTA is whether children are living at home; median WTA of those with children was $0.15 lower than those without. As expected, perceptions of benefits and risks of GM food strongly influenced WTA: the lower the level of perceived risk, the lower the compensation demanded. People that were less trusting of new foods and less optimistic about technology, demanded more compensation to consume the GM cookie at the median.

The last rows report the effect of location on WTA, holding constant all the other factors in the table. Even after controlling for differences in age, income, trust, risk perceptions, and attitudes toward food, the environment, and technology, consumers in the US and England had significantly lower median WTA than French consumers. Estimates also suggest median WTA from the three US locations is also significantly different than median English WTA. An interesting question that arises is whether, and to what extent, differences in levels of demographic and attitudinal variables explain differences in WTA across location. Recognizing that the estimated location dummy variables show the effect of "location" when the levels of age, education, risk/benefit, etc. are held at the same levels across location, it is clear that the relatively large magnitudes of the estimated dummy variables imply that there is still a significant degree of unexplained variability in WTA across location that is not accounted for by differences in levels of demographics, knowledge, trust, and general attitudes, as measured in this study. In other words, if the estimated dummy variables were zero, differences in explanatory variables across location would fully explain unconditional differences in WTA across location. The regression model, however, can explain some of the unconditional difference in WTA across location. Comparing the "raw" unconditional bids from round 5 to the estimated dummy variables in Table 7.14 provides an indication of the extent to which differences in independent variables explain the differences in unconditional WTA across location. For example, the unconditional median bid (which does not hold constant differences in any explanatory variable) in Lubbock TX is $1.86 lower than that in France. However, the conditional median bid (i.e., the estimated dummy variable) in TX is only $1.46 lower than in France. Thus, differences in levels of demographics, knowledge, trust, and general attitudes, as measured in this study, explain $0.40 (or 21.7%) of the unconditional median difference in WTA across TX and France. Similarly, differences in explanatory variables across location explain 16.7% of the unconditional median difference in WTA across California and France and 20.7% of the unconditional median difference in WTA across Florida and France.

Although we are only able to explain roughly one-fifth of the difference in unconditional median WTA across the US and France, we find stronger results for England. Calculations imply that the model explains 55.0%, 27.5%, and 44.6% of the unconditional median difference in WTA across England and Texas, California, and Florida, respectively. These findings suggest that while differences in levels of demographics, trust, attitudes about food and technology, and perceptions of risks and benefits explain some of the variability in WTA across location, there is still much to learn about what drives differences in values for GM food across the US and EU, especially with regard to France.

7.8.3   Conclusions

Some US producer groups claim that the precautionary policies taken by the EU toward GM food represent non-tariff trade barriers. One key piece of information needed to help resolve this conflict is information about consumer demand for GM foods in the US and EU. Results of this study tend to lend credence to the argument made by EU regulatory agencies that Europeans are concerned about the new technology. The welfare analysis conducted by Lusk *et al.* (2005) using these auction bids implies, under a set of assumptions about prices and segregation costs, that, on average, consumers in the three US locations have benefited from the introduction of GM food even without a label, whereas consumers in the two European locations would have, on average, suffered welfare losses due to the advent of GM food had labeling not been implemented. Their results show that a labeling policy would be welfare-reducing in the US, with the opposite occurring in Europe. These findings correspond well with the policies actually enacted in the US and Europe.

7.9 Controversial goods II: irradiation

In two recent controversies over food irradiation and genetic modification, the public has had to decide between assertions made about food safety by advocacy groups and by scientific experts. In both cases the weight of the scientific evidence suggested these foods were safe, and in both cases the typical response from advocates was that "no-one knows what effect genetic organisms (or food irradiation) will have on our health" (Organic Consumers). These statements need not be mutually contradictory because the scientific evidence, properly evaluated, cannot guarantee that a particular food is completely safe. The general public must believe these statements are at odds.

7.9.1 *Experiment*

We now examine the experimental design of Fox *et al.* (2002) that explores how consumers respond to this type of controversy. They consider how favorable and unfavorable information about food-irradiation affects willingness to pay (WTP) for a reduction in the chance that *trichinella* is present in pork. The favorable description emphasizes the safety and benefits of the process while the unfavorable description stresses the potential risks. They elicit WTP values for the upgrade from typical pork to irradiated pork and examined the changes in elicited values following the introduction of new information about the technology. Values are elicited using a second price auction in which the binding trial is chosen at random at the end of the experiment.

From a randomly selected sample of 200 households, eighty-seven primary food shoppers were recruited to participate in a "consumer economics experiment." In return for participating, subjects were offered $40.00. No other information about the experiment was provided to avoid participation bias related to irradiation, or any other feature of the experiment. Participants were assigned to ten groups ranging in size from six to twelve. There were three treatments: the first examined the effect of positive information about irradiation (POS), the second examined the effect of negative information (NEG), and the third examined the effect of providing both positive and negative information simultaneously (BOTH). Two groups each were assigned to the POS and NEG treatments with the remaining six groups assigned to the BOTH treatment. All experiments were conducted in a food taste-testing lab at Iowa State University.

The experiment contained several controls to ensure that participants understood the auction procedures and to elicit *ex ante* and *ex post* attitudes. Initially, subjects received the following descriptions of two pork sandwiches:

- *Type I*. This is a typical pork sandwich. The pork in this sandwich has a typical chance of being contaminated with *trichinella*.
- *Type II*. The pork in this sandwich has been treated by irradiation to control *trichinella*. Because of this treatment we can guarantee that this pork will not cause trichinosis.

Subjects were informed that they had each been endowed with a typical pork sandwich (*Type I*), and that an irradiated (*Type II*) pork sandwich would be sold using a second price, sealed-bid auction in which the highest bidder wins and pays the second highest bid. The auction had ten rounds (or trials) of bidding, each with equal probability of being binding. In each trial, the monitor publicly displayed the identification number of the highest bidder and three bids: the second highest, average, and lowest bid. Subjects were informed that in order to complete the experiment and earn their participation fee they would have to consume, at the conclusion of the experiment, either: a) the typical pork sandwich which they had been given; or b) the irradiated pork sandwich which was available for purchase in the auction. Before the auction began, the monitor provided each subject with the following "neutral" description of the food irradiation process:

The U.S. Food and Drug Administration (FDA) has recently approved the use of ionizing radiation to control Trichinella in pork products and Salmonella in poultry. Based on its evaluation of several toxicity studies, the FDA concluded that irradiation of food products at approved levels did not present a toxicological hazard to consumers nor did it adversely effect the nutritional value of the product. Irradiation of pork products at approved levels results in a 10,000 fold reduction in the viability of *Trichinella* organisms present in the meat. The forms of ionizing energy used in food processing include gamma rays, x-rays, and accelerated electrons. Ionizing energy works by breaking chemical bonds in organic molecules. When a sufficient number of critical bonds are split in the bacteria and other pests in food, the organisms are killed. The energy levels of the gamma rays, accelerated electrons, and x-rays legally permitted for processing food do not induce measurable radioactivity in food. This description is based on a review of the scientific literature on food irradiation.

Subjects were provided with a description of the symptoms of trichinosis and were informed that the objective odds of contracting trichinosis from the *Type I* sandwich were approximately 1 in 2,628,000. The first five rounds of bidding (trials) were then conducted, with the second highest, mean, and lowest bid publicly posted following each trial. Following the fifth bidding trial, we provided the favorable description of irradiation to the groups in the POS treatment ($n = 18$), the unfavorable description to those in the NEG treatment ($n = 19$), and both, simultaneously, to those in the BOTH treatment ($n = 50$). Abbreviated versions of the favorable and unfavorable descriptions are provided below.

Favorable description

Food irradiation (also called ion pasteurization) is a process that destroys harmful bacteria and pathogens by treating foods with ionizing radiation. Food irradiation has been shown to be highly effective in destroying bacteria and parasites responsible for food poisoning. Extensive research has proven that irradiation is a safe and reliable process, and it has been approved by the Food and Drug Administration, the American Medical Association, and the World Health Organization. Each year as many as 9,000 people die in the US from food-borne illness. Millions more suffer short term illness due to pathogens such as salmonella, listeria and e.coli. By eliminating these pathogens from food, irradiation can help to greatly reduce the number of food-borne illnesses. This description is based on information supplied by the American Council on Science and Health, a consumer education association.

Unfavorable description

Food irradiation is a process whereby food is exposed to radioactive materials, and receives as much as 300,000 rads of radiation – the equivalent of 30 million chest x-rays – in order to extend the shelf life of the food and kill insects and bacteria. While it is unlikely that food products themselves will become radioactive, irradiation results in the creation of chemicals called radiolytic products, some of which are known carcinogens. Studies have also suggested that irradiation may be linked to cancer and birth defects. Food irradiation can kill most of the pathogenic bacteria present in food, but so can proper cooking. Food irradiation was developed in the 1950s by the Atomic Energy Commission. The objective was to seek potential uses for the byproducts of nuclear weapons production. Today's food irradiation industry is a private, for-profit business enterprise with ties to the US nuclear weapons and nuclear power industries. This description is based on information supplied by Food and Water, Inc., a consumer advocacy group.

7.9.2   Results

Figure 7.3 shows the effect of new information about irradiation in the POS and BOTH treatments on the bids for irradiated pork. Bids in trials 1 through 5 in

Table 7.15. *Effect of information on relative safety assessments*

| Safety of irradiated pork relative to typical pork. | Information treatment | | | | | |
| | Positive | | Negative | | Both | |
Assessment –>	Pre	Post	Pre	Post	Pre	Post
Far safer	1	6	6	0	19	8
Somewhat safer	12	10	7	1	20	11
About as safe	4	2	6	10	9	15
Somewhat less safe	1	0	0	4	2	11
Far less safe	0	0	0	4	0	5
Total	18	18	19	19	50	50

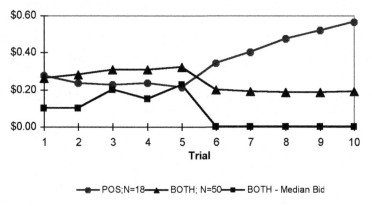

Figure 7.3   Effect of information on bids for irradiated pork

each treatment are based on common information about irradiation – i.e., the "neutral description" provided before any bids were submitted. To simplify the figure we omitted the NEG treatment – those results were as expected with bids for irradiated pork declining and with about 90% of participants bidding zero at the end of the experiment. The favorable information also has the expected effect and Figure 7.3 shows the increase in bidding following trial 5. But when the same favorable and unfavorable descriptions are presented simultaneously, the net impact is a significant reduction in bids for the irradiated product, with the median bid falling to zero.

In addition to bidding for the irradiated pork, participants were also asked to record their perception of its safety relative to the typical product. Table 7.15 summarizes those relative safety assessments both before and after the provision of new information. The favorable information reinforces the perception that the irradiated product is safe: following its presentation sixteen of eighteen subjects rate irradiated pork "safer" than typical pork, with 6 rating it "far safer." In the NEG treatment, participants downgrade their safety assessments with only one of nineteen continuing to rate the irradiated product as "safer" and eight of the nineteen (42%) rating it "somewhat less safe" or "far less safe." In the BOTH treatment the net effect is also a downgrading in the relative safety assessment. Prior to receiving the favorable and unfavorable descriptions thirty-nine of fifty (78%) participants rated irradiated pork either "safer" or "far safer." After reading the information, nineteen (38%) considered the irradiated product safer, and 32% considered it less safe.

The results show the effect of simultaneous provision of positive and negative information is qualitatively similar to that of providing only negative information. We tested this hypothesis by modeling the effect of information as a function of participant characteristics and experimental treatment. To create the dependent variable for the analysis we categorized the net effect of new information on each individual's perception of irradiation as positive (value $= 1$), neutral (value $= 0$), or negative (value $= -1$) depending on the change in bid and safety assessment. We regressed that categorical variable on a set of explanatory variables that included the participant's age, gender, education and prior attitude to irradiation in an ordered probit model. Table 7.16 reports the results. The only significant coefficient in the model is that associated with the POS treatment, but the interesting result is that the coefficient for the NEG treatment is relatively small and statistically insignificant. Because the base treatment in the model is BOTH, this suggests that the effect of providing both the favorable and unfavorable descriptions had essentially the same effect as that of providing only the unfavorable description.

7.9.3   Conclusions

The tendency to place more weight on negative information has potentially important implications for public policy. For processes such as food irradiation, genetic modification, and the use of growth hormones, even though the scientific evidence is favorable, claims by opponents, even if they are inaccurate and only suggest potential risks, will tend to reduce consumer demand. Because the media tends to provide both sides of every story, the negative descriptions created by advocacy groups tend to be widely available. In the US, even with favorable scientific and regulatory opinion about the safety and wholesomeness of irradiated foods, industry has been slow to introduce the process because it fears the impact of inaccurate claims on consumer demand. The direct implication for public policy is that if new food technologies are generally regarded to be in the public interest, then the anti-technology messages may reduce welfare.

Table 7.16. *Effect of new information*

Variables	Variable mean	Ordered probit
Constant		−1.04
		(0.766)
Prior attitude	0.08	0.487
1 = positive,		(0.344)
0 = neutral;		
−1 = negative		
Gender:	0.33	0.126
Male = 1		(0.370)
Age: Categorical	5.82	−0.126*
2 = 20–24;		(0.074)
4 = 30–34;		
6 = 40–44;		
8 = > 50; etc		
Education: Categorical	5.53	0.166
3 = High school grad		(0.101)
4 = Some trade school		
5 = Some college		
6 = BS/BA,		
9 = Ph.D, etc		
Positive treatment	N = 18	2.599***
		(0.472)
Negative treatment	N = 19	−0.184
		(0.469)
Correct predictions		74%

Note: * denotes significance at the 10% level, ** at the 5% level, and *** at the 1% level. N = 87.

An even larger issue is the tradeoff between the free speech rights of opponents of new technology compared with the potential loss in general welfare when promising new technologies are halted. The results also indicate the enormous responsibilities of those in the media who report on these controversies. If consumer opinion is sensitive to negative information by consumer advocates, it is likely they are sensitive to negative claims about food innovations made by governments – even if scientists, perhaps the government's own scientists, disagree. In that context, recognition of consumer preferences as legitimate grounds for protectionist trade policies may provide an incentive for governments to cast doubt on new technologies when the goal is to protect domestic producers. That scenario poses a legitimate threat to the expansion of world trade.

One open question is how such lab experiments on irradiated foods compare to retail behavior in the wilds. People in the lab still know that they are being monitored in a stylized setting, and the range of alternative purchases is more limited than in a retail setting. In response, Shogren *et al.* (1999) compare the similarity of lab valuation choices to retail store choices for irradiation. They also compare choices made in hypothetical surveys. All subjects came from the same small college town and made choices between typical chicken breasts versus chicken breasts irradiated to reduce the risk of food-borne pathogens.

Their results from both the survey and experimental market suggested significantly higher levels of acceptability of irradiated chicken than in the retail trial at an equal or discounted price for irradiation. Consumer choices were more similar across market settings at a price premium for irradiation. They observed that in a mail survey and a lab experiment, both of which included information about irradiation, 80% of participants preferred irradiated to non-irradiated chicken breasts when they were offered at the same price. When the irradiated product was offered at a higher price, the survey and experimental results predicted market share in a subsequent retail trial remarkably well. About thirty percent of survey respondents, experimental market participants, and shoppers were willing to pay a ten percent premium for the irradiated chicken, and fifteen to twenty percent were willing to pay a 20% premium. Retail purchases involved payment of real money for real products within an environment where thousands of products competed for the consumer's dollar. Any attempt to collect consumer information in a retail setting was liable to interfere with the realism of the market itself. The goal of the retail setting was to establish the most realistic baseline possible against which one could judge the lab or survey. Perfectly simulating a retail experience in the lab or a survey so as to control every nuance is unattainable. Rather the goal should be to compare lab and survey choices relative to a real world baseline. The research program that emerges for future work is to explore how comprehensive the lab or survey environments must be to come closer to replicate an actual market outcome.

7.10   Controversial goods III: food from animals treated with growth hormones

During the 1990s, the commercialization of some biotechnical products, such as bovine somatotropin (bST) and porcine somatotropin (pST), was delayed at the final stages of the Federal Drug Administration (FDA) approval process and by legislation designed in part to appease consumer concern. Consumers heard negative messages about bST, for example, in the "Stop bST" campaign by Ben and Jerry's ice cream. Although most scientists agree that milk produced with the aid of bST is completely safe, some groups, such as the Foundation on Economic Trends, contend that it poses potential health hazards.

The degree of concern consumers have about bST and other biotechnical products has been difficult to quantify. Smith and Warland (1992) summarized the results of several consumer surveys regarding beliefs about bST. They found that 56.7% of the survey respondents were negatively inclined toward bST. This negative reaction is not surprising, given that most people know little about bST; furthermore, Smith and Warland (1992) believe the contexts in which the surveys were conducted predisposed respondents somewhat negatively toward bST.

The situation faced by an interviewee in a survey differs from that which potential buyers will experience in retail settings. Many new products have both positive and negative attributes (cheaper or leaner versus biotechnological) that create ambiguity for consumers. Survey methods are hypothetical and the relative lack of information and time that constrain the survey approach makes it difficult to elicit accurate beliefs and can bias responses depending on how questions are asked. For example, a study by Pitman-Moore, a company that has developed a commercial pST, found that an average consumer would pay more for leaner pST-treated pork than for fattier pork from an untreated animal. In contrast, a study by Hoban and Burkhardt (1991) found that 45% of their respondents were very concerned, and 37% were somewhat concerned, about eating genetically engineered meat products.

7.10.1   Experimental design

Buhr *et al.* (1993) and Fox *et al.* (1994, 1995) constructed a series of experimental auctions to investigate consumers' awareness of and beliefs about growth hormones, pST and bST, and to examine the effect of providing consumers with information about the hormone. Consider here the Fox *et al.* (1995) experimental design regarding bST in milk production. Their experiments used a second price, sealed-bid auction mechanism and repeated trials to allow for learning. Each experiment consisted of two stages. The objective of stage 1 was to familiarize participants with the auction procedure. Each subject was initially endowed with a candy bar and $3. A different candy bar was then auctioned using the Vickrey method with five trials, one of which would be binding. At the end of stage 1, a number was randomly drawn to determine the binding trial and the highest bidder in that trial then exchanged his or her candy bar for the different bar and paid the posted price (the second highest bid in that trial). This transaction had the effect of making participants aware that their actions had monetary consequences.

In stage 2, each participant was initially endowed with a type 1 (bST) glass of milk and $15. A type 2 (normal) glass of milk was then auctioned. Participants were provided with the following descriptions: type 1: this glass of milk was produced by a typical dairy cow that received synthetic bST in research trials; type 2: this milk was produced by a typical dairy cow. Twenty trials were conducted. For the first ten trials, participants bid based on their pre-existing perceptions of the type 1 and type 2 milk. After the tenth trial, the following description of bST was provided:

Bovine somatotropin is a protein produced in the pituitary gland of a dairy cow that regulates and stimulates milk production. Through advances in genetic engineering, synthetic bST can now be manufactured using recombinant DNA technology. The bST is injected into cows to increase milk yields. The frequency of these injections may range from once a day to once every 14 to 28 days. Dairy cows treated with artificial bST have produced from 10 to 25% more milk in experimental trials. They have also shown an increase in feeding efficiency. The amount of bST in milk from treated cows has not been shown to differ from that found naturally in milk. However, there is concern by some people that too little research has been conducted to ensure the safety of milk and dairy products from cows treated with bST. Bovine somatotropin is currently under regulatory review and is expected to be approved soon by the Food and Drug Administration.

After twenty trials, a number was randomly drawn to determine which trial would be binding and who would purchase the type 2 milk. Subjects were required to drink the milk that they possessed at the end of the auction. The experiments were carried out at five universities in Iowa, Arkansas, Massachusetts, and California. Fifteen undergraduate students from a range of degree programs participated in an auction at each university. Because undergraduate students comprise a specialized segment of the milk consuming population, results are not generalizable to the results to the general population. Care was taken to replicate the experiments as closely as possible in a similar environment at all five locations. All experiments were conducted by the same investigator.

7.10.2   Results and discussion

Figure 7.4 shows the mean bid of each trial in all five experiments. The mean bid over the first ten (uninformed) trials was highest in urban California at $1.25. Over trials eleven through twenty, the highest mean bid was in Massachusetts at $0.80. The first bidding trial in each experiment represents the respondents' initial preferences for bST milk given the "compulsion to eat" factor. In trial 1, the mean bid at four of the locations was between $0.31 and $0.42 with the lowest mean bid of $0.12 at the rural California location. Through trials 1 to 10, the average bid increased in the urban California and Massachusetts experiments, indicating that many of those participants wanted to avoid the bST milk. At trial ten, the average bid in urban California was $1.63; in Massachusetts, it was $1.01. At the other locations the average bid also increased between trials one and ten but to a much lesser extent. This difference may reflect the level of prior knowledge of bST; in the urban California experiment, none of the participants indicated that they had heard of bST, but, in rural California four of fifteen had heard of it.

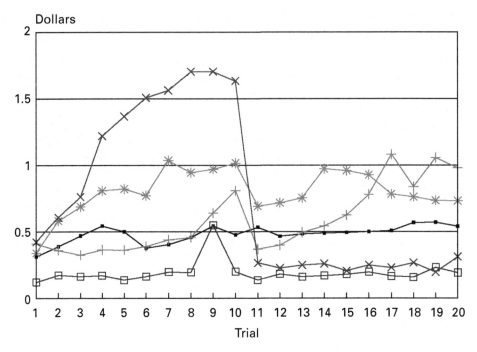

Figure 7.4 Average willingness to pay for "non-BST" milk in Iowa (■), Arkansas (+), Massachusetts (x), California (rural) (□), California (urban) (×)

With the exception of Iowa, the average bid fell between trials ten and eleven. The drop in bids was greatest in urban California and was also large for Arkansas and Massachusetts. This drop was most likely the result of the information provided after trial ten. Participants were informed that milk from cows treated with bST was very similar in composition to milk currently available at retail outlets and that the FDA was expected to approve bST in the near future. The effect of this information on the average bid of the urban California participants exceeded $1.00. People from urban California had the least prior information of any group of participants, and their behavior demonstrates the potential sensitivity of consumers to the way in which information is presented. The description of bST was a scientifically-balanced representation of the facts and it served to eliminate almost completely the concerns among these uninformed participants.

The behavior of the Massachusetts subjects was quite different. These participants may have had more exposure to negative publicity about bST (e.g., the Ben and Jerry's campaign, which focused on the northeastern United States), and had formed opinions they retained in spite of the information provided. Neither the rural California nor Iowa experiments demonstrated any participant sensitivity to the information, which was to be expected as these were

Table 7.17. *Frequency distribution of bids at trial 20*

Bid($)	California urban	California rural	Massachusetts	Arkansas	Iowa
0	6	9	6	7	12
0.01 to 0.25	4	0	2	1	0
0.26 to 0.50	2	4	0	1	0
0.51 to 0.75	1	2	0	1	0
0.76 to 1.00	1	0	0	1	0
≥ 1.00	1	0	7	4	3

students from Land-Grant universities (Iowa State University and University of California-Davis) where agricultural issues receive more attention.

Table 7.17 shows the frequency distribution of the bids for all five experiments at trial twenty. The bids appear to have a bimodal distribution with the majority of participants at all locations willing to pay $0.25 or less to avoid the bST milk. Between six and twelve participants (40 to 80%) would not pay anything to avoid the bST milk. Because some participants, particularly in Massachusetts, would bid more than $1.00 to avoid the bST milk this raises the possibility of a significant "niche" market for untreated milk products if bST is introduced. Overall, the results indicate that more than 50% of the participants would not require any price discount to purchase bST milk. The acceptability of the product (measured by the proportion bidding zero at the end of the auction) was highest in Iowa and rural California. The proportion of participants who would be very unlikely to purchase this product was greatest in Massachusetts. This may reflect an ongoing campaign against bST that has garnered some media attention in the Northeast. The results from the urban California group are most revealing. No participants had heard of bST prior to the experiment and they demonstrated a strong negative bias against the product until they learned more about it. Once they received a scientifically balanced description of the product, their concern almost disappeared, and about 70% of these participants then indicated a willingness to purchase the product at a zero or small discount.

7.10.3   Conclusions

These results suggest a relatively small group at each location would pay a large premium to avoid drinking bST milk but that more than 60% would purchase the product if it were available at the same price or at a slightly lower price than milk from untreated animals. The results also support the view that how information about these products is disseminated matters. In the absence of scientifically balanced information, many participants indicated that they were very reluctant to consume the product. This bias was overcome among the group of uninformed urban Californian participants but remained strong in the Massachusetts group, many of whom may have been exposed to some form of anti-bST publicity.

Interestingly, the FDA subsequently approved bST milk for sale after this study was conducted. Recognizing that the experiment was conducted with a very small and special segment of the population (i.e., 75 students) and that precise comparisons are very difficult, it is interesting to compare the experimental results presented herein to what has actually happened in the marketplace. Dhar and Foltz (2005) provide a summary of nationwide grocery store scanner data collected between 1997 and 2002 on sales of organic, bST-free, and conventional milk. Organic milk is free of bST and has other characteristics as well. Dhar and Foltz (2005) show that, on average, organic milk was priced at a $3.11 per gallon premium to conventional milk and that bST-free milk was priced at a $2.05 per gallon premium to conventional milk. At these price levels, organic and bST-free milk achieved market shares of 0.41% and 0.48%, or a combined total of slightly less than 1% market share. These data correspond reasonably well with that reported in Fox (1995). For example, only about 3% of the students bid more than $1.50 to exchange a glass of conventional milk for a glass of bST-free milk in the initial auction round.

7.11   Concluding comments

We have presented nine case studies using experimental auctions to value new goods and services. Each case study raised many specific design issues about the good on the auction block. But when thinking about these specific design features, it is vital to keep in mind the more *general lesson* to take away from these exercises: awareness of the subtle balance between *control* and *context*. Every experimental researcher works within these two poles: stripping away all real world elements aiming for complete and abstract control over the environment; or adding in all the real world context necessary to mimic real world decisions. But too much control can make the environment too sterile; too much context makes the environment too detailed, applying only to that case. Each researcher should understand and explain how much of the environment he or she wants to control and how much he or she wants to add context. This is the general challenge for all experimental auction work, including the case studies presented in this chapter. Readers hopefully questioned several design decisions made in these case studies, and hypothesized about the results if we have chosen another path. We support these challenges and encourage more experiments to test whether our results are robust to adding more control or more context. Because in the end, that is what experimentation is all about – exploring the boundaries of behavior given control over bidding struc-tures and given context over what this bidding means in broad social setting.

Appendix A7:   Instructions for beef steak auction experiments

A7.1   Introductory instructions identical for all treatments

Thank you for agreeing to participate in today's session. As you entered the room, you should have been given $40.00 and a packet. You should also have been assigned an ID number, which is located on the upper right hand corner of the packet. You will use this ID number to identify yourself during this research session. We use random numbers in order to ensure confidentiality.

Before we begin, I want to emphasize that your participation in this session is completely voluntary. If you do not wish to participate in the experiment, please say so at any time. Non-participants will not be penalized in any way. I want to assure you that the information you provide will be kept strictly confidential and used only for the purposes of this research.

In today's session, we are ultimately interested in your preferences for several different types of beef steaks. First, I would like you all to open your packets and take a minute to examine the "information sheet," which describes several types of beef steaks. When you have finished looking over the information sheet, take the "consumer survey" out of your packet. Take a few minutes to complete the survey.

I will now begin going through a set of instructions with you and will read from this script so that I am able to clearly convey the procedures. Importantly, from this point forward, I ask that there be no talking among participants. Failure to comply with these instructions will result in disqualification from the experiment.

Are there any questions before we begin?

A7.2   Information sheet

In today's session, we are interested in your preferences for several different types of beef steaks. Specifically, we have five different types of beef ribeye steaks that you will be asked to evaluate. The steaks are all the same size, weight (12 oz. or 0.75lbs.), packaging, and freshness, and differ only by characteristics identified by labels on the products. The first steak is generic and has no label. The second steak has a label identifying it as guaranteed tender. The third steak has a label identifying it as "natural" meaning it was raised with no added hormones or antibiotics. The fourth steak has a label identifying it as USDA Choice. The fifth steak is labeled as Certified Angus Beef. We realize that you may be unaware of some of these types of labels. To assist you in your evaluation, we have provided the following steak descriptions.

Generic steak

The generic steak has no label. Beyond the fact that the steak has been US Department of Agriculture (USDA) federally inspected, no other guarantees are given regarding the quality of the meat. For your information, steaks similar to this were selling at $8.09/lb last week at Dillon's Supermarket. This would be equivalent to $6.07 for a 12 oz. steak.

Guaranteed tender steak

This steak has been carefully selected to ensure that it is tender. Technology has been developed to categorize steaks by tenderness level. The classification system uses a shear force test to identify tenderness levels. Thus, steaks can be separated into different categories according to shear force values. The classification system has identified this steak as guaranteed tender.

Steak from animal raised with no added hormones or antibiotics (natural steak)

It is estimated that approximately 95% of all fed cattle in the US are administered added growth hormones during production. Animals that are administered growth hormones generally grow at faster rates and reach higher weights compared to animals which have not been administered growth hormones. In addition, cattle are routinely administered antibiotics during feeding to reduce the chance of illness. This steak comes from an animal that was raised with NO added hormones and was NOT fed antibiotics.

USDA choice steak

There are four primary USDA quality beef grades. In order of decreasing quality, these grades are: prime, choice, select, and standard. The primary determinant of the quality grade is the level of steak marbling. Marbling is the level of intra-muscular fat content in a steak. Steaks with higher levels of intra-muscular fat content receive higher quality grades. For example, prime steaks have the highest amount of intra-muscular fat and standard steaks have the lowest amount of intra-muscular fat. It has been shown in blind taste tests that consumers prefer steaks with higher levels of intra-muscular fat to steaks with lower levels of intra-muscular fat. Prime and Choice steaks are typically sold in restaurants; whereas, select, standard, and non-graded steaks are typically sold in grocery stores. This steak has been graded USDA choice.

Certified Angus beef steak

There are a wide variety of cattle breeds. This steak comes from an animal that met requirements for the Certified Angus Beef program. In addition to other specifications, this steak has been graded as being in the upper 2/3 of USDA Choice, and is from an animal that is predominantly Angus bred.

A7.3 Instructions for second price auction

7.3.1 Instructions for non-hypothetical practice auction with candy bars

Here in the front of the room, we have four candy bars: Butterfinger, Snickers, Nestlé Crunch, and Milky Way. We are interested in your preferences for each of these candy bars.

We will now conduct an auction for each of the candy bars, where you will have the opportunity to win *one* of the candy bars. In a moment, you will be asked to indicate the *most* you are willing to pay (if anything) to purchase each of the candy bars by writing bids on the enclosed bid sheets. Let me explain how the auction will proceed:

1) First, each of you has been given a bid sheet in your packet. On this sheet you will, in a moment, write the ***most*** you are willing to pay for each of the following: a) the Butterfinger, b) the Snickers bar, c) the Nestlé Crunch bar, and d) the Milky Way bar. Note: you will write four bids, one for each candy bar. Your bids are private information and should not be shared with anyone.

2) After you've finished writing your bids, the monitor will go around the room and collect the bid sheets.

3) In the front of the room, bids will be ranked from highest to lowest for each candy bar.

4) The person with the *highest* bid for each candy bar will win the auction and pay the *2nd highest* bid amount for the candy bar.

5) For each candy bar we will write the winning bidder number and the winning price on the chalkboard for everyone to see.

6) After posting the price, we will re-conduct the auction for five additional rounds.

7) At the completion of the 5th round, we will randomly draw a number 1 through 5 to determine the binding round. For example, if we randomly draw the number 5, then we will ignore outcomes in all other rounds and only focus on the winning bidder and price in round 5. Importantly, all rounds have an equally likely chance of being binding.

8) After the binding round has been determined, we will randomly draw a number 1 through 5 to determine which candy bar to actually auction (either the Butterfinger, Snickers, Nestlé Crunch, or Milky Way bar). For example, if we draw the number 1, we will only focus on bids for the Butterfinger and

will ignore bids for the other two candy bars. Importantly, all candy bars have an equally likely chance of being binding.

9) Once the binding round and candy bar have been determined, the winning bidder will come forward and pay the 2nd highest bid amount and receive winning candy bar. All other participants will leave with no candy bar.

Important notes

- You will only have the opportunity to win an auction for *one* candy bar. Because we randomly draw a binding round and binding candy bar, you *cannot* win more than one candy bar. That is, under no bidding scenario will you take home more than one candy bar from this experiment.
- The winning bidder **will actually pay money** to obtain the winning candy bar. This procedure is **not** hypothetical.
- In this auction, the best strategy is to bid **exactly** what it is worth to you to obtain each of the four candy bars. Consider the following: if you bid *more* than the candy bar is worth to you, you may end up having to buy a candy bar for more than you really want to pay. Conversely, if you bid *less* than the candy bar is really worth to you, you may end up not winning the auction even though you could have bought a candy bar at a price you were actually willing to pay. Thus, your best strategy is to bid *exactly* what each candy bar is worth to you.
- It is acceptable to bid $0.00 for any candy bar in any round.

Example

Suppose there were five people participating in an auction just like the one you are about to participate in. Suppose that these individuals participated in five auction rounds, as you will, and that the 5th round was randomly selected to be binding. Also, assume that the Nestlé Crunch bar was randomly selected to be the binding candy bar. Now, suppose in round 5, participant #1 bid $0.00 for the Nestlé Crunch bar, participant #2 bid $0.10, participant #3 bid $0.25, participant #4 bid $0.40, and participant #5 bid $0.50 for the Nestlé Crunch bar.

Who would win the auction? Participant #5 would win the auction because they bid the highest amount. How much would participant #5 have to pay for the Nestlé Crunch bar? Participant #5 would pay the 2nd highest bid amount, which was $0.40. Thus, participant #5 would come to the front of the room, pay $0.40 and obtain the Nestlé Crunch bar. Participants #1, #2, #3, and #4 would pay nothing and would leave with no candy bar.

Note: these dollar amounts were used for illustrative purposes only and should not in any way reflect what the candy bars may be worth to you.

Do you have any questions before we begin?

Please use the bid sheets, marked "candy bar auction."

7.3.2   Instructions for steak auction Now that you have had the chance to learn how the auction will work, we are interested in your preferences for five different ribeye steaks. Each of you should have been given an information sheet describing several different types of steaks. Please take a moment and read with me through the information sheet. <<now read through the information sheet>>

Now, we will give you the opportunity to participate in an auction to purchase the type of steak you desire. Here in the front of the room, we have five steaks as described in the information sheet. Again, other than differences in the labeled characteristics, the steaks are the same size, weight, packaging, etc.

We will now conduct an auction for each of the steaks, where you will have the opportunity to purchase *one* steak. In a moment, you will be asked to indicate the *most* you are willing to pay (if anything) for each of the steaks by writing bids on the enclosed bid sheets. The procedures for this auction are exactly the same as the candy bar auction. To refresh your memory as to how the auction works, I will go through the instructions again.

1) First, each of you has been given a bid sheet in your packet. On this sheet you will, in a moment, write the **most** you are willing to pay to for each of the following: a) the *generic* steak, b) the *guaranteed tender* steak, c) the *natural* steak, d) the *USDA choice* steak, and e) the *certified Angus beef* steak. Note: you will write five bids, one for each steak. Note: your bids are private information and should not be shared with anyone.

2) After you've finished writing your bids, the monitor will go around the room and collect the bid sheets.

3) In the front of the room, each of your bids will be ranked from highest to lowest for each steak.

4) The person with the *highest* bid for each steak will win the auction and pay the *2nd highest* bid amount for the steak.

5) For each steak we will write the winning bidder number and the winning price on the chalkboard for everyone to see.

6) After posting the price, we will re-conduct the auction for five additional rounds.

7) At the completion of the 5th round, we will randomly draw a number 1 through 5 to determine the binding round. For example, if we randomly draw the number 5, then we will ignore outcomes in all other rounds and only focus on the winning bidder and price in round 5. Importantly, all rounds have an equally likely chance of being binding.

8) After the binding round has been determined, we will randomly draw a number 1 through 5 to determine which steak to actually auction (either the *generic* steak, the *guaranteed tender* steak, the *natural* steak, the *USDA choice* steak, or the *certified Angus beef* steak). For example, if we draw the number 1, we will only focus on bids for the *generic* steak and will ignore

bids for the other four steaks. Importantly, all steaks have an equally likely chance of being binding.

9) Once the binding round and steak have been determined, the winning bidder will come forward and pay the 2nd highest bid amount and obtain the winning steak. All other participants will pay nothing and receive nothing.

Important notes

- You will only have the opportunity to win an auction for *one* steak. Because we randomly draw a binding round and binding steak, you *cannot* win more than one auction. That is, under no bidding scenario will you take home more than one steak from this experiment.

- The winning bidder **will actually pay money** to obtain the winning steak. This procedure is **not** hypothetical.

- In this auction, the best strategy is to bid **exactly** what each steak is worth to you. Consider the following: if you bid *more* than the steak is worth to you, you may end up having to buy a steak for more than you really want to pay. Conversely, if you bid *less* than the steak is really worth to you, you may end up not winning the auction even though you could have bought a steak at a price you were actually willing to pay. Thus, your best strategy is to bid *exactly* what the steak is worth to you.

- It is acceptable to bid $0.00 for any steak in any round.

- We realize that you may have errands to run after this experiment and may not be able to take your steak immediately home. We offer two services to accommodate your need. First, if you do not wish to take your steak home, we will give you a coupon that can be redeemed at the K-State meat lab. At some future date, you may come by and pick up the steak (your steak will be of the quality obtained in this experiment). Or, if you wish, we can give you a small styrofoam cooler to keep your steak cool until you get home.

Do you have any questions before we begin?

Please use the bid sheets marked "steak auction."

A7.4   Instructions for random nth price auction

A non-hypothetical auction with candy bars was held prior to the steak auction to help subjects learn about the mechanism; these instructions are not presented here as they very closely mirror the instructions for the steak auctions – see, for example, the detail in section A7.3 for the second price auction.

A7.4.1   Instructions for steak auction

Now that you have had the chance to learn how the auction will work, we are interested in your preferences for five different ribeye steaks. Each of you should have been given an information sheet describing several different types of steaks. Please take a moment and read with me through the information sheet. <<now read through the information sheet>>

Now, we will give you the opportunity to participate in an auction to purchase the type of steak you desire. Here in the front of the room, we have five steaks as described in the information sheet. Again, other than differences in the labeled characteristics, the steaks are the same size, weight, packaging, etc.

We will now conduct an auction for each of the steaks, where you will have the opportunity to purchase *one* steak. In a moment, you will be asked to indicate the *most* you are willing to pay (if anything) for each of the steaks by writing bids on the enclosed bid sheets. The procedures for this auction are exactly the same as the candy bar auction. To refresh your memory as to how the auction works, I will go through the instructions again.

1) First, each of you has been given a bid sheet in your packet. On this sheet you will, in a moment, write the **most** you are willing to pay to for each of the following: a) the *generic* steak, b) the *guaranteed tender* steak, c) the *natural* steak, d) the *USDA choice* steak, and e) the *certified Angus beef* steak. Note: you will write five bids, one for each steak. Note: your bids are private information and should not be shared with anyone.

2) After you've finished writing your bids, the monitor will go around the room and collect the bid sheets.

3) In the front of the room, each of your bids will be ranked from highest to lowest for each steak.

4) Next, a random number will be drawn to determine how many participants will win steaks. The random number will be somewhere between 1 and the total number of participants. Call this random number N.

5) The $N - 1$ highest bidders will win the auction and all winning bidders will pay the Nth highest bid amount for the exchange. For example, suppose there were 10 participants that submitted bids and the number 4 was randomly drawn by the monitor (i.e., $N = 4$). In this case, the 3 ($N - 1$) highest bidders will win the auction and each will pay the 4th highest bid amount for the winning steak.

6) For each steak we will write the winning participants' bidder numbers, the random number (N), and the winning price on the chalkboard for everyone to see.

7) After posting the prices and winning bidder numbers, we will re-conduct the auction for five additional rounds.

8) At the completion of the 5th round, we will randomly draw a number 1 through 5 to determine the binding round. For example, if we randomly draw the number 5, then we will ignore outcomes in all other rounds and only focus on the winning bidders and price in round 5. Importantly, all rounds have an equally likely chance of being binding.

9) After the binding round has been determined, we will randomly draw a number 1 through 5 to determine which steak to actually auction (either the *generic* steak, the *guaranteed tender* steak, the *natural* steak, the *USDA choice* steak, or the *certified Angus Beef* steak). For example, if we draw the number 1, we will only focus on bids for the *generic* steak and will ignore bids for the other four steaks. Importantly, all steaks have an equally likely chance of being binding.

10) Once the binding round and steak have been determined, the winning bidders will come forward and pay the Nth highest bid amount for the winning steak. All other participants will pay nothing and will not receive a steak.

Important notes

- You will only have the opportunity to win an auction for *one* steak. Because we randomly draw a binding round and binding steak, you *cannot* win more than one auction. That is, under no bidding scenario will you take home more than one steak from this experiment.
- The winning bidders **will actually pay money** for the winning steak. This procedure is **not** hypothetical.
- In this auction, the best strategy is to bid **exactly** what each steak is worth to you. Consider the following: if you bid *more* than the steak is worth to you, you may end up having to buy a steak for more than you really want to pay. Conversely, if you bid *less* than the steak is really worth to you, you may end up not winning the auction even though you could have bought a steak at a price you were actually willing to pay. Thus, your best strategy is to bid *exactly* what the steak is worth to you.
- It is acceptable to bid $0.00 for any steak in any round.
- We realize that you may have errands to run after this experiment and may not be able to take your steak immediately home. We offer two services to accommodate your need. First, if you do not wish to take your steak home, we will give you a coupon that can be redeemed at the K-State meat lab. At some future date, you may come by and pick up the steak (your steak will be of the quality obtained in this experiment). Or, if you wish, we can give you a small styrofoam cooler to keep your steak cool until you get home.

Do you have any questions before we begin?

Please use the bid sheets marked "steak auction."

A7.5   Instructions for English auction

A non-hypothetical auction with candy bars was held prior to the steak auction to help subjects learn about the mechanism; these instructions are not presented here as they very closely mirror the instructions for the steak auctions – see, for example, the detail in section A7.3 for the second price auction.

A7.5.1   Instructions for steak auction

Now that you have had the chance to learn how the auction will work, we are interested in your preferences for five different ribeye steaks. Each of you should have been given an information sheet describing several different types of steaks. Please take a moment and read with me through the information sheet. <<now read through the information sheet>>

Now, we will give you the opportunity to participate in an auction to purchase the type of steak you desire. Here in the front of the room, we have five steaks as described in the information sheet. Again, other than differences in the labeled characteristics, the steaks are the same size, weight, packaging, etc.

We will now conduct an auction for each of the steaks, where you will have the opportunity to purchase *one* steak. In a moment, you will be asked to indicate the *most* you are willing to pay (if anything) for each of the steaks. The procedures for this auction are exactly the same as the candy bar auction. To refresh your memory as to how the auction works, I will go through the instructions again.

1) In your packet each of you has been given a sheet with your participant ID number in large numbers. You will use this sheet, in a moment, to signal the *most* you are willing to pay for each of the following: a) the *generic* steak, b) the *guaranteed tender* steak, c) the *natural* steak, d) the *USDA choice* steak, and e) the *certified Angus beef* steak. Note: we will conduct five sequential auctions, one for each steak.

2) First we will conduct an auction to determine how much you are willing to pay for the *generic* steak.

3) To start the auction, the monitor will write a price on the chalkboard. The monitor will start with $0.25. Every ten seconds, the monitor will increase the price by $0.25.

4) If you *are* willing to pay the price (currently written on the chalkboard) for the *generic* steak, indicate this by keeping the sheet with your participant ID number flat on the desk. If you *are not* willing to pay the price (currently written on the chalkboard) for the *generic* steak, indicate this by raising the sheet with your participant ID number. Please keep the sheet raised until the end of the auction.

5) The last person to not raise the sheet with their participant ID number will win the auction. This is the last person to keep their sheet flat on the desk. This person will pay the last price written on the blackboard.

6) After this auction is completed, we conducted an identical auction for the *guaranteed tender, natural, USDA choice,* and *certified Angus beef* steaks. Then we will randomly draw a number 1 through 5 to determine which

steak auction is binding. For example, if we draw the number 1, we will only focus on the winner of the *generic* steak auction and will ignore winners of the other four steaks. Importantly, all steak auctions have an equally likely chance of being binding.

7) Once the binding steak has been determined, the winning bidder will come forward and pay the market price for the winning steak. All other participants will pay nothing and will not receive a steak.

Important notes

- You will only have the opportunity to win an auction for *one* steak. Because we randomly draw a binding round and binding steak, you *cannot* win more than one auction. That is, under no bidding scenario will you take home more than one steak from this experiment.
- The winning bidder ***will actually pay*** for the winning steak. This procedure is **not** hypothetical.
- In this auction, the best strategy is stay in the auction until the point at which the price is ***exactly*** equal to what the steak is worth to you.
- It is acceptable to immediately raise the sheet with your participant ID number when the auction begins. In this case, you are willing to pay $0.00 for the steak.
- We realize that you may have errands to run after this experiment and may not be able to take your steak immediately home. We offer two services to accommodate your need. First, if you do not wish to take your steak home, we will give you a coupon that can be redeemed at the K-State meat lab. At some future date, you may come by and pick up the steak (your steak will be of the quality obtained in this experiment). Or, if you wish, we can give you a small styrofoam cooler to keep your steak cool until you get home.

Do you have any questions before we begin?

A7.6   Instructions for BDM

A non-hypothetical auction with candy bars was held prior to the steak auction to help subjects learn about the mechanism; these instructions are not presented here as they very closely mirror the instructions for the steak auctions – see, for example, the detail in section A7.3 for the second price auction.

A7.6.1   Instructions for steak auction

Now that you have had the chance to learn how the auction will work, we are interested in your preferences for five different ribeye steaks. Each of you should have been given an information sheet describing several different types of steaks. Please take a moment and read with me through the information sheet.
<<now read through the information sheet>>

Now, we will give you the opportunity to participate in an auction to purchase the type of steak you desire. Here in the front of the room, we have five steaks as described in the information sheet. Again, other than differences in the labeled characteristics, the steaks are the same size, weight, packaging, etc.

We will now conduct an auction for each of the steaks, where you will have the opportunity to purchase *one* steak. In a moment, you will be asked to indicate the *most* you are willing to pay (if anything) for each of the steaks by writing bids on the enclosed bid sheets. The procedures for this auction are exactly the same as the candy bar auction. To refresh your memory as to how the auction works, I will go through the instructions again.

1) First, each of you has been given a bid sheet in your packet. On this sheet you will, in a moment, write the *most* you are willing to pay for each of the following: a) the *generic* steak, b) the *guaranteed tender* steak, c) the *natural* steak, d) the *USDA choice* steak, and e) the *certified Angus beef* steak. Note: you will write five bids, one for each steak. Note: your bids are private information and should not be shared with anyone.

2) After you've finished writing your bids, the monitor will go around the room and collect the bid sheets.

3) Then, the monitor will draw a number, 1 through 5, to determine which steak to actually auction. For example, if we draw the number 1, we will only auction the *generic* steak and will ignore your bids for the other steaks. Importantly, all steak bids have an equally likely chance of being binding.

4) Next the monitor will randomly draw a price, ranging from $0.00 to $20.00.

5) If your bid for the randomly selected steak is **greater** than the randomly drawn price, then you will win the auction, purchase the randomly selected steak at a price equal to the randomly drawn number.

6) If your bid for the randomly selected steak is **less** than the randomly drawn price, then you **will not purchase** the randomly selected steak.

7) Once the binding steak and random price have been determined, the winning bidders will come forward and pay the random price for the winning steak. All other participants (those with bids less than the randomly selected price) will pay nothing and will receive no steak.

Important notes

- You will only have the opportunity to win an auction for *one* steak. Because we randomly draw a binding round and binding steak, you *cannot* win more than one auction. That is, under no bidding scenario will you take home more than one steak from this experiment.
- The winning bidder *will actually pay money* for the winning steak. This procedure is **not** hypothetical.
- In this auction, the best strategy is to bid *exactly* what each steak is worth to you. Consider the following: if you bid *more* than the steak is worth to you,

you may end up having to buy a steak for more than you really want to pay. Conversely, if you bid *less* than the steak is really worth to you, you may end up not winning the auction even though you could have bought a steak at a price you were actually willing to pay. Thus, your best strategy is to bid *exactly* what the steak is worth to you.

• It is acceptable to bid $0.00 for any steak in any round.
• We realize that you may have errands to run after this experiment and may not be able to take your steak immediately home. We offer two services to accommodate your need. First, if you do not wish to take your steak home, we will give you a coupon that can be redeemed at the K-State meat lab. At some future date, you may come by and pick up the steak (your steak will be of the quality obtained in this experiment). Or, if you wish, we can give you a small styrofoam cooler to keep your steak cool until you get home.

Do you have any questions before we begin?

Please use the bid sheets marked "steak auction."

Appendix B7:   Instructions for financial records auction

B7.1   *Instructions for introductory willingness to accept second price candy bar auction*

Each of you will be given one candy bar. Everyone will receive the same type of candy bar. We are interested in how much you value the candy bar. We will now conduct an auction for the candy bars, where you will have the opportunity to sell back the candy bar in your possession. In a moment, you will be asked to indicate the *least* amount of money you would be willing to accept (if anything) in exchange for the candy bars in your possession. You will write your bids on the enclosed bid sheets. Let me explain how the auction will proceed:

Auction procedures

1) First, each of you has been given a bid sheet in your packet. On this sheet you will, in a moment, write the **least** amount of money you are willing to sell your candy bar for. Your bids are private information and should not be shared with anyone.
2) After you've finished writing your bids, the monitor will go around the room and collect the bid sheets.
3) In the front of the room, bids for the candy bar will be ranked from lowest to highest.
4) The person with the *lowest* bid for selling their candy bar will win the auction and be paid the *2nd lowest* bid selling price.
5) We will write the winning bidder number and the winning price on the chalkboard for everyone to see.

6) The winning bidder will come forward and be paid the 2nd lowest bid amount in exchange for his/her candy bar. All other participants will be able to keep their candy bar, but will not be given any other chance to sell their candy bar for money.

Important notes

- The winning bidder *will actually receive real money* and *forfeit their candy bar*. This procedure is not hypothetical.
- In this auction, the best strategy is to bid *exactly* what your candy bar is worth to you. Consider the following: if you bid *less* than the candy bar is worth to you, you may end up selling your candy bar for less than you really value it. Conversely, if you bid *more* than the candy bar is really worth to you, you may end up not winning the auction even though you could have sold the candy bar at a price you were willing to receive. Thus, your best strategy is to bid *exactly* what each candy bar is worth to you.
- It is acceptable to bid $0.00 if the candy bar has no worth to you.

Example

Suppose there were five people participating in an auction just like the one you are about to participate in. Now, suppose in the bidding round, participant #1 bid $0.00, participant #2 bid $0.10, participant #3 bid $0.25, participant #4 bid $0.40, and participant #5 bid $0.50 for the sale of their candy bar.

Who would win the auction? Participant #1 would win the auction because they bid the lowest amount. How much would participant #1 be paid for the Snickers bar? Participant #1 would be paid the 2nd lowest bid amount, which was $0.10. Thus, participant #1 would come to the front of the room, receive $0.10 in exchange for their candy bar. Participants #2, #3, #4, and #5 would receive nothing and would leave with their candy bar.

Note: these dollar amounts were used for illustrative purposes only and should not in any way reflect what the candy bars may be worth to you. Do you have any questions before we begin? Please use the bid sheets, marked "candy bar auction."

B7.2   Instructions for financial records auction

Now that you have had the chance to learn how the auction will work, we are interested in your valuation for your own personal financial records. You will now be able to participate in an auction where you will be able to sell your personal financial records in exchange for money.

Now each of you has been given an inventory sheet for the financial record auction where you list what financial statements and information you calculate, have in your possession, and are willing to sell. The items listed are the balance sheet, statement of cash flows, income statement, statement of owner's equity, checkbook register, and tax records. Let's take the first item listed, the balance sheet, as an example. First, if you do not formulate balance sheets for your farming operation, you would circle *no* under the *Do you calculate this?* column, and go on to the next item. If you did create balance sheets for your farm, you next say how many years of your annual balance sheet you have calculated and are part of your farm records. If you have only started to create balance sheets in the last two years, you would only circle the years 2004 and 2003. We are only interested in your most recent records, so only 2000–2004 are listed. The next column entitled *Document's Form* is simply asking if you created your balance sheet on a computer or if you did it by hand. If you made your balance sheet by hand, circle the word *handwritten*, if you created the balance sheet by computer circle the word *electronic*. You will proceed to fill out the other types of financial records the same way you did with the balance sheet.

After you have filled out your financial records inventory sheet, you will then decide the price you are willing to sell all the documents you listed in the inventory. You must truly ask yourself how much you value your financial document. If I only have one year's worth of tax records and a 2004 balance sheet that I created in less than an hour, I would probably be willing to sell my financial information at a lower price. On the other hand, if I have five years of annual balance sheets, income statements, statements of owner's equity, and cash flow statements that I have created with an accounting software package, and I use those statements to help analyze my profitability and make decisions about my operations, I would more highly value those documents and submit a high bid price. After deciding what is the *lowest* amount of money you are willing to accept for the forfeit of your financial information, write that amount in the blank under your *Bid Price* blank on the *Bid Sheet for the Financial Records Auction*.

Once you have decided your bid price, you are asked to explain how you came to that valuation price. Since your final bid price is made up of several different types of financial information, please record what weight each type of information had in your total bid price. You are asked to show how important each document type was in your total bid price by assigning each document type the percentage it was worth in your total evaluation. For example, if my financial records inventory included a balance sheet, an income statement, a checkbook register, and tax records, I might say that the balance sheet was worth 30% of my total valuation, my income statement 25%, my checkbook register 15%, and my tax records were worth 30%. When I add up my percentages from each type, it should equal 100%.

There will only be one round of bidding – so you only have one chance to sell your financial records. There will only be one winner of the auction. The procedures for this auction are exactly the same as the candy bar auction.

To refresh your memory as to how the auction works, I will go through the instructions again.

Auction procedures

1) You will fill out your financial records inventory sheet which will be collected by the monitor.

2) You will then fill out your bid sheets by submitting your total selling price for your financial information listed on the inventory sheet. You will also fill out on the bid sheet how much each financial document counted towards your final valuation.

3) In the front of the room, each of your bids will be ranked from lowest to highest.

4) The person with the *lowest* bid for their financial records will win the auction and will be paid the *2nd lowest* bid amount.

5) We will write the winning bidder number and the winning price on the chalkboard for everyone to see.

6) The winning bidder will come forward and identify himself/herself.

Important notes

• This experiment will take place in several different locations across Indiana. The lowest bidder from all of the experiments combined will receive money in exchange for their records. The winner at each auction site will need to identify themselves and give their contact information in case they are the overall winner.

• The overall winner *will actually receive money* for their financial records. This procedure is **not** hypothetical. We will expect the winner to give us all of their original records and all duplicative copies of the records they sold. We will keep the records in our possession for five years and then destroy them. Only <<project director>> will have access to the records that are sold. The winner of the auction will no longer have access to your financial records once they are in our possession. The winner will be allowed to have access to his/her tax and employment records if he/she is audited.

• In this auction, the best strategy is to bid *exactly* what your financial records are worth to you. Consider the following: if you bid *less* than your records are worth to you, you may end up losing your financial records. Conversely, if you bid *more* than your records are really worth to you, you may end up not winning the auction even though you could have sold your records at a price you were willing to take. Thus, your best strategy is to bid *exactly* what your financial records are worth to you.

Please use the sheets marked "Financial Records Inventory" and "Bid sheet for Financial Records Auction."

B7.3   Financial records inventory sheet

Financial Records Inventory

	Do you calculate this?		Which years of records are in your possession?	Document's Form	
Balance Sheet	Yes	No	2004 2003 2002 2001 2000	Handwritten	Electronic
Statement of Cash Flows	Yes	No	2004 2003 2002 2001 2000	Handwritten	Electronic
Income Statement	Yes	No	2004 2003 2002 2001 2000	Handwritten	Electronic
Statement of Owner's Equity	Yes	No	2004 2003 2002 2001 2000	Handwritten	Electronic
Checkbook Register	Yes	No	2004 2003 2002 2001 2000	Handwritten	Electronic
Tax Records	Yes	No	2004 2003 2002 2001 2000	Handwritten	Electronic

Are you a member of a farm records data bank?   ☐ Yes   ☐ No
(Example: Illinois Farm Business Farm Management Association)

Figure B7.1   Financial records inventory sheet

B7.4   Financial records bid sheet

Bid Sheet for Financial Records Auction

For the financial records you recorded on your inventory sheet, how much are you willing to sell them for?

Bid Price_____

☐ There is **no** amount of money I am willing to accept in exchange for my financial records.

In that bid price, how much did each type of record count towards the total valuation? Assign a percentage to each record type based on its contribution to your final bid price decision. If the percentage you wish to assign is not listed, you may write it down under the *other* column. **Remember that your added percentages from the six different types of records need to total to 100%.**

												Other
1) Balance Sheet	0%	10%	20%	30%	40%	50%	60%	70%	80%	90%	100%	____
2) Statement of Cash Flows	0%	10%	20%	30%	40%	50%	60%	70%	80%	90%	100%	____
3) Income Statement	0%	10%	20%	30%	40%	50%	60%	70%	80%	90%	100%	____
4) Statement of Owner's Equity	0%	10%	20%	30%	40%	50%	60%	70%	80%	90%	100%	____
5) Checkbook Register	0%	10%	20%	30%	40%	50%	60%	70%	80%	90%	100%	____
6) Tax Records	0%	10%	20%	30%	40%	50%	60%	70%	80%	90%	100%	____

Reminder: Make sure your percentages from the six types of records total to 100%.

Figure B7.2   Financial records bid sheet

Appendix C7: Appendix instructions for GM food auction

C7.1   Beginning candy bar auction

For agreeing to participate in this research session, we are giving each of you one free large Snickers bar. The large Snickers bar is yours to keep, but please do not eat it just yet.

Although you have been given a free large Snickers bar, in a moment we will give you the opportunity to participate in an auction to obtain a different size of candy bar if you so desire. Here in the front of the room, I also have a small Snickers bar.

I will now conduct an auction, where you will have the opportunity to exchange your Large Snickers bar for the Small Snickers bar. Obviously, you would probably prefer to have your larger Snickers bar rather than the smaller Snickers bar. Therefore, I'm interested in how much money I would have to give you so that you would be willing to exchange your larger Snickers for the smaller Snickers.

In a moment, you will be asked to indicate the *least* amount of money I must pay you to exchange your Large Snickers bar for the Small Snickers bar by writing bids on the enclosed bid sheets. Naturally, I do not want to pay out a large amount of money, so I am interested in finding the lowest bidders.

Let me explain how the auction will proceed:

Auction procedures

1) First, each of you has been given a bid sheet in your packet. On this sheet you will, in a moment, write the *least* amount of money you must be paid to *exchange* your Large Snickers bar for the Small Snickers bar. This is the amount of money I must pay you so that you'd be willing to give up your Large Snickers bar and take the Small Snickers bar instead. Note: Your bids are private information and should not be shared with anyone.
2) After you've finished writing your bids, the monitor will go around the room and collect the bid sheets.
3) In the front of the room, bids will be ranked from lowest to highest.
4) The *four lowest* bids for the Small Snickers bar will win the auction. The individuals that submitted the four lowest bids will be paid the *5th* **lowest** bid amount to exchange their Large Snickers bar for the Small Snickers.
5) The numbers of the winning bidders and the winning price (the 5th lowest bid) will be written on the chalkboard for everyone to see.
6) After posting the price, I will re-conduct the auction for two additional rounds.
7) At the completion of the 3rd round, I will randomly draw a number 1 through 3 to determine the binding round. For example, if we randomly draw the

number 3, then we will ignore outcomes in all other rounds and only focus on the winning bidder and price in round 3. Importantly, all rounds have an equally likely chance of being the winning round.

8) Once the binding round has been determined, the winning bidders will come forward and will be paid the 5th lowest bid amount and exchange their Large Snickers for the Small Snickers. All other participants will be paid nothing and will keep their Large Snickers.

Important notes

- You will only have the opportunity to win an auction for *one* candy bar. Because we randomly draw a binding round, you *cannot* win more than one candy bar. You will either leave with one Large Snickers if you are a high bidder or one Small Snickers and some amount of money if you are a low bidder.

- I **will actually pay money** to the winning bidders to exchange their Large Snickers for the Small Snickers bar. This procedure is **not** hypothetical.

- In this auction, the best strategy is to bid *exactly* what it is worth to you to *exchange* your Large Snickers for the Small Snickers. Consider the following: if you bid *more* than it is worth to you to exchange your Large Snickers bar for a Small Snickers bar, you may end up not winning the auction even though you could have exchanged your Large Snickers at a price you were actually willing to be paid. Conversely, if you bid *less* than it is worth to you to exchange your Large Snickers for the Small Snickers, you may end up having to exchange your Large Snickers at a price lower than you really wanted to. Thus, your best strategy is to bid *exactly* what it is worth to you to exchange your Large Snickers bar for the Small Snickers bar.

- It is acceptable to bid $0.00 for the Small Snickers in any round. This would mean that you are willing to give up your Large Snickers for the Small Snickers without any compensation from me.

- Importantly, we are interested in what it is worth to you to **exchange** your Large Snickers for the Small Snickers. We are not interested in your *total value* of the Small Snickers, only the amount of the **exchange**. In other words, what is the premium you would place on your Large Snickers versus the Small Snickers?

Auction example

Suppose there were ten people participating in an auction just like the one you are about to participate in. Suppose that these individuals participated in three auction rounds, as you will, and that the 2nd round was randomly selected to be binding. Now, suppose in round 2, participant #1 bid $0.00 to exchange their Large Snickers bar for the Small Snickers, participant #2 bid $0.03, participant #3 bid $0.06, participant #4 bid $0.09, and participant #5 bid $0.12, participant

#6 bid $0.15, participant #7 bid $0.18, participant #8 bid $0.21, participant #9 bid $0.24, and participant #10 bid $0.27 to exchange their Large Snickers bar for the Small Snickers. To further illustrate, the bids in round 2 were as follows:

Participant Number	#1	#2	#3	#4	#5	#6	#7	#8	#9	#10
Bid Amount	$0.00	$0.03	$0.06	$0.09	$0.12	$0.15	$0.18	$0.21	$0.24	$0.27

Who would win the auction? Participants #1, #2, #3, and #4 would win the auction because they were the **four lowest** bidders. How much would I pay participants #1, #2, #3, and #4 to give up their Large Snickers bar and take the Small Snickers? I would pay them the **5th lowest** bid amount, which was $0.12. Thus, participants #1, #2, #3, and #4 would come to the front of the room, be paid $0.12 and exchange their Large Snickers bar for a Small Snickers. Participants #5, #6, #7, #8, #9 and #10 would be paid nothing and would leave with their free Large Snickers bar.

* Note: these dollar amounts were used for illustrative purposes only and should not in any way reflect what the candy bars may be worth to you*

Do you have any questions before we begin?

Please use the bid sheets marked "candy bar auction."

7.11.1   GM cookie auction

Now that you have had the chance to learn how the auction will work, we are interested in your preferences for two types of cookies.

For agreeing to participate in this research session, we are giving each of you a free cookie. This cookie is yours to keep. We also want you to know that the cookie you have been given contains *NO* genetically modified ingredients.

Although you have been given this cookie for free, we will give you the opportunity to participate in an auction to obtain a different type of cookie if you so desire. Here in the front of the room, we have another type of cookie. This cookie was made *with* genetically modified ingredients. Specifically, this cookie was made with vegetable oil that came from vegetable seeds that were genetically modified. Other than differences I just described, the cookies are the same size, weight, and taste as the cookie that you have been given.

We will now conduct an auction, where you will have the opportunity to exchange your cookie that contains *NO* genetically modified ingredients for the cookie *with* genetically modified ingredients. In a moment, you will be asked to indicate the *least* amount of money I must pay you to exchange your cookie for the cookie *with* genetically modified ingredients by writing bids on the enclosed bid sheets. The procedures for this auction are exactly the same as the candy bar auction, with one exception: we request that all participants **eat** their cookies at the end of the auction. To refresh your memory as to how the auction works, I will go through the instructions again.

Auction procedures
1. First, each of you has been given a bid sheet in your packet. On this sheet you will, in a moment, write the *least* amount of money you must be paid so that you would be willing to *exchange* your cookie for the cookie that contains genetically modified ingredients. This is the least amount of money I must pay you to take the cookie *with* genetically modified ingredients instead of the cookie you now have, which contains *NO* genetically modified ingredients. Note: your bids are private information and should not be shared with anyone.
2. After you've finished writing your bids, the monitor will go around the room and collect the bid sheets.
3. In the front of the room, each of your bids will be ranked from lowest to highest.
4. The *four lowest* bids will win the auction. The individuals with the four lowest bids will be paid the *5th lowest* bid amount for the exchange.
5. We will write the winning bidder numbers and the winning price on the chalkboard for everyone to see.
6. After posting the price, we will re-conduct the auction for nine additional rounds.
7. At the completion of the 10th round, we will randomly draw a number 1 through 10 to determine the binding round. For example, if we randomly draw the number 5, then we will ignore outcomes in all other rounds and only focus on the winning bidder and price in round 5. Importantly, all rounds have an equally likely chance of being binding.
8. Once the binding round has been determined, the winning bidders will come forward and be paid the 5th lowest bid amount and exchange their cookie for the cookie made *with* genetically modified ingredients. All other participants will keep their cookie made *without* genetically engineered ingredients.

Important notes
• You will only have the opportunity to win an auction for *one* cookie. Because we randomly draw a binding round, you *cannot* win more than one cookie from this auction.
• The winning bidder *will actually be paid money* to exchange their cookie with no genetically modified ingredients for the cookie with genetically modified ingredients. This procedure is **not** hypothetical.
• We will also expect every participant to eat their cookie at the conclusion of the auction.

- In this auction, the best strategy is to bid *exactly* what it is worth to you to *exchange* your cookie for the cookie with genetically modified ingredients.
- It is acceptable to bid $0.00 in any round. This would mean that you are willing to accept the cookie made with genetically modified ingredients for no compensation.
- Importantly, we are interested in what it is worth to you to *exchange* your cookie for the cookie made with genetically modified ingredients.

  Do you have any questions before we begin?

8   Auction design: case studies*

8.1   Introduction

Results from experimental auctions frequently generate as many questions as
answers about bidding behavior and auction design. Creating an auction that
balances experimental control and real-world context can raise fundamental
questions about how experience with a good and the market affects bidding,
whether preferences are fixed or fungible with different market interaction,
how incentive structures can affect bidding behavior, and how hypothetical
payments affect bidding behavior. This chapter reports on some of our own
work to explore questions of auction design; queries triggered by attempts
to value new food products and other basic goods. We focus on eight case
studies related to auction design: preference learning, auction institution and the
willingness to pay/willingness to accept gap, second price auction tournaments,
fixed or fungible preference, gift exchange, calibration of real and hypothetical
bidding, and bidding behavior in consequential auctions.

8.2   Preference learning

Evidence from experimental auctions suggests the average person will pay a
price premium for many new products. But some observers have pointed out
that this premium frequently exceeds expectations of what they think people
would actually pay in a real retail market. In the case of food safety, for instance,
the average person was willing to pay a one-time $0.70 per meal price premium
to reduce the health risk from food-borne pathogens – a premium that some
observers familiar with the market for safer food believe to be unduly high
(Hayes *et al.*, 1995).

   The question is why price premia are greater than expected by some
in the experimental auction. One explanation is the *novelty of the experiment experience*. Experimental auctions are usually designed as a one-time

* This chapter draws on material worked on over the past decade with colleagues and students
  including Dermot Hayes, Sean Fox, Greg Parkhurst, Chris McIntosh, Bob Wilhelm, Sara Gunnersson, Todd Cherry, Cannon Koo, Michael Margolis, John List, and Lucine Tadevosyan.

experience in which a person submits bids in multiple trials in one treatment on one day. Some bidders might be able to afford a high price premium in a new and singular setting. A second explanation is the *novelty of the good*. Many bidders have never experienced the new goods up for auction, e.g., irradiated meat or genetically modified food. Theory predicts a bid will reflect two elements of value: the consumption value of the good and the information value of learning how the good fits into his or her preference set (Grossman *et al.*, 1977; Crocker and Shogren, 1991). *Preference learning* exists if people bid large amounts for a good because they wanted to learn about an unfamiliar good.

Shogren *et al.* (2000) tested these two explanations by auctioning three goods varying in familiarity (candy bars, mangos, and irradiated pork) to subjects in four consecutive experimental auctions over a two-week period. If experimental novelty tells the story, average bids should decline as the novelty wears off for all three goods, familiar or unfamiliar. But if preference learning is the explanation, average bids should remain relatively stable for the familiar goods and should decline for unfamiliar goods once people become familiar with them. Once a person learns by actually eating the good, his bid should decline.

The experimental design had each student subject attend four sessions over a two-week period in a taste-testing room at a meat laboratory. They were paid $10 for each session and a $50 bonus for perfect attendance. Each session had three stages. In stage 1, the monitor endowed each subject with a brand name candy bar. Each subject submitted a bid stating what he or she would pay to exchange their candy bar for an alternative brand of candy bar. All auctions were second price and were conducted over five rounds. The monitor displayed the identification number of the highest bidder and the second highest bid (i.e., market price) each round, and after all five rounds, one round was randomly selected as binding.

In stage 2, the monitors displayed two types of pork meat, the only difference was one had been irradiated to control for *trichinella*. Subjects were endowed with a non-irradiated pork sandwich, and then were given information on the likelihood and severity of *trichinella* and the irradiation process. Each subject bid to 'upgrade' from the non-irradiated to the irradiated pork sandwich. Subjects knew that to receive their participation fee, they would eat the sandwich at the end of the session. In stage 3, each subject was endowed with an apple and bid to exchange it for a mango.

Since each subject gave fifteen bids in four sessions, the following panel data model was estimated for each of the three goods:

$$Bid_{it} = \alpha_i + \sum_{1}^{3} \beta S_t + \sum_{1}^{2} CX_{it} + \varepsilon_{it} \tag{8.1}$$

Table 8.1. *Fixed-effects estimation results of bid function*

Variable	Candy	Mango	Pork
Session 1	−0.005	−0.01	0.051*
	(−1.48)[a]	(−1.45)	(5.54)
Session 2	−.001	0.005	0.024*
	(−0.30)	(0.74)	(2.88)
Session 3	0.003	0.011	0.011
	(0.76)	(1.59)	(1.44)
Winner	−0.033*	−0.141*	−0.10*
	(−5.55)	(−13.19)	(−6.72)
Lagged price	0.18*	0.14*	−0.08
	(3.05)	(4.21)	(−1.60)
R^2	0.57	0.66	0.75
Adjusted R^2	0.54	0.64	0.73
$F(\alpha_i = 0)$	19.1*	32.6*	39.2
(d.f.)	(29,534)	(29,534)	(29,534)
N	570	570	570

[a] t-ratios in parentheses beneath coefficient estimates.
* Significant at the p < .01 confidence level.

where Bid_{it} denotes subject i's bid in trial t, α_i represents a fixed/random bidder effect, which controls for individual-specific time-invariant effects such as subjects' private values and subjective risk perceptions for the good; S_t are dichotomous variables that represent each of the four data gathering sessions (excluding Session 4 as the baseline reference category); and X_{it} are other factors that may affect bidding behavior. In X_{it}, we include lagged price to control for any posted price effects, and a dichotomous variable that indicates whether the participant was a winner of the item in a previous session (winner = 1; otherwise 0).

Table 8.1 contains our panel data estimation results. The results suggest that bidding behavior differed across sessions, but only for unfamiliar goods. Coefficient estimates in the candy and mango regressions show that bidding behavior did not significantly change across the four sessions for these two goods. These results imply bidders were not enticed to bid differently on familiar goods when they are confronted with the novel lab environment. Empirical estimates in the pork regression differ. Subjects tend to decrease their bids slowly over the four sessions. For example, a coefficient estimate of 0.051 for the session 1 dummy variable indicates that controlling for price, whether the subject was a previous winner, and subject-specific effects, participants bid about a nickel higher in the first session compared to the fourth. Given that the mean bid in all four sessions was approximately nine cents, this decrease is dramatic.

Combining empirical results from the pork regression with estimates from regressions of the familiar goods suggests that people tend to bid in an aggressive manner in early sessions, but only for unfamiliar goods. For familiar goods that the bidder may have had past experience, there appears to be little evidence of a lab novelty effect. We reject the novelty of the experiment experience hypothesis.

The results also show that conditional bids from winners significantly decrease after experience with the good. Estimates related to the coefficient of *winner* in each auction imply that winners tend to reduce their bids significantly in the next session. Conditioning on subject-specific effects, lagged price, and session number, our estimates imply that winning subjects decrease their bid by about 3.3, 14.1, and 10 cents in the sessions after they purchased the candy, mango, and pork. Because the sessions were held several days apart for goods that are probably consumed in or shortly after the experiment, the bid reduction is probably not a result of movement down the demand curve. Instead, results support the notion that people are trying to learn their preference for the unfamiliar good.

The results of this study indicate that preference learning about unfamiliar goods explains the "high" bids in experimental auctions, not the novelty of the experimental experience. Behavior is consistent with the view that a person's bid includes an information value that reflects his desire to learn more about unfamiliar goods, i.e., preference learning. Of course, this information value is a real value that might be expected to be present in the marketplace. Depending on the purpose of an auction, the information value may be an important economic component to measure (say when estimating market share of a novel good). Other studies may be more interested in longer-run valuations when all consumers are fully informed; if so, the design of the study presented in this section provides a way to disentangle the preference learning value from the underlying value for the good. Additional research on the relationship between individual measures of familiarity with a good and bidding behavior would help to further resolve this issue.

8.3   Willingness to pay, willingness to accept, and the auction mechanism

A key question is whether the choice of auction mechanism is responsible for generating the reported behavioral anomalies in elicited values. One on-going debate is over the driver of the unexpected gap between willingness to pay (WTP) and willingness to accept (WTA) measures of value. Rational choice theory suggests that with small income effects and at least one perfect substitute, WTP for a commodity and WTA to sell the same commodity should be about equal (Hanemann, 1991).

Evidence has accumulated over the past two decades suggesting a significant gap exists between WTP and WTA. Consider the conflicting results from two visible papers. First, Kahneman *et al.* (1990) report evidence to support their idea of the *endowment effect* as why WTP diverges from WTA. The idea behind the psychological argument for the endowment effect is that people treat gains and losses asymmetrically: the fear of a loss weighs more heavily than the enjoyment from an equal gain. The effect exists if people offer to sell a commonly available good in their possession at a substantially higher amount than they will pay for the identical good not in their possession. Their results make a case for the existence of a fundamental endowment effect as WTA exceeded WTP in all treatments over all iterations. People's preferences seemed to depend on initial endowments of resources, a violation of rational choice theory.

In contrast, Shogren *et al.* (1994) designed an experimental auction to test the proposition that with positive income elasticity and repeated market participation, WTP and WTA will converge for a market good with close substitutes (e.g., candy bars and mugs) but will not converge for a good with imperfect market substitute (a sandwich with health risk). They also considered whether transaction costs could explain the WTP-WTA gap by providing the market goods (e.g., candy bars and mugs) immediately outside the lab door that could be purchased by the subjects once the experiment ended. Their results showed that WTP and WTA values converged after several repeated trials for candy bars and mugs (goods with many available substitutes), but that the values continued to diverge for the reduced health risks from safer food.

The question is why different results were obtained in these two studies. One major distinction between Kahneman *et al.* (1990) and Shogren *et al.* (1994) is their choice of auction mechanism. Kahneman *et al.* (1990) used the BDM mechanism to elicit preferences whereas Shogren *et al.* (1994) used a second price auction. The choice of auction should not matter in theory since a bidder's weakly dominant strategy is to state their true WTP or WTA in both mechanisms. Evidence exists, however, which reveals differences in bids across incentive-compatible auctions. Rutström (1998), for instance, detected WTP bid differences elicited in the BDM and Vickrey style auctions. Differences in auction mechanism might be one cause of the differences in results between these two studies.

Did the choice of auction mechanism generate the different findings on the WTP-WTA gap? Too many differences exist across the two original experimental designs to say for sure. In response, Shogren *et al.* (2001b) addressed this issue by designing an experiment in which the auction mechanism was varied as a treatment variable. If the endowment effect accounts for observed behavior, the effect should be observable and persistent for any mechanism used to elicit WTP and WTA, provided the mechanism is incentive compatible. Shogren *et al.* (2001b) tested this thesis by evaluating the impact of three auction mechanisms in the measurement of WTP and WTA for goods with close substitutes: the BDM mechanism with exogenous price feedback, second price auction with endogenous market-clearing price feedback, and a random nth price auction with endogenous market-clearing price feedback.

Table 8.2 summarizes the design parameters in Kahneman *et al.* (1990), Shogren *et al.* (1994), and the new Shogren *et al.* (2001b) study. The key experimental parameters in the new design are: (i) *auctioned goods*: a brand-name candy bar in Stage 1 and an Iowa State University coffee mug in Stage 2; (ii) *initial monetary endowment*: $15 paid up-front; (iii) *number of trials*: ten trials per experiment, in which wealth effects were controlled by randomly selecting one of the ten trials to be the binding trial; (iv) *retail price information on the commodities*: none was provided; (v) *subject participation*: voluntary participants from the student population at Iowa State University; (vi) *number of subjects per session*: eight to ten subjects in the second price auctions and twenty for the BDM mechanism; and (vii) the *auction mechanism*: either the BDM, second price, or random nth price.

For the auction mechanisms, the BDM mechanism in Kahneman *et al.*'s fifth experimental treatment was used. The BDM mechanism worked as follows. *Step 1:* Twenty subjects were randomly divided into two subgroups of ten buyers and ten sellers. *Step 2:* Monitors gave each seller a candy bar in Stage 1 (a coffee mug in Stage 2), which he or she could take home or sell at the auction. *Step 3:* Each buyer had the option to buy the commodity in the auction. *Step 4:* Each buyer and seller were asked to determine independently and privately their maximum WTP or minimum WTA by marking an "X" on a recording sheet listing a price schedule such as:

I will buy (sell)   I will not buy (sell)

	I will buy (sell)	I will not buy (sell)
If the price is $ 0.40	_____	_____
If the price is $ 0.30	_____	_____
If the price is $ 0.20	_____	_____

Step 5: After collecting all recording sheets from buyers and sellers, one price from the sheet was selected randomly. *Step 6:* If a buyer was willing to pay at least the exogenous random price, he or she bought the commodity. If the seller was willing to accept less than or equal to the random price, he or she sold the commodity. *Step 7:* The random price along with the number of buyers and sellers willing to buy and sell at the random price were recorded on the blackboard as public information. *Step 8:* After the tenth trial in each stage, one of the ten trials was randomly selected as the binding trial that determined take-home pay.

The second price auction was the same as in Shogren *et al.* (1994). In the WTP treatment, bidders were asked to record, privately and independently, the

Table 8.2. *Summary of experimental design parameters*

Design parameter	Original experimental designs		New experimental design	
	Original Kahneman *et al.* (1990)	Original Shogren *et al.* (1994)	New experiments	Random *n*th price auction
Auctioned goods	Tokens, pens, & mugs	Candy bar, sandwich, & mugs	Candy bar & mugs	Candy bar & mugs
Initial monetary endowment	None	$3: candy bar $15: sandwich or mug	$15	$15
Number of trials	Varied between 3 and 7	5: candy bar 20: sandwich 10: mugs	10: candy bar 10: mugs	10: candy bar 10: mugs
Retail price information	Provided for some treatments	None provided	None provided	None provided
Subject participation	In-class	Voluntary	Voluntary	Voluntary
Number of subjects per session	Varied between 30 & 44	12 to 15	8–10: second price auction 20: BDM	10: random *n*th price auction
Auction institution	Simon Fraser U. Becker-DeGroot-Marschak Mechanism (BDM)	Iowa State U. Second price auction (SPA)	Iowa State U. Both the BDM and the second price auction	U. Central FL Random *n*th price auction

maximum he or she was willing to pay for the candy bar (Stage 1) or coffee mug (Stage 2) on a recording sheet in ten repeated trials. In each trial, the monitors collected the recording cards, and then posted the identification number of the highest bidder and the market-clearing price (the second highest bid) on the blackboard as public information. One of the ten trials was randomly selected as binding at the conclusion of the session. In the WTA treatments, monitors gave each subject a candy bar (Stage 1) or a coffee mug (Stage 2). Subjects wrote their minimum WTA to sell the commodity on their recording sheet in each of ten trials and for both stages. Again monitors posted the identification number of the lowest bidder and the market-clearing price (the second lowest bid) after each trial. After the tenth trial in each stage the monitors randomly selected one of the ten trials as the binding trial. The auctions were conducted in three sessions on the same day at Iowa State University. There were 78 participants. Different subjects participated in each session. Each session was completed within two hours.

Tables 8.3 and 8.4 present the summary statistics of the experimental results on the BDM and second price auction treatments. In the BDM treatment, the average selling price exceeded the average buying price for all ten trials in both the candy bar and coffee mug stages. The same is true of the median bids. The average and median WTA/WTP ratios remain relatively constant throughout the ten trials, ranging from 1.5 to 1.8 for the candy bar and 1.4 to 1.6 for the coffee mug. The null hypothesis that the mean WTP and WTA are equal can be rejected at the $p < 0.01$ level ($p = 0.05$ and $p = 0.10$) for candy bars (coffee mugs) using a small sample t-test and a Mann-Whitney U-test.

The bidding behavior in the second-price auction followed a different pattern. As illustrated in Table 8.4, bidding behavior in trial 1 does not contradict Kahneman $et\ al.$'s (1990) concept of an endowment effect. The average and median WTA bid was significantly greater than the average or median WTP bid in trial 1. Unlike the BDM treatment, however, WTA offers decreased and WTP bids increased after the initial trial in each second price auction. The average and median WTA/WTP ratios decline throughout the ten trials, decreasing from 1.4 in trial one to 0.88 in trial nine for the candy bar (the ratio in trial ten was 4, including an extreme outlier bid of $50).[1] The average WTA-WTP ratio decreased from 2.5 in trial one to 1.05 in trial ten for the coffee mug. In trials two to ten for the candy bar, we cannot reject the null hypothesis that the mean WTP and WTA are equal at the 10% level using a t-test and at the 5% level using a Mann-Whitney U-test. For the coffee mug, we cannot reject the null in trials three to seven and nine to ten at the 5% level using the t-test, and we cannot reject the null in trials two to ten at the 1% level using the Mann-Whitney U-test. The value disparity faded away in the second-price auction with feedback on the endogenous market-clearing price: average WTP and WTA value measures

---

[1] The second price auction was clearly not demand revealing in trial ten for this subject.

Table 8.3. *Summary statistics of the Becker-DeGroot-Marschak Mechanism*

Good	Value measure		Trial 1	2	3	4	5	6	7	8	9	10
Candy	WTP	Mean	$0.58	$0.50	$0.54	$0.54	$0.53	$0.53	$0.47	$0.48	$0.51	$0.51
	N = 20	Median	0.50	0.50	0.50	0.50	0.50	0.50	0.50	0.50	0.50	0.50
		Variance	0.121	0.093	0.071	0.070	0.080	0.084	0.097	0.092	0.075	0.079
	WTA	Mean	0.92	0.90	0.86	0.82	0.83	0.78	0.80	0.79	0.78	0.78
	N = 20	Median	0.90	1.00	0.95	0.85	0.80	0.80	0.80	0.80	0.80	0.80
		Variance	0.067	0.086	0.072	0.105	0.073	0.067	0.087	0.092	0.091	0.114
	Ratio of mean WTA/WTP		1.59	1.80	1.59	1.52	1.57	1.47	1.70	1.65	1.53	1.53
	t-test of means		−3.5[a]	−4.2[a]	−3.8[a]	−2.9[a]	−3.4[a]	−2.9[a]	−3.4[a]	−3.2[a]	−2.9[a]	−2.7[a]
Mug	WTP	Mean	$2.40	$2.40	$2.25	$2.28	$2.25	$2.25	$2.23	$2.23	$2.10	$2.18
	N = 20	Median	1.75	1.75	1.75	1.75	1.75	1.75	1.75	1.75	1.25	1.50
		Variance	4.200	4.700	4.540	4.144	3.961	3.961	3.802	3.802	3.085	3.928
	WTA	Mean	3.68	3.55	3.50	3.40	3.40	3.35	3.40	3.43	3.35	3.13
	N = 20	Median	3.25	3.50	3.25	3.00	3.00	3.00	3.00	3.00	3.00	3.00
		Variance	5.955	5.287	5.553	5.726	5.674	5.134	5.463	5.349	5.108	5.628
	Ratio of mean WTA/WTP		1.53	1.46	1.56	1.49	1.51	1.49	1.52	1.54	1.60	1.44
	t-test of means		−1.8[b]	−1.6[c]	−1.8[d]	−1.6[e]	−1.6[e]	−1.6[e]	−1.7[b]	−1.8[d]	−2.0[d]	−1.4[e]

H_0: $MEAN_{WTP} - MEAN_{WTA} = 0$; H_A: $MEAN_{WTP} - MEAN_{WTA} < 0$.

[a] *t*-test: reject H_0 at the 1% level; Mann-Whitney *U*-test: reject H_0 at the 1% level.
[b] *t*-test: reject H_0 at the 5% level; Mann-Whitney *U*-test: reject H_0 at the 10% level.
[c] *t*-test: reject H_0 at the 10% level; Mann-Whitney *U*-test: reject H_0 at the 5% level.
[d] *t*-test: reject H_0 at the 5% level; Mann-Whitney *U*-test: reject H_0 at the 5% level.
[e] *t*-test: reject H_0 at the 10% level; Mann-Whitney *U*-test: reject H_0 at the 10% level.

Table 8.4. *Summary statistics of the second price auction*

Good	Value measure		Trial									
			1	2	3	4	5	6	7	8	9	10
Candy	WTP N = 18	Mean	$0.56	$0.62	$0.63	$0.70	$0.68	$0.72	$0.69	$0.71	$0.73	$0.75
		Median	0.53	0.63	0.62	0.75	0.72	0.80	0.70	0.78	0.86	0.90
		Variance	0.090	0.086	0.092	0.102	0.098	0.174	0.103	0.114	0.118	0.123
	WTA N = 20	Mean	0.78	0.84	0.65	0.62	0.89	0.67	0.51	0.64	0.64	3.00
		Median	0.75	0.60	0.50	0.45	0.43	0.37	0.29	0.29	0.29	0.26
		Variance	0.169	1.033	0.376	0.363	4.631	1.199	0.530	1.267	1.278	123.57
	Ratio of mean WTA/WTP		1.39	1.35	1.03	0.89	1.31	0.93	0.74	0.90	0.88	4.00
	t-test of means		-1.9^b	-0.9	-0.1	0.5	-0.4	0.2	1.0	0.3	0.3	-0.9
Mug	WTP N = 18	Mean	$2.22	$2.73	$2.90	$3.19	$3.38	$3.34	$3.33	$3.58	$3.42	$3.28
		Median	1.75	3.00	3.25	3.40	3.63	3.53	3.74	3.80	3.87	3.73
		Variance	2.142	1.407	1.573	1.805	1.855	2.821	2.726	2.276	2.918	2.687
	WTA N = 20	Mean	5.52	4.56	3.77	3.58	3.52	3.16	3.08	2.45	3.33	3.44
		Median	4.88	5.00	4.48	3.75	4.01	3.18	3.25	1.13	3.50	4.00
		Variance	15.912	13.397	6.971	6.775	5.749	6.364	6.448	5.498	7.073	8.304
	Ratio of mean WTA/WTP		2.49	1.67	1.30	1.12	1.04	0.95	0.92	0.68	0.97	1.05
	t-test of means		-3.4^a	-2.1^c	-1.3^d	-0.6	-0.2	0.3	0.4	1.8^c	0.1	-0.2

H_0: $MEAN_{WTP} - MEAN_{WTA} = 0$; H_A: $MEAN_{WTP} - MEAN_{WTA} < 0$.
[a] t-test: reject H_0 at the 1% level; Mann-Whitney U-test: reject H_0 at the 1% level.
[b] t-test: reject H_0 at the 5% level; Mann-Whitney U-test: reject H_0 at the 5% level.
[c] t-test: reject H_0 at the 5% level.
[d] t-test: reject H_0 at the 10% level.

are not statistically different. If the idea that the effect should persist across auctions and trials is correct, our results suggest no fundamental endowment effect exists.

Although compelling, one could challenge the results with notions of *affiliated bidding behavior* and a *top dog effect*. First, concern has been voiced that most bidders walk into a valuation auction cold, and thus the common uncertainty about the value of the good might create "affiliated" values or beliefs (see Milgrom and Weber, 1982). Affiliation exists if high bids induce low bidders to increase their bids. The posted bid affects behavior because prices send information to bidders about commonly perceived, but unknown, characteristics of the product. List and Shogren (1999) reject this affiliation hypothesis for familiar goods in second price auctions with feedback. Second, some observers have suggested that the second price auction creates an environment that is too competitive to elicit people's true WTA and WTP. People might be submitting bids to win for winning's sake. They might bid WTP up and WTA down to leave the experiment as the "top dog" among their peers. While this is a theoretical possibility, experimental evidence at this time provides little support for this conjecture (see Shogren *et al.*, 2001b). The evidence suggests that the top dog effect is not a universal phenomenon in valuation experiments, and the case remains unarticulated by its supporters as to why it should exist for one set of goods over another.

But these retorts do not explain the observations of Knetsch *et al.* (2001) who ran second price and ninth price auctions with repeated trials for a familiar good. They found large gaps in WTP and WTA values for the ninth price auction, but not for the second price auction. They concluded that the "endowment effect remains robust over repeated trials, and that contrary to common understanding the Vickrey auction may not be demand revealing." They make the reasonable case that the uniform auction is not necessarily the preferred mechanism if it fails to engage *off-the-margin bidders*, i.e., bidders whose value is far below or above the market-clearing price. They argue something is fundamentally flawed about the mechanism, that is, the endowment effect is not the "problem" the mechanism is the "problem."

These off-the margin bidders in the second and ninth price auctions might have less incentive to make sincere bids if they believe they have no chance to win or to lose the auction and profit. The second price auction might not engage low value bidders, while the ninth price auction might not engage high value bidders. Ninth price auction bidders realize the support of bids is significantly below their value and therefore can afford to submit false bids without being punished by the market. Evidence using induced values does not contradict this conjecture: bidders off-the-margin of the market-clearing price frequently do not bid sincerely (e.g., Miller and Plott, 1985). Off-margin low value bidders in the second price auctions are bounded from above by the high value bidders;

off-margin high value bidders in the ninth price auction are unbounded from above. This suggests that the off-margin bidding behavior has greater chance for more variability in the ninth price auction.

To address this question of unengaged bidders, Shogren *et al.* (2001b) tested the random *n*th price auction. The auction attempts to engage all bidders by combining the best parts of the BDM and second price mechanisms: a random but endogenously determined market-clearing price. Randomness to keep all bidders in the auction and reduce their incentive to chase a particular market-clearing price; endogenous to guarantee that the bidders themselves determine the market-clear price.

The random *n*th price auction works as follows: (i) each bidder submits a bid (offer); (ii) each bid (offer) is rank-ordered from lowest to highest; (iii) the monitor selects a random number, the *n* in the *n*th price auction, uniformly distributed between two and *N* (*N* bidders); and (iv) in the WTP case, the monitor sells one unit of the good to each of the $(n - 1)$ highest bidders at the *n*th price; in the WTA case, the monitor buys one unit each from the $(n - 1)$ lowest bidders and pays the *n*th lowest bid. Lab evidence suggests the auction can work: bidders revealed sincere bids, and off-the-margin bidders were more engaged relative to the standard second price mechanism (Shogren *et al.*, 2001a).

Shogren *et al.* (2001b) constructed the random *n*th price treatment to match the two other treatments except for the obvious switch of the auction mechanism. Table 8.2 summarizes the random *n*th price experiments, which were run in four sessions on the same day at the University of Central Florida with a total of forty subjects. Table 8.5 summarizes the experimental results. Bidding behavior was similar to that observed in the second price auction. The initial WTA-WTP gap disappears with experience. The average and median WTA and WTP bids are significantly different through trial three for the candy bar and trial four for the coffee mug, which does not contradict Kahneman *et al.*'s (1990) concept of an endowment effect.

The results then show the WTP and WTA values converged in the last seven trials for candy bars and six trials for coffee mugs. For the candy bar, the median WTA/WTP ratio dropped from nearly two to one from trial one to trial ten. We cannot reject the null hypothesis that the mean WTP and WTA are equal at even the 10% confidence level using a *t*-test or a nonparametric Mann-Whitney *U*-test in trials four to ten. For the coffee mug, the average WTA/WTP ratio decreased to 0.78 in trial ten from 2.42 in trial one. We cannot reject the null in trials five to ten at the 10% level using the *t*-test, and we cannot reject the null in trials two to ten at the 5% level using the Mann-Whitney *U*-test. Like behavior in the second price auction, little value disparity is observed in the random *n*th price auction after minimal market experience: average WTP and WTA value measures are not statistically different in the later trials.

Table 8.5. *Summary statistics of the random nth price auction*

Good	Value measure		Trial									
			1	2	3	4	5	6	7	8	9	10
Candy	*WTP*	Mean	$0.69	$0.70	$0.68	$0.74	$0.68	$0.88	$0.91	$0.93	$1.01	$0.99
	N = 20	Median	0.53	0.58	0.50	0.50	0.61	0.75	0.77	0.88	1.00	1.00
		Variance	0.30	0.26	0.33	0.45	0.31	0.45	0.48	0.51	0.47	0.52
	WTA	Mean	1.29	1.33	1.26	1.07	0.93	1.05	1.06	1.05	0.88	0.88
	N = 20	Median	1.00	1.13	1.12	1.00	1.00	0.99	0.88	0.87	0.99	1.00
		Variance	0.67	0.64	0.56	0.45	0.21	0.98	1.14	1.20	0.22	0.20
	Ratio of mean WTA/WTP		1.87	1.90	1.85	1.44	1.36	1.20	1.15	1.13	0.87	0.89
	t-test of means		−2.7[a]	−2.9[a]	−2.8[a]	−1.5	−1.5	−0.67	−0.48	−0.41	0.70	0.58
Mug	*WTP*	Mean	$2.15	$2.21	$2.32	$2.21	$2.27	$2.76	$2.99	$2.77	$2.99	$3.83
	N = 20	Median	1.00	1.00	1.23	1.55	2.00	2.25	2.00	3.00	2.50	3.25
		Variance	6.07	6.06	6.22	4.55	2.88	3.72	7.38	2.76	3.10	4.96
	WTA	Mean	5.21	4.62	4.19	4.29	3.63	3.35	3.37	2.63	2.98	3.02
	N = 20	Median	5.03	4.50	3.75	3.53	3.00	2.50	2.03	2.00	2.35	2.00
		Variance	12.69	11.83	10.98	12.94	11.72	5.97	6.09	4.64	5.70	5.80
	Ratio of mean WTA/WTP		2.42	2.08	1.81	1.93	1.60	1.21	1.12	0.95	0.99	0.78
	t-test of means		−3.1[a]	−2.5[a]	−2.0[d]	−2.2[b]	−1.6	−0.84	−0.46	0.23	0.01	1.10

H_0: $MEAN_{WTP} - MEAN_{WTA} = 0$; H_A: $MEAN_{WTP} - MEAN_{WTA} < 0$.

[a] *t*-test: reject H_0 at the 1% level; Mann-Whitney *U*-test: reject H_0 at the 1% level.

[b] *t*-test: reject H_0 at the 5% level; Mann-Whitney *U*-test: reject H_0 at the 5% level.

[c] *t*-test: reject H_0 at the 5% level.

[d] *t*-test: reject H_0 at the 10% level.

In conclusion, Shogren *et al.* (2001b) find that while initial bidding behavior does not contradict the endowment effect concept, the effect can be eliminated with repetitions of a second price or random *n*th price auction. These results provide little support that the endowment effect exists insofar as the endowment effect is perceived as an effect that should persist across auction mechanisms and across trials. These findings suggest the auction mechanism could have accounted for the conflicting observations in Kahneman *et al.* (1990) and Shogren *et al.* (1994). These results raise the question of whether the endowment effect is a fundamental part of choice or simply an artifact of a weak exchange environment (see also Plott and Zeiler, 2005). The weaker the exchange institution, the weaker the socialization of rational behavior and the stronger the potential hold of asocial anomalies on choice. Determining exactly why three theoretically incentive compatible mechanisms are not all demand-revealing suggest more research is needed to develop a theory of auction-dependent bidding behavior and more experimental work to test out its predictions.

8.4   Second price auction tournaments

Vickrey's (1961) second price auction has been frequently used in experiments because of three attractive properties: the auction is weakly demand revealing in theory, bidders set the market-clearing price, and the allocation and pricing rules are easy to explain to bidders. But whether bidders understand these rules in practice is another question. Evidence from induced value studies suggests bidders do not always bid their induced value, especially bidders with induced values far away from the market-clearing price (see the discussion in Chapter 2 and in Kagel, 1995). Insincere bidding occurs when people do not understand the incentives or the incentives are not salient.

These findings triggered us to explore whether a second price auction tournament with a non-linear payoff schedule could induce people to bid more sincerely relative to the standard auction design. Shogren *et al.* (2006) consider a tournament setting for three reasons. First, real world tournaments are used to induce people to pay attention to small differences in measurable performance, see for instance Lazear and Rosen (1981), Ehrenberg and Bognanno (1990), Jensen and Murphy (1990), and Drago *et al.* (1996). Second, some research suggests people in a tournament act more like rational choice theory predicts, especially when the winner earns a significant prize ($150+) relative to a standard experimental design in which earnings accumulate round by round (e.g., see Shogren, 1997, Bull *et al.*, 1987, Drago and Heywood, 1989, and Baik *et al*, 1999). Third, recasting the second price auction as a tournament rewards rational bidding by providing a reason for both on-margin and off-margin bidders to pay attention to the incentives.

To investigate whether tournaments might generate behavior more consistent with theoretical predictions, an experiment was designed following typical procedures, in which the standard and tournament auction were the treatments. Instructions were purposefully kept simple and included a one-page description of the auction rules and payoff structure along with a one-page quiz to test bidders' understanding. Bidders knew that their take-home pay in a session depended on the total points they earned over twenty trials. They also knew that they earned points by bidding in the auction. The information feedback in each round was identical across treatments: players only got to see if they won an auction and how many points they earned; no one saw what anyone else had bid or earned.

The seven rules in both treatments were:
1. Each bidder was randomly assigned a resale value (note: each bidder could get a different resale value in each trial, and the values could differ across bidders).
2. Each bidder then submitted a bid.
3. The monitor ranked the bids from highest to lowest.
4. The bidder with the highest bid won the auction for that trial.
5. The price paid by the winner was the second-highest bid in that trial.
6. The amount of points earned by the highest bidder equaled the resale value minus price.
7. Non-winners in that trial earned zero points.

The standard and tournament auction designs were identical except for the payoff scheme. In the standard auction, take-home pay was: $5 + $5* (total individual points earned over all trials). In the tournament, take-home pay depended on points earned by the person relative to points earned by all other participants over all trials. Tournament payments were:

$120   Winner: the player with most total points at the end
$80   Runner up: the player with 2nd most points
$50   3rd place: the player with 3rd most points
$30   4th place: the player with the 4th most points
$15   Players ranked 5th, 6th, and 7th
$5   Players ranked 8th, 9th, and 10th.

For the standard auction, the expected payoff was $21.85, with maximum and minimum earnings of $25.50 and $18.50, including the flat $5 participation fee for each subject. For the tournament treatment, the expected payoff was $30.00, with a maximum and minimum of $120 and $5.[2]

---

[2] Some evidence exists that subjects react differently to differences in absolute payoffs provided differences are substantial enough. This could suggest the expected payoff difference for the tournament treatment could induce bidders to pay more attention to bidding just because of

Table 8.6. *Descriptive statistics (all rounds)*

	Standard auction design with linear payoffs	Tournament auction design with non-linear payoffs
Mean bid	$16.26	$10.94
(S.D.)	(64.28)	(7.10)
Mean induced value	9.98	9.98
(S.D.)	(5.74)	(5.74)
Mean [bid – induced value]	6.28	0.96
(S.D.)	(63.51)	(4.14)
Mean [bid/induced value]	1.70	1.21
(S.D.)	(4.52)	(1.23)
Mean percent of maximum surplus: Rounds 1–10	−470.2%	−435.7%
(S.D.)	(1311.7)	(664.1)
Mean percent of maximum surplus: Rounds 11–20	66.1%	−142.6%
(S.D.)	(69.5)	(515.1)

For each round, induced values were randomly drawn from a uniform distribution on [$0.00, $20.00] in ten-cent increments. Each auction had ten bidders; two sessions were run for each treatment for a total of forty bidders. Each session lasted about forty minutes. Table 8.6 summarizes bidding behavior for all rounds across both treatments. The unconditional results suggest the tournament induced more sincere bidding than the standard design. Mean bids were more accurate, and the variation was smaller with the tournament. The mean bid in the standard treatment exceeded the mean induced value (i.e., resale value) by $6.28 (standard deviation = $63.51); the mean bid in the tournament was only $0.96 larger than induced value (standard deviation = $4.14).

Using conditional panel regression analysis, three key results emerge. First, bidders bid more sincerely in the second price auction tournament than in the standard second price auction. Sincere bidding in the tournament is tested with a two-way random effects model:

$$Bid_{it} = \phi IN_{it} + \alpha_i + \varphi_t + \varepsilon_{it}, \tag{8.2}$$

where Bid_{it} denotes subject i's bid in trial t; IN_{it} denotes subject i's induced value in trial t; α_i represents subject-specific characteristics; φ_t represents

the absolute level effect. It remains an open question whether the less than twofold difference we have in our treatments is *substantial* enough to make a difference. Interestingly, one could have equated expected payoffs by increasing the show-up fee to $12.15 in the standard auction treatment; but it is unclear whether this would have made the incentives for sincere bidding better or worse given an even flatter payoff in the standard auction. In addition, the tournament payoffs were stated in dollar terms, whereas the standard auction was presented as points to be converted to dollars.

Table 8.7. *Panel data estimation results (two-way)*

Variable	Tournament auction sample		Standard auction sample		Pooled sample	
	Random effects	Fixed effects	Random effects	Fixed effects	Random effects	Fixed effects
Constant	0.86	0.84*	−4.55	−6.80	−1.87	−2.98
	(0.68)[a]	(0.34)	(7.22)	(6.25)	(3.68)	(3.14)
Induced value	1.01*	1.01*	2.09*	2.31*	1.55*	1.66*
	(0.03)	(0.03)	(0.53)	(0.55)	(0.29)	(0.28)
$F(\alpha_i = 0, \varphi_t = 0)$		7.26*		1.87*		2.12*
(d.f.)		(39, 360)		(39, 360)		(59, 740)
Breush-Pagan	$\chi_2^2 = 484.6^*$		$\chi_2^2 = 16.54^*$		$\chi_2^2 = 36.17^*$	
(p-value)	(0.00)		(0.00)		(0.00)	
Hausman	$\chi_1^2 = 0.11$		$\chi_1^2 = 3.38$		$\chi_1^2 = 3.35$	
(p-value)	(0.74)		(0.07)		(0.07)	
R^2	0.65	0.81	0.03	0.19	0.03	0.17
Sum of squares	6839	3817	1597160	1324560	1615820	1380509
N	400	400	400	400	800	800

[a] Numbers in parenthesis are standard errors.

trial-specific random effects, including learning or other trends in bidding behavior; and ε_{it} is iid error. For (8.2), perfect demand revealing bids requires $\phi = 1$, $\alpha_i = 0 \, (\forall i)$, and $\varphi_t = 0 \, (\forall t)$.

First, consider expression (8.2) estimated for the tournament data. Assuming α_i and φ_t are drawn from a bivariate normal distribution, the estimated equation is (standard errors in parenthesis):

$$Bid_{it} = \underset{(0.68)}{0.86} + \underset{(0.03)}{1.01 IN_{it}}$$

The equation was estimated with both fixed and random effects (see Table 8.7), but Hausman and Lagrange Multiplier tests support the random effects specification. Using a Wald test, the null hypothesis of truthful bidding ($\alpha = 0$ and $\varphi = 1$) cannot be rejected at the $p = 0.29$ level. The tournament is demand revealing.

Now consider behavior in the standard auction. Estimating expression (8.2) using the random effects specification for the standard auction treatment yields:

$$Bid_{it} = \underset{(7.22)}{-4.55} + \underset{(0.53)}{2.09 IN_{it}}.$$

The slope of the regression equation is twice as steep as theory predicts, and the intercept term below zero. The null hypothesis (that $\alpha = 0$ and $\varphi = 1$) is rejected at the 6% significance level. The rejection of the null hypothesis is the first indication that the tournament with the non-linear payoff may be structurally different than the standard auction with linear payoffs. Indeed, using a Chow test, we find the estimated models differ significantly across the two treatments: bidders were less likely to bid sincerely in the standard auction ($F_{1,796} = 5.87$, p-value $= 0.02$).

Second, the tournament auction design is more effective at engaging on-margin and off-margin bidders than the standard auction design. The effectiveness of the tournament relative to the standard auction to engage both on- and off-margin bidders is examined by separating the induced values into three groups: off-margin low values [\$0, \$5]; off-margin mid values (\$5, \$10]; and on-margin values (\$10, \$20]. Extending (8.2), the following equation is estimated to disentangle the treatment effects on sincere bidding:

$$
\begin{aligned}
Bid_{it} = \alpha_i &+ \phi_1 IN_{it} + \phi_2 (NL_{it}) + \phi_3 (IN_{it}{}^* NL_{it}) \\
&+ \phi_4 (mid_{it}) + \phi_5 (mid_{it}{}^* IN_{it}) + \phi_6 (mid_{it}{}^* NL_{it}) \\
&+ \phi_7 (mid_{it}{}^* IN_{it}{}^* NL_{it}) + \phi_8 (low_{it}) + \phi_9 (low_{it}{}^* IN_{it}) \quad (8.3) \\
&+ \phi_{10} (low_{it}{}^* NL_{it}) + \phi_{11} (low_{it}{}^* IN_{it}^* NL_{it}) + \varepsilon_{it},
\end{aligned}
$$

where the dependent variable, Bid_{it}, is subject i's bid in trial t, α_i is a subject-specific fixed/random effect that accounts for systematic differences in bidding patterns and controls for ordering of the experiment types; IN_{it} is subject i's induced private value in trial t; $NL_{it} = 1$ for non-linear pay (tournament) treatment, 0 otherwise; and $mid_{it} = 1$ for bidder i in trial t if his value was in the range (\$5, \$10] in trial t, 0 otherwise; and $low_{it} = 1$ for bidder i in trial t if his value was in the range [\$0, \$5] in trial t, 0 otherwise. The remaining variables $IN_{it}{}^* NL_{it}$, $mid_{it}{}^* IN_{it}$, $mid_{it}{}^* NL_{it}$, $mid_{it}{}^* IN_{it}{}^* NL_{it}$, $low_{it}{}^* IN_{it}$, $low_{it}{}^* NL_{it}$, and $low_{it}{}^* IN_{it}{}^* NL_{it}$, are interaction terms and allow slope and intercept changes across payment method and bidder type (i.e., off- or on-the-margin bidders).

Table 8.8 presents the regression results. Based on the Hausman test, we estimate a random effects model, which includes the NL dummy variable (column 3). Evaluating the estimated regression equations for high induced values, indicates the slope on the standard treatment is roughly four times that of the tournament treatment, 3.90 versus 0.92 (the tournament slope is close to demand revelation, i.e., unity). The intercept of the regression line is 2.7 for the tournament and -32.35 for the standard auction. A Wald test is used to test the joint hypothesis of demand revelation, intercept $= 0$, slope $= 1$. We reject the null hypothesis for the standard treatment ($\chi_2^2 = 13.32$, p-value < 0.01), but fail to reject the null hypothesis for the tournament ($\chi_2^2 = 0.10$, p-value $= 0.95$). For

Table 8.8. *On margin/off margin panel data estimation results (two-way)*

Variable	Random effects	Fixed effects	Random effects W/treatment variable
Constant	−15.04	−13.90	−32.35**
	(12.22)[a]	(12.10)	(16.22)
IN	2.84*	3.88*	3.90*
	(0.79)	(1.08)	(1.02)
NL			35.07***
			(22.34)
NL*IN	−0.83**	−3.02**	−2.98**
	(0.41)	(1.49)	(1.42)
Mid	−2.39	4.18	12.67
	(26.06)	(28.85)	(27.04)
Mid*NL	11.26	−19.59	−22.03
	(32.39)	(39.63)	(37.50)
Mid*NL*IN	−0.92	0.86	1.18
	(4.10)	(4.37)	(4.13)
Mid*IN	0.62	0.71	−0.26
	(3.04)	(3.18)	(2.98)
Low	18.43	34.42**	35.06**
	(15.19)	(19.19)	(18.00)
Low*NL	−3.20	−37.12***	−36.82***
	(13.50)	(26.26)	(24.90)
Low*NL*IN	1.03	3.22	3.15
	(4.31)	(4.56)	(4.31)
Low*IN	−2.02	−3.22	−3.10
	(3.21)	(3.35)	(3.13)
$F(\alpha_i = 0, \varphi_t = 0)$[b]		2.13*	
(d.f.)		(59,731)	
Breush-Pagan	$\chi_2^2 = 34.07^*$		$\chi_2^2 = 34.56^*$
(p-value)	(0.00)		(0.00)
Hausman	$\chi_1^2 = 10.77$		
(p-value)	(0.38)		
Standard and tournament equal	$\chi_5^2 = 5.29$	$\chi_5^2 = 6.57$	$\chi_6^2 = 7.83$
	(0.62)	(0.75)	(0.75)
R^2	0.05	0.19	0.05
Sum of squares	1600980	1363070	1596800
N	800	800	800

[a] Standard errors in parenthesis

* significant at the 5% level.

[b] The null hypothesis that $\alpha_i = 0$ and $\varphi_t = 0$ for all i and t is rejected at the p < 0.05 level of significance

Table 8.9. *Efficiency in the tournament and standard second price auction*

Treatment session	Winner of the auction		Price-setter of the auction	
	Highest value bidder (predicted winner)	Second highest value bidder	Highest value bidder	Second highest value bidder (predicted price-setter)
Tournament A	10	3	10	8
Tournament B	12	4	7	11
n = 40				
Total	**22**	7	17	**19**
Percentage	55%	17.5%	42.5%	47.5%
Standard Auction A	6	7	9	4
Standard Auction B	11	4	5	5
n = 40				
Total	**17**	11	14	**9**
Percentage	42.5%	27.5%	35%	22.5%

on-margin, high-induced values, the tournament is demand revealing, whereas the standard treatment is not.

Turning to the mid level induced values, we see the standard treatment has an intercept of -19.68 and a slope of 3.64. Alternatively, the tournament has an intercept of -6.64 and a slope of 1.84. We fail to reject the null hypotheses of demand revelation for either treatment (Standard: $\chi_2^2 = 0.93$, p-value $= 0.63$; Tournament: $\chi_2^2 = 0.09$, p-value $= 0.96$). Finally, for low induced values, in the standard treatment the intercept is 2.71 and the slope is 0.80. The tournament treatment has an intercept of 0.96 and a slope of 0.97. Again, we fail to reject the null hypotheses of demand revelation for both treatments (Standard: $\chi_2^2 = 0.15$, p-value $= 0.93$; Tournament: $\chi_2^2 = 0.02$, p-value $= 0.99$). Note, although off-margin bidders in the standard treatment are not statistically different from the demand revelation baseline, intercept and slope coefficients differ from demand revelation by greater magnitudes than the tournament counterparts (i.e. larger variances exist for estimated coefficients in the standard treatments). These results lend strong support for the hypothesis that the tournament performs better at engaging on-margin bidders relative to the standard auction; weak support is evident for off-margin bidders.

Third, the second price auction tournament is more efficient than the standard auction. The bidder with the highest value was more likely to win, and the bidder with the second highest value was more likely to set the price in the tournament as compared to the standard auction. Table 8.9 shows the bidder that should have won the auction (e.g., the highest value person) did so 55% of the time in the auction tournament; and 42.5% in the standard auction. Second, in the auction tournament, the high-value bidder either won or set the price in 97.5% of all rounds; in the standard auction, this occurred in only 77.5% of rounds. Third, in the tournament, the bidder that should have set the market-clearing price did so 47.5% of the time, compared to just 22.5% in the standard auction. For *strict efficiency* – the auction is strictly efficient when the highest value bidder wins the auction and pays the bid of the player with the second highest induced value – we observe the auction tournament accurately predicts the winner and price setter in 45% of all rounds, whereas this only occurs half as frequently (22.5%) in the standard auction. Focusing on the last ten rounds, the predicted winner and the price setter was observed 75% in the tournament, and 25% in the standard auction.

If one also considers efficiency as measured by the percentage of maximum surplus captured (max surplus = highest induced value – second highest induced value), we find that efficiency is highest for the last ten rounds in the tournament, capturing 66% of the potential surplus. By this measure of efficiency, the standard treatment was negative in rounds one to ten and eleven to twenty, which suggests the gains captured by a winning highest induced value bidder were more than offset by the losses of winning bidders with low induced values.

Why did the second-price tournament generate more rational behavior relative to the standard auction? On the surface, a tournament setting should create a more complex strategic setting than a standard auction. The fear as stated by Camerer and Hogarth (1999, p. 36) is "in theory, tournament incentives should induce more status-seeking and risk-taking and hence, does not lead subjects to incentive-compatibly maximize expected profit (which is why economists usually eschew them). Whether tournaments actually do have those unintended effects have not been carefully investigated." We did not see such unintended effects: we found the opposite.

These results are consistent with three behavioral explanations. First, the tournament payoffs were framed such that winning points as clearly indicated in the dollar payoffs (not just points to be converted into dollars) made points appear more valuable in the tournament. Earning points in the tournament could be viewed as more valuable so the typical mistake of overbidding and occasionally suffering losses had more impact in the tournament. Four players in the tournament stood to earn more than the average, where the winner and runner up would earn substantially more. That the contingent expected payoffs were slightly higher in the tournament could have been enough to trigger more sincere bidding. Second, we purposefully created our auction tournament as a repeated game of incomplete information with almost common knowledge. Players did not know their relative position in the tournament regardless of the round. The set of induced values differed randomly in each trial, only the winning bidder knew he or she had won and the market price and cumulative profits were private. While such a game can lead to multiple equilibria, the logic of a unique focal equilibrium arises based on risk dominance (e.g., select the safest strategy: the one that maximizes one's payoff independent of what the other players do) and iterated deletion of dominated strategies (Kajii and Morris, 1997). As points accumulate across rounds, the dominant strategy in the last round of the second price tournament is to follow Vickrey's initial strategy: bid one's induced value. Overbidding is dominated because it increases the risk of paying too much and losing accumulated points; underbidding is dominated because it increases the risk of missing out on profitable opportunities. Since a bidder only learns his relative ranking at the game's end, if he or she works backwards eliminating dominated strategies, this leads to a weakly dominant strategy of bidding one's induced value in each round.

A third behavioral explanation rests in Heiner's (1983) theory on the origins of predictable behavior. This theory suggests the more uncertainty, the more predictable a person's behavior. He notes "'behavioral rules' . . . arise because of uncertainty in distinguishing preferred from less-preferred behavior. Such uncertainty requires behavior to be governed by mechanisms that restrict the flexibility to choose potential actions, or which produce a selective alertness to information that might prompt particular actions to be chosen. These mechanisms simplify behavior to less-complex patterns, which are easier for an observer to recognize and predict" (p. 561). Here the only information each player had in a bidding round was his or her induced value (and own accumulated points). Without information on relative ranking or the current "tournament leader", a player had no legitimate chance to strategize against an opponent; rather he or she had to rely on a behavioral rule. Our results do not contradict that the behavioral rule is to bid one's induced value. Given the limited ability of people to eliminate simple dominated strategies (see Camerer, 2003), our results do not contradict the Heiner story. One implication is that rather than trying to explain irrational bidding *ex post* with new restrictions on preferences, one can construct *ex ante* a second price auction environment where sincere bidding is a good predictor of behavior.

8.5   Preferences: fixed or fungible?

In experimental auctions with active market feedback, an open question is whether a person's preferences for new goods and risky events are fixed or fungible. Most economists view fixed preferences as a valuable precept, a fundamental building block that has served them well in describing behavior within active exchange institutions (e.g., see Krugman, 1998). Many psychologists counter that preferences are fungible, more affected by non-economic contextual cues than economists have acknowledged or admitted (e.g., see Slovic, 1991; Tversky and Simonson, 1993). The question of preference stability matters for theory and public policy because if preferences are "transient artifacts" contingent on context, so are the welfare measures used in cost-benefit analyses to rationalize or reject regulations to protect health and safety.

Gunnarsson *et al.* (2003) investigate the stability of preferences of people who fall prey to the classic anomaly of preference reversals (e.g., a person prefers lottery A to lottery B, but then puts greater monetary value on B than A). In Chapter 9, we discuss how preference reversals have been documented for isolated individuals in numerous lab experiments run by both economists and psychologists (Grether and Plott, 1979; Tversky *et al.* 1990). One explanation of preference reversals argues that the decision maker constructs preferences on the spot instead of ranking the options. The strategies when constructing preferences include (Slovic, 1991, p. 500), "anchoring and adjustment, relying on prominent dimension, eliminating common elements, discarding nonessential differences, adding new attributes into the problem frame in order to bolster one alternative, or otherwise restructuring the decision problem to create dominance and thus reduce conflict and indecision."

Gunnarsson *et al.* (2003) used experimental data to estimate an empirical model of preferences for risk and skewness, the love of the long shot, in market-like and non-market settings. Their results show that preferences remained stable even as arbitrage removed preference reversals. People stopped reversing preferences with arbitrage not because their preferences were fungible, but because they initially overpriced the risky long shot.

We use data from a lab experiment with 123 subjects (Cherry *et al.*, 2003). After entering the lab, participants signed a consent form acknowledging their voluntary participation while agreeing to abide by the instructions. Written protocols ensured uniformity across sessions, and all subjects were inexperienced with preference reversal experiments. The protocol included randomly seating the subjects as they entered the room, disallowing any communication whatsoever among subjects, reading the experimental instructions aloud as the subjects followed along, administering a test of comprehension, addressing any questions or concerns raised by the subjects, and conducting the market sessions.

Treatment 1: In this baseline treatment, subjects faced two independent settings that create conditions likely to induce people to reverse their preferences. In each setting, subjects were faced with two monetary lotteries: a *p-bet* lottery and a *$-bet* lottery. A *p-bet* is a relatively safe lottery with a high probability of winning a smaller reward; a *$-bet* is a relatively risky lottery with a low probability of winning a larger reward. Subjects were asked which lottery they preferred, and how much they valued each of the two lotteries. Preferences and values were binding in both settings, e.g., subjects were sold lotteries for their indicated value using a BDM mechanism. But inconsistent preferences and values were not arbitraged. The process was repeated with fifteen different lotteries.

Treatment 2: Subjects faced the same setting as in the baseline treatment except now in one of the two settings – the *market-like* setting, reversals were subject to arbitrage. In this market-like setting, if a subject's preference ranking did not match their stated values, a simulated market would engage the person in buys, sells and trades to extract profits from the inconsistency. For instance, if a person said he preferred lottery A to B, but valued A at $2 and B at $5, the market would sell him B for $5, then exchange B for A (as they indicated a preference ranking for B over A), and buy back A for $2. The net result is no lottery is owned and the person was $3 poorer. Previous work has documented that this type of money pump forces a person to reconsider and realign the inconsistencies of her preferences and values (see Chu and Chu, 1990). Choices and reversals in the *non-market* setting were not subject to arbitrage.

Treatment 3: Subjects faced the same setting as in treatment 2 except that the non-market setting without arbitrage was hypothetical. In the market-like setting, the subjects' indicated preferences and values over the monetary lotteries were binding and subject to arbitrage. In the non-market setting, the subjects' preferences and values were non-binding, i.e., hypothetical.

The resulting data provides observed behavior of 123 people indicating preferences and stated values over two lottery pairs in fifteen periods: 3,690 choices over lottery pairs and 7380 values over individual lotteries.

Golec and Tamarkin's (1998) and Garret and Sobel's (1999) empirical model was used to test for a preference for skewness (also see Ali, 1997; Woodland and Woodland, 1999). In the model, each player has an identical utility function and bets her entire wealth. Losing a lottery bet returns zero to the bettor. Player i's expected utility depends on the top prize payouts of each lottery game in option j, and she only plays those lottery games available in option j. Player i's expected utility for option j is:

$$E(U_{ij}) = P_{Gj} \cdot U_{ij}(X_{Gj}) + \sum_{g=1}^{n} P_{gj} \cdot U_{ij}(X_{gj}) \tag{8.4}$$

where g denotes all lottery games except G which is the highest top prize game, P_{Gj} is the probability of winning the highest top prize game G in option j, $U_{ij}(X_{Gj})$ is player i's utility from winning the top prize X_{Gj} in game G in option j, and $\sum_{g=1}^{n} P_{gj} \cdot U_{ij}(X_{gj})$ captures all other lottery games g offered in option j except the highest top prize game in game G in option j. This term is the probability of winning the top prize in any game g multiplied by player i's utility from winning the top prize, X_{gj}, in any game g summed over all n of g games. The two terms in equation 8.4 reflect the expected utility for player i for all lottery games available in option j, U_{ij}.

Normalize utility $U_{ij}(X_{Gj}) = 1$ and impose the preferences restriction that the odds between the gambles are selected to make the lottery players indifferent between the outcomes of game g or G, which allows us to rewrite equation (8.4) as:

$$E(U_{ij}) = P_{Gj} = P_{1j} \cdot U_{ij}(X_{1j}) = P_{2j} \cdot U_{ij}(X_{2j}) = \ldots\ldots$$
$$= P_{nj} \cdot U_{ij}(X_{nj}). \tag{8.5}$$

Given any lottery game g or G in option j,

$$E(U_{ij}) = P_{Gj} = P_{gj} \cdot U_{ij}(X_{gj}), \text{ or} \tag{8.6}$$

$$\frac{P_{Gj}}{P_{gj}} = U_{ij}(X_{gj}). \tag{8.7}$$

The expected utility for any player in option j is represented by equating the probability ratio of the highest top prize game G and any other lottery game g to player i's utility from winning the top prize any game g. To empirically estimate equation (8.7), the following cubic approximation is used:

$$\frac{P_{Gj}}{P_{gj}} = \left[\beta_0 + \beta_1 X_{gj} + \beta_2 X_{gj}^2 + \beta_3 X_{gj}^3\right] \tag{8.8}$$

where β_1 measures the bettor preferences over the mean of returns, β_2 measures bettor risk aversion ($\beta_2 > 0$ risk loving; $\beta_2 < 0$ risk aversion; $\beta_2 = 0$ risk neutrality), β_3 measures the bettor's preference for skewness ($\beta_3 > 0$ favorable preference for skewness; $\beta_3 < 0$ unfavorable preference for skewness; $\beta_3 = 0$ indifferent preference for skewness). If $\beta_1 > 0$, $\beta_2 < 0$, and $\beta_3 > 0$, then lottery players are risk averse, and choose to play those lotteries with greater skewness of returns. Because the experiment generates panel data, results expand on previous work by modifying the empirical specification in two ways. First, the independent variables are interacted with period indicator variables to estimate any change in subject preference and risk aversion over time. Second, time invariant subject attributes are controlled with a random effects specification.

Table 8.10 reports the results and shows the existence of the preference reversal phenomenon in this laboratory setting. Results also show how the introduction of arbitrage significantly decreases the rate of reversals (i.e., increases the rate of rational choices). Prior to arbitrage (round 6), reversal rates across treatments were not significantly different at any standard level. After four rounds of arbitrage, reversal rates were significantly lower in the arbitrage treatments relative to no-arbitrage baseline (p-values < 0.02). In the later rounds, the discipline from arbitrage was highly significant in generating more rational choices.

Now we turn to the issue of subjects' love of skewness and whether preferences remained stable when people adjusted behavior to act more rationally. Tables 8.11–8.13 report panel estimates of equation 8.8 across treatments. For each treatment, the market and non-market setting, a separate model is estimated. To estimate how preferences and risk aversion change within a setting

Table 8.10. *The impact of arbitrage on preference reversal rates (%)*

	Market			Non-market		
	Treatment 1	Treatment 2	Treatment 3	Treatment 1	Treatment 2	Treatment 3 Hypothetical
	Real & no arbitrage	Real & arbitrage	Real & arbitrage	Real & no arbitrage	Real & no arbitrage	& no arbitrage
Round 1	0.317	0.341	0.317	0.317	0.317	0.366
Round 2	0.34	0.366	0.268	0.366	0.317	0.341
Round 3	0.39	0.317	0.342	0.341	0.293	0.39
Round 4	0.293	0.341	0.293	0.39	0.366	0.341
Round 5	0.366	0.39	0.268	0.293	0.317	0.39
Round 6	0.317	0.366	0.317	0.317	0.341	0.317
Round 7	0.341	0.317	0.244	0.39	0.31	0.366
Round 8	0.317	0.219	0.22	0.341	0.244	0.317
Round 9	0.268	0.146$^\blacklozenge$	0.171	0.415	0.244	0.244†
Round 10	0.341	0.122‡	0.146†	0.341	0.22	0.190$^\blacklozenge$
Round 11	0.317	0.122†	0.122†	0.366	0.170†	0.190†
Round 12	0.268	0.098†	0.122†	0.317	0.122†	0.170$^\blacklozenge$
Round 13	0.317	0.049‡	0.146†	0.39	0.090‡	0.122‡
Round 14	0.268	0.073‡	0.098†	0.366	0.090‡	0.090‡
Round 15	0.341	0.024‡	0.073‡	0.34	0.049‡	0.120‡

$\blacklozenge$, $\dagger$, and $\ddagger$ indicate significance at the 10, 5 and 1 percent levels with the null being the reversal rate in the arbitrage treatment (2 or 3) is equal to the rate in the non-arbitrage baseline (treatment 1).

Note: arbitrage was introduced in round 6.

over time, we interact the measures (β_1, β_2, & β_3) with time period indicator variables. Recall β_1 measures the preferences over the mean of returns, β_2 measures the preference for risk, and β_3 measures the preference for skewness. We expect subjects are risk averse and prefer lotteries with greater expected payoffs and higher skewness ($\beta_1 > 0$, $\beta_2 < 0$, and $\beta_3 > 0$). Our null hypothesis is that risk aversion and skewness preferences remain stable even as people correct preference reversal behavior in the face of a new context: market-like arbitrage.

Results in the market-like and non-market settings across all three treatments confirm our expectations. In each model, estimated coefficients for the early periods were significantly different than zero and carried signs consistent with our expectations. Subjects preferred lotteries with higher expected returns ($\beta_1 > 0$), were risk averse ($\beta_2 < 0$), and preferred lotteries with higher skewness ($\beta_3 > 0$). One might imagine a link between the love for skewness and preference reversals, but the results from the later periods contradict this notion. In the later periods, estimated coefficients remained significantly different than zero indicating that subjects were still risk averse and preferred higher expected returns and skewness. But as the reversal rates declined in the market and

Table 8.11. *Random-effects estimates for treatment 1*
(Real arbitrage/real no-arbitrage)

	Market			Non-market		
	β_1	β_2	β_3	β_1	β_2	β_3
Round 1	2.95[‡]	−0.61[‡]	0.041[‡]	2.93[‡]	−0.58[‡]	0.036[‡]
	(0.37)	(0.092)	(0.0075)	(0.37)	(0.092)	(0.0075)
Round 2	2.83[‡]	−0.56[‡]	0.035[‡]	3.03[‡]	−0.62[‡]	0.04[‡]
	(0.37)	(0.094)	(0.0079)	(0.37)	(0.092)	(0.0077)
Round 3	2.76[‡]	−0.52[‡]	0.03[‡]	2.98[‡]	−0.59[‡]	0.036[‡]
	(0.37)	(0.090)	(0.0073)	(0.36)	(0.088)	(0.0072)
Round 4	2.75[‡]	−0.52[‡]	0.029[‡]	3.2[‡]	−0.70[‡]	0.049[‡]
	(0.38)	(0.093)	(0.0077)	(0.37)	(0.092)	(0.0076)
Round 5	2.93[‡]	−0.59[‡]	0.039[‡]	2.98[‡]	−0.59[‡]	0.036[‡]
	(0.37)	(0.091)	(0.0074)	(0.37)	(0.090)	(0.0074)
Round 6	2.94[‡]	−0.60[‡]	0.038[‡]	2.94[‡]	−0.57[‡]	0.035[‡]
	(0.37)	(0.090)	(0.0074)	(0.37)	(0.092)	(0.0076)
Round 7	2.89[‡]	−0.58[‡]	0.037[‡]	2.84[‡]	−0.54[‡]	0.032[‡]
	(0.36)	(0.089)	(0.0074)	(0.37)	(0.093)	(0.0078)
Round 8	2.8[‡]	−0.55[‡]	0.034[‡]	3.04[‡]	−0.62[‡]	0.04[‡]
	(0.37)	(0.092)	(0.0076)	(0.37)	(0.092)	(0.076)
Round 9	2.76[‡]	−0.52[‡]	0.03[‡]	2.93[‡]	−0.57[‡]	0.034[‡]
	(0.37)	(0.093)	(0.0078)	(0.37)	(0.092)	(0.077)
Round 10	2.89[‡]	−0.57[‡]	0.035[‡]	2.79[‡]	−0.51[‡]	0.028[‡]
	(0.37)	(0.094)	(0.0079)	(0.37)	(0.093)	(0.0079)
Round 11	2.78[‡]	−0.54[‡]	0.033[‡]	2.97[‡]	−0.58[‡]	0.035[‡]
	(0.38)	(0.094)	(0.0073)	(0.37)	(0.089)	(0.0073)
Round 12	2.74[‡]	−0.52[‡]	0.03[‡]	2.97[‡]	−0.59[‡]	0.036[‡]
	(0.37)	(0.087)	(0.0073)	(0.37)	(0.092)	(0.0074)
Round 13	2.82[‡]	−0.56[‡]	0.035[‡]	2.96[‡]	−0.59[‡]	0.036[‡]
	(0.38)	(0.093)	(0.0077)	(0.37)	(0.091)	(0.0075)
Round 14	2.73[‡]	−0.52[‡]	0.031[‡]	2.96[‡]	−0.59[‡]	0.037[‡]
	(0.38)	(0.096)	(0.0081)	(0.37)	(0.091)	(0.0075)
Round 15	2.93[‡]	−0.59[‡]	0.039[‡]	2.93[‡]	−0.57[‡]	0.035[‡]
	(0.38)	(0.096)	(0.0082)	(0.37)	(0.092)	(0.0073)
$\chi^2_{(45)}$	701.26			672.22		
(p-value)	(<0.000)			(<0.000)		
$\bar{R}^2$	0.552			0.542		
N	615			615		

Standard errors in parentheses unless stated otherwise.
[‡] indicates significance at the 1 percent level.

Table 8.12. *Random-effects estimates for treatment 2*
(Real arbitrage/real no-arbitrage)

	Market			Non-market		
	β_1	β_2	β_3	β_1	β_2	β_3
Round 1	2.98[‡]	−0.61[‡]	0.039[‡]	2.94[‡]	−0.60[‡]	0.038[‡]
	(0.36)	(0.085)	(0.0071)	(0.37)	(0.091)	(0.0074)
Round 2	2.97[‡]	−0.61[‡]	0.039[‡]	2.75[‡]	−0.52[‡]	0.03[‡]
	(0.38)	(0.097)	(0.0088)	(0.37)	(0.092)	(0.0076)
Round 3	2.89[‡]	−0.58[‡]	0.036[‡]	2.96[‡]	−0.60[‡]	0.038[‡]
	(0.37)	(0.093)	(0.0077)	(0.36)	(0.089)	(0.0073)
Round 4	2.89[‡]	−0.58[‡]	0.036[‡]	2.88[‡]	−0.57[‡]	0.035[‡]
	(0.38)	(0.097)	(0.0082)	(0.37)	(0.091)	(0.0073)
Round 5	2.77[‡]	−0.52[‡]	0.029[‡]	2.86[‡]	−0.56[‡]	0.034[‡]
	(0.37)	(0.093)	(0.0076)	(0.37)	(0.093)	(0.0076)
Round 6	2.91[‡]	−0.58[‡]	0.036[‡]	2.67[‡]	−0.49[‡]	0.028[‡]
	(0.36)	(0.087)	(0.0073)	(0.38)	(0.096)	(0.0082)
Round 7	2.97[‡]	−0.61[‡]	0.039[‡]	2.96[‡]	−0.60[‡]	0.039[‡]
	(0.36)	(0.087)	(0.0074)	(0.37)	(0.091)	(0.0074)
Round 8	2.94[‡]	−0.60[‡]	0.038[‡]	2.77[‡]	−0.52[‡]	0.031[‡]
	(0.37)	(0.091)	(0.0074)	(0.37)	(0.092)	(0.0074)
Round 9	2.75[‡]	−0.52[‡]	0.03[‡]	2.98[‡]	−0.61[‡]	0.039[‡]
	(0.37)	(0.092)	(0.0076)	(0.36)	(0.088)	(0.0071)
Round 10	2.96[‡]	−0.60[‡]	0.038[‡]	2.97[‡]	−0.61[‡]	0.039[‡]
	(0.36)	(0.089)	(0.0073)	(0.38)	(0.01)	(0.0088)
Round 11	2.88[‡]	−0.57[‡]	0.035[‡]	2.89[‡]	−0.58[‡]	0.036[‡]
	(0.37)	(0.091)	(0.0073)	(0.37)	(0.093)	(0.0077)
Round 12	2.87[‡]	−0.56[‡]	0.034[‡]	2.89[‡]	−0.58[‡]	0.036[‡]
	(0.37)	(0.093)	(0.0076)	(0.38)	(0.097)	(0.0082)
Round 13	2.69[‡]	−0.49[‡]	0.028[‡]	2.77[‡]	−0.52[‡]	0.029[‡]
	(0.38)	(0.096)	(0.0082)	(0.37)	(0.093)	(0.0076)
Round 14	2.96[‡]	−0.60[‡]	0.039[‡]	2.91[‡]	−0.579[‡]	0.036[‡]
	(0.37)	(0.088)	(0.0074)	(0.36)	(0.087)	(0.0073)
Round 15	2.77[‡]	−0.53[‡]	0.031[‡]	2.97[‡]	−0.61[‡]	0.039[‡]
	(0.37)	(0.092)	(0.0074)	(0.36)	(0.087)	(0.0074)
$\chi^2_{(45)}$	666.87			666.87		
(p-value)	(<0.000)			(<0.000)		
$\bar{R}^2$	0.540			0.540		
	615			615		
N						

Standard errors in parentheses unless stated otherwise.
[‡] indicates significance at the 1 percent level.

Table 8.13. *Random-effects estimates for treatment 3
(Real arbitrage/hypothetical no-arbitrage)*

	Market			Non-market		
	β_1	β_2	β_3	β_1	β_2	β_3
Round 1	2.87[‡]	−0.58[‡]	0.037[‡]	2.74[‡]	−0.53[‡]	0.032[‡]
	(0.37)	(0.093)	(0.0076)	(0.38)	(0.094)	(0.0077)
Round 2	2.73[‡]	−0.53[‡]	0.031[‡]	2.91[‡]	−0.6[‡]	0.038[‡]
	(0.38)	(0.093)	(0.0076)	(0.38)	(0.093)	(0.0077)
Round 3	2.9[‡]	−0.6[‡]	0.039[‡]	2.76[‡]	−0.53[‡]	0.032[‡]
	(0.37)	(0.093)	(0.0079)	(0.38)	(0.096)	(0.0080)
Round 4	2.75[‡]	−0.54[‡]	0.032[‡]	2.74[‡]	−0.53[‡]	0.031[‡]
	(0.38)	(0.094)	(0.0077)	(0.37)	(0.096)	(0.0079)
Round 5	2.8[‡]	−0.55[‡]	0.034[‡]	2.81[‡]	−0.56[‡]	0.035[‡]
	(0.37)	(0.090)	(0.0074)	(0.37)	(0.092)	(0.0075)
Round 6	2.73[‡]	−0.53[‡]	0.032[‡]	2.86[‡]	−0.58[‡]	0.037[‡]
	(0.38)	(0.095)	(0.0076)	(0.37)	(0.091)	(0.0075)
Round 7	2.81[‡]	−0.56[‡]	0.035[‡]	2.78[‡]	−0.55[‡]	0.034[‡]
	(0.38)	(0.093)	(0.0075)	(0.40)	(0.010)	(0.0089)
Round 8	2.74[‡]	−0.53[‡]	0.032[‡]	2.73[‡]	−0.53[‡]	0.032[‡]
	(0.38)	(0.094)	(0.0077)	(0.38)	(0.092)	(0.0074)
Round 9	2.91[‡]	−0.59[‡]	0.038[‡]	2.87[‡]	−0.58[‡]	0.037[‡]
	(0.38)	(0.093)	(0.0077)	(0.37)	(0.093)	(0.0076)
Round 10	2.76[‡]	−0.53[‡]	0.032[‡]	2.73[‡]	−0.53[‡]	0.031[‡]
	(0.38)	(0.096)	(0.0080)	(0.38)	(0.093)	(0.0076)
Round 11	2.74[‡]	−0.53[‡]	0.031[‡]	2.9[‡]	−0.6[‡]	0.039[‡]
	(0.39)	(0.096)	(0.0079)	(0.37)	(0.093)	(0.0079)
Round 12	2.81[‡]	−0.56[‡]	0.035[‡]	2.75[‡]	−0.54[‡]	0.034[‡]
	(0.37)	(0.092)	(0.0075)	(0.38)	(0.094)	(0.0077)
Round 13	2.86[‡]	−0.58[‡]	0.037[‡]	2.8[‡]	−0.55[‡]	0.034[‡]
	(0.37)	(0.091)	(0.0075)	(0.37)	(0.091)	(0.0074)
Round 14	2.78[‡]	−0.55[‡]	0.034[‡]	2.73[‡]	−0.53[‡]	0.032[‡]
	(0.40)	(0.010)	(0.0089)	(0.38)	(0.095)	(0.0078)
Round 15	2.73[‡]	−0.53[‡]	0.032[‡]	2.81[‡]	−0.56[‡]	0.035[‡]
	(0.38)	(0.092)	(0.0074)	(0.38)	(0.093)	(0.0075)
$\chi^2_{(45)}$	647.86			647.86		
(p-value)	(<0.000)			(<0.000)		
$\bar{R}^2$	0.532			0.532		
N	615			615		

Standard errors in parentheses unless stated otherwise.
[‡] indicates significance at the 1 percent level.

non-market setting due to the introduction of arbitrage, people maintained their preferences and aversion to risk. Arbitrage caused people to reconsider and correct the inconsistency of their preferences and values, but the reconciliation of preferences and values arose from *value adjustments* not *preference adjustments*. The average subject did not change his or her preference ordering with market-like experience. Rather he or she reversed the preference reversal not by changing preferences but by reducing their willingness to pay for the risky lottery.

Are preferences for skewness fixed or fungible across context? The results presented here suggest they are fixed. We find evidence that supports the economist's presumption that preferences are stable across market-like arbitrage and non-market contexts. People preferred skewness both before and after market-like arbitrage stopped them from reversing their preferences. Preference reversal behavior stopped not because people change their predilection for skewness; rather people stopped overpricing the long shot once arbitrage put a cost on this behavior. Additional research exploring the robustness of our findings would be useful.

8.6   Gift exchange

Research findings emerging from experimental auctions are relevant for more general economic questions. One such question we have addressed is whether there was a deadweight loss from gift-giving at Christmas. Waldfogel (1993, 1996) and Solnick and Hemenway (1996) previously provided conflicting answers. Waldfogel (1993) found a welfare loss as his average recipient valued her gifts at 87% of the cost to the giver. Solnick and Hemenway (1996) found a welfare gain; their average recipient valued her gifts at 214% of the cost. But based on work in experimental auctions both their estimates can be challenged on two fronts. First, their loss/gain estimates are hypothetical, and ample evidence exists to suggest that hypothetical values are sensitive to systematic bias. Second, the surveys were not framed as demand revealing auctions; thus the signals to induce subjects to truthfully reveal their preferences are weak.

List and Shogren (1998) re-estimated the deadweight loss of gift-giving in a real random *n*th price auction. They find a welfare gain: the average subject valued her gifts at 121% to 135% of the cost to the giver. The average subject understated her actual *material* value by about 21% to 28% in the hypothetical scenarios, with or without a demand revealing decision framework. Our results provide some positive evidence that in-kind transfers do not always destroy value, but these welfare gains are lower than those reported by Solnick and Hemenway (1996).

Table 8.14 illustrates the general experimental design. The rows reflect the value of a gift: *material value* + *sentimental value* = *total value*. The

Table 8.14. *Experimental design*

	Hypothetical survey	Hypothetical random *n*th price auction	Actual random *n*th price auction
Material value	A		D
Sentimental value			
Total value	*x*	B	C

columns reflect the study treatments: the hypothetical open-ended survey, the hypothetical demand revealing auction, and the actual demand revealing auction. Cell A represents the hypothetical material value elicited in the Waldfogel (1993; 1996) and Solnick and Hemenway (1996) surveys. Cell D reflects the real material value we use to estimate the welfare loss/gain from gift giving. Moving to cell D from cell A is complicated because the real auction occurs in cell C. In cell C, we elicit total value because the credibility of the auction would be stretched beyond reasonable limits to force a subject to forego his or her sentimental value in a real sale. Since sentimental values are embedded in the real offers, we use a three-stage experimental design to move from cell A to cell D via cells B and C.

In Stage 1 (February 4), a monitor administered Waldfogel's original survey (cell A) to a group of 46 undergraduate students at the University of Central Florida. After reading the experimental instructions and answering all relevant questions, the monitor asked each subject to complete the holiday gift giving survey. Information gathered from the survey included a description of all the gifts the subject received at Christmas, the relationship the subject had with each gift giver, and the estimated price the giver paid for each gift. Each subject also stated the hypothetical material values to sell his or her gifts. A subject who received ten gifts submitted ten values. Finally, each subject revealed the additional sentimental value for each gift.

In Stage 2 (February 6), the monitor introduced the hypothetical Vickrey-style uniform price, sealed-bid auction. Since most subjects received several gifts, we used the random *n*th price auction to provide incentive for a subject to take care in valuing each of his or her gifts. A second price auction was not used because such a mechanism might cause a subject to focus on selling only his or her lowest-valued gift. The goal was to increase the odds that gifts could actually be sold that would otherwise be off-the-margin, and thereby give a person more incentive to submit sincere offers for these gifts.

By using the random *n*th price auction, each subject could potentially sell more than one gift at the uniform price. While truth-telling can be a (non-unique) Nash equilibrium in a multiple-unit, uniform price auction, in general this need not be the case (see Forsythe and Isaac, 1982). A multi-good, uniform price auction does not necessarily inherit the same demand revealing properties as a second price or nth price auction in which subjects can only sell one gift (Vickrey, 1962). While subjects have incentive to bid sincerely on the first gift sold, their incentive to inflate the value of subsequent gifts increases because winning sellers affect the market price with positive probability (see Ausubel and Cramton, 1996). The subject can increase the expected selling price on the first gift by inflating offers for additional gifts. Experimental evidence suggests that nth price auctions do a reasonable job of empirical demand revelation on aggregate (see Franciosi et al., 1993). Offers off the margin are less likely to reveal demand truthfully, however, than those on the margin, as suggested by theory. Alternative designs to remove this incentive include a variation of the auction in which a bidder who sells K gifts receives the amount of the kth lowest rejected offer other than his or her own offer for the kth object won, or a descending-offer design that replicates the Vickrey auction (see Ausubel and Cramton (1996) for details).

The auction works as follows: (i) for each gift received, a subject states his or her total value to sell the gift; (ii) all gifts, g_i, from each subject are then pooled together to create the set of total available gifts, $G = \sum_{i \in M} g_i$, where M is the total number of subjects; (iii) all gifts, G, are then rank-ordered from lowest to highest total value; (iv) the monitor selects a random number uniformly distributed between 2 and 21 (21 was the most gifts received by a subject); and (v) the monitor then purchases the $(n - 1)$ lowest total value gifts overall and pays the nth lowest total value for each gift. For example, suppose $G = 500$ gifts overall and #6 was chosen as the random nth price, then only the five lowest valuation gifts overall would be purchased at the sixth lowest offer.

After the instructions were read, the monitor ran a candy bar pre-auction to give the subjects some experience with the random nth price auction. Next, we ran the hypothetical auction in which each subject offered a selling price, or her total value for each gift (cell B). Finally, the monitor asked the subject to split this hypothetical total value into its sentimental and material value components for each gift.

In Stage 3 (February 11), we ran the actual random nth price auction for the gifts. After the monitor read the instructions and stated that this auction was real, each subject submitted her real total value for each gift (cell C). The subject again divided total value into its sentimental and material value (cell D) components for each gift. The random price was #4, and the monitor made arrangements with the sellers to purchase the three lowest total value gifts each priced at the fourth lowest total value. Three distinct subjects sold one gift each at a uniform price of $2.00. Although some attrition occurred over the eight days of the three stage experiment, this is not a substantive issue since students were unaware that a real auction would occur after the first two stages. Also, gifts that were used before the experiment (e.g., candy, gift certificates, cash)

Table 8.15. *Experimental results*

	Hypothetical survey	Hypothetical random *n*th price auction	Actual random *n*th price auction	Waldfogel (1993) [1996][a]	Solnick and Hemenway (1996) [Partial Sample][b]
	Mean	Mean	Mean	Mean	Mean
Total cost (TC)	$362.55	$362.55	$362.55	$508.90 [NA]	$167.00 [$167.00]
Material value (MV)	$365.50	$368.13	$464.86	$462.10 [NA]	$6,667.00 [$202.00]
Ratio of mean value to mean cost (MV/TC)	100.8	101.5	128.2	90.8 [NA]	3992 [121.0]
Percent yield across subjects[d]	99.2 (2.0)[c]	100.6 (1.9)	121.0 (3.4)	87.1 (3.2) [NA]	10,100 (120,000) [214] [345]
Across gifts[e]	97.8 (2.5)	106.4 (6.7)	134.9 (7.6)	83.9 (2.8) [92.9] [1.0]	10,100 (120,000) [214] [345]
Subjects (N)	36	36	36	58 [455]	155 [150]
# Gifts	244	244	244	278 [2950]	155 [150]

[a] Waldfogel's (1996) results are in brackets under his (1993) estimates; NA denotes not available.
[b] Solnick and Hemenway's trimmed sample results are in brackets under full sample estimates.
[c] Standard error of the mean in parentheses beneath the yield estimates.
[d] "Mean yield across subjects" is the mean MV/TC for each subject averaged over all subjects.
[e] "Mean yield across gifts" is the MV/TC for each gift averaged over all gifts.

were trimmed from the analysis for obvious reasons. Our final sample consists of 244 gifts across thirty-six recipients.

According to Waldfogel's hypothetical survey given in Stage 1, gifts generate a welfare loss: average yields across subjects and gifts were 99% and 98% (see Table 8.15). Percentage yield across subjects is computed as the mean ratio of material values to the total costs for each subject averaged over all subjects;

percentage yield across gifts is the same ratio for each gift averaged over all gifts. Although our results do not exactly replicate Waldfogel's in that they do not differ significantly from 100% at conventional levels, the point estimates do not refute his finding that a deadweight loss may exist from gift-giving at Christmas. These findings suggest that sample selection may not be the pivotal issue in this debate. Subjects from the University of Central Florida respond as those at Yale.

At issue is the gap between hypothetical and actual behavior. In the actual random nth price auction, we estimate a welfare gain: average yields were 121 and 135% (Table 8.15). Our results support Solnick and Hemenway's intuition that gift-giving does not universally destroy value, but our results suggest their estimated gains of 214 to 10,100% (partial and full sample) are an upper bound. Plausible value creation can occur with gift-giving.

The welfare gains are driven more by the actual auction than framing the offers as demand revealing. This finding is illustrated in Columns 1–3 of Table 8.16, in which summary statistics for the revealed total cost and material value are shown for each of the treatments. Although mean yields differ across the two hypothetical instruments, using a Wilcoxon signed-rank test for matched pairs we cannot reject the hypothesis that the revealed values (material value, sentimental value, or total value) in the hypothetical survey were derived from the same parental population as the values from the hypothetical auction (see Table 8.16, Wilcoxon test, $W = 3281$ ($z = -0.46$); $W = 1120$ ($z = -1.09$); $W = 4752$ ($z = -0.66$)), we can reject the hypotheses that revealed values in the actual auction are derived from the same parental populations as the two hypothetical treatments (Table 8.16). The change to real economic commitments from a hypothetical scenario seems to be the catalyst for the welfare gain. If we calibrated Waldfogel's results by increasing his material values with the estimated mean real-hypothetical gap of 26.5–27.4% (from Table 8.16), his deadweight loss becomes a surplus. Similar implications are drawn if the calibration factor is taken from Table 8.15.

These results indicate that hypothetical surveys show a welfare loss from Christmas gift giving, whereas the actual auction produced a plausible welfare gain, as real selling prices were at least 27% higher than hypothetical prices. The subjects reacted differently when the auction was real, a common phenomenon noted in much of the non-market valuation literature. The relationship between in-kind transfers and value is not immune to the gap between intentions and actions, suggesting lessons learned in experimental auctions have implications for broader economic questions of general public interest.

8.7   Calibration of real and hypothetical auction bids

Experimental auctions can help better understand the question of the gap between what people say they will pay and what they actually do pay when

Table 8.16. *Experimental results – across gifts*

	Hypothetical survey	Hypothetical random nth price auction	Actual random nth price auction	Hypothetical auction vs. hypothetical survey	Actual auction vs. hypothetical auction	Actual auction vs. hypothetical survey
				Wilcoxon Test	Wilcoxon Test	Wilcoxon Test
	Mean	Mean	Mean			
Gift cost	$53.90 $(58.96)^a$	$53.90 (58.96)	$53.90 (58.96)	–	–	–
Material value	$53.92 (71.07)	$54.31 (71.30)	$68.68 (95.38)	3281^b $z = -0.46$	9404* $z = -3.84$	9560* $z = -13.25$
Sentimental value	$41.85 (147.21)	$42.02 (145.07)	$68.42 (174.31)	1120 $z = -1.09$	5482* $z = -4.91$	5272* $z = -5.10$
Total value	$95.77 (191.85)	$96.34 (194.87)	$136.87 (239.98)	4752 $z = -0.66$	6570* $z = -5.76$	7376* $z = -5.62$
N	244	244	244	–	–	–

[a] Standard deviations in parentheses.
[b] Wilcoxon test is a signed-rank test for matched pairs across gifts. Since the number of paired observations is larger than 30, the large-sample z-test is used. The large sample z-test's null and alternative hypotheses are given by:
H_0: Two sampled populations have identical probability distributions.
H_a: The probability distribution for population A is shifted to the right or to the left of that for population B. Critical z-values are computed as follows: $z = (W - (n(n + 1)/4))/(n(n + 1)(2n + 1)/24)^{1/2}$, where n is the number of non-tied differences between the two samples.
* Significantly different values at the 1% level.

required. The majority of research shows the average person exaggerates his actual willingness to pay when asked a hypothetical question (e.g., Bohm, 1972, Bishop and Heberlein, 1979, Dickie *et al.*, 1987, Shogren, 1990, Seip and Strand, 1992, Neill *et al.*, 1994). This hypothetical bias has motivated research into whether one can calibrate hypothetical and actual values using experimental markets (e.g., Fox *et al.*, 1998).

We now consider the experiment auctions in List and Shogren (1998), who explored calibration by comparing bidding behavior in a hypothetical and actual second price auction for baseball cards: deliverable objects with an intangible quality. Baseball cards have many favorable characteristics for a calibration exercise including familiarity, the ability to deliver, and an abstract quality beyond the normal market good. List and Shogren (1998) ran three treatments at a sports card show in Denver, CO: one card, one card among ten, and one card bid on by sports card dealers presumed more experienced with the market than the general population (the Dealer treatment).

For the one-card and Dealer treatments, the auctioned good was a Cal Ripken Jr. 1982 Topps Traded PSA graded nine rookie baseball card. All treatments displayed the same Cal Ripken Jr. card to ensure comparability of bids. An independent agency, Professional Sports Authenticators (PSA), graded the Cal Ripken Jr. card to avoid complications of participants not understanding the grade (i.e., substance and quality) of the card. We selected the Cal Ripken Jr. card to reduce the valuation issues encountered when subjects do not understand the substance of the good they are asked to value (Cummings *et al.*, 1986). For the ten-good treatment, we used the Cal Ripken Jr. card plus nine other sports cards (or sets of cards) that could act as potential substitutes or complements, e.g., Billy Ripken's 1989 rookie PSA graded card, three Troy Aikman cards, one complete set (without Aikman), and one Michael Irvin card. Bidders submitted a separate bid for each of the ten cards.

The experimental auction for the one-good and ten-good treatments used a four-step experimental design: (i) inspection of the good(s), (ii) hypothetical bid(s), (iii) actual bid(s), and (iv) debriefing. In *Step 1*, monitor A approached a person entering the show and asked if he or she would like to participate in a hypothetical auction that would take about ten minutes. If the person agreed, the monitor briefly explained that we were hypothetically auctioning off the baseball card(s) displayed on the table. The participant could pick up and visually examine each card. All cards were sealed with the PSA grade clearly marked on each cardholder. The monitor worked one-on-one with the participant and no time limit was imposed on his or her inspection of the card(s). We did not give the participants any financial incentives or gifts to participate, thus we avoid any claims of the results being influenced by "found money" effects.

In *Step 2*, monitor A gave the participant an instruction sheet that consisted of two parts: (i) a short socio-economic survey (e.g., age, education, years trading), and (ii) a bidding sheet. The participant was asked to submit a hypothetical bid stating the maximum that he or she was willing to pay for the card(s). The instructions for the bidding sheet stated that the hypothetical exchange mechanism was a sealed-bid second price auction. The bidding sheet reported:

A sealed bid second price auction will be used to determine the winner of this item. Thus, if your bid of $X for this item is the highest bid and the next highest bid is $X-5, you win this item but will only pay $X-5. Under this bidding mechanism it is best for you to bid your true value for this item because overbidding may cause you to pay too much and underbidding decreases your odds of winning the item.

Note: You will not be required to pay this amount and all bids are hypothetical. Also, the winner will not receive this card.

After the participant filled out the survey and hypothetical bidding sheet privately, he or she folded the bidding sheet and placed it in an opaque box. The monitor told the participant that his or her bid would not be opened until after the show and that all bids would be destroyed when our research project was complete. Monitor A then asked the participant to go over to monitor B at a second table fifteen feet away for a follow-up auction.

In *Step 3*, monitor B told the participant that he or she now has the chance to actually bid on the card(s) that he or she had just examined in Step 2. Monitor B gave the participant a second bidding sheet for the actual auction. Again the sealed bid second price auction was used as the exchange mechanism. After the monitor answered all questions about the auction, the participant placed his or her sealed bid into a second opaque box. To guarantee that we did not get a second hypothetical bid monitor B asked each participant to acknowledge their actual bid with a signature and valid telephone number where they could be contacted. Care was taken to avoid contamination of the results by any ordering effects (e.g., sealed boxes, monitors not handling or observing bids).

Finally, in *Step 4* monitor B debriefed the participant. The monitor explained that the participant would be contacted within three days after the show if he or she was the highest bidder. Monitor B also explained that if the participant won the auction, he or she would receive the card(s) after he or she had sent a check or money order for the amount of the second highest bid. After any remaining questions were answered, monitor B asked the participant not to discuss the auction with anyone else until after the show, and then thanked him or her for participating in the project. Within three days, the winner of each auction was notified by phone, and when the monitors received the checks, they mailed out the cards.

The one-good and ten-good treatments took approximately twelve hours to complete (9 am to 9 pm). On the top of each hour the auction treatment was switched from the one-good to the ten-good treatment and vice versa the next hour. No participant took part in both auctions. Participation rates were 82% (99 agreed to participate of 121 approached) for the one-good treatment, and 84% (93 of 111) for the ten-good treatment.

The Dealer treatment was similar to the one-good treatment except that a monitor visited each dealer at his or her booth the night before the sports card show. The monitor first gave each dealer an instruction sheet for the hypothetical auction, and then administered the follow-up actual auction, on the promise they would not leak any information to potential subjects. The treatment took about two hours (6:30 pm to 8:30 pm), and the participation rate was 91% (30 of 33).

Let (b^i_{Hk}, b^i_{Ak}) represent bidder i's hypothetical and actual bids for the Cal Ripken, Jr. Topps Traded card, where subscript H and A represent the hypothetical or actual bid, $k = one$ or ten represents the one-good or ten-good case, and the superscript i is the bidder ranked in terms of their bid ($i = 1, 2, \ldots, n$). Given these two institutions, the hypothetical and actual market prices could then be compared to Beckett's October 1995 book value for the cards (Cal Ripken, Jr. Topps Traded card = $350).

Two measures of internal consistency of bidding were considered. First, List and Shogren (1998) tested how other goods affect hypothetical and actual bidding behavior. Bids for the Cal Ripken, Jr. Topps Traded card should be lower in the ten-good case relative to the one-good case because values decline with more substitution possibilities, holding the binding budget constraint constant (i.e., the Le Chatelier principle). Second, dealer bids, those people with more intense experience with market prices, will be more clustered than non-dealer bids. Evidence from lab valuation suggests that as bidders gain experience with the market and the going market price, the variability of bids declines as many see the market price as an informative signal (e.g., Plott, 1996). Bids cluster as bidders learn about the market within which they trade. One should reject the hypothesis that the bid variability of dealers is similar to the variability of non-dealers in the 1-good auction.

We consider three hypotheses to explore whether the context of choice affects the calibration functions for the Cal Ripken Jr. card, $b^i_{Aone} = f(b^i_{Hone})$, $b^i_{Aten} = f(b^i_{Hten})$, and $b^i_{Adealer} = f(b^i_{Hdealer})$. First, for all three calibration functions, we test the notion that no bias exists in hypothetical behavior, i.e., that the regression intercept is zero and the regression slope coefficient on hypothetical bid b^i_{Hone} or b^i_{Hten} is one. Second, the no-bias hypothesis implies that bids are symmetrical in that no extra bias exists when other goods are present in the value elicitation process. We use a likelihood ratio test to determine if the coefficients generated from the one-good treatment equal the coefficients from the ten-good treatment. Finally, we test whether experience affects the calibration function. Again a likelihood ratio test is used to determine if the auction coefficients generated from non-dealers are the same as the coefficients generated from dealers.

Consider the general pattern of bidding behavior in the three treatments. Table 8.17 shows the mean and median bids and the demographic characteristics for participants in the one-good, ten-good, and dealer treatments. A one way ANOVA test indicates that the respective samples for the three treatments do not differ by the socio-economic characteristics listed in Table 8.17, thereby assuring that bids across treatments differ due to treatment rather than demographic differences. The results show that the distribution of hypothetical bids lies to the right of the distribution of actual bids. A Wilcoxon matched-pairs signed ranks test rejects equality of the distributions at the 1% level for each treatment (1-good: $Z = -6.9$; 10-good: $Z = -7.7$; Dealer: $Z = -5.9$). Additionally, bias as revealed by mean central tendency shows the ratio of hypothetical-to-actual overbidding ranges from 2.2 to 3.5, depending on auction type. This level of overbidding is within the range of 1.0 to 10.0 observed in earlier work

Table 8.17. *Selected characteristics of auction participants*

	1-Card auction (N = 99)	10-Card auction (N = 93)	Dealers (N = 30)
Age[a]	34.2	31.4	33.9
Gender (% male)[b]	0.94	0.93	1.00
Education[c]	3.9	3.4	4.1
Income[d]	4.2	3.5	4.6
Experience[e]	8.9	9.4	9.8
Average hyp. bid	142.02	91.71	208.8
(standard deviation)	(126.67)	(102.6)	(81)
Median bid	125.0	40.0	190.0
Average actual bid	55.87	26.4	95.5
(standard deviation)	(82.9)	(52.2)	(88.1)
Median bid	5.0	0.0	92.5
Excluding 0s	75.0	35.0	140.0
Zero bids (%)	47 (47.4)	53 (56.9)	9 (30)

[a] Age denotes actual age in years.
[b] Gender (0–1): 0, if female, 1 = if male.
[c] Education (1–6): 1 = grade 8 or less; 2 = high school graduate; 3 = 2 years college; 4 = other post-high school education; 5 = 4 year college; 6 = graduate school.
[d] Income (1–8): 1 = less than $10,000; 2 = $10,000–$19,999; 3 = $20,000–$29,999; 4 = $30,000–$39,999; 5 = $40,000–49,999; 6 = $50,000–$47,999; 7 = $75,000–$99,999; 8 = $100,00 > or over.
[e] Experience denotes actual years involved with sports cards.

on hypothetical-actual bidding (see Diamond and Hausman's overview, 1994). These results reinforce the argument that people overstate their actual willingness to pay. Table 8.17 also shows that hypothetical bids from the one-good auction required (0.39) less deflation than in the 10-good auction (0.28).

The auction market prices were reasonably close to the listed book value from Beckett. Table 8.18 presents the highest and second-highest hypothetical and actual bids for the Cal Ripken Jr. TT card in the three treatments and Beckett's book value, $350 (as of October 1995). For the Ripken 1982 TT card, hypothetical bids captured 143%, 100%, and 93% of the book value for the 1-good, 10-good and Dealer treatments, while the actual bids garnered 97%, 71%, and 73% of the book value. The table also lists the top two bids for the other nine goods with their book values. Overall, the average percentage of book value captured by the auctions was over 162% for the hypothetical bids and about 94% for the actual bids.

Overall, the results suggest bidding behavior is broadly consistent with theoretical predictions. First, the inclusion of other goods reduced bids, both hypothetical and actual; mean and median hypothetical bids fell by 35% ($142.02 to

Table 8.18. *Top two hypothetical and auction bids*

Treatment card	Hyp. bid (% of book)	Actual bid (% of book)	Book value
1-Carl Cal Ripken 1981 TT	(1) $600	$350	$350
	(2) $500 (143)	$340 (97)	
Dealer Cal Ripken 1981 TT	(1) $330	$260	$350
	(2) $325 (93)	255 (73)	
10-Card Cal Ripken 1981 TT	(1) $450	$300	$350
	(2) $350 (100)	$250 (17)	
Cal Ripken 1981 Topps	(1) $110	$80	$80
	(2) $110 (138)	$75 (94)	
Cal Ripken 1981 Donruss	(1) $80	$50	$55
	(2) $60 (109)	$45 (82)	
1982 TT Without Ripken	(1) $70	$50	$65
	(2) $70 (108)	$45 (96)	
Billy Ripken 1989 Fleer	(1) $100	$50	$40
	(2) $90 (225)	$35 (88)	
Troy Aikman 1989 Score	(1) $110	$60	$40
	(2) $100 (222)	$55 (122)	
Troy Aikman 1989 TT	(1) $10	$5	$3
	(2) $7 (233)	$3 (100)	
Troy Aikman 1989 Proset	(1) $12	$7	$5
	(2) $8 (160)	$4 (80)	
1989 TT without Aikman	(1) $15	$8	$6
	(2) $13 (217)	$5 (83)	
Michael Irvin 1989 Topps	(1) $10	$6	$3
	(2) $8 (267)	$5 (167)	
Percent of book value (12 card mean)	167.9	93.84	

$91.71) and 68% ($125 to $40), and mean and median actual bids fell by 53% ($55.87 to $26.40) and 100% ($75 to $0); excluding zero bids, the median fell by 53% ($75 to $35). Using a Wilcoxon test, we reject the hypothesis that the populations for bids, hypothetical and actual, elicited in the one-good auction were similar to bids elicited from the ten-good auction at the 5% level or better (hypothetical: $Z = -2.61$; actual: $Z = -2.06$). Second, using a Moses test, we also reject the equal variance hypothesis at the 1% level for hypothetical and actual bids (hypothetical: $M = 121$; actual: $M = 96$). The dealers' knowledge of the common market value reduced the dispersion of their bids.

Table 8.19 presents estimates of the Tobit and OLS calibration functions, $b^i_{Aone} = f(b^i_{Hone})$, $b^i_{Aten} = f(b^i_{Hten})$, and $b^i_{Adealer} = f(b^i_{Hdealer})$ across the three different auctions. Models 1–2, 3–4, and 5–6 reflect the 1-good, 10-good, and Dealer treatments. The OLS estimates suggest the calibration functions are concave for both one-card auctions (dealer and non-dealer), suggesting the relationship

Table 8.19. *Calibration functions*

	Model					
	One-card auction		Ten-card auction		Dealers	
	(1)	(2)	(3)	(4)	(5)	(6)
Variable	OLS	Tobit	OLS	Tobit	OLS	Tobit
Constant	−8.3	−20.0*	0.25	−0.19	3.1	6.8
	(−0.7)	(−1.9)	(0.1)	(−0.8)	(0.3)	(0.1)
Hyp. Bid	0.65**	0.39**	0.16	0.30**	0.20	.27
	(4.7)	(5.1)	(1.8)	(5.8)	(1.9)	(1.4)
Hyp. Bid²	−0.8E-03**	–	0.7E-03**	–	−0.8E-03**	–
	(−2.5)		(2.5)		(−2.2)	
Log likelihood	−559	−334	−448	−234	−210	−136

Note: Dependent variable is actual bid.
[a] t-statistics in parentheses.
** Significant at the 99-percent level.
* Significant at the 95-percent level.

between hypothetical and actual reported valuations is an inverted-U shape. Since these estimates may be biased and inconsistent, further investigation is warranted. In all Tobit specifications, the quadratic and square root terms are insignificant, suggesting a linear calibration function is appropriate. Focusing on the Tobit estimates, the no-bias hypothesis (i.e., zero intercept and unit slope) is rejected at the 1% level for all treatments.

Using a likelihood ratio statistic, we reject the hypothesis that the coefficients from the one-good treatment equal those from the ten-good treatment at the 1% level ($\chi^2 = 16.46$). A Mann-Whitney test also rejects pooling the data at the 5% level ($Z = -2.06$). The null hypothesis that the coefficient on hypothetical bid is equal across the two auctions is rejected at the 12% level. To avoid constraining the variances to equality across auction types we use the dummy variable interaction approach within a heteroscedastic model. These results suggest that subjects bidding in the one-good treatment have more tendencies to overstate the hypothetical bid relative to bidding in the ten-good case. This result suggests that calibration is good-specific: each good might need its own auction to capture the particular correlation between actual and hypothetical bidding. This raises a problem for calibration of non-deliverable goods.

Mixed support is provided for the null hypothesis that market experience does not affect the calibration function. Using the Likelihood ratio statistic, we cannot reject the null at any reasonable level of significance ($\chi^2 = 1.5$). Results from the Mann-Whitney test, however, reveal that the null should be rejected at the 5% level ($Z = -2.77$). Also, we reject the hypothesis of identical slope coefficients across dealer/non-dealer auction types at the 5% level. More market experience implies, weakly, that the adjustment required is less stringent: knowledge dampens but does not eliminate the tendency to overstate hypothetical bids.

In conclusion, List and Shogren's (1998) results support the view that people overstate actual bids, and the estimated calibration function to correct for this exaggeration is both good- and context-specific, i.e., other goods and market experience. The calibration factors were 0.39 in the one-good auction, 0.28 in the ten-good auction, and 0.46 in the dealer auction, all more stringent than the 0.6–0.9 range for irradiated meat products found in the CVM-X method developed in Fox *et al.* (1998).

CVM-X works in four steps: *Step 1:* Use a survey to elicit hypothetical values for the good in question. *Step 2:* Bring subsamples of the survey respondents into the laboratory and elicit real bids for the actual good in an incentive-compatible auction that employs real goods, real money, and repeated market experience. *Step 3:* Estimate a calibration function relating the auction market bids of the subsample to the hypothetical survey bids. *Step 4:* Use the estimated calibration function to adjust the values of the survey respondents who did not participate in the laboratory auction. CVM-X could be a cost-effective tool that combines the advantages of the stated preference, contingent valuation method (CVM) and experimental auction markets (X). The method could be used to increase the validity and accuracy of surveys while broadening the scope of non-market valuation in the lab.

The CVM-X application studied by Fox *et al.* (1998) is the reduction in health risk from the parasite *Trichinella* achieved with food irradiation. Irradiated foods are not yet widely available in the US and most people are unfamiliar with the process, which gives it a feature common to many nonmarket environmental goods like biodiversity. Nearly 200 randomly selected households participated in the survey. They were asked the maximum they would be willing to pay to upgrade from their less-preferred sandwich to their sandwich of choice in an open-ended elicitation question. At the end of the interview, participants who were pork eaters were asked if they would be interested in participating in a consumer economics experiment.

In the lab experiment, participants were assigned to one of two treatments: the irradiated or the non-irradiated treatment. The experimental auction procedures followed those in Hayes *et al.* (1995). Stage I was the candy bar auction (second price); stage II was the food auction. The results suggest that an upward bias in hypothetical bids exists, and that the lab can be used to correct for this bias, but the calibration function might be commodity specific.

Two other attempts to calibrate hypothetical and real values include the cross-commodity "bias function" approach of Blackburn *et al.* (1994), which rests on the empirically testable presumption that bias for a good in one context is measurable and transferable to another good in another context (also see

Swallow's discussion of their calibration method, 1994); and the two bias function method used by Harrison *et al.* (1997): one to account for the downward bias due to free riding and the other to account for hypothetical bias. The free riding bias function is measured in a comparison of two real valuation situations for a nature calendar, one of which features public provision of the calendar. While intuitively appealing, the approach rests on little tested assumptions about the transferability of bias functions between different contexts: real versus hypothetical values, private versus public goods; and the untested presumption that these biases are additive.

Good- and context-specific calibration suggests that one might be tempted to skip over the hypothetical question and go directly to the actual auction. But for policy debates over public goods, actual experimental auctions are constrained by one's ability to deliver the good. Randall (1997, p. 200) is more skeptical about the general usefulness of calibration: "[t]he calibration issue, it seems to me, is an audacious attempt to promote a Kuhnian paradigm shift. . . . I would argue vigorously that the essential premise is unproven and the question is therefore premature and presumptuous. The proposed new calibration paradigm is at this moment merely a rambunctious challenger to the dominant external validation paradigm." On a good day, one could interpret his statement as a call for more work on calibration. If so, future research in experimental auctions and calibration should explore whether private goods can serve as reasonable proxies for public good preferences, and the burden of calibration can be reduced by clustering goods into a limited set of functions defined by the context of choice.

Calibration work has been a series of exercises in pattern recognition without apology. One should not confuse pattern recognition with doodling. Rather observations are a formal and organized model of the structure and functions of a complex process: in this case, value formation. Researchers should be concerned with Smith and Mansfield's (1998, p. 210) admonition that lab valuation work has thus far provided "little systematic treatment of how the circumstances of choice influence the analyst's ability to describe preference relations from choice functions" – if, in fact, this claim were supported by the evidence. But this is an overstatement. A review of the growing laboratory valuation literature reveals some of the patterns observed about choice and valuation: context matters (Kahneman *et al.*, 1990; Buhr *et al.*, 1993), the good matters (Hayes *et al.*, 1995, Fox *et al.*, 1998), information matters (Melton *et al.*, 1996; Cummings and Taylor, 1999; Fox *et al.*, 2002), exchange institutions matter (Bohm, 1972, Rutström, 1998), market experience matters (Shogren, 1990, Shogren and Crocker, 1994), price information sometimes matters (List and Shogren, 1999), substitutes and complements matter (List *et al.*, 1998). The interested reader can find more examples in the literature.

The question remains *why*? Is it the exchange institution? The subject pool? The good? The context? All the above? The answer is not immediately obvious.

But it is unanswered questions like these that continue to make the gap between intentions and actions a challenge in non-market valuation. This is probably because the perception of a hypothetical stain has never really been systematically removed by an industrial-strength theory in over two decades of debate. We agree with Mansfield's (1998, p. 680) point that "the power of the calibration model could be improved by a better understanding of how individuals answer [contingent valuation] questions, including the traits or attitudes that inspire individuals to give more or less accurate answers." No camp has a completely convincing and axiomatic explanation as to what creates or removes the wedge between intentions and actions. And the lack of an analytical framework increases the likelihood that this discussion will remain stagnate as a "did not, did too" spat. The debate will likely be palliated only when a robust theoretical or behavioral reason emerges as to why the wedge happens and whether it can be controlled systematically.

Calibration research may eventually lead to generalizations about behavior that convert experimental results into theory. Such a conversion requires that we understand how and why the context of choice matters, as the literature on experimental economics has revealed time and again. Restructuring calibration models to include context-dependent preferences might be a place to start (see Tversky and Simonson, 1993). If context matters, people might think about values in both hypothetical and real terms, and the interaction of these two representations might affect the gap between intentions and actions (see, for example, Shafir et al.'s (1997) work on money illusion). Designing an experiment to understand whether a model of context-dependent preferences can help organize behavior in valuation exercises is a worthwhile next step.

8.8 Hybrid auctions and consequential bidding

In response to the arguments asserting that hypothetical surveys do not elicit truthful measures of economic value, Carson, Groves, and Machina (2000) argue the relevant distinction is not between *real* versus *hypothetical* valuation. Rather they argue one should consider the difference between values elicited in *consequential* versus *inconsequential* mechanisms. If people believe an incentive compatible valuation survey is *consequential*, one that might actually affect realized policy, they will truthfully state their preferences. This theory of consequential valuation, if supported, could provide a missing link between traditional demand theory and stated preference exercises.

The key behavioral assumption underlying this theory, however, remains untested: do people who believe an incentive compatible mechanism *might* yield a binding outcome with a positive probability (but less than 100%) reveal their preferences truthfully? Herein we test this assumption in the lab using a classic second price auction, which is weakly demand revealing in theory, in

Table 8.20. *Summary of experimental design*

Experimental variable	Parameter
The good	Redeemable token
Value measured	Willingness to pay bid
Auction institutions	Real, hypothetical and consequential second price auctions
Monetary endowment	$10 flat participation fee, plus the individual earning
Trials	3 sessions, 20 rounds per session
Number of participants	6–15 per session, n = 30
Induced values ($)	0.4, 1.8, 2.5, 3.2, 3.8, 4.0, 5.3, 6.1, 6.3, 6.5, 7.0, 7.6, and 8.4
A values (%)	88, 41, 100, 39, 85, 91, 0, 15, 24, 100, 0, 100, 65, 55, 0, 50, 0, 6, 10, 100

an induced value setting. While Carson *et al.* (2000) focus on a voting referendum mechanism for a public good, the idea underpinning the consequential mechanism should be robust to any incentive compatible device.[3] Shogren and Tadevosyan (2006) implemented a second price auction in which the probability the auction is binding is the treatment – real, hypothetical, or consequential.

Table 8.20 summarizes the design used by Shogren and Tadevosyan (2006). An induced value, second price auction was used to test for rational bidding behavior under consequential conditions. Let α represent the probability the auction is binding, in which case the highest bidder buys the good at the second highest bid; $(1 - \alpha)$ is the probability the auction is not binding, i.e., hypothetical or inconsequential. Based on this probability the auction is binding, we create three treatments: *real* ($\alpha = 100\%$), *hypothetical* ($\alpha = 0\%$), and *consequential*, a positive probability the auction is binding ($0\% < \alpha < 100\%$). For consistency we follow the auction design of Shogren *et al.* (2001a), in which the sets of induced values were randomly drawn from a uniform distribution on [$0.10, $10.0] in 10 cent increments, the utilized induced values were (0.4, 1.8, 2.5, 3.2, 3.8, 4.0, 5.3, 6.1, 6.3, 6.5, 7.0, 7.6, and 8.4). Each participant was assigned each value twice during the twenty rounds.

Standard second price auction experimental instructions were used, with the additional explanation of the *consequential* auction. Before starting the auction, the monitor read the experimental instructions and addressed any questions.

[3] In a consequential voting model, no one person can believe he or she alone can actually change the probability of the outcome – he or she just has to believe that there is some positive probability the action will be implemented given his or her vote. This is the essence of the voter's paradox – no one vote matters on the margin, but all matter in the final tally. The probability of public good provision is positive but exogenous to the voter. In theory, this exogenous probability makes the vote *consequential* and provides the needed incentives to induce truthful responses in an incentive compatible mechanism. Similarly, no bidder in the second price auction has to believe his or her individual bid affects the probability the auction is binding to induce truthful bidding, only that some exogenous positive probability exists that the auction will be binding.

The bidders knew the winner was the highest bidder, and he or she paid the second highest bid for the good. The experiment was run in three sessions with twenty rounds; the probability, α, was as follows for the twenty rounds: 88%, 41%, 100%, 39%, 85%, 91%, 0%, 15%, 24%, 100%, 0%, 100%, 65%, 55%, 0%, 50%, 0%, 6%, 10%, 100%.

Each round had five steps:

Step 1: Each participant had a recording sheet showing his or her ID number, induced value in that round (i.e., the price the monitor will pay to buy the good back from the player if they win), the probability ($0 \leq \alpha \leq 100\%$) the auction was binding in that round (identical for all bidders), and a place to write his or her bid.

Step 2: The bidders submitted their bids. Before doing so, we purposefully told bidders about the potential risks from bidding too high or too low, i.e., pay too much or miss out on a profitable opportunity. The monitor revealed the optimal bidding strategy information since the purpose is to test bidding behavior in a consequential auction relative to the benchmark cases of real or hypothetical auctions. Any deviation in bidding behavior from rationality or treatment can be attributed to the notion of consequentialism, not a bidder's generic confusion about the best bidding strategy in the second price auction.

Step 3: The monitor collected and ranked bids from highest to lowest bid.

Step 4: The monitor announced whether the auction was binding based on a random draw. The auction was binding if the random number was less than or equal to the probability for that round. If the auction was binding, the highest bidder was the winner, and he or she paid the second highest bid. The difference between induced value and the second highest bid is the profit for the winner for that round; no one else made any profits during that round.

Step 5: The next round started and Steps 1–4 were repeated. After twenty rounds, the monitor paid the subjects their profits and a flat participation fee of $10.

Table 8.21 summarizes bidding behavior for all rounds across treatments. The unconditional results suggest the *real* auction induced more sincere bidding than either the *hypothetical* or *consequential* auction. Mean bids were more accurate, and the variation was smaller. In the *real* treatment, the mean bid minus induced value was −0.08 (S.D. = 2.21); the mean bid minus induced value was −$2.73 (S.D. = 5.25) for the *hypothetical* (outliers excluded) and −$0.91 (S.D. = 6.59) for the *consequential*.

Using conditional panel regression analysis, three results emerge. First, bidders bid sincerely more frequently in the *real* second price auction relative to either the *hypothetical* or *consequential* auctions. We test sincere bidding with a two-way random effects model:

$$Bid_{it} = \beta_0 + \beta_1 I V_{it} + \beta_2 \alpha_1 + \beta_3 \alpha_p + \beta_4 \alpha_1 \times I V_{it}$$
$$+ \beta_5 \alpha_p \times I V_{it} + \gamma_i + \varphi_t + \varepsilon_{it}$$

Table 8.21. *Descriptive statistics (all rounds)*

	Real ($\alpha = 100\%$)	Hypothetical (all obs.) ($\alpha = 0\%$)	Hypothetical (7 outliers excluded)[a]	Consequential ($0\% < \alpha < 100\%$)
Mean bid	$4.16	$2610.65	$2.46	$4.35
(S.D.)	(2.91)	(15687.4)	(4.90)	(6.60)
Mean induced value	$4.96	$5.28	$5.19	$5.26
(S.D.)	(2.35)	(2.28)	(2.31)	(2.34)
Mean [Bid/Induced value]	−0.08	2605.37	−2.73	−0.91
(S.D.)	(2.11)	(15687.1)	(5.25)	(6.59)
Mean [Bid/induced value]	0.82	389.98	0.55	1.41
(S.D.)	(0.35)	(2390.3)	(1.33)	(5.49)
Mean percent of maximum surplus	153.2%	−20600.9%	−26.8%	27.7%
(S.D.)	(2.754)	(482.7)	(8.26)	(4.13)
N	120	120	113	360

[a] Bids of $1000 or more were excluded.

Table 8.22. *Panel data estimation results (7 outliers excluded)*

Variable		Parameter estimate	Standard error	Mean value	Pr > |z|
Intercept	(β_0)	1.3006	0.7960	–	0.1010
IV	(β_1)	0.5548*	0.1160	5.188	0.0000
α_1	(β_2)	−1.2725	1.3517	0.202	0.3465
α_p	(β_3)	0.3771	1.4253	0.191	0.7913
$\alpha_1 \times IV$	(β_4)	0.2551	0.2298	1.003	0.2269
$\alpha_p \times IV$	(β_5)	0.3696	0.2375	0.989	0.1196
N = 593					

* Significant at the 1% level.

where Bid_{it} is the bid submitted by ith player in tth round, β_0 is the intercept term, IV_{it} is the induced value for the ith player in tth round, α_1 equals 1 when $\alpha = 100\%$ (*real*), otherwise 0; α_p equals 1 if $0 < \alpha < 100\%$ (*consequential*), otherwise 0, γ_i represents subject-specific characteristics, φ_t represents round-specific random effects, including learning or other trends in bidding behavior, and ε_{it} is iid error. The interaction terms capture how slopes change for *real* and *consequential* relative to the *hypothetical* behavior.

Table 8.22 shows the regression results. The joint hypothesis that the constant was zero and the slope was one was tested to determine whether bidding

Table 8.23. *Wald test results*

	Hypothesis	Num DF	Den DF	**Wald Stats**	Chi-squared	Results
I						
Test 1	H_1: in **hypothetical** treatment the regression line has intercept $= 0$, slope $= 1$	2	586	**18.868**	0.00008	Reject H_0
Test 2	H_2: in **real** treatment the regression line has intercept $= 0$ and slope $= 1$	2	586	**2.565**	0.27739	Fail to reject H_1
Test 3	H_3: in **consequential** treatment regression line has an intercept $= 0$ and slope $= 1$	2	586	**27.868**	0.00000	Reject H_2
II						
Test 4	H_4: **hypothetical** and **real** behavior is the same	2	586	**18.019**	0.00012	Reject H_4
Test 5	H_5: **hypothetical** and **consequential** behavior is the same	2	586	**41.815**	0.00000	Reject H_5
Test 6	H_6: **real** and **consequential** behavior is the same	2	586	**7.845**	0.01979	Could reject or fail to reject the H_6

behavior in each treatment differs from the optimal bidding, i.e., bid one's induced value:

$$H_1 : \beta_0 = 0; \beta_1 = 1 \text{ (hypothetical)}$$
$$H_2 : \beta_0 + \beta_2 = 0; \beta_1 + \beta_4 = 1 \text{ (real)}$$
$$H_3 : \beta_0 + \beta_3 = 0; \beta_1 + \beta_5 = 1 \text{ (consequential)}$$

Based on the Wald statistics, we cannot reject the H_2: bidding behavior in the *real* treatment was not significantly different from the optimal bidding behavior of truth telling (see Table 8.23, Part 1). The *real* auction is demand revealing. In contrast, both hypotheses H_1 and H_3 are rejected; bidding in the *hypothetical* and *consequential* treatments was significantly different than rational truth-telling behavior.

The second main result is that bidding behavior was significantly different across the auction treatments. Three additional hypotheses were tested:

$$H_4 : \beta_0 - \beta_2 = 0; \beta_1 - \beta_4 = 0 \text{ (hypothetical vs. real)}$$
$$H_5 : \beta_0 - \beta_3 = 0; \beta_1 - \beta_5 = 0 \text{ (hypothetical vs. consequential)}$$
$$H_6 : \beta_2 - \beta_3 = 0; \beta_4 - \beta_5 = 0 \text{ (real vs. consequential)}$$

Using a Wald statistic, all three hypotheses were rejected (see Table 8.23, Part 2). Bidding behavior was not the same across treatments.

Table 8.24. *Winners and price-setters in second price auction treatments*

Treatment Session	Winner		Price-setter	
	Highest value bidder	Second highest Value bidder	Highest value bidder	Second highest value bidder
Real				
n = 12	7	2	2	3
Percentage	58%	17%	17%	25%
Hypothetical				
N = 12	1	1	3	0
Percentage	8%	8%	25%	0%
Consequential				
N = 36	14	7	6	8
Percentage	39%	19%	17%	22%

The third primary finding is that the *real* second price auction had the greatest percentage of highest-value winners and captured more of the potential surplus than either the hypothetical or consequential auction. The bidder with the highest value was more likely to win, and the bidder with the second highest value was more likely to set the price in the *real* treatments. Table 8.24 shows the highest bidder won 58% of the real auctions, but only 8% and 39% of the *hypothetical* and *consequential* auctions, respectively. Measuring efficiency by the percent of maximum surplus captured (max surplus = highest induced value – second highest induced value) we see the real auction captured 153% of the potential surplus (see Table 8.21). The maximum surplus captured in *hypothetical* treatment was negative (gains captured were overwhelmed by the losses of winning bidders with low induced values); the surplus captured in *consequential* treatment was positive but low, 29%.

While a *consequential* second price auction outperformed the *hypothetical/inconsequential* auction, it did not generate truth revealing bidding behavior. Rather rational bidding behavior was more likely to be observed when the auction was real (100% binding) relative to either the consequential or hypothetical auctions. Most evidence in the extant literature finds people tend not to state their real intentions in a hypothetical or *inconsequential* setting relative to a real economic commitment.

The theoretical possibility we consider herein is whether bidding behavior becomes more truth revealing if the auction is *consequential*, a positive probability of being binding, as argued by Carson *et al.* (2000). These results do not support that notion: bidding behavior in the consequential auction was neither optimal nor identical to real auction bidding. Rather bidding behavior was truth revealing only if the auction was 100% binding. In response, one might attempt to look for a consequential probability less than 100% that generates the optimal bidding behavior. But based on past experience in the calibration literature (see Fox *et al.*, 1998), this search could end up being either good- or context-specific or both, which would limit the general usefulness of the theory. This search remains an open empirical question.

8.9   Concluding remarks

Experimentalists know from experience that experiments generate as many questions as answers about human behavior and basic experimental design. Plott (1991) calls this *Say's Law of Experimentation* – supply creates its own demand. This chapter examined different experiments designed to explore eight questions that have emerged in our auction valuation work. Do people learn with experience about their preferences for unfamiliar goods and is this reflected in bidding behavior? Yes, the results suggest people who initially bid high in an experiment for a new good reduce their bids once they gain the desired information about how the good fits into their preference ordering. Can the choice of auction mechanism affect the gap between willingness to pay and willingness to accept measures of value? Yes, the results suggest that second price and random nth price auctions repeated over time lead to a convergence in WTP and WTA for a good with many substitutes (convergence occurs because WTA falls over time toward a relatively stable WTP), whereas no such convergence occurs with the BDM mechanism.

Does transforming the second price auction into a tournament setting create more incentives for all bidders – those on the margin of the market clearing price and those off the margin – to bid more sincerely? Yes, the results suggest that all bidders were more likely to bid truthfully in the auction tournament relative to a standard second price auction, even if the auction tournament was a theoretically more complex environment to predict a unique equilibrium. Are preferences for monetary lotteries fixed or fungible once any anomalies in behavior are eliminated with market-like experience? Fixed. Preferences for lotteries did not change once a preference reversal was *corrected* with market-like arbitrage. Rather stated values to buy and sell low probability-high payoff lotteries decreased toward their expected value. People tended to initially overstate their willingness to buy and sell these low-probability, high-payoff lotteries; once arbitraged, their value statements declined while their preferences over lotteries remained consistent.

Do people value the gifts they receive in a real incentive compatible auction? Yes, the results suggest that people do value an actually received Christmas gift;

however, the evidence does not support the idea that a deadweight loss arises in gift giving. Can one calibrate real and hypothetical bidding behavior using *ex post* regressions? Yes, there is some correlation between what people say they will do and what they actually do, but there is no general rule of thumb to guide generic calibration. The calibration factors seem to be both good-specific and context-specific. Finally, is the possibility that the valuation mechanism is *consequential* – a chance the information gathered could influence policy – sufficient to induce sincere bidding in a second price auction? No, the evidence suggests that only a real auction (100% binding) was sufficient to trigger sincere bidding behavior; consequential auctions (0% < binding probability < 100%) did not induce sincere bidding.

The general lesson to take away from this chapter is that one need be prepared to chase down the answers to many new questions piqued by your own curiosity or by colleagues who raise legitimate questions about why you did what you did. And while you do not have to run *their* untested experimental design for them, you do have to support your decision of why you choose the particular design route you did. These decisions can require auxiliary experiments such as those presented in this chapter. The good news is that these new experiments force you to think outside your normal spheres and will open doors to new theories, new patterns, and new designs: all leading to deeper and more general observations about human behavior.

9 Validity of experimental auctions

9.1 Introduction

This chapter addresses the question of whether experimental auctions are valid in the sense that they accurately measure the theoretical notions of values laid out in Chapter 3. Determining whether a measurement instrument is valid is a complex concern for social scientists – made more difficult in that the theoretical constructs we seek to measure are latent and unobservable. *Validity* refers to the extent to which a measurement instrument actually measures what it purports to measure. We must be clear about the object of measurement in experimental auctions. Many psychologists have attacked traditional economists' view of preferences arguing that valuations are malleable, contextual, and even constructed on the spot (e.g., see Bettman, Luce, and Payne, 1998; Gunnarsson *et al.*, 2003). This argument is about the appropriateness of a given theoretical model or construct; not with the validity of a measurement device *per se*.

We follow the economists' notion of value as the theoretical construct of interest (e.g., Chapters 2 and 3) and we seek to determine the validity of experimental auctions in measuring these latent variables. Our goal is to explore whether experimental auctions provide an accurate measure of value and whether elicited values respond in ways predicted by economic theory. Our focus on economists' views of values and preferences serves as benchmark behavior against which one can assess the validity of experimental auctions. We saw in Chapter 2 that bidding behavior in induced value auctions generally conforms to what is predicted by auction theory: many studies find that bids in incentive-compatible auctions are not statistically different than induced values. Unfortunately, the real world might not be as stark or have values as well defined as in induced value experiments. This chapter investigates the validity of experimental auctions conducted with homegrown values; those values that people bring into an experiment. This presents a unique challenge because we do not know true homegrown values (if we did there would be no need for the study) and cannot confirm whether bids match values. We must use indirect means of determining the validity of experimental auctions with homegrown values.

The psychology literature has identified several types of validity and has defined a variety of validity tests (see e.g., Nunnally and Bernstein, 1994). Although, most of the discussion in such literature is focused on determining the validity of multiple-items scales that are formed from aggregating individual responses to series of Likert "agree/disagree" statements, the general principles are relevant here. Consider a variable with a true value given by x_T and a measurement of that variable, given by x_M. The issue of validity can be conceptualized by recognizing that $x_M = x_T + e_s + e_r$ where e_s is systematic error and e_r is random error. A measurement is *valid* if $e_s = e_r = 0$, which implies $x_M = x_T$. A measurement is said to be *reliable* when $e_r = 0$. Reliability is a necessary but not sufficient condition for validity. In large samples, if e_r is a mean-zero random error (i.e., the measurement is reliable), a measurement is valid if there is no systematic error.

We organize the findings regarding the validity of experimental auctions around several key ideas. First, we investigate whether auction bids behave as predicted by economic theory. Second, we examine whether auctions are *reliable* measures of value. Third, we consider the *convergent validity* of auctions. Finally, we look at a three key behavioral anomalies.

9.2   Auction bids and economic theory

Auction theory makes several predictions about bidding behavior and the manner in which bids should change when other exogenous factors are altered. Most tests of economic theory can be thought of as a test of *internal validity* which focuses on cause-effect relationships between independent and dependent variables. We now examine the empirical evidence for seven predictions of economic theory: 1) market price increases as demand increases, 2) diminishing marginal utility, 3) more is preferred to less, 4) demand is affected by price/availability of complement and substitute goods, 5) values rise (fall) with positive (negative) information, 6) willingness to pay (willingness to accept) is increasing (decreasing) in the perceived difficulty in delaying the decision and decreasing (increasing) in the perceived difficulty in reversing the transaction, and 7) the value of a dollar to a person is exactly $1.00.

First, we start by asking whether market prices increase when the demand curve shifts out as is predicted by economic theory. Several factors might cause a demand curve to shift outward such as positive information about the good or advertising, factors we discuss momentarily. A more basic demand shifter is "population" or the number of auction participants. In econometric studies that estimate consumer demand using aggregate time-series data, population is frequently used as an explanatory variable. The intuition for including such a variable is that increased population, *ceteris paribus*, shifts the demand curve outward leading to higher quantity purchased at higher price levels.

A straightforward way to investigate this issue in the context of experimental auctions is to determine whether increasing the number of participants in an auction increases the market price. In an experimental auction, the supply curve is perfectly inelastic as the number of products for sale is fixed. For example, in a second price auction the supply is fixed at one unit. Shifting the demand curve out and to the right should increase the market price (i.e., the second highest bid in a second price auction). Umberger and Feuz (2004) tested this proposition. They used a fourth price auction to elicit bids for various beef steaks. They report results showing that increasing the number of subjects in an auction (from six to twelve people) was associated with a statistically significant increase in market price (i.e., the fourth highest bid) as would be predicted by economic theory. The addition of one additional person in an auction session was associated with a $0.28/lb increase in the market price for a beef steak.

Second, a firmly held tenet of economic theory is that people experience diminishing marginal utility. The utility from consuming $(n + 1)$ units of a good provides less additional utility than consuming n units of a good. Corrigan and Rousu (2006a) directly tested this proposition in the context of experimental auctions. They elicited bids to purchase one and two units of a good. They show that the mean bid for two units of a good was less than twice the bid for one unit of a good; a finding consistent with diminishing marginal utility and downward sloping demand curves. For example, the mean bid for two bags of plain-labeled chips was only $0.95, whereas two times the mean bid for one bag of chips was $1.02. Similarly, the mean bid for two jars of salsa was $1.13, whereas two times the mean bid for one jar of salsa was $1.30. Results in Hoffman *et al.* (1993) also support the notion that bidding behavior responds to diminishing marginal utility. People participated in a series of six binding auctions for beef steak. They found that the average price for steak was declining in the number of auctions in which a person participated. This finding is consistent with people moving down their demand curve as they purchased more steak. The average price in the sixth auction was about 20% lower than the average price in the first auction: people reduced their bids the more they purchased. Horowitz *et al.* (2006) also provide several tests of diminishing marginal utility in auctions for flashlights and coffee mugs. They show that the compensation demanded to give up one unit of a good (i.e., WTA) was falling in the number of units of the good a person was endowed with. For example, when the people were endowed with only one flashlight, mean WTA to give up the one flashlight was $6.30; however, when people were endowed with three flashlights, WTA to give up one flashlight fell to $5.50.

Third, although economic theory predicts diminishing marginal utility, it also posits non-satiation (e.g., more is preferred to less). This is the so-called "scope test," a test that value is increasing in the quantity/quality of the good provided. Corrigan and Rousu (2006a) observed just such a result. Although the mean bid for two units of a good was less than twice than the mean bid for one unit (e.g., people exhibit diminishing marginal utility), the mean bid for two goods was higher than the mean bid for one good. For example, they show that the mean bids for one bag of plain corn chips, USA branded corn chips, and salsa were $0.51, $0.58, and $0.65, and the mean bids for two bags of plain-labeled corn chips, American-labeled corn chips, and salsa were $0.95, $1.07, and $1.13; the results pass the "scope test" as more is preferred to less. List (2002) also finds that bids are increasing in the quantity of goods when people simultaneously bid on smaller and larger bundles of sports cards. The mean bid for non-dealers (dealers) for a bundle of ten sports cards was $3.72 ($3.09) whereas the mean bid for a bundle of thirteen sports cards was $4.52 ($3.45); however the effect disappeared when people viewed the bundles in isolation rather than simultaneously, a finding we discuss later in this chapter.

Fourth, a concept closely related to diminishing marginal utility and downward sloping demand curves is that economists expect demand to be affected by the price/availability of substitutes and complements. Corrigan and Rousu (2006c) investigated this issue by auctioning two substitute goods (plain-labeled corn chips and American-labeled corn chips) and a complementary good (salsa) in a variety of treatments that differed according to the quantity of each of the goods that was available for sale. They found that, as predicted by economic theory, bids were affected by the presence and availability of substitutes and complements. For example, the mean bid to obtain both the American- and plain-labeled corn chip bags was less than the sum of the bids to buy each good individually (i.e., the goods were substitutes). By contrast, the mean bid to jointly purchase American-labeled chips and salsa was $1.31, whereas the sum of the bids to purchase each item individually was only $1.23. As predicted by economic theory, demand was increasing in the availability of complements and decreasing in the availability of substitutes. Cherry et al. (2004) also investigated this issue in an induced value auction. They showed that auction bids were significantly influenced by the price of a non-auctioned good that was a perfect substitute for the auctioned good. They found that people reduced their auction bids when their value exceeded the price of the outside option and that a decrease in the price of the outside option resulted in greater bid reduction.

Fifth, it would be expected that bidding behavior responds to positive and negative information. Many of the goods that are sold in auctions can be characterized by risk in that there is uncertainty regarding the quality or safety of a novel auctioned good. Auction bids can be viewed as the certainty equivalent of a lottery. The bid depends on a person's belief or subjective probability that the auctioned good will generate a particular outcome. This conceptualization predicts that people will react to the introduction of new information by updating their prior probabilities concerning the likelihood of observing good and bad outcomes. A number of studies have investigated how auction bids respond to positive and negative information. As would be expected, and as is predicted by theory, people tend to increase their valuations when positive information is provided and decrease their valuations when negative information is provided. For example, Lusk *et al.* (2004a) showed for all but one treatment/location in their study people decreased the amount they demanded to consume a genetically modified food when provided information about the benefits of genetically modified food to health, the environment, and the developing world.

In another example, Fox *et al.* (2002) found that when provided with negative information about irradiation, people decreased their bid to exchange a typical pork sandwich for an irradiated pork sandwich whereas positive information had the opposite effect. Interestingly, those people provided with both positive and negative information behaved as if they had only received the negative.

Hoffman *et al.* (1993) found that providing information on the benefits of vacuum packaging increased the premium people placed on vacuum packaged meat over traditional over-wrapped meat. Hayes *et al.* (1995) auctioned pork sandwiches that varied by the likelihood and severity of illness. They found people generally reacted in the predicted direction when objective information was provided about probability of illness; valuations of a pork sandwich tended to decrease when people were told the objective probability of illness was greater than their own prior subjective probabilities and to increase when people were told the objective probability of illness was less than their prior subjective probability.

These findings seem rather obvious, but they do emphasize that auction bids are not arbitrary in the sense that they respond to new information in a way that is expected. Still, a critic might respond that because these are within-subject designs that people are responding in an intuitive way so as to not look foolish to the experimenter. A few studies have investigated the effect of information in between-subject designs in which such a concern is non-existent. Hayes *et al.* (1995) also conducted between-subject experiments and showed that holding the severity of illness constant, sandwich valuations were generally decreasing in the probability of illness; although the relationship between probability of illness and valuations was non-linear. Rousu *et al.* (2004a) and Huffman *et al.* (2004) conducted a between-subject study and found that the premium people placed on non-genetically modified food over genetically modified food was higher in treatments in which people were given information from anti-biotechnology organizations than in treatments in which subjects were given information from pro-biotechnology organizations.

The sixth prediction of economic theory comes from Zhao and Kling (2004), who took a page from the finance literature and applied the options value concept to consumer valuations arguing that willingness to pay and willingness to accept are dynamic constructs if there is uncertainty and reversibility. They argue that willingness to pay (willingness to accept) should be increasing (decreasing) in the perceived difficulty in delaying the decision and decreasing (increasing) in the perceived difficulty in reversing the transaction. Kling *et al.* (2003) tested this proposition in a field experiment using random nth price auctions with sports cards and Corrigan (2005) tested this proposition in a laboratory experiment in which coffee mugs were sold via a random nth price auction. Both studies asked people to indicate their perceived difficulty in selling/buying the items outside the experiment using scale questions. They found via regression analysis that willingness to pay and willingness to accept were related to the perceived difficulties in delay and reversal in the expected directions. In addition, Kling *et al.* (2003) conducted additional treatments in which they exogenously manipulated the difficulty of reversing the transaction by offering buy-back guarantees and other opportunities for re-sale one week after the initial experiment. Again, bids responded in the expected direction, e.g., the buy-back guarantee decreased willingness to accept.

Finally, we end this sub-section with the findings of Corrigan (2005), who conducted a random nth price auction in which people bid to obtain a one dollar bill. Although the auction is a homegrown value auction it permits a test of whether people bid truthfully as predicted by auction theory. The value of a one dollar bill should be exactly one dollar to all people. Because the random nth price auction is theoretically incentive compatible, all subjects should bid exactly one dollar. This is what Corrigan found; the mean bid for the dollar bill was $0.97 and the median bid was $0.99.

9.3   Reliability

We now investigate whether auctions generate *reliable* measures of value. *Reliability* refers to the extent to which repeated measures of value relate to one another. Reliability is a necessary but not sufficient condition for validity. A common measure of reliability in psychology is a test-retest measure, where the same person is given the same test at two points in time. To our knowledge, Shogren *et al.* (2000) is the only experimental auction study to carry out a strict test-retest procedure. In their study, each subject participated in four experimental sessions over a two-week time period. In each session, subjects bid in second price auctions to exchange an endowed: i) candy bar for another type of candy bar, ii) non-irradiated pork sandwich for an irradiated pork sandwich, and iii) apple for a mango. They found support for test-retest reliability as they could not reject the hypothesis of equality of mean bids across all four sessions for the candy bar and mango auctions; the only good for which bidding was not stable across sessions was irradiated pork, the more exotic good. Although they found little to no difference in mean bids across sessions, they did find that regardless of the good, winning subjects significantly reduced their bids the next session;

Table 9.1. *Correlation coefficients between auction bids for Certified Angus Beef steaks across five bidding rounds (n = 70)[a]*

	Round 1	Round 2	Round 3	Round 4	Round 5
Round 1	1.00				
Round 2	0.84	1.00			
Round 3	0.76	0.94	1.00		
Round 4	0.72	0.92	0.96	1.00	
Round 5	0.71	0.89	0.93	0.97	1.00

[a] Data taken from second and random nth price auctions from the no endowment treatment in Lusk *et al.* (2004); all correlation coefficients are statistically different than zero at the 0.01 level of significance.

an effect they attribute to preference learning where people bid higher to learn how a new good fits in their preference set.

Other findings in the literature indicate that auctions are reliable: a) in auctions with repeated rounds, bids are strongly correlated across rounds – this is a quasi application of the test-retest method and is also related to internal consistency reliability, b) different incentive compatible auction mechanisms tend to generate similar measures of value in between-subject experiments, and c) auction bids are reasonably stable across context (field versus lab) in between-subject experiments.

Although still debated, it has been common practice to conduct auctions over repeated rounds in which people submit bids for the same product(s) after obtaining market information from the previous round. At issue here is whether people are reasonably consistent in their bidding behavior across bidding rounds. If people pulled random numbers from their head each round to submit as bids, one would expect no correlation between bidding behavior across rounds, but people's bids tend to be strongly correlated across bidding rounds. For example, Table 9.1 uses the data from Lusk *et al.* (2004a) and shows the correlation coefficients between bids for Certified Angus Beef steaks across five bidding rounds. All correlation coefficients are positive and statistically different than zero; the lowest correlation is between the first and last bidding rounds, but the magnitude of the coefficient (0.71) is still reasonably large indicating a high degree of reliability. While Table 9.1 presents bidding behavior for one good in one study, we observe a similarly high degree of consistency in bids across rounds in virtually all repeated round auctions we have conducted.

Another type of reliability is called *parallel-forms reliability* which tests whether different, parallel measures are highly related. In the psychology literature, this test is conducted by creating a large set of agree/disagree scale questions designed to measure the same construct and then randomly dividing the questions into two sets given to the same set of people. The correlation between the two parallel forms is the estimate of reliability. Different incentive compatible auctions can be considered parallel forms. We are unaware of any studies in which the same people bid on the same good in two different auction institutions (a strict test of parallel-form reliability). A few between-subject studies exist, however, that compare bids across auction institutions. Lusk *et al.* (2004a) found that the second price, random *n*th price, English, and BDM all generated similar results in initial bidding rounds, but that market dynamics caused second price (random *n*th price) auction bids to exceed (fall below) bids from the English and BDM mechanisms which were single-shot auctions.

Rutström (1998) found that the English auction and the BDM mechanism generated similar results, but the second price auction generated bids in excess of either of the other mechanisms. In contrast, Rozan *et al.* (2004) found that mean bids from a BDM mechanism were statistically higher than bids from a second price auction. Knetsch *et al.* (2001) found that bids from second price WTP (WTA) auctions were significantly higher (lower) than bids from ninth price auctions. The extant literature is in disagreement about the reliability of bids across parallel forms.

To shed more light on this issue, Table 9.2 shows the correlation coefficient between the mean (round 1) bids for the five beef steaks from Lusk *et al.* (2004a). Table 9.2 indicates a high degree of agreement between mechanisms in terms of the relative quality of the five beef steaks as all correlation coefficients exceed 0.95. This leads us to believe that even in instances in which one might reject the hypothesis of equality of bids across mechanisms (a finding which can occur even if the differences are not economically important), bids across mechanisms are likely to be highly correlated.

A final form of reliability that is of interest is the consistency of auction bids across context. At least one study has investigated the stability of auction bids across an elicitation environment (e.g., the field versus the lab). In some ways, such an investigation could be considered a test of external validity as it tests the extent to which behavior in the laboratory corresponds to behavior in a different context – the field. For present purposes, we are primarily considering whether auction bids are stable enough across settings that they can be considered reliable. Lusk and Fox (2003) compared bids for novel cookies in an on-campus bakery to bids for the same cookies in a laboratory or classroom setting. They found that lab and in-store valuations were not statistically different when one investigated the entire bid distribution. When only the behavior of engaged bidders (those bidding at least something for one of the goods) was considered, they found that bids in the retail store were significantly greater than that in the lab. They attribute this finding to the notion that people were

Table 9.2. *Correlation coefficients between mean bids for five beef steaks across four auction institutions (n = 5)*[a]

	Second price auction	Random nth price auction	English auction	BDM
Second price auction	1.00			
Random nth price auction	0.98	1.00		
English auction	0.97	0.99	1.00	
BDM	0.95	0.98	0.97	1.00

[a] Data taken from the no endowment treatment in Lusk *et al.* (2004); all correlation coefficients are statistically different than zero at the 0.01 level of significance.

less uncertain about the value of the cookies in the store as other substitute prices were readily available. People were more likely to make a purchase in the store setting because they came to the store hungry.

9.4 Convergent validity

Convergent validity refers to whether measures that should be related are actually related. Our discussion in section 9.2 focusing on whether auction bids were consistent with economic theory can be categorized as tests of convergent validity. Now we delve into the issue a bit more and ask whether auction bids are related to other measures they should be related to such as preferences from taste tests, preference from hedonic rating scores, other measures of value obtained from different elicitation methods, and sales from a field market.

9.4.1 Auction bids and taste tests

A number of studies have investigated the link between preferences from taste tests and auction bids. A set of studies have focused on whether bids for beef steaks varied by tenderness levels. Lusk *et al.* (2001a), Fuez *et al.* (2004), and Platter *et al.* (2005) requested that participants take part in a blind taste test of several beef steaks. Unbeknownst to the experimental participants in these studies, the tenderness levels of steaks had been objectively measured using Warner-Bratzler shear force tests, which measures the amount of force required to penetrate a cut of meat. Lusk *et al.* (2001a) used only two types of steaks: tough (very high shear force ratings) and tender (very low shear force ratings). They showed that although the taste tests were blind, consumers bid about $0.44/lb on average to exchange the tough for the tender steak. Rather than categorizing steaks into tough or tender categories, Fuez *et al.* (2004) and Platter *et al.* (2005) used regression analysis to show that auction bids were significantly decreasing in shear-force value (toughness). This finding is noteworthy because people based their valuations only on the taste test – they did not know one steak was objectively deemed more tender than another.

In a similar study, Umberger and Feuz (2004) also show that bids for steaks are related to other palatability ratings obtained in the blind taste tests in anticipated directions, e.g., people bid more on steaks they thought were juicer. Melton *et al.* (1996a and 1996b) elicited bids for pork chops that varied by color, size, and marbling level. Marbling refers to the amount of intramuscular fat content in a cut of meat and higher marbling levels are associated with increased levels of juiciness and tenderness. Melton *et al.* (1996b) found that after participating in blind taste tests, people's bids and market prices were increasing in the level of marbling as would be expected. Platter *et al.* (2005) also had people bid on steak of differing marbling levels. They found, as did Melton *et al.* (1996a), that bids were increasing in the level of marbling (see also the studies by Killinger *et al.*, 2004a, 2004b, 2004c).

9.4.2   *Comparison of auction bids with hedonic ratings*

Lange *et al.* (2002) conducted a comparison of preferences for champagne expressed through auction bids to preferences for champagne expressed through hedonic ratings (on a scale of 0 – would certainly dislike to 10 – would certainly like). People were either assigned to participate in an auction or a hedonic rating treatment wherein they evaluated five different champagnes in three different information conditions (blind taste test, bottle, and full information). They found that both preference elicitation methods generated similar rankings of the five drinks within an information treatment. Although the two methods generated similar results, Lange *et al.* (2002) argued that the effect of champagne type and information was greater with auctions than with the rankings (i.e., the auction was more discriminative). They also found that people altered their preferences upon the introduction of new information in near identical manners across the two methods; preferences increased and became more heterogeneous in the bottle viewing treatment versus the blind taste treatment for both preference elicitation methods. They concluded (p. 607), "In conclusion, in this study both hedonic measurement and the auction procedure lead to the same result in terms of product differences."

Noussair *et al.* (2004b) used a within-subject design to compare hedonic ratings for different varieties of orange juice, cookies, and chocolate bars to auction bids for the same goods. On average, they found near identical preference hierarchy for varieties for each good – i.e., for cookies both methods indicate that brand S was preferred to brand N, which was preferred to brand C.

The ratio of average rating to the average bid was virtually equivalent across varieties with a product category. At the individual level, just over 60% of subjects have a weakly consistent ordering of varieties between the two measures, in which a weakly consistent ordering occurs when the rating for product A was greater than or equal to the rating for product B, the auction bid for product A was also greater than or equal to the auction bid for product B. About three-quarters of participants were consistent in identifying their most and least preferred varieties with their bids and ratings.

Wertenbroch and Skiera (2002) elicited bids to obtain Coca-Cola and Cake using a BDM mechanism. They found that bids for Coke and cake were significantly correlated with responses to the statements "how thirsty/hungry are you right now" and "How much do you like Coca-Cola/cake" in which people responded on a 5-point scale (1 = not much; 5 = a lot). They further found that the correlations between the auction bids and the two ratings were significantly higher than the correlations between hypothetical statements of value and the two ratings. They state (p. 233), "As predicted, these results suggest that WTPs from BDM provide a more valid measure of subjects' preferences than do WTPs from price matching." They also showed that bids for ball-point pens were significantly related to the attractiveness of the pen as determined by responses to a nine-point scale.

Menkhaus (1992) did not specifically collect hedonic ratings in their beef steak auctions, but they did collect similar information that should be related to bids. For example, people that indicated a recent increase in poultry consumption had lower auction bids for beef steak, people that were more concerned about cholesterol bid less for beef steaks, and people that regularly froze steaks prior to consumption placed a higher value on vacuum-packaged steaks over steaks on over-wrapped styrofoam packages than people that did not typically freeze steaks.

Like Menkhaus (1992), numerous studies exist that show auction bids related to other hedonic-type information. For example, Lusk et al. (2001b) showed that bids to exchange a bag of genetically modified corn chips for a bag of non-genetically modified corn chips were increasing in concern for biotechnology (as measured on a 10-point scale). Lusk et al. (2006) found that people's bids to avoid consuming a genetically modified food were increasing in the perceived risks and decreasing in the perceived benefits of genetically modified food (as measured on a 9-point scale). Overall, results from these studies imply strong convergent validity between preferences expressed through auction bids and preferences expressed through hedonic ratings and other "survey" measures of preference.

At least one study, however, has not found strong correlation between hedonic ratings taken after a taste test and subsequent auction bids. Jaeger and Harker (2005) found that although responses to two different hedonic scales taken after tasting two Kiwi fruits were significantly correlated with each other, neither were significantly related to bids for the fruit. Jaeger and Harker (2005) indicate (p. 2523), "Clearly, the two types of data provide different information. Equally clearly, the WTP data supplement the information gained through traditional sensory and consumer testing." These results indicate that while hedonic ratings can be and frequently are related to auction bids, they need not be. Such a result might arise when the hedonic ratings relate to preferences for one attribute, say taste, whereas the auction bids encompass multi-attribute preferences, say taste and visual appeal.

9.4.3   Comparison of auction bids with purchase decisions and other measures of value

Research also has been conducted in which hypothetical auction bids or other hypothetical statements of value have been compared to non-hypothetical bids. The purpose of such studies almost always rests with testing for hypothetical bias and many studies implicitly or explicitly assume that the non-hypothetical auction bids are the "correct" measure of value. The overwhelming majority of these studies find that hypothetical statements of value exceed non-hypothetical auction bids. For example, the review conducted by Harrison and Rutström (2008) shows that thirty-four of thirty-nine empirical tests find evidence of hypothetical bias, in which hypothetical values exceed real values by a range of 2 to 2,600 percent. While this finding is interesting and important in its own right, it sheds little light on the validity of experimental auctions. What is more relevant is that in the subset of these studies that contained within-subject comparisons one can investigate whether the two measures of preference are highly correlated recognizing, as previously stated, that we know the mean levels are likely to differ. This is what most studies find. For example, Fox *et al.* (1998) showed that hypothetical open-ended statements of WTP for irradiated pork elicited by phone survey were positively correlated with the same auction bids several days later. List *et al.* (1998) and List and Shogren (1998) show similar results in which the elapsed time between the two elicitation questions was much shorter (e.g., minutes); in general, hypothetical auction bids for sports cards were positively correlated with auction bids for sports cards. These findings imply a reasonable degree of convergent validity across the two measures of preference, but they still do not identify which measure of preference is "better."

A few studies shed light on this issue. Wertenbroch and Skiera (2002) found that while BDM bids for ball-point pens were significantly related to the stated attractiveness of the pen (determined via responses to a 9-point scale), WTP from a hypothetical choice task was not. Further, WTP from the auction mechanism was much closer to the prices people stated they normally paid for pens,

whereas WTP from the choice task significantly exceeded the stated price normally paid. Perhaps the most telling result is that WTP from the hypothetical
choice task was significantly related to the amount people normally paid for
pens whereas BDM bids were not. This led Wertenbroch and Skiera (2002)
to conclude (p. 237), ". . . this suggests that WTP is driven by subjects' price
memories rather than their assessment of the value of the good in the current
purchase context when it is elicited under a hypothetical response format. It is
as if subjects start with what they normally pay and then adjust that estimate
upward to derive their WTP. In contrast, WTP under the BDM was predicted
by the weighted attractiveness . . . which suggests . . . that BDM leads subjects
to derive their WTP as a function of the perceived value of the good in the specific purchase situation." More support for auctions comes from another part
of Wertenbroch and Skiera's study which compared BDM bids for Coke and
cake to hypothetical open-ended statements of WTP. They found that whereas
people tended to round their hypothetical statements of value, auction bids were
more differentiated.

Wertenbroch and Skiera (2002) found that bids from an auction mechanism
(the BDM) were greater than WTP implied by a hypothetical stated choice task.
Their study does not permit one to isolate the effect of elicitation institution
(auction versus choice) and binding commitments. The inflation of valuations
in the choice task relative to the auctions could simply be due to the hypothetical
nature of the former. Lusk and Schroeder (2006) removed this confound and
compared non-hypothetical auction bids to non-hypothetical purchase decisions
using a between-subject design. In the auctions, people bid to obtain one of five
different types of beef steak and in the purchasing task, people chose one of the
five steaks, each of which was assigned a price (people were also allowed to
choose not to make a purchase at all). A series of discrete choices were made and
one was randomly selected as binding. Results indicated that valuations implied
from the choice task were significantly higher than auction bids (four different
auction mechanisms were used and the result persisted across all mechanisms).
This result is somewhat troubling as it implies that people frequently chose to
buy steaks at higher prices than what they would likely have bid in an auction.
One positive note is that the preference ordering of the five steaks was consistent
across the choice and auction elicitation mechanisms. Data from Lusk and
Schroeder (2006) show that preferences expressed through auctions and choices
were different, but they do not imply which is a "better" measure of value.
Frykblom and Shogren (2000) also compared auction bids for a book to non-
hypothetical purchase decisions to obtain the book at a given price. Unlike the
findings in Lusk and Schroeder (2006), they could not reject the hypothesis of
the equality of WTP from the auction and choice tasks.

Ding *et al.* (2005) also compared auction and choice data. Their investigation focused on conjoint-type elicitation mechanisms. In a typical conjoint

exercise people are shown a series of product profiles or descriptions that differ along several attributes (e.g., brand, price, package size, etc.) and people are typically asked to (hypothetically) rate or rank the desirability of each product profile or to choose the one profile out of a set of profiles they most prefer. They studied typical conjoint formats in addition to "incentive-aligned" (e.g., non-hypothetical) conjoint elicitation methods. In one treatment, people stated their maximum buying price for each product profile, one of these profiles was randomly chosen, and a BDM mechanism was used to determine whether the profile was actually purchased. Another non-hypothetical treatment was similar to Lusk and Schroeder (2006) in that people made a series of choices between profiles and one of the choices was randomly selected as binding.

Ding *et al.* (2005) conducted a field experiment in a Chinese restaurant. Each individual participated in one of four treatments in Part 1 of the experiment: a hypothetical choice task, a non-hypothetical choice task, a non-hypothetical stated price task that used the BDM bidding mechanism to determine whether a purchase was made, or a hypothetical open-ended stated price task. After completing this task, then regardless of treatment people moved to Part 2 of the experiment and then made a single (non-hypothetical) choice of one Chinese dinner out of twenty possible alternatives. Performance of the elicitation mechanisms was judged primarily on the ability of preferences expressed in Part 1 to predict the choice in Part 2. For clarity when Part 1 involved a non-hypothetical task, a random draw determined whether the decisions in Parts 1 or 2 were actually binding. In the experiment, the treatment in Part 1 that involved non-hypothetical choices was virtually identical to the decision task in Part 2; the two tasks differed only in the options made available to people. The results were that the two non-hypothetical tasks generated significantly better out-of-sample predictions than the respective hypothetical tasks. The non-hypothetical choice treatment showed the best out-of-sample predictive performance (it predicted the correct purchase 48% of the time as compared to the naïve predictions which would only be correct 5% of the time). This result is not terribly informative or surprising given that the hypothetical choice task exactly mirrored the task used as the basis of performance. What is more interesting is the relative performance of the other treatments: the non-hypothetical choice, non-hypothetical stated price with BDM, and hypothetical stated price tasks correctly predicted the Part 2 dinner purchase 26%, 15%, and 7% of the time. Ding *et al.* (2005) attribute the finding that the non-hypothetical BDM mechanism did not perform as well as the hypothetical choice task to their design choice of screening participants for interest in the study. They indicated (p. 74), "According to the pilot study, it is almost certain that had we not screened out participants who were not serious about the purchase decision the [non-hypothetical pricing task with the BDM] would have performed better than the . . . hypothetical choice conjoint."

9.4.4   External validity

In addition to comparing values obtained from auctions to that obtained from other value elicitation methods, it is important to determine how well auction bids relate to actual retail behavior. A few studies have investigated this issue. As just discussed, Ding *et al.* (2005) investigated how bids obtained from a BDM mechanism predicted an actual subsequent choice of which Chinese meal to eat. Their findings implied that the auction mechanism performed three times better than a naïve prediction and twice as well as a hypothetical open-ended pricing task at predicting a subsequent non-hypothetical choice and would likely have had better predictive performance than non-hypothetical choices were it not for the vagaries of the particular experimental design.

List and Shogren (1998) tackled this issue from a slightly different angle. They compared the market prices from experimental auctions (i.e., the second highest bid in a second price auction) for several sports cards to actual book values for the cards. These results were previously shown in Table 8.18. On average, across twelve different sports cards, the second highest bid from the real-money auctions was 94% of the book value. This shows a very high degree of external validity in that the auction generated prices very consistent with a credible estimate of the market value of the card.

In one of the few studies carrying out a strict test of external validity, Brookshire, Coursey, and Schulze (1987) compared demand curves constructed from bids for strawberries collected in a laboratory auction to implied demand curves from actual purchases of strawberries made via door-to-door sales. They were unable to reject the hypothesis that the valuations from the auction were different than the field sales data. This is an important finding as it implies valuations were stable across setting (the lab versus the field) and elicitation method (auction versus purchases at a stated price).

9.5   Anomalies

We now discuss some findings that question the validity of experimental auctions. To be more precise, the contention is not with experimental auctions as a method to elicit values *per se*, but with the economists' notion of preferences. Most economic models assume preferences are stable and independent of context. But numerous studies stemming from psychology suggest malleable preferences that are shaped or wholly constructed by frame and context. An extreme view of wholly constructed preferences would argue against auctions as a measure of value because such a view presupposes there is no "real" value that exists to elicit. A more moderate view of contextual preferences would limit the applicability of valuations obtained from auctions because such valuations would only be "valid" in the context in which they were elicited and would therefore be useless in predicting consumer choice, cost/benefit analysis, and so on.

We now briefly cover three challenges that have been brought to the table: a) the willingness to pay (WTP) versus willingness to accept (WTA) disparity, b) preference reversals, and c) coherent arbitrariness. We begin our discussion of the WTP/WTA disparity as it represents a case in which repeated experiments and development of economic theory have provided insight into what was once seen as major challenge to economic theory. As for the preference reversal and coherent arbitrariness phenomena, it is still too soon to fully understand under what conditions economic theory and auction valuations "fail" and how economic theory might evolve to address the concerns. But even in these instances in which violations of individual rationality have been observed, we believe there is evidence to suggest that the power of auctions and the discipline of markets have the potential to generate rational behavior.

9.5.1   Willingness to pay versus willingness to accept

Early theoretical literature on non-market valuation operated under the theory that WTP and WTA should be approximately equal except for a small income effect (e.g., Randall and Stoll, 1980). Early contingent valuation surveys and economic experiments found large differences between WTP and WTA – much larger than could be explained by an income effect (e.g., Bishop and Heberlein, 1979; Knetsch and Sinden, 1984). Such findings were (and still are to some extent) seen as a failure of economic theory to adequately describe behavior and as a condemnation of valuation methods. Many posited that the findings required a modification of standard utility theory. Thaler (1980) coined the term "endowment effect" which has been used to explain the WTA/WTP disparity based on Kahneman and Tversky's (1979) prospect theory and the concept of loss aversion. Although a number of findings have been published supposedly in support of the endowment effect, modifications, extensions, or further explanations of standard utility theory and enhanced experimental protocol have served to explain the apparent anomaly quite well.

Several studies suggest theoretical reasons exist for WTP and WTA to differ without abandoning standard utility theory. For example, Hanemann (1991) showed theoretically that WTP and WTA should differ not only by an income effect but by a substitution effect. Shogren et al. (1994) tested this notion using experimental auctions and found that WTP and WTA were similar for goods with close substitutes but differed for goods that had imperfect substitutes, findings which supported Hanemann's observations. In addition to theoretical explanations for the divergence, Shogren et al. (1994) and Shogren et al. (2001b) showed that much of the divergence in WTP and WTA that had previously been observed dissipated when people participated in an active auction market with repeated trials. List (2003) also showed the WTP/WTA disparity disappeared with market experience as sports card dealers had similar value measures, but inexperienced traders exhibited significant differences in WTP and WTA. Such findings are generally consistent with the theoretical model put forth by Kolstad and Guzman (1999), which implies that the WTP/WTA divergence can be caused by costly information acquisition. Because people with greater market experience have gained more information, one might expect WTP and WTA to be more similar for such people according to the model in Kolstad and Guzman (1999).

Zhao and Kling (2001) argued that if people are uncertain about the value of a good and reversibility exists, WTP and WTA should diverge. Their "commitment cost" theory suggests that the difference between WTP and WTA should decrease when people are more certain of a good's value, expect to obtain less information about the good in the future, are more impatient, expect that reversing the transaction becomes easier, and have more freedom in choosing when to make the decision. Zhao and Kling (2001) reviewed much of the empirical literature on the WTP/WTA divergence and most of the findings were supportive of the theory's predictions. Kling *et al.* (2003) tested the theory by conducting WTP and WTA auctions and measuring perceptions about the ease of delaying the decision and reversing the transaction. When the perceived difficulty of reversing the transaction was greater than the perceived difficulty in delaying the decision, they observed the common result that WTA > WTP. When the perceived difficulty in reversing the transaction was less than the perceived difficulty in delaying the decision, however, they actually found that WTP > WTA – exactly what is predicted by the commitment cost theory.

Plott and Zeiler (2005) argue that the empirical evidence of the WTP/WTA divergence is primarily due to subject misconceptions about the experiment. Proper experimental control, which includes a variant on the BDM elicitation procedure and extensive training with the elicitation mechanism, eliminate the WTP/WTA divergence. In particular, they show that they can turn the WTP/WTA divergence "on" and "off" by varying experimental procedures, a finding that suggests the endowment effect cannot be generated by a fundamental feature of preferences. They conclude ". . . observed differences in WTP and WTA cannot be explained as an endowment effect based on prospect theory and that broad implications based on such an interpretation and advanced in the literature are inappropriate. Moreover, given the nature of our results, claims that WTP-WTA gaps are unrelated to the experimental procedures are clearly misleading with respect to the interpretation of the gap and its implications."

9.5.2   *Preference reversals*

Preference reversals refer to the situation when a person chooses good A over good B in a task involving a straightforward choice, but places a higher monetary value on B than A in an auction-type setting. Preference reversals, which were first shown in psychology by Lichtenstein and Slovic (1971) and were introduced into the economics literature by Grether and Plott (1979), have primarily been demonstrated in decision making under risk, in which the "goods" are lotteries. Preference reversals are usually found by asking people to choose between one lottery with a high probability of winning a low dollar price and second lottery with a low probability of winning a high dollar prize. Consider an example out of Grether and Plott (1979), in which the first lottery consists of a 35/36 chance of winning $4.00 and a 1/36 chance of losing $1 and the second lottery consists of an 11/36 chance of winning $16 and a 25/36 of losing $1.5. A common response is for people to choose the first lottery over the second in a choice task but to state a higher buying/selling price for the second lottery in an auction-type mechanism.

The preference reversal phenomenon has been shown to be robust to the size (and presence) of payoffs, training, presentation format, and other various changes in experimental protocol. Such findings have led to criticism of the BDM elicitation method for non-expected utility preferences (e.g., Holt, 1986; Karni and Safra, 1987) and the development of a variety of competing theories, virtually all of which abandon classical preference theory (e.g., Goldstein and Einhorn, 1987; Tversky et al., 1990). So, what are we to make of these findings? There are three possibilities which are well articulated by Tversky and Thaler (1990) through the use of a baseball analogy. A baseball umpire may have one of three philosophies in judging the merits of a pitch: "I call them as I see them" (e.g., values exist and people perceive them indirectly as best they can and possibly with bias), "I call them as they are" (e.g., values exist and people know their values directly), and "They ain't nothing till I call them" (e.g., values are constructed in the process of elicitation).

At the onset, one might question how "special" the paired lotteries must be for a reversal to be observed. Harrison et al. (2003) argued that one must control for risk preferences before deciding whether preference reversals are economically meaningful. They elicited risk preferences from a sample of people and showed that at the estimated levels of risk aversion, people were practically indifferent between the two lotteries in certainty equivalent terms; small errors in decision making, which are not costly, could cause reversals. Despite this contention, they observed preference reversals even for tasks which would be "costly" given the estimated risk preference. Still, "costly" is a subjective measure and it is difficult to know the psychic opportunity cost of putting cognitive effort into deciding between lotteries with expected values around $3. Berg et al. (2004) provide useful results related to the hypothesis of decision making with error. They find that in experiments without monetary incentives, models that require task-dependent preferences provide the best fit to the data. When incentive compatible mechanisms are used with real money, however, models based on standard expected utility theory with error best explain the data.

Another interesting observation that has arisen is that people who reverse preferences are subject to arbitrage in market settings. For example, suppose a person chose lottery A over B but stated a monetary value of $3 for A and $5 for B. The person could be sold B for their stated value ($5). Because the person preferred A over B, however, they should be willing to give up B to have A. Once in possession of A, the lottery can be bought back at the stated value of $3. The end result is that the person has no lottery in their possession and has lost $2. Chu and Chu (1990) and Cherry et al. (2003) have shown that when people are vulnerable to arbitrage in a market-like setting they stop reversing preferences. Chu and Chu (1990) show that people do not reverse preferences even when they are not subject to arbitrage so long as they have previously been exposed to arbitrage opportunities.

Cherry et al. (2003) showed that the rationality generated by arbitrage in preference reversal experiments can "spill over" to non-market valuation settings. Cherry and Shogren (2006) showed that rationality from such arbitrage can "cross over" to other decision-making tasks. Another interesting observation from Cherry et al. (2003) is that after arbitrage, people do not change their preference ordering but revise their stated values (bids) for high-risk lotteries to conform to their choices.

Based on these findings Cherry et al. (2003) argue that rationality should not necessarily be considered an individual-level phenomenon, but that markets and other institutions induce rationality. If people have constraints on cognitive abilities or must ration scarce cognitive resources, markets are necessary to induce rationality. Markets can "create" rationality either by natural selection, in which irrational people are forced out of the market due to bankruptcy or by creating greater incentives for people to devote scarce resources to more precisely articulate their preferences.

The good news is that experimental auctions naturally put people in a market-like context and expose people to the discipline that markets impose. To the extent that one believes preferences and values exist, auction markets provide incentives for people to carefully consider and state their preferences.

9.5.3   Coherent arbitrariness

Ariely et al. (2003) recently argued that preferences and valuations are arbitrary in the sense that they can be manipulated by non-informative signals such as social security numbers. Once a valuation has been stated, however, Ariely et al. (2003) show that the preferences are coherent in the sense that they respond in intuitive and predictable ways. Such findings cast doubt on whether "comparative static" tests illustrate the validity of experimental auctions.

In their first experiment, they asked people to first state whether they would purchase six products such as wines, computer accessories, and luxury chocolates at a price equal to the last two digits of their social security numbers. People were subsequently asked to state their maximum WTP for each item. A random device was used to determine whether the first or second exercise was binding; if the second was binding a BDM mechanism was used to determine if purchase was actually made. At odds with economists' view of preferences, Ariely *et al.* found that the WTP bids were significantly correlated with social security numbers; higher social security numbers led to higher bids. For example, subjects with above median social security numbers bid from 57 to 107% above people with below median social security numbers. Despite the apparent malleability of absolute valuations, however, the relative valuations exhibited remarkable stability as over 95% of subjects bid more on high rated wine than low rated wine.

In a second set of experiments, Ariely *et al.* investigated valuations to avoid listening to an annoying high-pitched sound delivered through headphones. As in the previous experiment, people first answered a yes/no question about whether they would listen to the sound for a given price (people were randomly offered $0, $0.10, or $0.50) and then participated in a BDM mechanism in which they bid an amount to avoid listening to the sound. The results suggest that bids were influenced by the initial price indicating arbitrariness in preference; but the relative valuations responded in intuitive ways, e.g., people increased valuations when the sound was to last for longer periods of time.

List (2002) generated similar findings in a sports card market. He found that the mean bid for a package of ten sports cards was significantly less than the mean bid for a package of thirteen sports cards, when people viewed one and only one of the packages. When viewed side-by side, however, people appeared rational by stating higher bids for the package of thirteen sports cards than the package of ten sports cards. This demonstration of a preference reversal shows, as do the findings in Ariely *et al.*, that relative valuations can appear rational and coherent even if absolute valuations are not.

Ariely *et al.* argue that people may appear to behave rationally by avoiding intransitive preferences so long as they remember all past transactions. Their point is that the initial choice was not a "true preference" but was arbitrary and influences all subsequent valuations. This argument in and of itself is not terribly troubling for economists. Economics is silent about where preferences come from. It only supposes that preferences exist and are not endogenous to the problem at hand. Economics also has little to say about how preferences are formed for a new good that people have never experienced, such as an annoying noise. Only time will tell whether the apparent arbitrariness in preferences holds up in market-like contexts in which people are subject to incentives and arbitrage and whether the finding is isolated to "unfamiliar goods." While List's (2002) preference reversal result held up for card dealers and non-dealers, one would be hard pressed to say that dealers are experienced in trading cards in bundles of ten and thirteen.

It is also important to mention that several empirical findings suggest preferences are less arbitrary than indicated in Ariely *et al.* In particular, studies that show "rational" changes in bidding behavior across treatments in between-subject experiments would provide an indication that preferences are not entirely constructed (e.g., Gunnersson *et al.*, 2004). To that point, virtually countless contingent valuation studies have been published showing that the frequency of people that would affirmatively vote for a policy is falling in price – this is despite each person in such studies only receiving a single price. These are between-subject demonstrations that demand curves are downward sloping. It is also helpful to consider between-subject studies such as Rousu *et al.* (2004a) which show that people who receive positive information about a good bid more for the good than people who receive negative information. If preferences were entirely arbitrary, valuations would be randomly distributed in positive and negative treatments.

9.6   Summary

This chapter reviewed the literature to examine the question of the *validity* of experimental auctions. Several studies have tested whether bidding behavior conforms to basic tenets of economic theory, e.g. diminishing marginal utility and downward sloping demand curves. Overall, the results support the notion that bidding behavior is consonant with the comparative static predictions of basic economic theory. Comparing bidding behavior with predictions of economic theory is a test of convergent validity (a test that establishes whether bids are related to other constructs they should be related to) and internal validity (tests of the cause-effect relationship between independent and dependent variables).

Several studies have investigated convergent validity of auction bids in other ways by comparing bids to preference ratings in taste tests, hedonic product ratings, and other measures of value. The results suggest people tend to bid higher for products they indicate as tasting better and for products given higher hedonic rating scores. While the mean bid from experimental auctions differs from mean willingness to pay inferred from non-incentive compatible contingent valuation purchase questions, the value measures from the two approaches are highly correlated. There is some conflict in the literature regarding whether willingness to pay inferred from non-hypothetical choices is consistent with auction bids; however, in the one study that found bids to be significantly lower that willingness to pay from choice, the rank-ordering of goods was consistent in both approaches.

Only a few studies have investigated the external validity of auction values by comparing whether auction bids correctly predict out-of-sample purchasing behavior. In one such study, Ding *et al.* (2005) found that the BDM mechanism performed three times better than a naïve prediction and twice as well as a hypothetical open-ended pricing task at predicting a subsequent non-hypothetical choice. They also concluded that the BDM mechanism would likely have had better predictive performance than non-hypothetical choices were it not for the vagaries of their particular experimental design. In another study, Brookshire *et al.* (1987) compared demand curves implied from bids in experimental auctions to demand curves calculated from actual purchases of strawberries made via door-to-door sales and were unable to reject external validity.

Taken together, these results lend strong support for the notion that experimental auctions are valid measurement instruments and that the values elicited in auctions are a valid theoretical construct. Some evidence exists to contradict this view. For example, mean bids can differ across competing auction mechanisms, all of which should be incentive compatible, a finding which undercuts the reliability of the method. Such findings, however, only imply a weakness in a particular implementation of the method or a weakness with one particular mechanism, not necessarily with the entire valuation paradigm. There are other "anomalies" presented as a challenge to the validity of experimental auctions and economists' notion of values. But repeated experiments and development of economic theory have served to address some such challenges. In other cases, we do not have enough information to understand under what conditions economic theory and auction valuations "fail" and how economic theory might evolve to address the concerns. Even in the instances in which violations of individual rationality have been observed, other studies provide evidence to suggest that the power of auctions and the discipline of markets have the potential to generate rational behavior.

10 The future of experimental auctions

10.1 Introduction

Today researchers use experimental auctions to examine incentive and contextual questions that arise in eliciting values through stated preferences methods. The initial work developing the experimental valuation method was pioneered decades ago by researchers interested in estimating the demand for public goods, e.g., Bohm (1972), Bennett (1983), Knetsch and Sinden (1984), and Cummings *et al.* (1986). Most experimental auctions follow a process similar to that described by physicist James Conant (1951; p. 56): "[a]bout three centuries ago the trial-and-error experimentation of the artisan was wedded to the deductive method of reasoning of the mathematician; the progeny of this union have returned after many generations to assist the 'sooty empiric' in his labors." By combining pattern recognition with theoretical insight, the "sooty empiric" uses experimental auctions to help clarify how incentives and context affect how people state their preferences for real and hypothetical goods and services.

This book has assimilated the current state of knowledge on the use of experimental auctions to elicit values for goods. Our goal is to provide a resource to practitioners interesting in designing and using experimental auctions in applied economic, psychology, and marketing research. We have covered the basics on value and auction theory to provide the analytical background for the experiments. We then addressed specific issues related to design and implementation of experimental auctions. In many cases, we offered specific advice. Other times, we provided guidance but no specific advice since there is too little information in the extant literature to draw firm conclusions about the appropriateness of a particular design issue. Implementation questions still exist, e.g., whether to use repeated bidding rounds with price feedback and whether to endow subjects with a good prior to bidding remain debatable topics. Likewise, while the general conclusion is that experimental auctions exhibit a high degree of validity, several unresolved issues remain.

Uncertainties about the "appropriate design" or questions on validity arise because research on experimental auctions is still in its early stages. Although a few research programs have explored the nature of experimental auctions for nearly two decades, this is a relatively short period of time relative to that devoted to other value elicitation research methods such as conjoint analysis and contingent valuation. Only recently have papers on experimental auctions appeared in outlets outside general and applied economics journals. For instance, Hoffman *et al.* published their original work in *Marketing Science* in 1993, but almost ten years passed until another paper appeared in a major marketing journal on the topic (e.g., Wertenbroch and Skiera's paper on the BDM mechanism appeared in the *Journal of Marketing Research* in 2002).

Anecdotal evidence suggests researchers are increasingly interested in the method as experimental auctions are discussed in work published in marketing outlets. A recent paper by Ding *et al.* (2005), for instance, provides evidence that marketing researchers should seriously consider using incentive compatible value elicitation mechanisms. Also, experimental auctions are now showing up in applied life science journals by non-economists. Examples of the method have appeared in the *Journal of Animal Science, Food Safety*, the *Journal of Muscle Foods*, the *British Food Journal*, the *Journal of Food Quality and Preference, Nicotine and Tobacco Research, Radiation Physics and Chemistry*, and the *Journal of Dairy Science* (see Table 1.1). While the use of experimental auctions is increasing, we can always learn more as researchers apply the method in more diverse contexts and for varied purposes.

10.2   Ten questions worthy of future research

We conclude the book by offering ten research questions worthy of future examination. Addressing these questions can provide insight into the validity of the method and into the appropriateness of implementation and design techniques.

First, do experimental auctions elicit rational statements of value? Addressing this behavioral question is the most important direction for future work on experimental auctions. If one believes that choices and values emerge in the social context of an active exchange institution, estimates of value should not be separated from the interactive experience provided by an exchange institution, either directly or indirectly. Institutions matter because experience can make rational choice more transparent to a person (e.g., Plott, 1994). Institutions also dictate the rules under which exchange occurs, and these rules can differ across allocative settings. People can interpret differently the information conveyed by such settings. The institutional context matters for economic choices and values. The reality is that most people make allocation decisions in several institutional settings each day: markets, missing markets, and unidentified markets. How does this institutional mix affect how people make their choices and form/state their preferences for new goods and services? This question is fundamental because it gives reason for purposeful actions underlying all valuation work. The contact with others who are making similar decisions in an exchange institution puts in context the economic maxim that choices have consequences and stated values have meaning for valuation and demand estimation. Relying on rational theory to guide valuation and policy makes more sense if people make, or act as if they make, consistent and systematic choices toward certain and risky events. Experimental auction work should address the economic circumstances under which the presumption of rationality is supported and when it is not.

The impact of rational valuation might be better understood if a person could choose his preferred exchange institution, and if the researcher measures whether a person's stated value is based on a *complete* and *coherent* set of beliefs. Completeness implies a person's risk neutral beliefs that measure value are equal to the no-arbitrage price, if it exists (de Finetti, 1974). Coherence or the no-arbitrage condition implies that the person does not accept a strictly negative gamble, i.e., a sure loss or Dutch book. Implementing choice of an exchange institution or some mix of institutions could be straightforward to test in the lab. Let a person first select the auction or exchange institution that he or she wants to participate in, and then elicit his or her value for the good in question. Allowing for the choice of multiple exchange institutions complicates a person's decision problem, but it is necessary in a world of incomplete beliefs about environmental values.

Second, do experimental auctions mimic real world behavior? Perhaps the greatest impediment to increased use of experimental auctions in disciplines outside economics is the dearth of studies testing the external validity of the method. The following comments received by an anonymous reviewer of a recent journal article emphasizes the point well, "My background is in psychology . . . I do not believe that economists should be using such auctions to study choice behavior or to elicit preferences that will be used to inform policy. Until such time as economists undertake rigorous, systematic comparisons of auction-revealed preferences and choices . . . in real markets, then people like me . . . will continue to ask for evidence of external validity." This comment ignores the theory behind experimental auctions outlined in Chapters 2 and 3, the extant empirical evidence for validity in Chapter 9, and the studies by Ding *et al.* (2005) and Brookshire *et al.* (1987) that have tested for external validity. The comment also ignores that bids in experimental auctions are revealed preferences obtained in a real market with real products and real money.

Still, this concern has some merit. The pertinent question is whether the preferences revealed in an experimental auction market are related to preferences that govern other decisions in life such as daily shopping decisions. More research is needed to determine the external validity of experimental auctions. Forecasted market share or estimated demand curves obtained from experimental auction bids might be compared to market shares and estimated demand curves from retail sales data. Such findings would serve to determine whether the findings of Brookshire *et al.* (1987) and Shogren *et al.* (1999) are robust. Relaxing the assumption of single unit demand and using multiple-unit variants of the Vickrey auction could be useful to elicit demand schedules for each person.

Third, how well do experimental auctions forecast retail behavior relative to other research methods? We need to understand better how our preference measures help predict and explain various behaviors of everyday life. Examples of behaviors of interest include the distribution of consumption within a family, savings decisions, investment choices, and decisions about human capital investment. Preference measures should be collected on the same people for which we have extensive household survey data on choices. Even if one could reject external validity of experimental auction bids could another method do any better? A common approach in marketing studies is to construct a "hold-out" choice as the last question in a survey/experiment and compare the ability of different methods and models to forecast this hold-out choice, see, e.g., Ding *et al.* (2005). The problem with using this approach to test external validity is that while the hold-out choice is external to the initial decision making exercise, it differs from a choice in a retail market in which individuals' decisions are not being scrutinized. It is not surprising that Ding *et al.* (2005) found that a non-hypothetical choice task better predicted a subsequent non-hypothetical choice than bids from a BDM mechanism because the hold-out choice was essentially another replication of the previous choice-based decision task. A more informative experiment would compare the performance of models estimated from choice-based conjoint-type tasks to experimental auctions in terms of their ability to predict market share and demand in a retail setting.

It is important to recognize that the goal of value elicitation is not always to predict retail shopping behavior. One reason economists turn to primary data collection methods such as experimental auctions is to measure externalities that cannot be measured by analyzing retail purchases. The only feasible way to measure externalities or the value of public goods is to put people in a decision-making environment in which the public good or externality can be directly traded. For example, consider the value a person places on a program provided by public radio. It can easily be determined whether the person actually makes donations to public radio, a practice akin to retail shopping behavior. Donations to public radio in the "real world", however, do not always reflect their true value for the program. One reason is people might not donate because they perceive their individual gift as having too small an impact on the viability of public radio. Probably a more likely reason that donations do not reflect value is that people can free ride off contributions of others, enjoying free public radio without having to pay the price. The only way to truly measure a person's value for a program is to charge a price for the program and investigate whether the person is willing to pay the price to listen. This is when an experimental auction is useful. In an experimental auction, people could bid for the right to listen to a program that would be otherwise unavailable. People have a dominant strategy to bid their true value for the program; they can no longer free ride off others' contributions. Experimental auctions provide a measure of value in a real market. Experimental auction markets may differ in terms of structure and style from a traditional retail market, but they are real markets nonetheless.

Fourth, how do experimental auctions compare to choice-based value elicitation methods and can the methods be combined to improve estimates of people's values? Auctions are not the only "game in town" when it comes to constructing real markets. Some non-hypothetical choice-based methods are also incentive compatible. It is important to realize that competing value elicitation methods each have advantages and disadvantages. Experimental auctions have several weaknesses including presenting a bidding task unfamiliar to some people, participating in the auction can be cognitively burdensome, and the decision task in an experimental auction (stating a bid) differs from shoppers' routine tasks of choosing a product at a posted price. Non-hypothetical discrete choice tasks, in which people choose a product they wish to purchase at a given price, avoid these weaknesses. Such discrete choice tasks are straightforward for most people to answer because they mimic the natural environment.

Discrete choice tasks, however, have their own weaknesses. Discrete choices only provide an approximate indication of preferences: one can only determine whether one option is more preferred than another, but cannot necessarily determine how much more preferred one option is to another. People can be requested to respond to repeated choice questions to gain more precision, but such a procedure entails a tradeoff between statistical precision, saliency, and participant boredom. Further, when discrete choices are elicited one must assume some functional form for utility and a form for the stochastic nature of the random utility model such that choice data yields meaningful insight into willingness to pay or market share. In contrast, auctions provide a point estimate of each individual's willingness to pay; auctions yield a continuous distribution of valuations independent of functional form assumptions.

No research method is a universal panacea. Auctions and discrete choice tasks have their own relative advantages and disadvantages. More research is needed to focus on combining the advantages of both methods to better characterize preferences or to better forecast individual and market behavior. A body of literature has begun to develop arguing for the combined estimation of revealed and stated preference models, e.g., see Louviere *et al.* (2000) for a review, and several empirical studies show that such joint models exhibit better performance than either individual model (Azevedo *et al.*, 2003). Such arguments are also based on statistical literature showing that combined forecasts tend to outperform the forecasts of any individual model or individual, e.g., Clemen (1989). Future research should focus on developing methods for combining auction and discrete choice data into a single prediction model. For example, perhaps a model can be constructed in which auction data can be used to reduce the comparatively large variance in choice-based models that arises because discrete choices only provide bounds on preferences. Future research might also seek to identify conditions under which auction data might outperform choice data and vice versa.

Fifth, can experimental auctions be more broadly employed to test economic theory? One of the unique advantages of experimental auctions is that detailed information can be gained about preferences without requiring strong *a priori* assumptions about utility functionals. Experimental auctions are an excellent method to use if one wishes to test the tenets of consumer theory in economics. Chapter 9 discussed the results of several studies that have used experimental auctions to perform such tests, but much more could be done. More research is needed that focuses on using auction bids to estimate traditional systems of demand curves used by economists (e.g., food, labor, health) even though experimental auctions have rarely been used in such applications. More work would be useful because most demand systems are estimated and consumer theory tested using aggregate time series data even though the theory is meant to hold at the individual level. Only when certain aggregation properties can demand relationships be expected to hold at the aggregate level. Conditions such as homogeneity and symmetry, commonly rejected in aggregate models, can be more effectively tested in demand curves estimated from auction data. Properties such as the weak axiom of revealed preferences (WARP) might also be tested with auction data. Interest also lies in testing for alternative preference structures, such as separability tests which focus on whether preference rankings between two goods are affected by the price of a third good. Because auctions can be used to construct individual-level demand curves, it might be possible to discover significant heterogeneity in the degree to which different consumers consider different bundles of goods as separable. Further, analysis of demand systems frequently focuses on determining whether structural changes in demand have occurred. If a panel of people routinely participated in auctions, such tests of structural change could be more effectively tested. Aggregate time series estimates of demand are plagued with concerns over the endogeneity of price and quantity; experimental auctions suffer from no such concern.

Sixth, can debates over design issues in experimental auction methods be settled with non-experimental data? One advantage of additional research on the external validity of auctions would be that such work would serve to solve some of the controversies regarding the appropriateness of particular experimental design issues. Arguments can be made for and against conducting repeated bidding rounds with price feedback. Similarly, arguments could be made for and against endowing participants with a good and eliciting bids to upgrade to a substitute. Knowledge of the relative ability of each method to forecast out-of-sample retail shopping behavior would identify the appropriateness of each method.

Even if such out-of-sample data are unavailable or are irrelevant for a given context, many interesting research questions remain. Consider the issue of whether multiple bidding rounds should be held with price information released at the end of each round. The argument for such an approach is that the procedure helps participants learn about the mechanism and forces them to abandon heuristics such as "buy low." The argument against is that values might become affiliated, a problem which would interfere with incentives for truthful bidding. Future research might help resolve this issue by comparing the bidding behavior of people that have had extensive training with the mechanism, even perhaps with induced value versions of the auction, to the bidding behavior of people without such training. As a control, both groups might be exposed to similar price posting, perhaps with the use of confederate bidders. If the trained people respond to price information differently than the untrained, learning and not affiliation is the likely cause for the changes in bidding behavior across rounds. As another example, consider the design quandary as to whether people should bid to exchange an endowed good for a substitute or whether they should bid full value for each good. A potential problem when no endowment is provided is that prices and availability of non-laboratory goods can interfere with incentives to bid true value in the laboratory. Studies could be designed to experimentally manipulate the price and availability of outside substitutes to directly determine the extent to which such issues might be problematic. Corrigan and Rousu (2006a) argue that a potential problem with endowing subjects with a good is that people will now bid higher for the substitute to reciprocate for receiving the endowment. Future research in this area might force people to pay for or earn their endowments to determine if such a procedure causes bidding behavior to differ from the standard approach of freely endowing subjects with a good.

Seventh, how useful are experimental auctions for pattern recognition? There are a wealth of interesting issues yet to be addressed in the extant literature on experimental auctions relating to the psychology of individual decision making. A few studies have begun to use "thought listing" exercises in experimental auctions, in which people are requested to write down each thought that comes to mind during the auction (e.g., Kassardjian et al., 2005). Such research has the potential to uncover the processes by which people arrive at their valuations and their bids. These methods have limits. People find it hard to articulate why they behaved in certain ways, e.g., Wilson and Schooler (1991), Wilson and LaFleur (1995). People will rationalize their behavior even though their explanation may not match the true cause for the decision. The possibility arises that the presence of a thought listing exercise may influence the valuation and bidding formation processes, a conjecture which can be easily tested. This is the classic Hawthorne effect: people are more productive when they know they are being measured for their productivity. However, results from thought listing exercises could serve as an initial way to look into decision makers' black boxes.

Eighth, how do personality traits affect bidding behavior in experimental auctions? It would be interesting to determine whether people with certain personality traits exhibit differences in bidding behavior compared to people with a different set of traits. Such work might investigate whether personality has a stronger influence on valuations or on how people react to the auction market. One personality trait of direct relevance for experimental auctions relates to the competitiveness of a person. Mowen (2004) found consumers are heterogeneous in their degree of competitiveness. He related measures of competitiveness to people's interests in situations in which people directly compete against one another (e.g., sports). Mowen also found that competitiveness affected preferences for products in which competition is vicarious (e.g., watching a drama movie) and preferences for products that may be purchased for conspicuous motives (e.g., a new innovation). Competition regards one's standing relative to others. Competitiveness is related to one's concern for social standing and the desire for social approval. For example, Ashworth et al. (2005) show that people refuse to use coupons in the market place so as to not "look cheap," but will use coupons in settings in which they believe their actions will not be perceived as "looking cheap." Such findings have important implications for experimental auctions and suggest new avenues for study. For example, are more competitive people more likely to attend and participate in experimental auctions? Do more competitive people bid higher in auctions because they value the act of winning? Are certain products viewed as being more competitive or conspicuous than others? Are people worried they might "look cheap" if they bid too low? Research designs that vary the degree of anonymity, the degree of information revealed about the distribution of individual bids, the competitiveness of the mechanism, e.g., BDM versus second price auction, the wording of instructions, e.g., using the term buyer instead of winner, might provide interesting observations on this issue. One could measure personality traits and competitiveness in pre- or post-surveys and use regression analysis to identify the effect on bidding behavior.

Ninth, how do emotions and auction institutions interact? There remains an open question about whether values are accentuated or attenuated by emotions like the "fun of participation." Several studies exist suggesting that emotions can affect willingness to pay and willingness to accept valuations (e.g., Peters et al., 2003; Lerner et al., 2004). For example Lerner et al. (2004) showed that emotions induced by having people watch movie clips carried over to valuation exercises – if people experienced the emotion of disgust, WTP measures of value can exceed WTA measures of value, whereas the opposite was the case for other induced emotions. The challenge is that economists usually work by adding in only *one* emotion into a model as an extra degree of freedom; they rarely if ever add two or three or more. If multiple emotions were added to make *homo economicus* more human, either separability must be assumed across emotions or assumptions must be made about how one emotion affects the marginal productivity of another emotion (e.g., does envy increase or decrease the marginal product of regret?). This challenge goes beyond what economists usually know about behavior or have tried to address in modeling. Adding in one emotion at a time or assuming separability is convenient but in the end rather unsatisfying from the perspective of moving from *homo economicus* toward a more human bidder.

Finally, can experimental auctions predict the future? A body of literature has developed showing that prediction markets, where individuals buy and sell contracts with values contingent on election outcomes, significantly outperform polls in predicting election outcomes (e.g., Berg *et al.*, 2006; Forsythe *et al.*, 1992). For example, in such a market, people buy and sell contracts that pay $1 if Candidate A wins an election and $0 if Candidate B wins. Participants in the market buy and sell the contracts depending on the expected success of each candidate. If the "going price" of the contract is $0.60, this indicates that the market predicts a 60% chance that Candidate A will win the presidential election. Contracts can also be constructed that pay out the vote share of the respective candidates, where the market prices can be interpreted as the market consensus of the candidates expected vote share. Other studies have shown that prediction markets are successful in forecasting the outcome of football games (Servan-Schreiber *et al.*, 2004), technological development (Pennock *et al.*, 2001), firm sales (Plott and Chen, 2002) and sales receipts from opening weekends of Hollywood movies (Wolfers and Zitzewitz, 2004).

The typical prediction market is a continuous double auction with buyers submitting bids to buy (perhaps multiple) contracts and sellers submitting asks to sell (perhaps multiple) contracts with transactions occurring when a bid exceeds an ask at a price equal to the last bid or ask. The exchange institution could be simplified to match the types of auctions considered in this book. For example, a single contract that pays out $1 if an event happens prior to a given date could be auctioned off in a second price auction. With such a procedure, each person bids, and in so doing, provides an estimate of their value for the contract. If risk neutrality can be assumed or induced through experimental procedures, a person's value for the contract should equal their expectation of the probability that the event will happen before the given date. As described by Davis and Holt (1993), risk neutrality can be induced by conducting the auction in two stages where (1) earnings from the auction are determined in "points" rather than money and (2) each person plays a lottery for a fixed monetary prize where the chance of winning the prize is increasing in the number of points earned. Aggregating bids for a contingent contract provides an estimate of a group's expectation of the likelihood of observing future events.

10.3   Concluding remarks

Over the past two decades, we have learned about the pros and cons of experimental auctions to elicit demand for new goods and services. Researchers understand better now how people learn about and react to incentives, institutions, and information. They have and continue to compare how decisions are made with and without real economic commitments, within and without active exchange institutions, and with and without signals of value. They can and continue to explore what the results suggest for *ex ante* questionnaire design, *ex post* statistical evaluation, and more importantly perhaps economic theory itself. Some of what was learned reinforced previously held views, other findings sparked interest in developing models that better characterized consumer behavior. Other findings, which showed that subtle changes in experimental design can have significant effects on bidding behavior, have led to refinements in the method.

This book surveyed the current state of knowledge on experimental auctions and provides guidance about experimental design based on economic theory and empirical research. Many important questions remain to be addressed. Experimental auction work is an active and growing area of research. Our hope is that over time, and as designs are refined and as more research is conducted, experimental auctions and the variants on the method that emerge will become a useful method to better understand consumer behavior so as to improve business decision making and public policy.

We believe that if you want to learn about the method, try running an experimental auction yourself. Inventing and implementing an experiment is still the best way to discover the power and limits of the method. Ask the question you are interested in, study previous attempts to address similar questions, design your experimental auction, look for a balance of control and context, think about options outside the lab since we cannot create a perfect "people" vacuum, think about incentives in light of intrinsic and extrinsic motives, prepare to explain yourself to others who might have wanted you to ask a different question, have fun, and get ready to do it again because you might end up finding more questions than answers.

References

Ackert, L., B. K. Church, and G. P. Dwyer (2005) 'When the Shoe is on the Other Foot: Experimental Evidence on Evaluation Disparities' Federal Reserve Bank of Atlanta, Working Paper.

Addelman, S. (1962) 'Orthogonal Main-Effect Plans for Asymmetrical Factorial Experiments.' *Technometrics* 4: 21–46.

Aldenderfer, M. S. and R. K. Blashfield (1984) *Cluster Analysis*. University Paper Series on Quantitative Applications in the Social Sciences. Newbury Park, CA: Sage Publications.

Alfnes, F. and K. Rickertsen (2003) 'European Consumers' Willingness to Pay for U.S. Beef in Experimental Auction Markets' *American Journal of Agricultural Economics* 85: 396–405.

Ali, M. M. (1997) 'Probability and Utility Estimates for Racetrack Bettors' *Journal of Political Economy* 85: 803–815.

Allenby, G. M. and P. E. Rossi (1999) 'Marketing Models of Consumer Heterogeneity' *Journal of Econometrics* 89: 57–78.

Ariely, D., G. Loewenstein, and D. Prelec (2003) 'Coherent Arbitrariness: Stable Demand Curves without Stable Preferences' *Quarterly Journal of Economics* 118: 73–105.

Arnold, C. R. (1931) 'The Place of Farm Accounting in Extension' *Journal of Farm Economics* 13: 57–64.

Ashworth, L., P. R. Darke, and M. Schaller (2005) 'No One Wants to Look Cheap: Trade-Offs Between Social Disincentives and the Economic and Psychological Incentives to Redeem Coupons' *Journal of Consumer Psychology* 15: 295–306.

Ausubel, L. M. and P. C. Cramton (1996) 'Demand Reduction and Inefficiency in Multi-Unit Auctions' Working Paper, Department of Economics, University of Maryland.

Azevedo, C. D., J. A. Herriges, and C. L. Kling (2003) 'Combining Revealed and Stated Preferences: Consistency Tests and Their Interpretations' *American Journal of Agricultural Economics* 85: 525–537.

Baik, K. H., T. Cherry, S. Kroll, and J. Shogren (1999) 'Endogenous Timing in a Gaming Tournament' *Theory and Decision* 47: 1–21.

Balistreri, E., G. McClelland, G. Poe, and W. Schulze (2001) 'Can Hypothetical Questions Reveal True Values? A Laboratory Comparison of Dichotomous Choice and Open-Ended Contingent Values with Auction Values' *Environmental and Resource Economics* 18: 275–292.

Bateman, I., A. Munro, B. Rhodes, C. Starmer, and R. Sugden (1997) 'A Test of the Theory of Reference-Dependent Preferences' *Quarterly Journal of Economics* 112: 479–505.

Becker, G. M., M. H. DeGroot, and J. Marschak (1964) 'Measuring Utility by a Single-Response Sequential Method' *Behavioural Science* 9: 226–32.

Bennett, J. W. (1983) 'Validating Revealed Preferences' *Economic Analysis and Policy* 13: 2–17.

(1987) 'Strategic Behavior: Some Experimental Evidence' *Journal of Public Economics* 32: 355–368.

Berg, J. E., R. Forsythe, F. Nelson, and T. Rietz (2006) 'Results from a Dozen Years of Election Futures Markets Research' in *Handbook of Experimental Economics Results*. C. Plott and V. Smith (eds.) Amsterdam: Elsevier, forthcoming.

Berg, J., J. Dickhaut, and K. McCabe (2005) 'Risk Preference Instability Across Institutions: A Dilemma' *Proceedings of the National Academy of Sciences* 102: 4209–4214.

Berg, J., J. W. Dickhaut, and T. A. Rietz (2004) 'Preference Reversals: The Impact of Truth-Revealing Incentives' Working Paper, Department of Accounting, University of Iowa, June.

Bernard, J. C. (2005) 'Evidence of Affiliation of Values in a Repeated Trial Auction Experiment' *Applied Economics Letters* 12: 687–691.

(2006) 'Finding and Retaining the Dominant Strategy: The Second-Price, English, and "Sealed Offer" English Auctions' *Journal of Economic Behavior and Organization* forthcoming.

Bernard, J. C. and W. Schulze (2005) 'The Next New Thing: Curiosity and the Motivation to Purchase Novel Products' *Economics Bulletin* 3: 1–8.

Berry, S., J. Levinsohn, and A. Pakes (1995) 'Automobile Prices in Market Equilibrium' *Econometrica* 63: 841–890.

Bettman, J. R., M. F. Luce, and J. W. Payne (1998) 'Constructive Consumer Choice Processes' *Journal of Consumer Research* 25: 187–203.

Bishop, R. and T. Heberlein (1979) 'Measuring Values of Extramarket Goods: Are Direct Measures Biased?' *American Journal of Agricultural Economics* 61: 926–930.

Blackburn, M., G. Harrison, and E. E. Rutström (1994) 'Statistical Bias Functions and Informative Hypothetical Surveys' *American Journal of Agricultural Economics* 76: 1084–1088.

Blondel, S. and M. Javahéri (2004) 'Valuing Organic Farming: An Experimental Study of the Consumer' *Acta Horticulturae* 655: 245–252.

Boardman, A. E., D. Weimer, D. Greenberg, and A. Vining (2005) *Cost Benefit Analysis: Concepts and Practice*. 3rd edn Upper Saddle River, N. J.: Prentice-Hall.

Bohm, P. (1972) 'Estimating Demand for Public Goods: An Experiment' *European Economic Review* 3: 111–130.

(1984) 'Are There Practicable Demand-Revealing Mechanisms?' in *Public Finance and the Quest for Efficiency*, H. Hanusch (ed.) Detroit: Wayne State U. Press.

(1994) 'Behavior under Uncertainty without Preference Reversal: A Field Experiment' *Empirical Economics* 19: 185–200.

Bohm, P., J. Lindén, and J. Sonnegård (1997) 'Eliciting Reservation Prices: Becker-DeGroot-Marschak Mechanisms vs. Markets' *Economic Journal* 107: 1079–1089.

Boyce, R. R., T. C. Brown, G. H. McClelland, G. L. Peterson, and W. D. Schulze (1992) 'An Experimental Examination of Intrinsic Values as a Source of the WTA-WTP Disparity' *American Economic Review* 82: 1366–1373.

Bradley, R. A. and M. E. Terry (1952) 'Rank Analysis of Incomplete Block Designs. I. The Method of Paired Comparisons' *Biometrika* 39: 324–345.

Brookshire, D. S. and D. L. Coursey (1987) 'Measuring the Value of a Public Good: An Empirical Comparison of Elicitation Procedures' *American Economic Review* 77: 554–566.

Brookshire, D. S., D. L. Coursey, and W. D. Schulze (1987) 'The External Validity of Experimental Economics Techniques: Analysis of Demand Behavior' *Economic Inquiry* 25: 239–250.

Brown, J., J. A. L. Cranfield, and S. Henson (2005) 'Relating Consumer Willingness-to-Pay for Food Safety to Risk Tolerance: An Experimental Approach' *Canadian Journal of Agricultural Economics* 53: 249–263.

Brown, T. C. (2005) 'Loss Aversion Without the Endowment Effect, and Other Explanations for the WTA–WTP Disparity' *Journal of Economic Behavior and Organization* 57: 245–379.

Brundtland, G. (2001) *How Safe is Our Food?* Statement by the Director-General, World Health Organization [http://www.who.int/fsf/].

Buchinsky, M. (1994) 'Changes in the U.S. Wage Structure 1963–1987: Application of Quantile Regression' *Econometrica* 62: 405–459.

Buhr, B. L., D. J. Hayes, J. F. Shogren, and J. B. Kliebenstein (1993) 'Valuing Ambiguity: The Case of Genetically Engineered Growth Enhancers' *Journal of Agricultural Resource Economics* 18: 175–184.

Bull, C., A. Schotter, and K. Weigelt (1987) 'Tournaments and Piece Rates: An Experimental Study' *Journal of Political Economy* 95: 1–33.

Buzby, J., T. Roberts, C. T. J. Lin, and J. MacDonald (1996) 'Bacterial Foodborne Disease: Medical Costs and Productivity Losses' Agricultural Economics Report No. 741, August.

Camerer, C. (2003) *Behavioral Game Theory*. Princeton, NJ: Princeton University Press.

Camerer, C., and R. Hogarth (1999) 'The Effects of Financial Incentives in Experiments: A Review and Capital-Labor-Production Framework' *Journal of Risk and Uncertainty* 19: 7–42.

Carlson, A., J., Kinsey, and C. Nadav (1998) 'Who Eats What, When, and From Where?' Working Paper 98–05, St. Paul, MN: University of Minnesota, Retail Food Industry Center.

Carpenter, J. P., J. Holmes, and P. H. Matthews (2004) 'Charity Auctions: A Field Experimental Investigation' IZA Discussion Paper No. 1330. October.

Carson, R., T. Groves, and M. Machina (2000) 'Incentive and Informational Properties Preference Questions.' Paper presented at the Kobe Conference on Theory and Application of Environmental Valuation. Kobe: Kobe University, January.

Cherry, T. L. and J. F. Shogren (2006) 'Rationality crossovers' *Journal of Economic Psychology* forthcoming.

Cherry, T. L., P. Frykblom, J. F. Shogren, J. A. List, and M. B. Sullivan (2004) 'Laboratory Testbeds and Non-Market Valuation: The Case of Bidding Behavior in a Second-Price Auction with an Outside Option' *Environmental and Resource Economics* 29: 285–294.

Cherry, T. L., T. Crocker, and J. F. Shogren (2003) 'Rationality Spillovers' *Journal of Environmental Economics and Management* 45: 63–84.

Chu, Y. P, and R. L. Chu (1990) 'The Subsidence of Preference Reversals in Simplified and Marketlike Experimental Settings' *American Economic Review* 80: 902–911.

Clemen, R. (1989) 'Combining Forecasts: A Review and Annotated Bibliography' *International Journal of Forecasting* 5: 559–583.

Cochrane, W. G. and G. M. Cox (1957) *Experimental Designs*, 2nd edn. New York: NY, Wiley & Sons.

Conant, J. (1951) *Science and Common Sense*. New Haven, CT: Yale University Press.

Coppinger, V. M., V. L. Smith, and J. A. Titus (1980) 'Incentives and Behavior in English, Dutch, and Sealed-Bid Auctions' *Economic Inquiry* 43: 1–22.

Corrigan, J. R. (2005) 'Is the Experimental Auction a Dynamic Market?' *Environmental and Resource Economics* 31: 35–45.

Corrigan, J. R. and M. Rousu (2006a) 'The Effect of Initial Endowments in Experimental Auctions' *American Journal of Agricultural Economics* 88: 448–457.

(2006b) 'Posted Prices and Bid Affiliation: Evidence from Experimental Auctions' *American Journal of Agricultural Economics*, forthcoming.

(2006c) 'Demand Curve Shifts in Multi-Unit Auctions: Evidence from a Laboratory Experiment' Working Paper, Department of Economics, Kenyon University.

Coursey, D. L., J. L. Hovis, and W. D. Schulze (1987) 'The Disparity Between Willingness to Accept and Willingness to Pay Measures of Value' *Quarterly Journal of Economics* 102: 679–690.

Cox, R. C., B. Roberson, and V. L. Smith (1982) 'Theory and Behavior of Single Object Auctions' in V. L. Smith (ed.), *Research in Experimental Economics* Vol. 2. Greenwich: JAI Press.

Cox, J. C., V. L. Smith, and J. M. Walker (1992) 'Theory and Misbehavior of First-Price Auctions: Comment' *American Economic Review* 82: 1392–1412.

Cragg, J. G. (1971) 'Some Statistical Models for Limited Dependent Variables with Application to the Demand for Durable Goods' *Econometrica* 39: 829–844.

Crocker, T. and J. F. Shogren (1991) 'Preference Learning and Contingent Valuation Methods' in F. Dietz, R. Van der Ploeg, and J. van der Straaten (eds.) *Environmental Policy and the Economy*. Amsterdam: North-Holland pp. 77–93.

Crocker, T. D., J. F. Shogren, and P. R. Turner (1998) 'Incomplete Beliefs and Nonmarket Valuation' *Resource & Energy Economics* 20: 139–163.

Crutchfield, S. J., T. Buzby, M. Ollinger Roberts, and C.-T. J. Lin (1997) 'An Economic Assessment of Food Safety Regulations: The New Approach to Meat and Poultry Inspection' Agricultural Economic Report Number 755, ERS, USDA, Washington, DC.

Cummings, R., D. Brookshire, and W. Schulze (1986) *Valuing Environmental Goods: An Assessment of the Contingent Valuation Method*. Totowa, NJ: Rowman and Allanheld.

Cummings, R. and L. Taylor (1999) 'Unbiased Value Estimates for Environmental Goods: A Cheap Talk Design for the Contingent Valuation Method' *American Economic Review* 83: 649–665.

Cummings, R., C. Holt, and S. K. Laury (2004) 'Using Laboratory Experiments for Policymaking: An Example from the Georgia Irrigation Reduction Auction' *Journal of Policy Analysis and Modeling* 23: 342–363.

Dasgupta, P. and E. Maskin (2000) 'Efficient Auctions' *Quarterly Journal of Economics* 115: 341–388.

Davis, D. D. and C. A. Holt (1993) *Experimental Economics*. Princeton, NJ: Princeton University Press.

de Finetti, B. (1974) *Theory of Probability*, Vol. I, New York, NY: John Wiley & Sons.

Dhar, T. and Foltz, J. D. (2005) 'Milk by Any Other Name . . . Consumer Benefits from Labeled Milk' *American Journal of Agricultural Economics* 87: 214–228.

Diamond, P. A. and J. A. Hausman (1994) 'Contingent Valuation: Is Some Number Better Than No Number?' *Journal of Economic Perspectives* 8: 45–64.

Dickie, M., A. Fisher, and S. Gerking (1987) 'Market Transactions and Hypothetical Demand Data: A Comparative Study' *Journal of American Statistical Association* 82: 69–75.

Dickinson, D. L. and D. Bailey (2002) 'Meat Traceability: Are U.S. Consumers Willing to Pay for It?' *Journal of Agricultural and Resource Economics* 27: 348–364.

(2005) 'Experimental Evidence on Willingness to Pay for Red Meat Traceability in the United States, Canada, the United Kingdom, and Japan' *Journal of Agricultural and Applied Economics* 37: 537–548.

Di Mauro, C. and A. Maffioletti (1996) 'An Experimental Investigation of the Impact of Ambiguity on the Valuation of Self-Insurance and Self-Protection' *Journal of Risk and Uncertainty* 13: 53–71.

Ding, M., R. Grewal, and J. Liechty (2005) 'Incentive-Aligned Conjoint Analysis' *Journal of Marketing Research* 42: 67–83.

Drago, R. and J. Heywood (1989) 'Tournaments, Piece Rates, and the Shape of the Payoff Function' *Journal of Political Economy* 97: 992–998.

Drago, R., G. Garvey, and G. Turnbull (1996) 'A Collective Tournament' *Economics Letters* 50: 223–227.

Ehrenberg, R., M. Boganno (1990) 'Do Tournaments have Incentive Effects?' *Journal of Political Economy* 98: 1307–1324.

Eigenraam, M., L. Strappazzon, N. Lansdell, A. Ha, C. Beverly, and J. Todd (2006) 'EcoTender: Auction for Multiple Environmental Outcomes' *National Action Plan for Salinity and Water Quality National Market Based Instruments Pilot Program. Project Final Report*. Department of Primary Industries, Victoria, Australia, February.

Feldkamp, T, T. C. Schroeder, and J. L. Lusk (2005) 'Determining Consumer Valuation of Quality Differentiated Beef Steak Attributes' *Journal of Muscle Foods* 16: 1–15.

Feuz, D. M., W. J. Umberger, C. R. Calkins, and B. Sitz (2004) 'U.S. Consumers' Willingness to Pay for Flavor and Tenderness in Steaks as Determined with an Experimental Auction' *Journal of Agricultural and Resource Economics* 29: 501–516.

Food Traceability Report (2002) 'EU Parliament Approves Strict Traceability for GM Foods' <http://www.foodtraceabilityreport.com/>. Accessed August 1.

Forsythe, R. and Isaac, R. M. (1982) 'Demand-Revealing Mechanisms for Private Good Auctions,' in Vernon Smith (ed.) *Research in Experimental Economics*. Greenwich, CT: JAI Press, Inc., Vol. 2, pp. 45–61.

Forsythe, R., F. Nelson, G. R. Neumann, and J. Wright (1992) 'Anatomy of an Experimental Political Stock Market' *American Economic Review* 82: 1142–1161.

Fox, J. A., D. J. Hayes, J. B. Kliebenstein, and J. F. Shogren (1994) 'Consumer Acceptability of Milk from Cows Treated with Bovine Somatotropin' *Journal of Dairy Science* 77: 703–707.

Fox, J. A., B. L. Buhr, J. F. Shogren, J. B. Kliebenstein, and D. J. Hayes (1995) 'A Comparison of Preferences for Pork Sandwiches Produced from Animals with and without Somatotropin Administration' *Journal of Animal Science* 73: 1048–1054.

Fox, J. A. and D. G. Olson (1998) 'Market Trials of Irradiated Chicken' *Radiation Physics and Chemistry* 52: 63–66.

Fox, J. A., J. F. Shogren, D. J. Hayes, and J. B. Kliebenstein (1998) 'CVM-X: Calibrating Contingent Values with Experimental Auction Markets' *American Journal of Agricultural Economics* 80: 455–465.

Fox, J. A., D. J. Hayes, and J. F. Shogren (2002) 'Consumer Preferences for Food Irradiation: How Favorable and Unfavorable Descriptions Affect Preferences for Irradiated Pork in Experimental Auctions' *Journal of Risk and Uncertainty* 24: 75–95.

Franciosi, R., R. M. Isaac, D. E. Pingry, and S. S. Reynolds (1993) 'An Experimental Investigation of the Hahn-Noll Revenue Neutral Auction for Emissions Licenses' *Journal of Environmental Economics and Management* 24: 1–24.

Friedman, D. and S. Sunder (1994) *Experimental Methods: A Primer for Economists.* Cambridge University Press.

Frykblom, P. (1997) 'Hypothetical Question Modes and Real Willingness to Pay' *Journal of Environmental Economics and Management* 34: 275–287.

Frykblom, P. and J. F. Shogren (2000) 'An Experimental Testing of Anchoring Effects in Discrete Choice Questions' *Environmental and Resource Economics* 16:3: 329–341.

Garret, T. and R. Sobel (1999) 'Gamblers Favor Skewness, Not Risk: Further Evidence from United States Lottery Games' *Economics Letters* 63: 85–90.

Gaskell, G., M. W. Bauer, J. Durant, and N. C. Allum (1999) 'Worlds Apart? The Reception of Genetically Modified Foods in Europe and the U.S.' *Science* 285: 384–387.

Giannakas, G. and M. Fulton (2002) 'Consumption Effects of Genetic Modification: What if Consumers are Right?' *Agricultural Economics* 27: 97–109.

Gloy, B. A. and E. L. LaDue (2003) 'Financial Management Practices and Farm Profitability' *Agricultural Financial Review* 63: 157–174.

Goldstein, W. M. and H. J. Einhorn (1987) 'Expression Theory and the Preference Reversal Phenomenon' *Psychological Review* 94: 236–254.

Golec, J. and M. Tamarkin (1998) 'Bettors Love Skewness, not Risk, at the Horse Track' *Journal of Political Economy* 106: 205–225.

Graff Zivin, J. S. (2006) 'Ensuring a Safe Food Supply: The Importance of Heterogeneity' *Journal of Agricultural and Food Industrial Organization* 4, Article 2.

Greene, W. (2000) *Econometric Analysis.* Upper Saddle River, NJ: Prentice Hall.
    (2004) 'Interpreting Estimated Parameters and Measuring Individual Heterogeneity in Random Coefficient Models' Working Paper, Department of Economics, Stern School of Business, New York University, May 6.

Grether, D. and C. Plott (1979) 'Economic Theory of Choice and the Preference Reversal Phenomenon' *American Economic Review* 69: 623–638.

Grossman, S., R. Kihlstrom, and L. Mirman (1977) 'A Bayesian Approach to the Production of Information and Learning by Doing' *Review of Economic Studies* 46: 533–547.

Groves, R. M. (1987) 'Research on Survey Data Quality' *Public Opinion Quarterly* 51: S156–S172.

Gul, F. (1991) 'A Theory of Disappointment Aversion' *Econometrica* 59: 667–686.

Gunnersson, S., J. F. Shogren, and T. L. Cherry (2003) 'Are Preferences for Skewness Fixed or Fungible?' *Economics Letters* 80: 113–121.

Hammitt, J. K. and J. D. Graham (1999) 'Willingness to Pay for Health Protection: Inadequate Sensitivity to Probability?' *Journal of Risk and Uncertainty* 18: 33–62.

Hanemann, W. M. (1984) 'Welfare Evaluations in Contingent Valuation Experiments with Discrete Responses' *American Journal of Agricultural Economics* 66: 332–341.

(1991) 'Willingness to Pay and Willingness to Accept: How Much Can They Differ?' *American Economic Review* 81: 635–647.

(1994) 'Valuing the Environment through Contingent Valuation' *Journal of Economic Perspectives* 8: 19–43.

Hanley, N., J. F. Shogren, and B. White (2006) *Introduction to Environmental Economics.* Oxford, UK: Oxford University Press.

Harless, D. W. (1989) 'More Laboratory Evidence on the Disparity between Willingness to Pay and Compensation Demanded' *Journal of Economic Behavior and Organization* 11: 359–379.

Harless, D., and C. Camerer (1994) 'The Predictive Utility of Generalized Expected Utility Theories' *Econometrica* 62: 1251–1289.

Harrison, G. W. (1989) 'Theory and Misbehavior of First-Price Auctions' *American Economic Review* 79: 749–762.

Harrison, G. W., R. Beekman, L. Brown, L. Clements, T. McDaniel, S. Odom, and M. Williams (1997) 'Environmental Damage Assessment with Hypothetical Surveys: The Calibration Approach' in M. Bowman, R. Brannlund, and B. Kriström (eds.) *Topics in Environmental Economics* Amsterdam: Kluwer Academic Publishers.

Harrison, G. W., E. Johnson, M. M. McInnes, and E. E. Rutström (2003) 'Individual Choice in the Laboratory: Paradox Reloaded' Working Paper, Dept. Economics, University of Central Florida, September.

Harrison, G. W., R. M. Harstad, and E. E. Rutström (2004) 'Experimental Methods and the Elicitation of Values' *Experimental Economics* 7: 123–140.

Harrison, G. W. and J. A. List (2004) 'Field Experiments' *Journal of Economics Literature* 42: 1009–1055.

Harstad, R. M. (2000) 'Dominant Strategy Adoption and Bidders' Experience with Pricing Rules' *Experimental Economics* 3: 261–280.

Hatcher, L. (1994) *A Step-by-Step Approach to Using SAS for Factor Analysis and Structural Equations Modeling* Cary, NC: SAS Institute.

Hayes, D. J., J. F. Shogren, S. U. Shin, J. B. Kliebenstein (1995) 'Valuing Food Safety in Experimental Auction Markets' *American Journal of Agricultural Economics* 77: 40–53.

Heckman, J. J. (2001) 'Micro Data, Heterogeneity, and the Evaluation of Public Policy: Nobel Lecture' *Journal of Political Economy* 109: 673–748.

Heiner, R. (1983) 'The Origin of Predictable Behavior' *American Economic Review* 76: 560–595.

Hey, J. D. and C. Orme (1994) 'Investigating Generalizations of Expected Utility Theory Using Experimental Data' *Econometrica* 62: 1291–1326.

Hoban, T. J., and J. Burkhardt (1991) 'Determinants of Public Acceptance in Meat and Milk Production: North America' in P. van der Wal, G. M. Weber, and F. J. van der Wilt (eds.) *Biotechnology for Control of Growth and Product Quality in Meat Production: Implications and Acceptability*. The Netherlands: Pudoc Wageningen.

Hobbs, J. E., D. Bailey, D. L. Dickinson, and M. Haghiri (2005) 'Traceability in the Canadian Red Meat Sector: Do Consumers Care?' *Canadian Journal of Agricultural Economics* 53: 47–65.

Hobbs, J. E., K. Sanderson, and M. Haghiri (2006) 'Evaluating Willingness-to-Pay for Bison Attributes: An Experimental Auction Approach' *Canadian Journal of Agricultural Economics* 54: 269–287.

Hoffman, E., D. Menkhaus, D. Chakravarti, R. Field, and G. Whipple (1993) 'Using Laboratory Experimental Auctions in Marketing Research: A Case Study of New Packaging for Fresh Beef' *Marketing Science* 12: 318–338.

Hofler, R. and J. A. List (2004) 'Valuation on the Frontier, Calibrating Actual and Hypothetical Statements of Value' *American Journal of Agricultural Economics* 86(1): 213–221.

Holt, C. A. (1986) 'Preference Reversals and the Independence Axiom' *American Economic Review* 76: 508–515.

Holt, C. A. and S. K. Laury (2002) 'Risk Aversion and Incentive Effects' *American Economic Review* 92: 1644–1655.

Hong, C. S. and N. Nishimura (2003) 'Revenue Non-Equivalence between the English and the Second-Price Auctions: Experimental Evidence' *Journal of Economic Behavior and Organization* 51: 443–458.

Horowitz, J. K. (2005) 'The Becker-DeGroot-Marschak Mechanism is not Always Incentive Compatible, even for Non-Random Goods' Working Paper, Department of Agricultural and Resource Economics, University of Maryland, March.

Horowitz, J. K. and K. E. McConnell (2000) 'Values Elicited from Open-Ended Real Experiments' *Journal of Economic Behavior and Organization* 41: 221–237.

Horowitz, J. K., J. A. List, and K. E. McConnell (2006) 'A Test of Diminishing Marginal Value' *Economica*, forthcoming.

Huber, J. and K. Train (2001) 'On the Similarity of Classical and Bayesian Estimates of Individual Mean Partworths' *Marketing Letters* 12: 259–269.

Huck, S. and G. Weizäcker (2002) 'Do Players Correctly Estimate What Others Do? Evidence of Conservation in Beliefs' *Journal of Economic Behavior and Organization* 47: 71–85.

Hudson, M. D., K. O. Coble, and J. L. Lusk (2005) 'Consistency of Risk Premium Measures' *Agricultural Economics* 33: 41–49.

Huffman, W. E., M. Rousu, J. F. Shogren, and A. Tegene (2003) 'Consumer Willingness to Pay for Genetically Modified Food Labels in a Market with Diverse Information: Evidence from Experimental Auctions' *Journal of Agricultural and Resource Economics* 28: 481–502.

(2004) 'Consumers' Resistance to Genetically Modified Foods in the US: The Role of Information in an Uncertain Environment' *Journal of Agricultural and Food Industrial Organization* 2: Article 8.

Ibehndahl G., S. Isaacs, and R. Trimble (2002) 'Financial Information Base of Participants in FSA Borrower Training' *Journal of Extension* 40.

Irwin, J. R., G. H. McClelland, M. McKee, W. D. Schulze, and N. E. Norden (1998) 'Payoff Dominance vs. Cognitive Transparency in Decision Making' *Economic Inquiry* 36: 272–285.

Jaeger, S. R. and R. Harker (2005) 'Consumer Evaluation of Novel Kiwifruit: Willingness-to-Pay' *Journal of the Science of Food and Agriculture* 85: 2519–2526.

Jaeger, S. R., J. L. Lusk, L. O. House, C. Valli, M. Moore, B. Morrow and W. B. Traill (2004) 'Acceptance of Genetically Modified Foods: Non-Hypothetical Experimental Markets' *Food Quality and Preference* 15: 701–714.

Jensen, M. and K. J. Murphy (1990) 'Performance Pay and Top-Management Incentives' *Journal of Political Economy* 98: 225–264.

Kachelmeier, S. J. and M. Shehata (1992) 'Examining Risk Preferences under High Monetary Incentives: Experimental Evidence for the People's Republic of China' *American Economic Review* 82: 1120–1140.

Kagel, J. H. (1995) 'Auctions: A Survey of Experimental Research' in *The Handbook of Experimental Economics*, J. H. Kagel and A. E. Roth (eds.) Princeton University Press, Princeton, NJ, pp. 501–585.

Kagel, J. H. and D. Levin (2002) *Common Value Auctions and the Winner's Curse.* Princeton, NJ: Princeton University Press.

Kagel, J. H., R. M. Harstad, and D. Levin (1987) 'Information Impact and Allocation Rules in Auctions with Affiliated Private Values: A Laboratory Study' *Econometrica* 55: 1275–1304.

Kagel, J. H. and D. Levin (1993) 'Independent Private Value Auctions: Bidder Behavior in First, Second-, and Third Price Auctions with Varying Numbers of Bidders' *Economic Journal* 103: 868–879.

Kahneman, D. and A. Tversky (1979) 'Prospect Theory: An Analysis of Decision under Risk' *Econometrica* 47: 263–291.

Kahneman, D. and A. Tversky (eds.) (2000) *Choices, Values, and Frames.* Cambridge, UK: Cambridge University Press.

Kahneman, D., J. L. Knetsch, and R. H. Thaler (1990) 'Experimental Tests of the Endowment Effect and the Coase Theorem' *The Journal of Political Economy* 98: 1325–1348.

Kajii, A. and S. Morris (1997) 'The Robustness of Equilibria to Incomplete Information' *Econometrica* 65: 1238–1310.

Kalaitzandonakes, N. and J. Bijman (2003) 'So Who's Driving Biotech Acceptance?' *Nature Biotechnology* 21: 336–339.

Karni, E. and Z. Safra (1986) 'Vickrey Auctions in the Theory of Expected Utility with Rank-Dependent Probabilities' *Economics Letters* 20: 15–18.

(1987) 'Preference Reversals and the Observability of Preferences by Experimental Methods' *Econometrica* 55: 675–685.

Kassardjian, E., J. Gamble., A. Gunson, and S. R. Jaeger (2005) 'A New Approach to Elicit Consumers' Willingness to Purchase Genetically Modified Apples' *British Food Journal* 107: 541–555.

Katsaras, N., P. Wolfson, J. Kinsey, and B. Senauer (2001) 'Data Mining: A Segmentation Analysis of U.S. Grocery Shoppers' Working Paper 01-01. St. Paul, MN: University of Minnesota, Retail Food Industry Center.

Kaufman, L. and P. J. Rousseeuw (2005) *Finding Groups in Data: An Introduction to Cluster Analysis*. Wiley-Interscience.

Killinger, K. M., C. R., Calkins, W. J. Umberger, D. M. Feuz, and K. M. Eskridge (2004a) 'Consumer Visual Preference and Value for Beef Steaks Differing in Marbling Level and Color' *Journal of Animal Science* 82: 3288–3293.

(2004b) 'Consumer Sensory Acceptance and Value for Beef Steaks of Similar Tenderness, but Differing in Marbling Level' *Journal of Animal Science* 82: 3294–3301.

(2004c) 'A Comparison of Consumer Sensory Acceptance and Value of Domestic Beef Steaks and Steaks from a Branded, Argentine Beef Program' *Journal of Animal Science* 82: 3302–3307.

Kim, J. O. and C. W. Mueller (1978) *Introduction to Factor Analysis: What it is and How to Do It*. University Paper Series on Quantitative Applications in the Social Sciences, Series No. 07–013. Newbury Park, CA: Sage Publications.

Kirby, K. N. (1997) 'Bidding on the Future: Evidence against Normative Discounting of Delayed Rewards' *Journal of Experimental Psychology: General* 126: 54–70.

Kirk, R. E. (1994) *Experimental Design: Procedures for Behavioral Sciences* (3rd edn.) Pacific Grove CA: Brooks Cole.

Klemperer, P. (1999) 'Auction Theory: A Guide to the Literature' *Journal of Economics Surveys* 13: 227–286.

(2004) *Auctions: Theory and Practice*. Princeton NJ.: Princeton University Press.

Kline, P. (2002) *An Easy Guide to Factor Analysis*. Routledge, New York, NY.

Kling, C. L., J. A. List, and J. Zhao (2003) 'The WTP/WTA Disparity: Have we been Observing Dynamic Values but Interpreting Them as Static?' Working Paper 03-WT 333, Center for Agricultural and Rural Development, Iowa State University, May.

Knetsch, J. L. and J. A. Sinden (1984) 'Willingness to Pay and Compensation Demanded: Experimental Evidence of an Unexpected Disparity in Measures of Value' *Quarterly Journal of Economics* 99: 507–521.

Knetsch, J. L., F. F. Tang, and R. H. Thaler (2001) 'The Endowment Effect and Repeated Market Trials: Is the Vickrey Auction Demand Revealing?' *Experimental Economics* 4: 257–269.

Koenker, R. and K. F. Hallock (2001) 'Quantile Regression' *Journal of Economic Perspectives* 15: 143–156.

Koenker, R. and G. Bassett (1978) 'Regression Quantiles' *Econometrica* 46: 33–50.

Kolstad, C. D. and R. M. Guzman (1999) 'Information and the Divergence between Willingness to Accept and Willingness to Pay' *Journal of Environmental Economics and Management* 38: 66–80.

Kraemer, H. C. and S. Thiemann (1987) *How Many Subjects?* Newbury Park, CA: Sage Publications.

Krishna, V. (2002) *Auction Theory*. Elsevier Science: Academic Press.

Krugman, P. (1998) 'Two Cheers for Formalism' *Economic Journal* 108: 1829–1836.

Kupper, L. L. and K. B. Hafner (1989) 'How Appropriate are Popular Sample Size Formulas?' *The American Statistician* 43: 101–105.

Lange, C., C. Martin, C. Chabanet, P. Combris, and S. Issanchou (2002) 'Impact of the Information Provided to Consumers on their Willingness-to-Pay for Champagne: Comparison with Hedonic Scores' *Food Quality and Preference* 13: 597–608.

Lazear, E. and S. Rosen (1981) 'Rank-Order Tournaments as Optimal Labor Contracts' *Journal of Political Economy* 89: 841–864.

Lerner, J., D. Small, and G. Loewenstein (2004) 'Heart Strings and Purse Strings: Carry-Over Effects of Emotions on Economic Transactions' *Psychological Science* 15: 337–341.

Levitt, S. D. and J. A. List (2005) 'What Do Laboratory Experiments Tell Us About the Real World?' Working Paper, Department of Economics, University of Chicago, September 12.

Levy, P. and S. Lemeshow (1991) *Sampling of Populations: Methods and Applications*, New York: John Wiley and Sons Ltd.

Lichtenstein, S. and P. Slovic (1971) 'Reversals of Preference Between Bids and Choices in Gambling Decisions' *Journal of Experimental Psychology* 89: 46–55.

Lin, T. and P. Schmidt (1984) 'A Test of the Tobit Specification Against an Alternative Suggested by Cragg' *Review of Economics and Statistics* 66: 174–177.

List, J. A. (2001) 'Do Explicit Warnings Eliminate the Hypothetical Bias in Elicitation Procedures? Evidence from Field Auctions for Sportscards' *American Economic Review* 91: 1498–1507.

(2002) 'Preference Reversals of a Different Kind: The "More is Less" Phenomenon' *American Economic Review* 92: 1636–1643.

(2003) 'Does Market Experience Eliminate Market Anomalies?' *Quarterly Journal of Economics* 118: 41–71.

(2004) 'The Nature and Extent of Discrimination in the Marketplace: Evidence from the Field' *Quarterly Journal of Economics* 119: 49–89.

List, J. A. and C. A. Gallet (2001) 'What Experimental Protocol Influence Disparities Between Actual and Hypothetical Stated Values?' *Environmental and Resource Economics* 20: 241–54.

List, J. A. and D. Lucking-Reiley (2000) 'Demand Reduction in a Multi-Unit Auction: Evidence from a Sportscard Field Experiment,' *American Economic Review* 90: 961–972.

List, J. A. and J. F. Shogren (1998) 'Calibration of the Differences Between Actual and Hypothetical Valuations in a Field Experiment' *Journal of Economic Behavior and Organization* 37: 193–205.

(1999) 'Price Information and Bidding Behavior in Repeated Second-Price Auctions.' *American Journal of Agricultural Economics* 81: 942–949.

List, J. A., M. Margolis, and J. F. Shogren (1998) 'Hypothetical-Actual Bid Calibration of a Multi-Good Auction.' *Economics Letters* 60: 263–268.

Loewenstein, G. (1988) 'Frames of Mind in Intertemporal Choice.' *Management Science* 34: 200–214.

Lou, G. Y. (2002) 'Collective Decision-Making and Heterogeneity in Tastes.' *Journal of Business and Economic Statistics* April, Vol. 20, No. 2; pp. 213–226.

Loureiro, M. L., W. J. Umberger, and S. Hine (2003) 'Testing the Initial Endowment Effect in Experimental Auctions' *Applied Economics Letters* 10: 271–276.

Louviere, J. J., D. A. Hensher, and J. D. Swait (2000) *Stated Choice Methods: Analysis and Application*. Cambridge: Cambridge University Press.

Luce, R. D. (1959) *Individual Choice Behavior*. New York, NY: John Wiley & Sons.

Lucking-Reiley, D. (1999) 'Using Field Experiments to Test Equivalence between Auction Formats: Magic on the Internet.' *American Economic Review* 89: 1063–1080.

(2000) 'Vickrey Auctions in Practice: From Nineteenth-Century Philately to Twenty-First-Century E-Commerce' *Journal of Economic Perspectives* 14: 183–192.

Lunander, A. and J. E. Nilsson (2004) 'Taking the Lab to the Field: Experimental Tests of Alternative Mechanisms to Procure Multiple Contracts' *Journal of Regulatory Economics* 25: 39–58.

Lusk, J. L. (2003) 'An Experimental Test of the Commitment Cost Theory' *American Journal of Agricultural Economics* 85: 1316–1322.

Lusk, J. L. and J. A. Fox (2003) 'Value Elicitation in Laboratory and Retail Environments' *Economics Letters* 79: 27–34.

Lusk, J. L. and D. Hudson (2004) 'Effect of Monitor-Subject Cheap Talk on Ultimatum Game Offers' *Journal of Economic Behavior and Organization* 54: 439–443, July.

Lusk, J. L. and C. H. Coble (2005) 'Risk Perceptions, Risk Preference, and Acceptance of Risky Food' *American Journal of Agricultural Economics* 87: 393–405.

Lusk, J. L. and B. Norwood (2005) 'Effect of Experimental Design on Choice-Based Conjoint Valuation Estimates' *American Journal of Agricultural Economics* 87: 771–785.

Lusk, J. L. and M. Rousu (2006) 'Market Price Endogeneity and Accuracy of Value Elicitation Mechanisms' *Experimental Methods in Environmental and Resource Economic* John List (ed.) Edward Elgar Publishing. forthcoming.

Lusk, J. L. and T. C. Schroeder (2006) 'Auction Bids and Shopping Choices' *Advances in Economic Analysis and Policy*, forthcoming.

Lusk, J. L., J. A. Fox, T. C. Schroeder, J. Mintert, and M. Koohmaraie (2001a) 'In-Store Valuation of Steak Tenderness' *American Journal of Agricultural Economics* 83 539–550.

Lusk, J. L., M. S. Daniel, D. Mark, and C. L. Lusk (2001b) 'Alternative Calibration and Auction Institutions for Predicting Consumer Willingness to Pay of Nongenetically Modified Corn Chips.' *Journal of Agricultural and Resource Economics* 26: 40–57.

Lusk, J. L., T. Feldkamp, and T. C. Schroeder (2004a) 'Experimental Auction Procedure: Impact on Valuation of Quality Differentiated Goods' *American Journal of Agricultural Economics* 86: 389–405.

Lusk, J. L., L. O. House, C. Valli, S. R. Jaeger, M. Moore, B. Morrow, and W. B. Traill (2004b) 'Effect of Information about Benefits of Biotechnology on Consumer Acceptance of Genetically Modified Food: Evidence from Experimental Auctions in United States, England, and France' *European Review of Agricultural Economics* 31 July: 179–204.

Lusk, J. L., L. O. House, C. Valli, S. R. Jaeger, M. Moore, B. Morrow, and W. B. Traill (2005) 'Consumer Welfare Effects of Introducing and Labeling Genetically Modified Food.' *Economics Letters* 88: 382–88, September.

Lusk, J. L., C. Alexander, and M. Rousu (2006a) 'Designing Experimental Auctions for Marketing Research: Effect of Values, Distributions, and Mechanisms on Incentives for Truthful Bidding.' Working Paper, Department of Agricultural Economics, Oklahoma State University.

Lusk, J. L., J. R. Pruitt and B. Norwood (2006b) 'External Validity of a Field Experiment' *Economics Letters* 931: 285–290.

Lusk, J. L., W. B. Traill, L. O. House, C. Valli, S. R. Jaeger, M. Moore, and B. Morrow (2006c) 'Comparative Advantage in Demand: Experimental Evidence of Preferences for Genetically Modified Food in the United States and European Union' *Journal of Agricultural Economics* 57: 1–21.

Machina, M. J. (1982) 'Expected Utility Analysis Without the Independence Axiom' *Econometrica* 50: 1089–1122.

Mansfield, C. (1998) 'A Consistent Method for Calibrating Contingent Value Survey Data' *Southern Economic Journal* 64: 665–681.

Marcellino, D. (2006) 'Valuing Farm Records'. Unpublished M. S. Thesis. Department of Agricultural Economics, Purdue University.

Marette, S., J. Roosen, S. Blanchemanche, and P. Verger (2006) 'Health Information and the Choice of Fish Species: An Experiment Measuring the Impact of Risk and Benefit Information' Iowa State University, Center for Agricultural and Rural Development (CARD) Publication 06-wp421, April.

Margolis, M. and J. F. Shogren (2004) 'Implementing the Efficient Auction: Initial Results from the Lab' *Economics Letters* 84: 141–147.

Masters, W. A. and D. Sanogo (2002) 'Welfare Gains from Quality Certification of Infant Foods: Results from a Market Experiment in Mali' *American Journal of Agricultural Economics* 84: 974–989.

McAfee, R. P. and J. McMillan (1987) 'Auctions and Bidding' *Journal of Economic Literature* 25: 699–738.

McClelland, G., W. Schulze and D. Coursey (1993) 'Insurance for Low-Probability Hazards: A Biomodal Response to Unlikely Events' *Journal of Risk and Uncertainty* 7: 95–116.

McDonald, J. F. and R. A. Moffitt (1980) 'The Uses of Tobit Analysis' *Review of Economics and Statistics* 62: 318–321.

Mead, P. L., V. Slutsker, L. Dietz, J. McCaig, C. Bresee, P. Shapiro, Griffin, and R. Tauxe (1990) 'Food-Related Illness and Death in the United States' *Emerging Infectious Diseases* 5: 607–625.

Melton, B. E., W. A. Colette, and R. L. Willham (1994) 'Imputing Input Characteristic Values from Optimal Commercial Breed or Variety Choice Decisions' *American Journal of Agricultural Economics* 76: 478–491.

Melton, B. E., W. E. Huffman, and J. F. Shogren (1996a) 'Economic Values of Pork Attributes: Hedonic Price Analysis of Experimental Auction Data.' *Review of Agricultural Economics* 18: 613–627.

Melton, B. E., W. E. Huffman, J. F. Shogren, and J. A. Fox (1996b) 'Consumer Preferences for Fresh Food Items with Multiple Quality Attributes: Evidence from an Experimental Auction of Pork Chops' *American Journal of Agricultural Economics* 78: 916–923.

Menkhaus, D. J. (1992) 'An Empirical Application of Laboratory Experimental Auctions in Marketing Research' *Journal of Agricultural and Resource Economics* 17: 44–55.

Milgrom, P. (2004) *Putting Auction Theory to Work*. Cambridge: Cambridge University Press.

Milgrom, P. R. and R. J. Weber (1982) 'A Theory of Auctions and Competitive Bidding' *Econometrica* 50: 1089–1122.

Miller, G. and C. Plott (1985) 'Revenue Generating Properties of Sealed-bid Auctions: An Experimental Analysis of One-price and Discriminative Auctions' in V. L. Smith (ed.) *Research in Experimental Economics* Greenwich, CT: JAI press, Inc, Vol 3. pp. 159–182.

Montgomery, D. C. (2000) *Design and Analysis of Experiments*. New York, NY: John Wiley & Sons Ltd.

Mowen, J. C. (2004) 'Exploring the Trait of Competitiveness and Its Consumer Behavior Consequences' *Journal of Consumer Psychology* 14: 52–63.

Mussa, M. and S. Rosen (1978) 'Monopoly and Product Quality' *Journal of Economic Theory* 18: 301–317.

Nalley, L., D. Hudson, and G. Parkhurst (2004) 'The Impacts of Taste, Location of Origin, and Health Information on Market Demand for Sweet Potatoes' Mississippi State University Department of Agricultural Economics Research Report 2004–001, July.

Neill, H., R. Cummings, P. Ganderton, G. Harrison, and T. McGukin (1994) 'Hypothetical Surveys and Real Economic Commitments' *Land Economics* 70: 145–154.

Neilson, W. (1994) 'Second Price Auctions without Expected Utility' *Journal of Economic Theory* 62: 136–151.

Nevo, A. (2001) 'Measuring Market Power in the Ready-to-Eat Cereal Industry' *Econometrica* 69: 307–342.

Norwood, F. B. and J. L. Lusk (2006) 'The Dual Nature of Choice: When Personality and Choice Collide' Working Paper, Department of Agricultural Economics, Oklahoma State University.

Noussair, C., C. Plott and R. Riezman (1995) 'An Experimental Investigation of the Patterns of International Trade' *American Economic Review* 85: 462–491.

Noussair, C., S. Robin and B. Ruffieux (2002) 'Do Consumers Not Care About Biotech Foods or Do They Just Not Read the Labels?' *Economics Letters* 75: 47–53.

(2004a) 'Revealing Consumers' Willingness-to-Pay: A Comparison of the BDM Mechanism and the Vickrey Auction' *Journal of Economic Psychology* 25: 725–741.

(2004b) 'A Comparison of Hedonic Rating and Demand-Revealing Auctions' *Food Quality and Preference* 15: 393–402.

(2004c) 'Do Consumers Really Refuse to Buy Genetically Modified Food?' *The Economic Journal* 114: 102–120.

Nunnally, J. C. and I. H. Bernstein (1994) *Psychometric Theory* 3rd edn. New York, NY: McGraw-Hill.

Organic Consumers Association. (2002) 'Irradiation Home Page.' http://organicconsumers.org/irradlink.html

Parkhurst, G., J. F. Shogren and D. L. Dickinson (2004) 'Negative Values in Vickrey Auctions' *American Journal of Agricultural Economics* 86: 222–235.

Pennock, D. M., S. Lawrence, C. L. Giles, and F. A. Nielsen (2001) 'The Real Power of Artificial Markets' *Science* 291: 987–988.

Pennings, J. M. E., B. Wansink, and M. T. G. Meulenberg (2002) 'A Note on Modeling Consumer Reactions to a Crisis: The Case of the Mad Cow Disease' *International Journal of Research in Marketing* 19: 91–100.

Perry, M. and P. J. Reny (2002) 'An Efficient Auction' *Econometrica* 70: 1199–1212.

Peters, E., P. Slovic, and R. Gregory (2003) 'The Role of Affect in the WTA/WTP Disparity' *Journal of Behavioral Decision Making* 16: 309–330.

Phaneuf, D. J., J. A. Herriges, and C. L. Kling (1998) 'Valuing Water Quality Improvements using Revealed Preference Methods when Corner Solutions are Present' *American Journal of Agricultural Economics* 80: 1025–1031.

(2000) 'Estimation and Welfare Calculations in a Generalized Corner Solution Model with an Application to Recreation Demand' *Review of Economics and Statistics* 82: 83–92.

Platter, W. J., J. D. Tatum, K. E. Belk, S. R. Koontz, P. L. Chapman, and G. C. Smith (2005) 'Effects of Marbling and Shear Force on Consumers' Willingness to Pay for Beef Strip Loin Steaks' *Journal of Animal Science* 83: 890–899.

Plott, C. R. (1991) 'Will Economics Become an Experimental Science?' *Southern Economic Journal* 57: 901–919.

(1994) 'Market Architectures, Institutional Landscapes and Testbed Experiments' *Economic Theory* 4: 3–10.

(1996) 'Rational Individual Behavior in Markets and Social Choice Processes' in K. Arrow *et al.* (eds.) *The Rational Foundations of Economic Behavior*. London, Macmillan, New York: St Martin Press.

Plott, C. R. and K. Y. Chen. (2002) 'Information Aggregation Mechanisms: Concept, Design and Implementation for a Sales Forecasting Problem' California Institute of Technology, Social Science Working Paper 1131, March.

Plott, C. R. and K. Zeiler (2005) 'The Willingness to Pay – Willingness to Accept Gap, The "Endowment Effect," Subject Misconceptions and Experimental Procedures for Eliciting Valuations' *American Economic Review* 95: 530–545.

Pond, G. A. (1931) 'The Place of Farm Accounting in Research' *Journal of Farm Economics* 13: 49–56.

Powell, J. (1984) 'Least Absolute Deviations Estimation for the Censored Regression Model' *Journal of Econometrics* 25: 303–325.

Pratt, J. W. (1964) 'Risk Aversion in the Small and in the Large' *Econometrica* 32: 122–136.

Quiggin, J. (1982) 'A Theory of Anticipated Utility' *Journal of Economic Behavior and Organization* 3: 323–343.

Randall, A. (1997) 'Calibration of CV responses: Discussion' in D. Bjornstad and J. Kahn (eds.) *The Contingent Valuation of Environmental Resources*, London: Edgar Elgar, 198–207.

Randall, A. and J. Stoll (1980) 'Consumer's Surplus in Commodity Space' *American Economic Review* 70: 449–455.

Romesburg, C. (1984) *Cluster Analysis for Researchers*. Belmont, Calif: Lifetime Learning Publications.

Roosen, J., D. A. Hennessy, J. A. Fox, and A. Schreiber (1998) 'Consumers' Valuation of Insecticide Use Restrictions: An Application to Apples' *Journal of Agricultural and Resource Economics* 23: 367–84.

Rousu, M., W. E. Huffman, J. F. Shogren, and A. Tegene (2004a) 'Estimating the Public Value of Conflicting Information: The Case of Genetically Modified Foods' *Land Economics* 80: 125–135.

Rousu, M., W. E. Huffman, J. F. Shogren, and A. Tegene (2004b) 'Are United States Consumers Tolerant of Genetically Modified Foods?' *Review of Agricultural Economics* 26: 19–31.

Rousu, M., D. C. Monchuk, J. F. Shogren, and K. M. Kosa (2005) 'Consumer Willingness to Pay for "Second-Generation" Genetically Engineered Products and the Role of Marketing Information' *Journal of Agricultural and Applied Economics* 37: 647–657.

Rozan, A., A. Stenger, and M. Willinger (2004) 'Willingness-to-pay for Food Safety: An Experimental Investigation of Quality Certification on Bidding Behaviour' *European Review of Agricultural Economics* 31: 409–425.

Rutström, E. E. (1998). 'Home-Grown Values and Incentive Compatible Auction Design' *International Journal of Game Theory* 27: 427–441.

Seip, K. and J. Strand (1992) 'Willingness to Pay for Environmental Goods in Norway: A Contingent Valuation Study with Real Payment' *Environmental and Resource Economics* 2: 91–106.

Servan-Schreiber, E., J. Wolfers, D. M. Pennock, and B. Galebach (2004) 'Prediction Markets: Does Money Matter?' *Electronic Markets* 14: 2443–2251.

Shafir, E., P. Diamond, and A. Tversky (1997) 'Money Illusion' *Quarterly Journal of Economics* 112: 341–374.

Shaw, W. D., R. M. Nayga, Jr., and A. Silva (2006) 'Health Benefits and Uncertainty: An Experimental Analysis of the Effects of Risk Presentation on Auction Bids for a Healthful Product' *Economics Bulletin* 4: 1–8.

Shin, S. Y., J. Kliebenstein, D. J. Hayes, and J. F. Shogren (1992) 'Consumer Willingness to Pay for Safer Food Products' *Journal of Food Safety* 13: 51–59.

Shipman, D. R. (2001) 'Marketing of Grains in Today's Evolving Markets' Paper presented at the meeting 'Strategies for Coexistence of GMO, Non-GMO, and Organic Crop Production,' Minneapolis, MN, November 28.

Shogren, J. F. (1990) 'The Impact of Self-Protection and Self-Insurance on Individual Response to Risk' *Journal of Risk and Uncertainty* 3: 191–204.

(1997) 'Self-Interest and Equity in a Bargaining Tournament with Non-Linear Payoffs' *Journal of Economic Behavior and Organization* 32: 383–394.

(2005) 'Experimental Methods and Valuation' in *Handbook of Environmental Economics.* K. G. Mäler and J. Vincent, (eds.) Amsterdam: North-Holland.

Shogren, J. F. and T. Crocker (1994) 'Rational Risk Valuation with Sequential Reduction Opportunities' *Economics Letters* 44: 241–248.

Shogren, J. and L. Tadevosyan (2006) 'Bidding Behavior in a Consequential Second Price Auction' Working Paper, University of Wyoming.

Shogren, J. F., J. A. Fox, D. J. Hayes, and J. B. Kliebenstein (1994) 'Bid Sensitivity and the Structure of the Vickrey Auction' *American Journal of Agricultural Economics* 76: 1089–95.

Shogren, J. F., S. Y. Shin, D. J. Hayes, and J. B. Kliebenstein (1994) 'Resolving Differences in Willingness to Pay and Willingness to Accept' *American Economic Review* 84: 255–270.

Shogren, J. F., J. A. Fox, D. J. Hayes, and J. Roosen (1999) 'Observed Choices for Food Safety in Retail, Survey, and Auction Markets' *American Journal of Agricultural Economics* 81: 1192–1199.

Shogren, J. F., J. A. List, and D. J. Hayes (2000) 'Preference Learning in Consecutive Experimental Auctions' *American Journal of Agricultural Economics* 82: 1016–1021.

Shogren, J. F., M. Margolis, C. Koo, and J. A. List (2001a) 'A Random *n*th-Price Auction' *Journal of Economic Behavior and Organization* 46: 409–421.

Shogren, J. F., S. Cho, C. Koo, J. List, C. Park, P. Polo, and R. Wilhelmi (2001b) 'Auction Mechanisms and the Measurement of WTP and WTA' *Resource and Energy Economics* 23: 97–109.

Shogren, J. F., G. M. Parkhurst, and C. McIntosh (2006) 'Second-Price Auction Tournament' *Economics Letters* 92: 99–107.

Slovic, P. (1991) 'The Construction of Preferences' *American Psychologist* 50: 364–371.

Smith, B. J. and R. H. Warland (1992) 'Consumer Responses to Milk from rbST-Supplemented Cows' *Bovine Somatotropin and Emerging Issues: An Assessment*, Milton C. Hallberg, (ed.) Westview Special Studies in Agriculture Science and Policy, Westview Press.

Smith, V. L. (1976) 'Experimental Economics: Induced Value Theory' *American Economic Review* 66: 274–280.

(1980) 'Experiments with a Decentralized Mechanism for Public Good Decisions' *American Economic Review* 70: 584–599.

(1982) 'Microeconomic Systems as an Experimental Science' *American Economic Review* 72: 923–955.

Smith, V. K. and C. Mansfield (1998) 'Buying Time: Real and Hypothetical Offers' *Journal of Environmental Economics and Management* 36: 209–224.

Soler F. and G. J. M. Sánchez (2002) 'Consumers' Acceptability of Organic Food in Spain: Results from an Experimental Auction Market' *British Food Journal* 104: 670–687.

Solnick, S. and Hemenway, D. (1996) 'The Deadweight Loss of Christmas: Comment' *American Economic Review* 86: 1299–1305.

Stoneham, G., V. Chaudhri, A. Ha, and L. Strappazzon (2003) 'Auctions for Conservation Contracts: An Empirical Examination of Victoria's BushTender Trial' *Australian Journal of Agricultural and Resource Economics* 47: 477–500.

Swallow, S. (1994) 'Value Elicitation in Laboratory Markets: Discussion and Applicability to Contingent Valuation' *American Journal of Agricultural Economics* 76: 1096–1100.

Thaler, R. (1980) 'Toward a Positive Theory of Consumer Choice' *Journal of Economic Behavior and Organization* 1: 39–60.

Tversky, A. and R. H. Thaler (1990) 'Anomalies: Preference Reversals' *Journal of Economic Perspectives* 4: 201–211.

Tversky, A. and D. Kahneman (1992) 'Advances in Prospect Theory: Cumulative Representation of Uncertainty' *Journal of Risk and Uncertainty* 5: 297–323.

Tversky, A. and I. Simonson (1993) 'Context-dependent Preferences' *Management Science* 39: 1179–1189.

Tversky, A. and C. R. Fox (1995) 'Weighting Risk and Uncertainty' *Psychological Review* 102: 269–283.

Tversky, A., P. Slovic, and D. Kahneman (1990) 'The Causes of the Preference Reversal Phenomenon' *American Economic Review* 80: 204–217.

Umberger, W. J. and D. M. Feuz (2004) 'The Usefulness of Experimental Auctions in Determining Consumers' Willingness to Pay for Quality Differentiated Products' *Review of Agricultural Economics* 26: 1–16.

Umberger, W. J., D. M. Feuz, C. R. Calkins, and K. Killinger-Mann (2002) 'U.S. Consumer Preference and Willingness-to-Pay for Domestic Corn-Fed Beef versus International Grass-Fed Beef Measured Through an Experimental Auction' *Agribusiness: An International Journal* 18: 491–504.

Umberger, W. J., D. M. Feuz, C. R. Calkins, and B. M. Sitz (2003) 'Country-of-Origin Labeling of Beef Products: U.S. Consumers' Perceptions' *Journal of Food Distribution Research* 34: 103–116.

U.S. Bureau of the Census. 'U.S. Census Bureau.' <http://www.census.gov/>

U.S. Food and Drug Administration (FDA) (1999) Progress and Perspective Food Safety Initiative FY Annual Report.

U.S. Dept. of Agriculture, National Agricultural Statistics Service (NASS), Acreage (2005) June 30.

Van Ravenswaay, E. O. (1988) 'How Much Food Safety Do Consumers Want? An Analysis of Current Studies and Strategies for Future Research' in *Demands in the Marketplace: Public Policy in Relation to Food Safety, Quality and Human Health*, Katherine L. Clancy, (ed.) Washington DC: Resources for the Future.

Vickrey, W. (1961) 'Counterspeculation, Auctions and Competitive Sealed Tenders' *Journal of Finance* 16 March: 8–37.

Vickrey, W. (1962) 'Auctions and Bidding Gamess' Recent Advances in Game Theory. Papers Delivered at a Meeting of the Princeton University Conference, October [sic] 4–6, 1961, Princeton University Conference, pp. 15–29.

Viscusi, W. K. (1989) 'Prospective Reference Theory: Toward an Explanation of the Paradoxes' *Journal of Risk and Uncertainty* 2: 235–263.

Viscusi, W. K., W. A. Magat, and J. Huber (1987) 'An Investigation of the Rationality of Consumer Valuations of Multiple Health Risks' *RAND Journal of Economics* 18: 465–479.

Waldfogel, J. (1993) 'The Deadweight Loss of Christmas' *American Economic Review* 83: 1328–1336.

Waldfogel, J. (1996) 'The Deadweight Loss of Christmas: Reply' *American Economic Review* 86: 1306–1308.

Wertenbroch, K., and B. Skiera (2002) 'Measuring Consumers' Willingness to Pay at the Point of Purchase' *Journal of Marketing Research* 39: 228–241.

Wilson, T. D. and J. W. Schooler (1991) 'Thinking Too Much: Introspection Can Reduce the Quality of Preferences and Decisions' *Journal of Personality and Social Psychology* 60: 181–192.

Wilson, T. D. and S. J. LaFleur (1995) 'Knowing What You'll Do: Effects of Analyzing Reasons on Self-Prediction' *Journal of Personality and Social Psychology* 68: 21–35.

Wolfers, J. and E. Zitzewitz (2004) 'Prediction Markets' *Journal of Economic Perspectives* 18: 107–126.

Woodland, B. M. and L. M. Woodland (1999) 'Expected Utility, Skewness, and the Baseball Betting Market' *Applied Economics* 31: 337–345.

World Health Organization (2000) *Food Safety – A Worldwide Public Health Issue* (http://www.who.int/fsf/fctshtfs.htm#Recognition of food safety at international level).

Zhao, J. and C. L. Kling (2001) 'A New Explanation for the WTP/WTA Disparity' *Economics Letters* 73: 293–300.

(2004) 'Willingness-to-Pay, Compensating Variation, and the Cost of Commitment' *Economic Inquiry* 42: 503–571.

Index

ABA and BAB design 52–53
affiliated values
  in incentive compatible auctions 25–26
  in repeated bidding rounds 80–88, 90, 92
aliased effects 49
anticompetitive behavior identification 5
assignment of units to treatments 48,
  51–52
auction bids
  comparison with hedonic ratings 256–258
  comparison with other measures of value
  258–260
  comparison with purchase decisions
  258–260
  comparison with taste tests 255–256
auction bids and economic theory, validity of
  predictions 248–252
auction design case studies
  calibration of real and hypothetical bidding
  229–239
  fixed or fungible preferences 217–222, 223,
  224, 225
  gift exchange 225–228, 229, 230
  hybrid auctions and consequential bidding
  239–245
  preference learning 196–199
  second price auction tournaments 209–214,
  215, 217
  WTP, WTA and the auction mechanism
  199–204, 205, 208, 209
auction mechanism
  and unengaged bidders (case study) 202,
  206–208, 209
  choosing 69–76
auction mechanism-dependent bidding
  behavior (case study) 199–204, 205, 208,
  209
auction theory, 19 see also economic theory

balanced design 49–51
baseball card auctions (case study) 230–237
Bayes models 4–5

BDM (Becker-Degroot-Marschak) mechanism
  17, 19–20, 69–70
  demand revealing performance 27–28,
  30–32, 33
  relaxation of expected utility theory 24–25
beef tenderness grading system (case study)
  113–121, 175–186
  analytical framework 114–115
  conclusions 120, 121
  data and methods 117–118
  instructions for beef steak auction
  experiments 175–186
  linking theoretical model to auction bids
  116–117
  marbling and tenderness 113–114
  results 118–121
  US beef quality grading system 113–114
behavioral economists, use of information on
  people's values 1–2
bidding behavior
  factors affecting 19
  in consequential auctions (case study)
  239–245
Bradley-Terry-Luce model 111
business managers, eliciting values for
  non-market goods 1
buyers, willingness-to-pay 1

calibration of real and hypothetical bidding
  (case study) 229–239
case studies see auction design case studies;
  valuation case studies
censored regressions with auction bids 95–100
  double hurdle model 98–100
  interval censored observations 96
  left censored observations 96
  likelihood function 97
  right censored observations 96
  Tobit model 97–100
  uncensored observations 96
censoring, quantile regression with auction
  bids 101, 102

Christmas gift giving, welfare effects (case study) 225–228, 229, 230
cluster analysis 108–109
coherent arbitrariness 265–267
collective auction 69, 70
commitment costs 43–44
conditional mean regression, comparison with quantile regression 100–102
confounding factors 47–49, 50, 52–54
conjoint analysis 4–5
consequential bidding (case study) 239–245
context and control issues 53–54, 57–60
   balance between 174–175
   balance in experimental auctions 6–16
context-dependent preferences 238–239
contingent valuation 4
control and context issues 53–54, 57–60
   balance between 174–175
   balance in experimental auctions 6–16
controversial goods case study (demand for GM food) 154–161, 163, 191–195
   conclusions 162–163
   EU stance on GM food 154–155
   experiment 155–157
   instructions for GM food auction 191–195
   results 157–161, 162
   US stance on GM food 154–155
   use of biotechnology in food production 154
controversial goods case study (food from animals treated with growth hormones) 169–174
   bovine somatotropin (bST) 169–170
   conclusions 173–174
   experimental design 170–171
   health controversy 169–170
   porcine somatotropin (pST) 169–170
   results and discussion 171–173
controversial goods case study (irradiation of food) 163–169
   conclusions 167–169
   experiment 163–165
   results 165–167, 168
   welfare effects of anti-technology messages 167–169
convergent validity 235, 255–261
   auction bids and hedonic ratings 256–258
   auction bids and other measures of value 258–260
   auction bids and purchase decisions 258–260
   auction bids and taste tests 255–256
   external validity 235, 261
cumulative prospect theory 42–43
CVM-X method 237

Dasgupta and Maskin mechanism 89
data analysis
   censored regressions with auction bids 95–100
   cluster analysis 108–109
   elementary statistical analysis 95, 112
   factor analysis 106–108
   market share simulation 109–112
   panel data regression with auction bids 103–106
   quantile regression with auction bids 100–102, 103
demand, effects of price/availability of substitutes and complements 79–80, 250
demand reduction 53, 76–80
demand revealing, performance of incentive compatible mechanisms 27–32, 33
diminishing marginal utility 76–80, 249
discrete choice models 4–5
double hurdle model 98–100
Dutch auctions, efficiency 28

eBay 62–63
econometric techniques 4–5
economic theory, evidence for predictions
   demand is affected by price/availability of substitutes and compliments 250
   diminishing marginal utility 249
   factors affecting WTP and WTA 251–252
   market price increases as demand increases 248–249
   more is preferred to less 249–250
   testing reliability at individual level 5
   the value of a dollar to a person is exactly $1.00 252
   values will rise (fall) with positive (negative) information 250–251
   see also auction theory
economic value of choices 1
economists, use of information on people's values 1–2
efficiency of design 49–51
endowment effect 262–263
   case study 199–204, 205, 208, 209
endowment versus full bidding 65–68
English auctions 17, 19–20, 24–25, 69
   demand revealing performance 27–32, 33
ex-post regression analysis 53
exchange institutions 1
expected utility theory 5
   relaxation of the independence axiom 24–25
experimental auctions
   active market environment 3–4

advantage over other value elicitation
methods 3–5
applications 6, 7–14
control/context balance 6–16
description of heterogeneity in valuations
4–5
determination of individual willingness to
pay 4
early work 5
elicitation of homegrown values 6–16
exchange mechanism 3–4
incentive compatible mechanisms 3–4,
16–17
induced value experiments 5–6, 15–16
purpose 5
two basic strategies 16
valuation of non-market goods 3–4
valuations are directly obtained 3–4
see also English auctions; BDM
mechanism; collective auctions; Dutch
auctions; nth price auctions; random nth
price auctions; second price auctions;
Vickrey's second price auctions
experimental auctions (conducting)
affiliation of values in repeated bidding
rounds 80–88, 90, 92
avoiding misperceptions in participants
62–65
BDM mechanism 69–70
best practices 62
choosing an auction mechanism 69–76
collective auction 69, 70
Dasgupta and Maskin mechanism 89, 90
demand reduction 76–80
diminishing marginal utility 76–80
endowment versus full bidding 65–68
English auction 69
field substitutes 79–80
focus groups 62
initial qualitative study 62
learning in repeated bidding rounds 80–88,
90, 92
multiple good valuation 76–80
negative values 92–94
nth price auction 69
random nth price auction 69, 70
repeated bidding round auctions 80–88, 90,
92
second price auction 69
training and practice for participants
62–65
experimental auctions (preliminaries)
experimental design 47–54
sample size determination 55–57
study objectives 46–47

study setting and context (field versus
laboratory) 57–60
use of students as subjects 46–47
experimental design 47–54
ABA and BAB design 52–53
aliased effects 49, 50
assignment of units to treatments 48, 51–52
balanced design 49–51
common expectation among participants 53
confounding factors 47–49, 50, 52–54
control of design variables 47–51
definition of experimental unit 51–52
demand reduction 53
efficiency of design 49–51
ex-post regression analysis 53
extraneous variables 52–54
finding designs 51
fractional factorial design 48–51
full factorial design 47–48, 49
issues of control and context 53–54
main-effects only design 48–51
orthogonal design 49–51
randomization 48, 52
replication of treatments 51–52
software 51
within-subject design 48, 52–53
experimental unit, definition 51–52
external validity 261

face validity of data 6–16
factor analysis 106–108
farm financial records valuation (case study)
149–154, 186–190
benefits of farm recordkeeping 149–150
conclusions 152–154
data and methods 150–151
instructions for financial records auction
186–190
results 151–152, 153
field substitutes, effects of 79–80, 250
'first choice' or 'highest utility' rule
110–111
first price auction 23–24
efficiency 28
fixed or fungible preferences (case study)
217–222, 223, 224, 225
focus groups 62
food from animals treated with growth
hormones (case study) 169–174
bovine somatotropin (bST) 169–170
conclusions 173–174
experimental design 170–171
health controversy 169–170
porcine somatotropin (pST) 169–170
results and discussion 171–173

forecasting market share of a new product
  (case study) 119, 137–141, 175–186
  calculating market share 137–139
  data and methods 119, 139
  instructions for beef steak auction
    experiments 175–186
  results 139–141
fractional factorial design 48–51
fresh food with multiple quality attributes
  (case study) 141–149
  experimental design 142–145
  results and discussion 145–149
  study objectives 141
  summary 149
full bidding versus endowment 65–68
full factorial design 47–48, 49
future research in experimental auctions
  ability to forecast retail behavior 272–273
  comparison with choice-based methods
    273–274
  diversification of purposes and contexts
    7–14, 269–270
  experimental design issues 274–275
  interaction of emotions and auction
    institutions 276–277
  personality traits and bidding behavior 276
  potential for pattern recognition 275–276
  prediction markets 277–278
  rationality of statements of value 270–271
  relationship to real world behavior 271–272
  testing economic theory 274

gift exchange, welfare effects (case study)
  225–228, 229, 230
GM (genetically modified) food demand (case
  study) 154–161, 163, 191–195
  conclusions 162–163
  EU stance on GM food 154–155
  experiment 155–157
  instructions for GM food auction 191–195
  results 157–161, 162
  US stance on GM food 154–155
  use of biotechnology in food production
    154
GM food tolerance (case study) 129–137
  conclusions 136–137
  controversy over GM foods 129–130
  experiment 130–134
  GM labelling and tolerance standards
    129–130
  results 134–136

hedonic ratings, comparison with auction bids
  256–258
homegrown values elicitation 6–16

explanation of the dominant strategy 33
  validity of measurements 247–248
hybrid auctions and consequential bidding
  (case study) 239–245
hypothetical bidding, tendency to overstate
  (case study) 229–239

incentive compatible auctions 19–20
  assumptions underlying the theory 24–27
  BDM (Becker-Degroot-Marschak)
    mechanism 19–20
  bidders' goals outside experimental context
    26–27
  effects of affiliated values 25–26
  English auction 19–20
  explanation of the dominant strategy 33
  nth price auction 19–20
  random nth price auction 19–20
  relaxation of expected utility theory 24–25
  second price auctions 19–20
  separate what people say from what they
    pay 19–20
  situations when not incentive compatible
    24–27
  theory of 20–27
  Vickrey's second price auction 19–23
  weakly dominant strategy 19–20
incentive compatible mechanisms 3–4
  BDM (Becker-Degroot-Marschak)
    mechanism 17
  demand revealing performance 27–32, 33
  English auction 17
  random nth price auction 17
  second price auction 16–17
  testing in induced value studies 27–32, 33
  Vickrey auction 16–17
  Vickrey nth price auction 17
induced value auctions, testing of incentive
  compatible mechanisms 27–32, 33
induced value experiments 5–6, 15–16
informing policy case study (beef tenderness
  grading system) 113–121, 175–186
  analytical framework 114–115
  conclusions 120, 121
  data and methods 117–118
  instructions for beef steak auction
    experiments 175–186
  linking theoretical model to auction bids
    116–117
  marbling and tenderness 113–114
  results 118–121
  US beef quality grading system 113–114
informing policy case study (tolerance for GM
  food) 129–137
  conclusions 136–137

controversy over GM foods 129–130
  experiment 130–134
  GM labelling and tolerance standards
    129–130
  results 134–136
informing policy case study (valuing safer
    food) 121–127, 128, 129
  conclusions 129
  experiment 124–125
  prevalence of food-borne diseases
    121–122
  results 126–127, 128, 129
  study objectives 122–124
insincere bidding, and auction treatment (case
    study) 209–214, 215, 217
irradiation of food (case study) 163–169
  conclusions 167–169
  experiment 163–165
  results 165–167, 168
  welfare effects of anti-technology messages
    167–169

learning in repeated bidding rounds 80–88,
    90, 92
likelihood function, censored regressions with
    auction bids 97
logit model 111

main-effects only design 48–51
market price increases as demand increases
    (theory) 248–249
market segmentation, effects of valuation
    heterogeneity 5
market share simulation 109–112
  Bradley-Terry-Luce model 111
  'first choice' or 'highest utility' rule
    110–111
  logit model 111
  money-metric utility 110
  share of preference model 111
marketing case study (forecasting market
    share) 119, 137–141, 175–186
  calculating market share 137–139
  data and methods 119, 139
  instructions for beef steak auction
    experiments 175–186
  results 139–141
marketing case study (fresh food with multiple
    quality attributes) 141–149
  experimental design 142–145
  results and discussion 145–149
  study objectives 141
  summary 149
marketing case study (value of farm financial
    records) 149–154, 186–190

benefits of farm record keeping 149–150
  conclusions 152–154
  data and methods 150–151
  instructions for financial records auction
    186–190
  results 151–152, 153
marketing experts, use of information on
    people's values 1–2
mixed logit models 4–5
money-metric utility 110
more is preferred to less (theory) 249–250
multiple good valuation 76–80

negative values, effects of 92–94
non-expected utility behavior 41–43
non-market goods
  valuation in experimental auctions 3–4
  value elicitation 1–2
nth price auctions 19–20, 69
  non-expected utility preferences 24–25
  see also random nth price auctions

off-the-margin bidders
  and auction mechanism (case study) 202,
    206–208, 209
  effects of tournament auction (case study)
    209–214, 215, 217
orthogonal design 49–51

panel data regression with auction bids
    103–106
  individual-specific model 88, 105–106
  one-way fixed and random effects models
    104–105
  random coefficients model 106
  two-way fixed and random effects models
    105
parallel-forms reliability 253–254, 255
participants
  affiliation of values in repeated bidding
    rounds 80–88, 90, 92
  avoiding misperceptions in 62–65
  create common expectation 53
  explanation of weakly dominant strategy
    33
  influenced by being watched 60
  learning in repeated bidding rounds 80–88,
    90, 92
  negative values 92–94
  training and practice 62–65
  use of students as subjects 46–47
policymakers, eliciting values for non-market
    goods 1 see also informing policy case
    studies
prediction markets 277–278

preference learning for unfamiliar goods (case
        study) 196–199
preference reversals 263–265
    case study 217–222, 223, 224, 225
preferences
    construction 218
    fixed or fungible (case study) 217–222,
        223, 224, 225
    stability (case study) 217–222, 223, 224,
        225
price discrimination models, effects of
        valuation heterogeneity 5
psychologists, use of information on people's
        values 1–2
public policy, determination of welfare effects
        5 see also informing policy case studies
purchase decisions, comparison with auction
        bids 258–260

quantile regression with auction bids
        100–102, 103
    censoring 101, 102
    comparison with conditional mean
        regression 100–102

random nth price auctions 17, 19–20, 69, 70
    demand revealing performance 27–28,
        30–32, 33
    see also nth price auctions
random parameter models 4–5
randomization 52
rank-dependent expected utility theory 24–25,
        42
reliability
    consistency across context 254–255
    consistency across repeated rounds 253
    definition 252
    of experimental auction measurements
        252–255
    parallel-forms reliability 253–254, 255
    relation to validity 252
    test-retest 252–253
repeated bidding round auctions 80–88, 90,
        92
    affiliation of values 80–88, 90, 92
    consistency across rounds 253
    learning in 80–88, 90, 92
replication of treatments 51–52
revealed preference methods, implicit values
        2–3
risk, definition 37
risk aversion 39–41
risk perception 39–41
risk preference 39–41
risk premium (WTP to avoid a risky good) 40

sample size determination 55–57
    comparison of means from two independent
        samples 55–56
    distribution of a valuation in the population
        56–57
second price auctions 16–17, 19–20, 69
    demand revealing performance 27–32, 33
    non-expected utility preferences 24–25
    see also Vickrey's second price auction
second price auction tournaments (case study)
        209–214, 215, 217
sellers, willingness to accept 1
share of preference model 111
stated preference methods 2–3
    unreliability of values elicited 3
students, use as subjects 46–47
study objectives 46–47
study setting and context (field versus
        laboratory) 57–60
    participants influenced by being watched 60
substitute availability, effects on demand
        79–80, 250

taste tests, comparison with auction bids
        255–256
test-retest reliability 252–253
Tobit model 97–100
tournament auction
    comparison with standard auction (case
        study) 209–214, 215, 217
    demand revelation (case study) 209–214,
        215, 217
    effects on insincere bidding (case study)
        209–214, 215, 217

unengaged bidders
    and auction mechanism (case study) 202,
        206–208, 209
    effects of tournament auction (case study)
        209–214, 215, 217
unfamiliar goods, preference learning (case
        study) 196–199

validity
    definition 247
    external 235, 261
validity of experimental auctions 247–248
    anomalies 261–267
    auction bids and economic theory 248–252
    coherent arbitrariness 265–267
    convergent validity 235, 255–261
    endowment effect 262–263
    measurement of homegrown values
        247–248
    object of measurement 247–248

preference reversals 263–265
reliability of measurements 252–255
WTP versus WTA disparity 262–263
valuation
  assumption that economic value does exist
    34
  WTA (willingness to accept) 34
  WTP (willingness to pay) 34
valuation case studies
  balance between control and context
    174–175
  controversial goods I (demand for GM food
    in three countries) 154–161, 163,
    191–195
  controversial goods II (irradiation of food)
    163–169
  controversial goods III (food from animals
    treated with growth hormones) 169–174
  informing policy I (beef tenderness grading
    system) 113–121, 175–186
  informing policy II (valuing safer food)
    121–127, 128, 129
  informing policy III (tolerance for GM
    food) 129–137
  marketing I (forecasting market share of a
    new product) 119, 137–141, 175–186
  marketing II (fresh food with multiple
    quality attributes) 141–149
  marketing III (value of farm financial
    records) 149–154, 186–190
valuation case studies (appendices)
  instructions for beef steak auction
    experiments 175–186
  instructions for financial records auction
    186–190
  instructions for GM food auction
    191–195
valuation heterogeneity, need to understand
  4–5
valuation in a dynamic environment with
    uncertainty, limited information and
    irreversibility
  commitment costs 43–44
  dynamic WTA 44
  dynamic WTP 43–44
valuation under certainty 34–37
  producer profit maximization 36
  WTA (willingness to accept) 34–35, 36–37
  WTP (willingness to pay) 34–36
valuation under uncertainty 37–43
  cumulative prospect theory 42–43
  effects of new information 38–39
  non-expected utility behavior 41–43
  rank-dependent expected utility theory 42
  risk (definition) 37

risk aversion 39–41
risk perception 39–41
risk preference 39–41
risk premium 40
threats with low-probability and high
    damage 41–43
  WTA (willingness to accept) 38
  WTP (willingness to pay) 37–38
  WTP to avoid a risky outcome 40
  WTP to obtain a risky good 39–40
value elicitation
  applications for information 1–2
  non-market goods 1–2
  WTA (willingness to accept) 34
  WTP (willingness to pay) 34
value elicitation methods
  revealed preference 2–3
  stated preference 2–3
value measures, comparison with auction bids
    258–260
values theory, rise (fall) with positive
    (negative) information 250–251
valuing safer food (case study) 121–127, 128,
    129
  conclusions 129
  experiment 124–125
  prevalence of food-borne diseases
    121–122
  results 126–127, 128, 129
  study objectives 122–124
variables
  control of 47–51
  extraneous 52–54
Vickrey, William 16–17, 19
Vickrey's nth price auction 17
Vickrey's second price auction 16–17,
    19–20
  comparison with first price auction
    23–24
  demonstration of incentive compatibility
    20–23
  formal utility maximization framework
    20–21
  intuitive, heuristic framework 21–23
  tournaments (case study) 209–214, 215,
    217
  see also second price auctions

weakly dominant strategy
  explanation to participants 33
  in incentive compatible auctions 19–20
  in second price auctions 16–17
willingness to accept see WTA
willingness to pay see WTP
within-subject design 48, 52–53

WTA (willingness to accept) 1, 38
   dynamic 44
   valuation under certainty 34–35, 36–37
   value measure 34
   when to use 34–35
WTP (willingness to pay) 1, 37–38
   determination of 4
   dynamic 43–44
   overstatement in hypothetical bidding (case
     study) 229–239

to avoid a risky good (risk premium) 40
to obtain a risky good 39–40
valuation under certainty 34–36
value measure 34
when to use 34–35
WTP and WTA
   disparity 262–263
   factors affecting 251–252
   gap and the auction mechanism (case study)
     199–204, 205, 208, 209